THEY FOUND THE BURIED CITIES

STELA AT COPÁN, HONDURAS

DRAWING BY FREDERICK CATHERWOOD

THEY FOUND THE BURIED CITIES

Exploration and Excavation in the
AMERICAN TROPICS

ROBERT WAUCHOPE

The University of Chicago Press
CHICAGO AND LONDON

(Frontispiece taken from John L. Stephens: *Incidents of Travel in Central America, Chiapas, and Yucatan*)

Library of Congress Catalog Card Number: 65-24433

The University of Chicago Press, Chicago & London
The University of Toronto Press, Toronto 5, Canada

© *1965 by the University of Chicago. All rights reserved. Published 1965*
Printed in the United States of America

TO BETTY

Contents

Introduction

The Initiation of an Archaeologist

The age of archaeological exploration in Central and South America is not yet past. Although one can now drive or fly to most of the famous ruins—trips that only recently required days of hard travel by muleback or on foot through jungle, thorny thickets, or rugged mountains—vast areas of tropical rain forest and remote highland are still seldom visited, and great regions are as yet wholly unexplored. There are doubtless scores—perhaps hundreds—of ruined Maya towns and cities, some of them of major size, that have never even been discovered.

Archaeological adventures in the American tropics are still being experienced, but one rarely reads more than the dry technical monographs that result from these explorations. In their published reports, few archaeologists reveal their hardships and adventures, or even their thoughts and emotions. Some of them keep personal journals, but I know of only two that have appeared in print. Perhaps some plan eventually to write about their experiences but never find the time to do so, and feel that these accounts do not properly belong in a scientific monograph. I do not agree. I like the old nineteenth-century accounts by Stephens, Morelet, Squier, and Maler—scientific reports that were widely read and enjoyed by the public, books that recounted adventures, were not afraid of expressing emotion, and frequently philosophized on matters entirely marginal to their technical theme.

Most travel reminiscences nowadays appear in books by professional "adventurers" and journalists posing as archaeologists; their writings strongly suggest that many of the tales are outright fabrications and the dialogue imagined rather than real. Not only are adventures themselves largely falsified, but the scanty archaeological content of these books is inaccurate and grossly misleading. The "newly discovered" ruins these men photograph are usually

1

well known and in most instances easily accessible; those they do not picture are generally "lost" again, along with all clues to their whereabouts—inexcusable for any self-respecting explorer! Native Indians in regions where they ordinarily wear khaki pants and manufactured shirts are photographed in jaguar skins and posed uncomfortably clutching a spear, while the author's chauffeur-driven car waits on a paved highway nearby. The dialogue is stereotyped "native talk" as imagined by the armchair explorer ("But, señor, why do you not fear death from the crocodiles?"), and the frequent brushes with disaster, if they actually took place, would reflect seriously on the explorer's experience, abilities, and good sense.

For the most part, we must go back half a century and more to find authentic reminiscences by real archaeological explorers. This book selects some of these incidents of travel and adventure, most of them widely read in their time but scarcely known today. Even the present-day professional archaeologist, finding it difficult to keep abreast of even current technical literature, is sometimes unfamiliar with the interesting narratives of his predecessors in the same fields of exploration and excavation.

J. Eric S. Thompson, in his fine account of incidents of archaeological excavation in the Maya region as he remembered them in the 1920's and 1930's, remarked that attitudes and the pattern of daily life in Central America then were perhaps closer to those which obtained when Maya civilization was collapsing under the impact of Spanish conquest than to those of the 1960's. "Life essentially was not too far removed from what it had been when John Lloyd Stephens wrote in 1841 and 1843. . . ."

The main purpose of this book is to illustrate Thompson's observation, first with some excerpts from my own diaries written between 1932 and 1947, and then with a series of anecdotes of travel and adventure recorded by archaeologists in the tropics during a period of one hundred and thirty-six years, beginning in 1805 with the travel narratives of Guillelmo Dupaix and ending with extracts from Louis Halle's excellent *River of Ruins*, published in 1941. Although I have no particularly startling adventures of my own to report, I hope that the reader will note the general and in many instances specific similarity between conditions that I encountered—as did all my Mayanist contemporaries—and those described in the earlier accounts on the following pages.

My first experience in the Maya area was as a beginning graduate student at Harvard in 1932, when I became a greenhorn staff member of a Carnegie Institution of Washington expedition to the ruins of Uaxactún in the Department of El Petén, Guatemala. The project was directed by A. Ledyard Smith, a seasoned veteran of many trips into the bush. The third member of the party was his brother, Robert E. Smith, who had also worked at Uaxactún before. This was the beginning of a lifelong friendship with these two men, and I shall be eternally grateful to both of them for their friendly patience with a young tenderfoot.

Bob Smith and I sailed from New Orleans on the United Fruit Company's old *Choluteca* and arrived early in February in Belize, British Honduras, where Ledyard met us. The city was a wreck, leveled only a few months earlier by a hurricane and tidal wave that took more than two thousand human lives. We put up at the Palace Hotel, at one dollar each per day. Its proprietor was a Syrian named Sabala. The hotel was straight out of Somerset Maugham; it could justifiably boast of only two good features: its bar, tended by a young Negro called Mac, and its fresh turtle soup, served in the dining room by the waitress, Nina. The hotel rooms were separated from each other by thin wooden walls, open and latticed near the ceiling. This helped the circulation of air in a torrid climate, but, as I noted in the first day's entry in my diary, not only air but loud snores from next door, punctuated with Spanish curses called down on their perpetrator by a Mexican in still another room, circulated during most of the night. The only other remark about the hotel that I find worth repeating is my pious notation that we were afraid to drink the water there, and so I very shortly became fast friends with Mac the bartender.

Ledyard was busy outfitting the expedition, and I trailed him from store to store, all eyes and ears on my first visit to a tropical port. He taught me my first lesson in practical archaeology: never buy your groceries just after a meal—nothing looks very appealing when you are not hungry. I purchased a splendid poncho for what seemed an outrageous price—ten dollars—but it, my machete (made in Connecticut), and my *pabellón* mosquito bar and hammock were perhaps the most useful things that I took with me into the bush.

Five nights after arriving in Belize we were ready to board the little river boat which Ledyard had chartered to carry us up the Belize River to the head of navigation at El Cayo, near the Guatemala frontier. That morning I had finished packing my *cayak*, a hard-leather box about the size of a large suitcase, but at the last minute I slipped in a couple of coconuts we had gathered during an outing to the offshore keys the day before. In the evening we paid a last call at the P. W. Shufeldts', who had been so kind to us during our stay in town, and then we dropped by the Perla del Oriente for a farewell drink—our last (with the exception of a cup of rum punch) that we would have for many months.

It was quite moving, that departure into what for me was truly the unknown. There were just the three of us and half a dozen Negroes. Enrique Shufeldt, son of an old-time chicle concessionaire, was there to see us off. The river boat lay quietly at its mooring, rocking a little in the slow wash of the stream. The night was black, and we worked by flashlight. A single tiny lantern shed flickering red on the dark face of the pilot. Santiago and

Walter Scott, the houseboy, were nervously fussing with this and that line or stopping to talk together in low undertones.

A slight breeze sprang up across the river and shattered the placid reflection of our lantern and flashlights. We could hear the wooden tinkle of a marimba nearby and the faint underbeat of dancers' shuffling feet. I tossed my own cayak aboard, slung my hammock alongside Bob's and Ledyard's, and then helped pack the supplies in the dugout "flatpan" that we would tow behind us. After what seemed a long time, we were ready to leave. A little bell rang, Enrique wished us good luck, a dim electric light went on over our hammocks. There was a sound of churning water, a jerk as the

Our Belize River boat, British Honduras, 1932. Ledyard Smith is in his hammock (*below*). Walter is second from left, and Dixon second from right, in group (*above*).

line from launch to the dugout flatpan went taut, and then the boat chugged out into the river and headed upstream.

Later there was a moon, and Bob and I climbed up on top to watch the thick mangrove swamps creep by, the willows, sapotes, and dark palm trees rising behind them scarcely visible in the moonlight. We sat there a long time in the cool night river breeze, talking to Dixon, the cook, who was half drunk and sang us songs in Spanish. The Negroes lay forward together, talking softly among themselves in their river dialect, which reminded me strongly of the low-country Gullah I had so often heard in South Carolina. All seemed quiet and strange and beautiful. I lay there and smoked and looked and wondered what lay ahead. Finally I climbed down, took off my shoes, settled in my hammock, and was asleep.

It was very cold on the river that night, and I used both my blankets. I spent most of the next day topside. The scenery had changed to jungle on both sides of the river—tremendous trees towering on each bank and thick undergrowth beneath them. Several blue and white herons flew ahead of the boat and perched near as it went by, repeating this action for hours at a time. I saw a young crocodile and an iguana. Ledyard taught me to distinguish coconut from corasal and cabbage palms. We passed several little settlements of thatch-roofed huts perched high on the banks, rejoicing under such names as Young Gal, Never Delay, Happy Home, and Beaver Dam. We stopped for a few minutes at most of them; at Happy Home, we took on corn, at $2.50 a barrel. During the day I passed some time by sketching Ledyard and Bob reading in their hammocks, while the pilot watched over my shoulder with great amusement.

By night the rain forest appeared much denser and more awe-inspiring. Above the palms, laurel, and smaller growth spread the great canopy of the jungle—breadnuts, sapodillas, and huesillos, almost blotting out the sky above us—and through this roof thrust the true forest giants—majestic mahogany, mastic and wild fig trees—all festooned with rope-like lianas which sometimes swept the top of our little boat. Moonlight glittered on the river, casting an unearthly glow on the jungle and playing strange light tricks on the vines that dropped straight down to the water from what seemed enormous heights.

We reached El Cayo long after midnight the second night, slept until six-thirty, and swam in the river. We hung our hammocks in the house of Mr. Hopún, a short, powerfully built man of Syrian, Mexican, and Indian descent who owned the general store in the village and who acted as our agent there, forwarding supplies to us in the bush via regular mule train between Uaxactún and El Cayo. My hammock was slung on his screened back porch overlooking the river. Hopún gave me a story he had written in English and Maya; he had learned the latter language from his grandmother, who was pure Indian.

On the third day in El Cayo we were up early, had breakfast, and boarded two dugouts which had been packed and were ready to take us to the place where the *mulada* was to start. Hopún and a Negro paddled the dugout I was in; another Negro boy paddled Bob and Ledyard. We saw two natives in a dugout spearing fish with a sharpened bamboo: one paddled downstream; the other stood in the bow with spear poised, and took several fish even while we passed.

Belize River, British Honduras, 1932

When we reached the appointed spot, the mules were already being packed. I had seen diamond hitches in New Mexico, but these fastenings here were different and seemed highly insecure to me. First they placed a soft matlike blanket on the mule's back. Then they doubled a rope twice and threw it across. Then they took two cayaks—or whatever the load happened to be—and held them against the mule's sides, forming with them an inverted V over the back, on top of the rope. They secured these with rapid turns of the rope, filled the space between the cayaks with other provisions, and then threw a waterproof canvas or tarpaulin over the whole load. They put another rope in a big loop over this and ran it through a hooked block of wood under the girth. One *arriero* placed his foot against the mule's side and tightened the rope while his helper took up the slack. A small piece of rope was left free; they gave the mule a swat with this to make it trot away while they watched to see whether the pack sat tight and was correctly balanced.

My mule was incongruously named Golondrina, and I came to wonder whether this very unbirdlike creature carried me safely through or whether I survived the journey in spite of her. I secured my saddle bags, machete, canteen of water, and a poncho within easy reach. I was weak from a long spell of diarrhea. Standing in that hot sun I felt faint, but I sat under a tree until the dizziness passed. Finally, amid tremendous shouting and cursing from the muleteers, pounding of hoofs, flourishing of lashes, and confused trotting of mules, we started off on the long, four-day trip through the jungle.

The first day we were in the saddle ten hours, not one minute of which could be called relaxed riding. Everything was new and strange to me. I was awed by the jungle's immensity, its sheer grandeur, and from the first it appealed to me as no other terrain had before or has since. Although it was beauty in its wildest magnificence, the forest seemed to fight us continuously, as if to keep us out and drive us back to where people "belonged"— in mild, orderly, but dirty villages and towns. All day long we tore through unbushed side trails, wallowed in mud up to the mules' bellies, were lashed by vines and ripped by thorns. Even the mules, in which I placed an unwarranted confidence, lost their footing, stumbled, or fell sprawling and kicking in apparent panic. We frequently held our booted legs out of the stirrups, high on the mule's neck, in order to leap clear if the animal fell or to avoid being crushed against the spiny tree trunks along the side of the trail. Time and again we had to cut the floundering mules clear of vines and lift them bodily from mudholes. My old felt hat, which I had borrowed from my brother-in-law before leaving the States, was almost in shreds after the first day's ride.

Then came the great thrill near the end of the day. Stiff and cramped from the long ride, hot, thirsty, and still weak from diarrhea, I suddenly heard far ahead the faint, ghostly hunting horn of the lead rider on the bell mare—she wore a bell around her neck to guide the following animals—announcing that we were nearing Yaloch, our first stop. Immediately all weariness left me. We kicked our mules to a fast trot, the shouting at the pack animals redoubled, and we began to catch little glimpses of water through the thinning bush. It was the Yaloch *laguna*. Then we emerged into a small open area covered with grass, and saw a fairly large, uninhabited thatch-roofed shelter, erected years ago by the *chicleros* who roam this wilderness, which was to be our shelter for the night.

We dismounted, unsaddled, opened our cayaks, hung our hammocks, took off our heavy boots, and removed our clothes. This is a rule of the mulada: you must do all these things before you relax, no matter how tired you may be. If not, you will be too tired or it will be too dark to do them later. Then I took soap and towel, bathed in the laguna—but did not swim because the men warned me against crocodiles—and came back to a fine dinner which Dixon had prepared: a delicious bird something like a partridge and a piece of venison (one of the arrieros had killed a deer). Four cups of steaming hot coffee did not quench my thirst. Then I lay in my hammock and smoked—pure heaven on earth!

Pack mule, cayaks, and other equipment at overnight camp, El Petén, Guatemala, 1932.

Before dropping off to sleep, I removed fourteen ticks from my body and, on the arrieros' expert advice, rubbed lard on my right knee, which was full of long thin spines from an escoba palm that my mule had bashed me against. I was still thirsty, and so I had two cups of hot tea. The insects set up such a drone that I stopped my ears with two scraps of cloth—an unnecessary precaution, since I was asleep before dark.

Next morning we were up at four, and off forty-five minutes later. The muleteers had been up much earlier, cutting *ramón* branches to feed the mules and packing the beasts. Sure enough, the larded spines had worked up to the surface during the night, and it was easy to extract them from my knee. The day was almost a duplicate of the previous one. We went through one long, difficult *bajo* before reaching a tiny thatched shelter called Dos Arroyos, where we camped. One of the men killed an armadillo with his machete—the first wild one I had ever seen. I was not as tired that night, and I read for a while in my hammock before going to sleep.

I gained strength steadily on the trip, and the third night—at San Clemente—I was scarcely weary at all. Most of the day I rode just behind the bell mare. Bob and Ledyard went on ahead and got to camp before us. On my first attempt to ride and catch up with them, I got off the trail and experienced a few moments of panic. Luckily, I was not out of sound of the bell mare when she came along; I soon rejoined the train, determined never to leave it again under any circumstances. Again, we slept under a small thatched shelter. I watched two of the arrieros build their palm-frond lean-to. They propped two nine-foot forked poles against each other to form an A-frame, laid one end of a ridgepole between the crossed tips, and secured the other end to a tree. Then they laid dozens of big palm fronds against one slope and hung their hammocks under the shelter, tying one end to the top of the A-frame, the other to the tree.

The last day we were up again at four. Bob and Ledyard, who knew the way, started almost immediately. I had learned my lesson the day before, and waited until Dixon and Walter Scott finished with the breakfast dishes; then we three started out, well ahead of the mulada. Although we were only a few hours on the trail, and by now I was strong and saddle-toughened, this last day was in some ways the hardest of all. We crossed one long, bad bajo—the worst of the trip—just before reaching Uaxactún. At one place Walter's mule, just ahead of me, fell, but Walter jumped clear and was not hurt. In another I had a narrow escape. We had turned off the trail for twenty or thirty feet to avoid an especially bad mudhole. Coming back to it, Golondrina carried me right into a trap—two fallen trees crossed a little above the height of my saddle, with a third tree so close to them that I could not slip through. I had been busy holding my hat jammed down on my head, warding off branches and lianas with arms and elbows, and shifting my knees constantly to avoid the fierce needle-like spines on the escoba palms on all sides. I had therefore relaxed the rein on Golondrina, and I did not see the trap until the mule's head had bent to go under it. Realizing my best chance was to turn Golondrina's head so I would slide along the trees instead of under them, I pulled on the right rein and back at the same time, shouting "whoa!" The mule turned right but did not slacken her pace; instead she lurched forward. It was too late to bend forward on the mule's neck—the crossed trees had reached the pommel of my saddle. I lay back as flat as I could force myself, pushed against the bottom of the log with upturned palms—not to try to lift these monsters but to force myself lower— and turned my face to one side. The log scratched my face as it passed over. When I looked back, I could not believe that the saddle, much less I in it, had ever squeezed beneath those trees.

Finally we emerged from the bajo. Dixon said, "Very close now, sah." A few moments later we trotted through opening woods, across a big, open, grassy clearing, and into Carnegie's camp at Uaxactún. There were several

Palm-frond shelter for overnight camp, Tikal, 1932

thatch-roofed structures in a group; on the front open "porch" of the biggest sat Ledyard and Bob drinking coffee. A man took my mule. I removed saddle bags, machete, canteen, hammock, and blanket roll, dumped them on the tamped marl flood of the *corredor,* and sat down to coffee and a cigarette. Next—wonder of wonders divine—Walter announced that my hot shower was ready. I luxuriated under warm water spraying through a real shower attachment, from a barrel suspended by a rope overhead.

Uaxactún was what used to be called an "Old Empire" Maya city, meaning that it was occupied during the earlier stages of Maya civilization. Today, "Classic period" is a more usual designation for this epoch, because here in the southern lowlands it marked the classic expression of Maya culture, when the Indians erected imposing temple-crowned pyramids and multi-room civic and religious buildings of stone masonry, their narrow chambers bridged overhead with corbeled vaults. The city plazas were studded with stone monuments elaborately carved with figures and hieroglyphic inscriptions recording their ruling dynasties, historical events, and the dates thereof, together with related astronomical and astrological observations. These monuments were often erected at traditional intervals of time—every twenty, ten, or even five years, for example—and there is growing archaeological evidence that the pyramids were rebuilt—larger, higher, and more imposing—over existing structures at these intervals or when important personages died.

These important personages—probably priest-rulers in a theocratic city-

The expedition's mulada arrives at the camp clearing, Uaxactún, 1932

state sort of political organization—were buried in deep shaft graves or vaulted masonry tombs, sometimes sunk far down into the heart of the pyramid itself. The tunneled entrances were sealed after the funeral, to protect—the Indians hoped—forever their deceased leaders and the wives, concubines, and slaves sacrificed to accompany them to the next world.

These royal tombs and the various caches and other offerings that archaeologists encounter during their investigations—as well as the refuse dumps, substructure fill, and domestic dwellings that are excavated—yield the jewelry, pottery, weapons, tools, ceremonial objects, and other artifacts from which we infer much of what we know about prehistoric cultures. Of these, pottery is by far the most useful, since it underwent constant changes in fashion and style; and since it is found in such large quantities—either whole vessels or broken fragments—an archaeologist can usually obtain a large sample of specimens to analyze and interpret. Pottery was also traded widely and its styles diffused over large areas. The pottery of the Early Classic period at Uaxactún, for example, does not differ radically from that found throughout the Petén. Its distinctive features of clay composition, vessel shape, and decoration can be traced far into Honduras, up into northern Yucatán, across the Guatemala highlands to the Pacific coast, and indeed in some features all the way to the valley of Mexico.

The years that the Carnegie Institution excavated at Uaxactún enabled its archaeologists—especially Oliver G. Ricketson, Jr., Edith Bayles Ricketson, and, later, Ledyard and Bob Smith—to reconstruct in minute detail the chronological sequence of architectural and ceramic changes that occurred at this one site during a period of more than eighteen hundred years. The history of its occupation was pushed back beyond the Early Classic period into the epoch known as the Formative or Preclassic, dating to the first millennium before Christ.

Uaxactún's ruined buildings are divided into half a dozen or more groups, some of them situated on the leveled summits of high, steep-sided acropolis-like natural eminences connected by great causeways bridging the intervening ravines and swampy areas. The immense forest now blankets the entire city. Low mounds covering minor structures and dwellings are scattered throughout the large area; our field headquarters, a large pole-and-thatch house in a clearing at the foot of one of these acropolises, was built on the summit of one of these low mounds.

I had gone to Uaxactún to excavate house mounds, the dwelling places of the common people, whose remains archaeologists had understandably neglected in their exploration of the more spectacular pyramids, temples, palaces, and royal graves. The first three weeks, however, I spent on odd jobs that needed doing, and which gave me opportunity to find my way about the widely scattered sectors of this large ruined city, to learn the ways of the workmen before I supervised a group of my own, and to become acclimated in general to life in the bush. I made a plan and cross-section drawings of

A-XV—the only standing temple at Uaxactún—copied mask panels from it and the famous E-VII sub-pyramid—the oldest known temple platform in the Maya lowlands—and recorded hieroglyphic inscriptions on newly dis-covered stelae. I also sank a fourteen-foot pipe into the center of the great bajo to get a cross section of its deposits, in an attempt to test the geologist Cooke's hypothesis that these swamps were once great freshwater lakes that had become silted through erosion from Maya *milpas*, the corn patches planted in cleared and burned forest areas.

By the time I was ready to begin my own excavations, most of them at considerable distances from the main ruins and our camp, I was almost at home in the great rain forest, and could even strike out confidently from the established trails to cut my way into more remote parts of the jungle. This last was the most fun of all. I learned to respect the wildness and im-mensity of the bush, but also to revel in its awesome beauty and to be amused by its teeming life. Groups of spider monkeys, those fantastically agile acrobats of the treetops, hurtled through the forest or occasionally stayed to play and feed high overhead; more than once big howler monkeys, hostile but curious, would fuss and fret in a tree above me, roaring their disapproval and shaking branches with such brute power that I would be showered with dead limbs and other arboreal ammunition. The all-devouring army ants once passed between me and camp when I was coming back after a day's work. On another occasion I watched astonished as an enormous wola, a boa constrictor, on being prodded from his water-filled resting place, unwound almost ten feet of body and slithered it all slowly into a hole under

Carnegie Institution's archaeological camp at Uaxactún.

a tree. (One of my workmen, Santiago, wanted to kill it because, he said, the wola was poisonous between 4:30 P.M. and 5:30 A.M. When I questioned him on this, he explained that the wola has always bitten something by 5:30 A.M., and thus used up its "poison" for most of the day, but by late afternoon it has accumulated a new supply.)

I learned to be wary of small things, especially after I spent an hour copying a glyphic inscription from a monument and then discovered a tarantula in a hole in the wall where I had propped myself. Dixon and Walter were stung almost daily by scorpions in the *bodega* where our food was stored, and we killed enough coral snakes for each of us to have pen staffs covered with their skins. To this day I sometimes automatically empty my shoes and shake my trousers before putting them on. I learned to make ticks back out with a lighted cigarette, and to put adhesive plaster over a beef worm for twelve hours before squeezing it out of the skin. In spite of all these minor wonders I do not think that anyone ever felt himself in real danger in the bush—the frightening tales of professional adventurers to the contrary notwithstanding. A bad accident, an attack of appendicitis, or something else demanding immediate treatment could have been serious, even fatal, but this threat arose from our remoteness from civilization, not from the ferocity of the jungle itself.

Wild deer occasionally wandered from the forest into our clearing; one of our men shot a *gato del monte,* a sort of wildcat, within yards of our

Stelae and unexcavated temple mounds, Uaxactún

house. (I still have the tanned skin.) Don Pancho, the caretaker, and his short-haired dog hunted deer, wild pig, turkey, guan, curassow, and coati; we had wild game on the dinner table almost every day. We took no liquor with us into the bush—except a few bottles of rum for the one fiesta of the season, to which all the workmen were invited; consequently Bob, Ledyard, and I spent an inordinate amount of time preparing *bocas* (hors d'oeuvres) before dinner and debating the relative merits of the various meat sauces to be served with the entree of the evening.

J. Eric S. Thompson quotes a Belize old-timer as saying that anyone who claimed to like the Central American bush was either a bloody fool or a bloody liar. He was doubtless referring to travel in the jungle, with its constant hardships, disappointments, and annoyances. I do not know anyone who has spent any time in a "permanent" camp in the bush who did not love it. I was young and stronger then, perhaps more impressionable, and of course I did not have the responsibilities, say, that Ledyard had, which made a big difference in attitude. But Ledyard has gone back enthusiastically to Guatemala almost every one of the more than thirty years that have elapsed since then, usually to the rain forests of the Petén, the Pasión, and the Usumacinta.

One day a raggedly attired Guatemalan army officer showed up at our camp and asked permission to leave some chicle there until he could come back for it. Ledyard agreed, but made him sign a paper releasing us from any responsibility for the chicle. The officer had just arrested a poor fellow for bleeding chicle without permission. This man, in dire financial straits, had come into the Petén and, half starving, had managed to bleed forty-one blocks of chicle—more than a thousand pounds—in this area. Being arrested was bad enough, but having his chicle confiscated was worse. Our workmen were sympathetic with him, and one of them tipped me off that he would try to escape that night.

Sure enough, next day the chiclero was gone. He had struck out on the trail to Flores on Lake Petén, where he would offer his chicle to a contractor who had influence with the officials and who could bribe them to say that the chicle was taken under his government concession. In return for this favor, the chiclero had confided, he would sell his blocks to the contractor at a much reduced price—I believe it was twelve or fifteen cents a pound— thus saving the chiclero from total loss and from a term in jail.

The officer, waking up to find the chiclero gone, went out and arrested another man who was camping near Uaxactún. They did not find any chicle in his possession, and so they charged him with being an accomplice. At least the officer would not return empty-handed.

A *chultún* is a small subterranean chamber cut into natural limestone. Originally, these may have been dug simply to provide *sascab*, the marl or rotted limestone with which the Maya, both ancient and modern, floored their huts and used in making mortar and plaster. But they also served a number of other purposes. In some parts of the Maya area they were well plastered and would probably hold water; that they may have been reservoirs is further suggested in these instances by the paved drainage platforms surrounding their mouth—about the size of a manhole. Most of the chultúns at Uaxactún were not plastered, however, and could not have been reservoirs. For the same reason it seems to me that they would not have provided satisfactory storage, especially for corn or other food. Modern Indians store their corn in wooden bins raised well above ground level to protect the contents from moisture, rats, pigs, chickens, or other foraging animals. A few chultúns were used as tombs, but this was not their primary function.

When we were clearing the floor of an ancient Maya dwelling at Uaxactún, Santiago came on a huge stone lying flat and imbedded in the marl floor. When we prized it up, we found that it was the "lid" of a chultún entrance; the neck below was filled with fine, soft earth. The next day I started digging—a slow and difficult job because of the cramped work space, barely enough to stand in, much less maneuver a pick or shovel. Just before lunch time, I had cleared to a depth halfway between my knees and hips, and found that I had reached the bottling-out part—that is, the bottom of the entrance shaft. Some flat rocks were wedged into the neck at this point. With the edge of my shovel I flipped two of these rocks out, and noticed that loose earth began to slide through a small hole leading downward. Gradually an area fourteen inches long and five inches deep opened, with a dark emptiness below it. This was a great stroke of luck; I had expected to have to dig out the entire chultún. The Indians had evidently sealed the entrance to the underground chamber, filled the neck of the shaft, and then covered it with a lid stone at ground surface. Why would they go to all this trouble? Was there something in the chultún to hide? My curiosity was now thoroughly aroused.

I had climbed out hastily when the small hole began to open under my feet; some chultúns are bottle-shaped, and I did not want to fall through and hurtle down into the room below. Now I lay flat on my stomach on the dwelling floor above, had the workman Archie hold my ankles, and I let myself slide headfirst slowly down the shaft. I had no flashlight, and only a faint glimmer of light penetrated the small opening at the base of the shaft. I peered and peered, and gradually made out the lighter color of the marl floor below, some dark objects that seemed to be bones, and, farther back in the underground room, some black circles. I could not see what they were, but I hoped they were vessels of pottery left with the dead. It was maddening—like a bad dream in which you want terribly to see something, but your vision is blurred and you can make out only the dim outlines.

I returned to camp for lunch, and took back with me to the digging a poncho and flashlight. It had rained off and on all morning, and Ledyard had called off work for the day; so I was alone. In the pouring rain and with half a dozen spider monkeys showering me with branches from overhead, I spread the poncho on the wet ground, flung myself on it, and slid headfirst into the neck of the chultún. I held on for dear life with my right hand; in my left hand I held the flashlight to the opening at the bottom of the shaft and pressed the button to turn a beam of light into the darkness below.

Far richer tombs have been discovered at Uaxactún and throughout the Maya area. My burial was probably at best a middle-class artisan or temple attendant who lived in the environs of the main ruins, laid to rest, so to speak, in his own house cellar. But this was my first "big" find, and I doubt that Lord Carnarvon felt a greater thrill when he opened the last treasure-laden crypt of Tutankhamen in Egypt. First I saw the large bones of a complete skeleton, in what appeared to be a state of almost perfect preservation. Obviously this had been a large male and the bones seemed enormous by Maya standards. The skeleton lay flexed on its right side. Near the skull was a polychrome tripod dish, painted on the interior with three series of six conventionalized hieroglyphs between three concentric painted bands above and below; there were traces of a central decoration on the bottom. Nearby was a bowl, which was most attractive in its symmetry, color, and decoration of painted orange and black stripes and zigzag triangular patterns.

I climbed down into the subterranean chamber gingerly. Several coils of what appeared, when I first looked into the chamber from above, to be snakes or heavy rope, turned out to be tree roots which had penetrated the ceiling of the chultún, then dried up and fallen to the floor. I killed a large spider which evidently fell into the shaft while I was at lunch. Then I cleaned everything with alcohol, painted the bones with a thin solution of ambroid, and drew a scale plan and two cross sections of the cave.

I mentioned that we took no liquor into the bush except a few bottles of rum for the annual fiesta, a party that Ledyard gave every year for the workmen. They paraded from their camp over to ours, led by an improvised band consisting of a cornet, clarinet, guitar, a cymbal made from the top of a gas can, and the jawbone of an ass. The last had loose teeth, so when the jaw was held at the chin in the player's left hand and struck on the sides with his right hand, the loose teeth vibrated and gave a strange nasal twanging, much like the sound of a jew's harp.

We had cakes and punch spiked with rum, and distributed cigarettes. The men sang together and in solos, sometimes in Spanish, sometimes in their Belize River English. Each could play fairly well by himself, but they had no idea whatsoever of harmony or of keeping in tune together. Ledyard, Bob, and I performed sleight-of-hand tricks, feats of skill and strength, hand wrestling, and other "entertainment." Adolphus, the *caporal* (headman), made a formal speech, and Ledyard congratulated the workmen before distributing metal stars for their belts. These stars are given one for each season and are prized highly throughout the year, the old-timers sporting as many as six as proof of their seniority. The party ended at 1:00 A.M.; just before they left for their camp, the men gave three cheers for each of us in turn, in good old English style.

To me, brought up in South Carolina, these British customs performed by our Negro workmen at Uaxactún never failed to be startling and intriguing. The Negroes were, after all, British subjects, and their "formal" English had a distinct British accent. Almost every afternoon I walked over to their camp to watch them play cricket. Some Sundays Ledyard and Bob and I improvised a sort of track and field meet in which we competed with them in various events—I was undefeated in the hammer throw, I remember, but Ledyard was undisputed hand-wrestling champion. Slightly built, deceivingly unathletic in appearance, he had—and still has, I suppose—a grip like iron, and in short order he could bring any of us to his knees or push us sprawling off balance.

On April 14, Dixon reported having seen two men sneaking around camp and taking the trail out toward Santa Cruz. He thought they were fugitives from justice, because they avoided everyone, camped nearby without even coming over to speak, and left before dawn. Two days later they were again seen, this time going in the opposite direction and driving seven mules with them as fast as they could.

Carnegie Institution staff at Uaxactún, 1932. *From left to right:* Wauchope, Ledyard Smith, Bob Smith.

Two days after that an American arrived at our camp with two arrieros and four mules. He worked near Pasa Caballo for the Chicle Development Company, and was in pursuit of the three men who had sneaked by our clearing earlier, and who, he said, had stolen seven mules from his company.

The American was a short, thin, sun-browned, hard-bitten man of about forty-five, who had worked down here for many years, most of them in the bush. He had not been back to the States since 1923. He had dinner with us, and then sat and talked and smoked with us until after nine o'clock (a late hour for us). When he left, he said he scarcely hoped to get the mules back—they would probably be sold by the time he reached El Cayo—but he did hope to meet the thieves on the road. He touched his holster.

Later still our huntsman and caretaker, Don Pancho, returned to camp after being away several days, and said that he had met the mule thieves on the trail. They first claimed the mules were theirs, but Pancho told them he recognized one of the mules. At this they admitted they were stolen, but warned Pancho, who was unarmed except for his machete, not to inform on them. Pancho said he knew one of the men—a bad character known to have killed several persons from ambush. I thought of Sylvanus Morley's account of the ambush murder of Dr. Lafleur near this same spot and of the many tales of robberies and killings among these tough chicleros of the Petén, many of them outlaws when they fled to the jungle. It occurred to me that if there were any true dangers in the rain forest, they were not of that magnificently wild land itself, but of its puny human occupants.

In 1934, after another year of graduate study, I was back in the Maya country, this time to study in detail the dwellings of the living Indians. In order to interpret better the ancient house sites, we needed to know more about the construction, the furnishings, the assemblages, and the social uses of Maya dwellings, which had apparently changed little since prehistoric times. Carnegie Institution of Washington gave me a budget of $1,200 (nowadays the cost of a week's work in this business), no time limits (I stretched it to nine months in three countries), and a completely free rein to go anywhere and do anything I wanted.

In Yucatán I bought a hammock, a mosquito bar, a small duffel bag, a canteen for water, and a knapsack for my notebooks, pencils, and first-aid kit. Next I obtained a pass that enabled me to go anywhere, any time, on the narrow-gauge wood-burning railroads whose four main lines could take me within striking distance of much of that low flat and rocky limestone plain, covered—where there were no henequen fields—with a dry, thorny, and dense scrub forest. I would get on a train with no particular destination in mind; when we passed through an interesting village, I would toss the duffel bag out the window, get off, and then, either by muleback or on foot, visit the more remote villages in the area. Sometimes horse-drawn flat cars on rails (*plataformas*) extended from the railroad toward these more distant places.

Usually the village officials would let me sling my hammock in the municipal offices or, more frequently, in the jail room adjoining. When these accommodations were lacking, I sought shelter in the Indians' own thatch-roofed dwellings, where I learned firsthand how they lived and especially how they used their houses and sparse homemade furnishings. Week in and week out I lived on rice, black beans, tortillas, and oranges; strangely enough, I came to love rather than hate this diet. At intervals, when my socks were worn out and my clothes no longer bearable and a hot bath could, in the interests of simple health, no longer be postponed, I would wander leisurely back to the nearest railroad town and a pension, or back to the comfortably appointed Carnegie headquarters at the ruins of Chichén Itzá, where they had cocktails before dinner, ate from real tablecloths, and slept on real cots.

I traced the life history of Maya dwellings from their first stages of construction to their last years after abandonment, always noting what traces they would leave in the ground long after timbers had rotted away: the patterns of postholes and wall-pole footings, the arrangements of pole shelves and tables, the three-stone fireplaces, the pottery wash basins embedded in marl floors or in the hard-packed yard outside, the exterior storerooms, corn bins, hollow-log beehive stacks, and boundary walls. I learned which woods were favored for main posts that were embedded in the earth, which for the A-frames, and which for the ridgepoles. I plotted the geographical distribution of different house types, and questioned all the old people about

Palm-thatched Indian hut with door of woven vines. Tizimín, Yucatán, 1934

their remembrances of houses in the past. Everywhere I noted the Indian names for each part of the house, in the hope of finding these in early Spanish-Maya dictionaries or of reconstructing the aboriginal house types through paleolinguistics.

This last approach yielded some fascinating information. I found that in terminology the house was thought of as a creature. Throughout Yucatán—and, as I learned later, in almost all parts of Guatemala in many widely separated and mutually unintelligible Maya dialects—the literal meanings of native house terms were the same: for example, main posts were always the "legs of the house," the ridgepole the "head of the house," the door the "mouth of the house." From northern Yucatán to the remote western highlands of Guatemala, one timber in the roof frame was "the road of the rat": *u beil cho* in Yucatec; *be ri cho* in Quiché, of the central Guatemala highlands; *t be itch* in Mam, near the Mexican border; *be cho* in Kekchi, of the Alta Verapaz. Occasionally there were variations, but the rat usually figured in all: in Zutuhil on Lake Atitlán, Guatemala, for instance, *warabal choi,* "sleeping place of the rat."

This was long before the science of glottochronology made it possible to estimate the age of dialects, but we all knew the Maya languages must have diverged from their common ancestral stock many centuries—more likely

Indian huts of sacate grass thatch, cornstalk-and-stone walls, and with inverted pots at peaks of roofs. Santiago Atitlán, Guatemala, 1934.

millennia—before the coming of the Spaniards. That an unusual slang term
was the same in all Maya tongues, long isolated from each other by vast
stretches of jungle and mountains, surely meant that the house of antiquity
had this same timber in it. Thus I hoped, timber by timber, word by word,
to reconstruct the appearance of the aboriginal Maya dwellings as they were
long before the mural artists painted them on the walls of the Temple of
the Warriors at Chichén Itzá or before graffiti doodlers scratched them, in
still more ancient times, on the temples at Tikal.

Some Indians were apparently ashamed to tell me some of these slang
terms, and they would rack their brains for more elegant expressions, which,
however, always came out in Spanish, not Maya. Similarly, I had a hard
time wringing from them information about some house customs of a ritual
nature. For example, did they dedicate the house in some way when it was
completed, other than having it blessed by a Roman Catholic priest if he was
available? Usually, they denied any such practice. Then I would say, "You
know, in my country we have the custom of placing certain mementos—
papers, pictures, coins, or other objects—in the cornerstone of a building."
Ah—well, then they recalled that perhaps, maybe, yes, sometimes they dug
a hole in the floor and placed in it some holy water, a sacrificed chicken,
an herb, and some silver; then they prayed for the safety of the house and
burned some incense so the smoke would drive away evil spirits; then they
sealed the floor cache with marl and earth. I remembered seeing A. V.
Kidder find a sub-floor cache in the room of an ancient pueblo in New
Mexico; in a small depression capped with a stone slab lay two parrot skeletons and some ceremonial objects. Is it not possible that some day we will
excavate something like this from the floor of an ancient Maya dwelling?

All sorts of superstitions center in Indian house building. In Valladolid,
Yucatán, I was told that materials for the house had been cut when the
moon was full. I made only casual note of this statement at the time. Later
at Tizimín, when another informant said the same thing, I asked whether
this was customary and why. My informant replied that if wood is cut when
the moon is not full, it will split, break, rot, or crumble to pieces; in short,
it is no good for house construction. On being asked why this was so, the
Indian said that he did not know exactly, but many believe that when the
moon is full, it is "complete, mature, and strong" and that plants are then
correspondingly strong and mature. He said that fruit trees, for instance,
do not bear good, sweet, mature fruit until the moon is full. The same information was given at San Cristóbal in the Alta Verapaz, Guatemala. Later,
on my return to the States, I read a report on Chan Kom by Robert Redfield
and Alfonso Villa Rojas, who wrote that in this village in Yucatán the new
moon was called "the green, or unripe, moon," the full moon being the
"full pot moon," and that fruit trees and root crops were best planted, in
Indian belief, three days after the moon is full.

The Maya dwelling is at the heart center of Maya domestic life, beliefs,

ubject of fleas reminds me of more places than I care to remembe
st of all of Cobán, in the Alta Verapaz, Guatemala, an otherwis
g town. I stayed at a German hotel where the mattresses were mad
ded bark or old corn husks—I cannot remember which—and the wil
them was varied and lively. I also encountered in Cobán the only
mariposas—to put it delicately—that I have seen in years of trave
America.

d spent a week in Cobán, recording the unique cornhusk-thatched
huts under the invaluable guidance of Mrs. R. W. Hempstead, who
Kekchi fluently and took me personally from house to house to inter-
he Indians. I had ridden horseback with her son Alan to a neighboring
, San Juan Chamelco, and I had gone with her by *camión* to Santa
From there I walked the one and three-quarters leagues to San
bal, a Pokonchi-speaking village, and recorded Indian houses and
terms all day long, walking back in the afternoon to meet the camión
return trip. Now, at the end of July it was raining so often that I
zed that if I was to get back to Guatemala City by automobile—having
to Cobán, I was determined to see something of the Baja Verapaz at
d level—I must leave soon, because streams would soon be too swollen
rd. I therefore made arrangements to drive to El Rancho with a man
said he would leave as soon as his other passengers were ready. On
ust 1, they told him that they could go the next day, and we set the
r of departure at 3:00 A.M.

Ve did not get away until 4:00. It was bitter cold, and I kept myself
pped in a poncho until we came down out of the mountains into the hot
i-desert south of Salama. In the meantime, however, with the driver and
other male passengers crowded into a small vehicle, I soon realized that
nething was strangely amiss. In a land where menfolk prided themselves
their *machismo*, the air in the car reeked with perfume. Soon I learned
at my fellow passengers were traveling actors who had just completed an
gagement in Cobán and, like me, were returning to Guatemala City.
As soon as it grew light enough, I concentrated on observing the house
pes as they changed through the dramatic shifts of environment. For ex-
mple, in Cobán, houses had been thatched with corn or sugar cane. As
e climbed upward and southward, sacate grass thatch began to appear
nd, around Tactic, wholly replaced the other. Still farther south, palm thatch
ecame more frequent—the small leaf of the *Palma real* rather than the
onger fronds of the corasal and other types more commonly used in the
owlands. We stopped for coffee at Patal, a small Pokonchi settlement in the
mountains just over the political line into the Baja Verapaz, then at Tactic
(it was still dark there), and had breakfast of sandwiches at the top of a
mountain overlooking Salama—a magnificent view, surpassing any I had
seen in the western highlands. To the left of the road, up on a little hillock,
was a large pile of rocks supporting a wooden cross. Some Indians had

and practices. Here the child is born; here the woman kneels much of the
day by her crude stone fireplace, fanning the three smoldering sticks to flame
and filling the home with stifling smoke; here she mills corn on a metate and
pats tall stacks of tortillas; here the man returns from his milpa, and only
within the intimacy of the home do husband and wife lower their outward
reserve and show affection for each other; here the children learn much of
how they should behave as adults; and here, usually, the old people die.
A pole-and-thatch hut lasts, literally, a lifetime.

One thing I found out very quickly: so much depends on your guide-
translator. I did not speak the Indian languages, and often the Indians spoke
no Spanish; so I had to have someone accompany me to act as translator.
Furthermore, in the Guatemala highlands (much less so in Yucatán) the
inhabitants of the dwellings refused to admit me or even talk to me unless
I was with someone they knew and trusted. Frequently the men were far
away tending their corn patches, and the women of the house were timid
and uncommunicative. I found to my sorrow that a poorly chosen guide
(often a *ladino* recommended to me by the *alcalde* or *presidente* of the
village) was worse than none at all, particularly if he was disliked by the
villagers. Usually a small boy, Indian or ladino, made an excellent guide;
everyone knew him, he was not overbearing and did not interrupt the in-
formants to correct them or ridicule them. Small boys were also willing to
walk their legs off all day with me and carry my camera tripod without
complaint or sullenness.

Even these generalities backfired at least once. I had always heard that the
Indians of Santiago Atitlán in Guatemala were suspicious of strangers—they
had stoned the archaeologist Samuel Lothrop when they disapproved of his
excavating at one spot—but I was not prepared for being turned away from
fifteen huts the first morning I was there. I was accompanied that day by
an eleven-year-old who had been recommended to me. Although a ladino,
he "knew everyone" (I was told) and he spoke Zutuhil. Apparently everyone
also knew him—too well—since we gained admittance to few dwellings. What
was worse, he had seen my camera and tripod and had the idea that all I
wanted was photographs. Although I impressed on him before approaching
every house not to mention photographs, and that I did not care if I did not
get a single picture all day, he persisted in telling each family that I was
there to photograph them. After reprimanding him a dozen times, to no
avail, I finally told him to keep quiet—absolutely quiet on pain of untold
punishment—and I did the best I could with the natives in Spanish, which
none of the women spoke and which the men spoke even worse than I.

Two days later I chartered a launch for the day and returned to Santiago,
this time my launch man acting as intermediary. What a difference! He was
an Indian himself; he spoke Zutuhil; he caught on at once to the nature of
my work; and, best of all, he had an easy, friendly, disarming way of treating the Indians of the village—joking with the women until they giggled and

let us enter their homes, talking with the men about things wholly unrelated to my research until the ice was broken and confidence established, and never taking no for an answer. His name was Osualdo Velázquez Ordoño; God bless him!

Intermediaries came in all shapes and all sizes. Much to my surprise, one of the best I happened on was a native policeman at San Lucas Tolimán, also on Lake Atitlán. I engaged him with many misgivings, since I suspected that most Indians were cop haters. But he was Indian; he wore the costume; and although he carried the policeman's long black leather whip of authority, he was quiet, friendly, not at all overbearing with the townspeople, and apparently known and liked by them all. I was particularly careful in San Lucas to ask permission to enter every house, so that the occupants would not feel that the law was forcing them to let me in.

One more note on intermediaries. When I was in Tecpán, Guatemala, I decided to walk about three and a half miles to an Indian village called Santa Apolonia. When I reached there, not a living soul was in town except three Indians whom I found working at the *pila* for the city—doubtless working off their taxes or a fine. Everyone else had gone to the market at Tecpán. Santa Apolonia was not a large village, but it was not small, either; it gave me a strange feeling to see a town absolutely deserted.

I asked the three Indians whether there was anybody to guide me around, because I could not go poking into houses even if no one was at home. One of the Indians—the only one who spoke Spanish—went in search of a

guide, but after a long time came back alone. I would not ordinarily have risked: I bribe job for an hour and take me to his house an whispered conference with the other two, an what I would pay him for an hour's work. I k for the three of them to split profitably, and so of thirty-five cents. He quickly accepted.

From then on he made me feel as much like had ever felt. He cast furtive glances all about hi he frequently stole to the door and peered about voices; and when he left, he implored me to kee as surreptitiously as possible. (I had included in t a provision allowing me to remain in his house af

After I paid him, he slipped out; I stayed and and sketched details. When I had finished, I stro again and noticed that a town official had returned eating lunch on the *cuartel* steps. When I came up to the official, they gave me agonized, imploring lo and completely ignored them, and I could imagine not mention to the official a word about the transacti

Walking back the three and a half miles to Tecpán had bought more than scientific data with my thirty quired in the Indian's house a truly remarkable collect

My Indian policeman-guide in hut at San Lucas

Tolimán, on Lake Atitlán, Guatemala, 1934

stopped here to rest, and one of them, kneeling before the cross, prayed for several minutes before he moved on.

We came down into the valley and drove through Salama, with its tile-roofed adobe ranchos, then southward and eastward through San Jerónimo, Jícaro, San Clemente, and Crucitas to Morazán, and finally almost due east to San Agustín, where we crossed the Motagua River and drove into Rancho on the railroad a few minutes later.

This country, the Baja Verapaz, forms the western boundary of El Oriente, a semi-desert of rocks, hot sand, cactus, and cottonwoods, drained by the Motagua and extending, over rugged mountain terrain, into western Honduras. It was the country traversed by Stephens when he visited Copán, the scene of his journal to be quoted later in these pages. It has always had the reputation of being the "Wild West" of Guatemala—or rather the "Wild East." Even when I visited it in the early 1930's once away from the larger towns, like Zacapa and Chiquimula, the country was much as I have pictured in my mind our own West or northern Mexico of the nineteenth century: the blistering stretches of arid wasteland; the deep rocky gorges and dry arroyos; the boulder-strewn trails over mountains supporting a sparse and scrubby flora; the isolated adobe ranchitos and tiny settlements where women, stripped to the waist, sat in the shade of a narrow corredor and simultaneously wrapped and smoked cigars; the hardbitten men who looked as if they belonged to a band of Pancho Villa's marauders.

I remembered Stephens' accounts of this lawless land of the 1830's, but that was a century before, and I was astonished when my landlady, Doña Conchita, who ran the only pension in Chiquimula, implored me not to undertake the relatively short horseback trip over the mountains to Jocotán, a Chorti-speaking town that I was anxious to see. She told me alarming tales of bandits and robberies and murders, and I could not decide whether she had heard old wives' tales, whether she felt a gringo was not up to a little rough riding, or whether she was simply being overprotective. When I had engaged horses and a guide and set the hour of departure, she urged me to go well armed at least, which of course I had no intention of doing. In a land where seemingly every male over the age of twelve carried a pistol at his belt, I knew that I could only come off second best—that is, dead— in any possible encounter. Besides, it seemed to me that dressed as I was in aged khaki pants, a frequently patched shirt, and shoes now held together with strips of dust-caked adhesive tape, and with luggage consisting chiefly of a rolled-up hammock, an old weather-beaten Voigtlander camera, and a rickety tripod, I would present slim pickings to any would-be robber. I was entirely right.

My guide and I left Chiquimula at 4:30 A.M. We rode along for some time in the dark. Then we forded the Río San José and followed the Río Zutuque up through San Esteban and Santa Elena. Here we crossed the river and rode up over the mountains—splendid views everywhere—in a generally eastern course, although the road wound around and about from valley to mountain top and down again in every conceivable direction. Finally we descended into the valley of the Río Carcar, passed through a little settlement of adobe ranchos called San Juan Ermita, and then through a splendid stretch of semi-desert to Jocotán.

We arrived there at 10:15 A.M., having established what my guide seemed to consider the world's speed record for the trip. Everywhere we went in Jocotán he bragged about the killing pace, which puzzled and considerably annoyed me in view of the fact that most of the way we had walked our horses at what seemed a snail's pace; I had ridden far ahead much of the time, shouting back to urge, cajole, or threaten him into pushing his mount to at least a slow jogging trot. In this respect he was no different from almost every guide I have had in Central America. They all seemed to figure that one trip, no matter how short, was a day's work, so why hurry? Sylvanus Morley, whose adventures in the Petén I shall quote later in this book, is said to have held the speed record from Chiquimula to Copán, very probably over the same route I was following. But his mule dropped dead on arrival.

I suppose that we often expect too much of saddle mules and horses in Latin America in areas where they are poorly fed, just as I am sure that we

Between Chiquimula and Jocotán, Guatemala, 1934

expect too much of undernourished human workers. I used to attribute the latter's intolerably slow work rate, long rest periods, and general goof-off attitude to sheer laziness; but after considering their low calorie and still lower vitamin intake, I wonder how they can work as long and as well as they do. I was always acutely aware of this when I would sit down to mid-day lunch with a guide or a group of laborers. My meager sandwiches, fruit, and (at excavation sites) thermos of hot coffee or tea seemed like a banquet compared to their little bowl of *posole* with possibly a tortilla to go with it. A corn-fed mule brought a high price in Latin America. In the jungle they were fed ramón branches, a fair substitute, but in El Oriente the grazing must be very spare.

Another thing that we are likely to forget is the strong tradition of "motor habits." As A. L. Kroeber has noted, the Japanese carpenter always pulls the plane toward himself, whereas the Western workman always pushes it away from his body centrifugally. A man's coat or shirt buttons from the left over the right, but in women's garments it is the reverse; each sex finds it difficult to use the other system. Even animals acquire motor habits conditioned by human culture. We mount to the saddle by the left stirrup, and most horses become disturbed by an attempt to mount them from the right. In spite of being trained in anthropology and learning these things from books or lectures, I was always impatient with my Guatemala highland workmen who persisted in moving earth with their big hoes instead of using the fine shovels that I had brought all the way from the States. They would fill a hoe with loose earth from one pile and then with an awkward, stiff-armed motion fling it in an arc to the next pile. This was inefficient and slow on flat ground; from a deep pit, it was practically impossible. Every year I would demonstrate the slow, easy swing of a shovel wielder and point out that it was less tiring, more accurate for aim, moved more dirt at a time, required less working room, and could be directed straight overhead as well as forward or sideways. My workmen were always deeply impressed, murmured admiration, and immediately went back to their hoes.

In Yucatán that same year I first met E. Wyllys Andrews and formed another of the lifetime friendships that have made my pursuit of archaeology so rewarding. Bill was a freshman at Harvard at the time, but was already an expert on Maya hieroglyphics and had published on this technical and most difficult subject in professional journals. Morley had of course spotted him, and had invited him to Yucatán to take part in Carnegie Institution's archaeological program there. Bill wanted to make a trip down to Lake Chichancanab, south of the Yucatán boundary, in Quintana Roo, an archaeologically little known area in which ruins had from time to time been reported. I was anxious to trace Indian house types in the same area, and so on May 12 we took the train from Mérida to Peto, the end of the line and what we thought was to be jumping-off place for our two-man expedition. Here we learned that the best way to get even farther south was via mule-drawn plataforma on a branch line that ran from Tzucacab to Catmis. We had passed Tzucacab on the train, and so next morning we took our same train back a little way to this town and obtained passage on the plataforma. Catmis was a chicle town, where chicleros sold their blocks of gum bled in the rain forests of the south, and was well known also for its sugar factory. It was therefore not very Indian, and I had some difficulty finding the Maya terms for parts of the house.

From Catmis we took another plataforma to Santa Rosa, a large chicle hacienda, where we were entertained graciously by the manager, Luís Maldonado. This gentleman not only made us his guests at the hacienda, but gave us mounts and a guide for the trip to the lake and provided us with shotgun and shells and provisions as well. I have known many kind and friendly people in Middle America, but none has exceeded Maldonado's hospitality.

After supper we left for Lake Chichancanab, late in the evening—after dark—to avoid the savanna flies, which were vicious and would have bitten the mules beyond endurance. That ride in the black of night was one of the weirdest I have ever experienced. We had four animals: two saddle horses, a saddle mule for the guide, and a pack mule. Except for the flickering light from a miner's lamp attached to the head of the guide, it was pitch dark. I rode third, and I had to keep my eyes glued on the arriero's hat and its light not only to follow it but also to see vines and branches in time to ward them off my head. As we had traveled south from Tzucacab we noticed the scrub forest becoming higher and higher; by now we were in real jungle, the first rain forest I had seen since two years earlier in the Petén. Occasionally the arriero's hat was brushed off, the light went out, and we would be in total darkness until it could be relit. Only the frequent flashes of lightning revealed what was around us. The jungle in broad daylight is awe-inspiring. At midnight, on the trail, it is frightening—or at least it was to me—and I found myself wondering what we would do if our little light failed or if our guide lost or deserted us.

It was therefore no little relief that I felt when we reached, late that night, deep in the forest, a *ranchito* called Dziuche. We slung our hammocks in a palm-thatched, dirt-floored, one-room bush hut. Bill and I both had large hammocks, and we took up more room than the Indians. Between us slept a little boy in a smaller hammock. A fourth person had rigged a sort of bed up on a platform of poles at the end of the hut.

Next morning we were up early. We reached the lake after a short ride, and had our first daylight view of the magnificent rain forest. Close to the lake's edge, near a small lean-to shelter of *guano* palm fronds, we encountered a lone native, who said that he supported himself by killing crocodiles in the lake and selling their skins in Catmis, whence I suppose they eventually found their way to the craftsmen and shops of the capital. He offered to take us in his dugout canoe on a tour of the lakeshore—for a fee—and we readily accepted, blessing the good fortune that had led us to apparently the sole inhabitant of this wilderness.

We loaded all our provisions in the canoe and climbed in. For some time our guide poled through the still water close to shore, inside a belt of reeds that protected us from the lake wind, while we reveled in the tropical scenery. Then he pushed the canoe through the reeds out into the lake. A sudden gust of wind whipped the waves high, and before we knew what was happening the canoe overturned, tossing us and all our belongings into the churning water. It all happened so suddenly that we could assess the seriousness of the situation only a little at a time. Comparing thoughts later, Bill and I agreed that each new thought we had only increased our alarm. First, could we recover the canoe? Second, could we get to shore? Third, what about our cameras, our borrowed shotgun, our knapsacks of field notes, money, passports, and railroad passes? And, finally, what about those crocodiles our guide hunted for a living!

We pushed the canoe nearer to the shore, to a point where we could splash water out of the canoe with one hand while holding it above the lake surface with the other. Then we began diving for our lost equipment. The water was murky and full of reeds, making visibility correspondingly poor; but it was not very deep, and eventually we recovered everything except our canteen of boiled water, which we were by now willing to abandon. We piled everything into the canoe again, an article at a time, and then pushed and swam with it back to still water where we could clamber back in.

This, as I say, was in 1934. I do not know whether it was true or not, but we were told locally that we were the third and fourth North Americans to visit Lake Chichancanab within memory—one man eight years before us, and another eighteen. Bill and I do lay claim, however, to being the first to reach the bottom of the lake. For brevity's sake, we have always referred, in our personal correspondence with each other, to this ill-fated jaunt as the 301CIWSXWJYQR&BLC—short for the Three Hundred and First Carnegie Institution of Washington Submarine Expedition, to the Wilds and Jungles of Yucatán and Quintana Roo, and the Bottom of Lake Chichancanab.

At my present age, this experience would be enough to persuade me that I needed a week's rest, physical and mental. To give some hint of how we young men were able to accomplish so much in so little time in those days, I want to summarize the schedule Bill and I kept during the following week. Our dunking in Chichancanab was on Monday, May 14. We realized that after their hour's soaking in the lake, our cameras with their Compur shutters, our watches, and the shotgun would not be of much further use to us unless they were rather promptly cleaned and adjusted. So in spite of the savanna flies we rode all the way back to Santa Rosa, stopping only briefly for coffee at Dziuche, then took a plataforma to Catmis after supper, caught there the late plataforma to Tzucacab, napped a couple of hours, breakfasted, and were on the six-o'clock train Tuesday morning again bound for Mérida. We searched the city for a camera repair shop but could find none. A watchmaker, however, who agreed to do a rush job on our watches, assured us that he could also clean and reset our camera shutter mechanisms. It took him most of the night and the next morning, but he was as good as his word. By Wednesday afternoon we were again on the train, this time for Oxkutzcab, arriving that same evening. We called on the presidente, who told us we could sling our hammocks in the *cuartel municipal*. Before nightfall, not only had we found and engaged an arriero and mules for further travel the next day, but I had ridden horseback around the town several times and recorded the house types there. On Thursday we rode muleback from Oxkutzcab to the ruins of Labná, stopping en route to record old ruined dwellings at Tabi, modern Indian huts in a little settlement called Sabbiche, and ancient ruins nearby. It was pouring rain when we reached Labná, but we spent the remaining daylight hours making short

Maya ruin, Labná, Yucatán. Roof structure was to achieve increased height as well as for ornamentation.

dashes from one room to the other of the larger structures. We continued our visit Friday morning, rode on to the ruins of Xlabpak, then to Sayil, where we ate lunch and inspected the famous "palace" and other buildings. Later that same afternoon we rode on to the ruins of Kabah.

We spent most of Saturday at Kabah and left late in the afternoon for Oxkutzcab again—all this, remember, by muleback. On Sunday we departed Oxkutzcab by train for Mérida, left there the same afternoon for Muna, where we settled in the *fonda;* we arranged for an ancient automobile to take us over rocky roads to the ruins of Uxmal the next day, and then I recorded the thatched huts and interviewed some old Indians about their childhood memories. Next day we rattled and shook over the rugged road to Uxmal, spent the day and night there, and returned Tuesday via Muna to Mérida, one week and a day after the 301CIWSXWJYQR&BLC.

Two days later, having returned to Chichén Itzá for a change of clothing, I was off on a fourteen-day trip that carried me by train, sailboat (*canoa*), plataforma, and *tranvía* (gasoline-run flatcar) to Campeche, Lerma (a picturesque little town squeezed between the cordillera and the sea), Champotón, and assorted inland villages. Our clothes and shoes wore out in those days, but we did not seem to.

Wauchope and Bill Andrews at Kabah, Yucatán, 1934

Another year of graduate study at Harvard and I was ready for the field again—this time scheduled to go as a field assistant on a survey of Coahuila, in northern Mexico, a little known region archaeologically and an important one because of its geographical position between the high civilizations of ancient Mexico and the archaeologically rich Southwestern United States. But less than five minutes' conversation changed the plans entirely.

We used to call the stone front steps of the old Peabody Museum of Harvard the anthropologists' travel bureau. You were not allowed to smoke in the museum or its library, and so a small group of graduate students and a professor or two were almost always standing on the front steps smoking and talking. Many of us felt that we learned more out there than we did in the classrooms and library, since the news and arguments ranged from physical anthropology and ethnology to linguistics and archaeology, from Siberia to Africa, China to the Americas. Alumni of the department and other professional anthropologists reporting back to the museum or there on other business stopped here to chat too, and we young fellows were always anxious to meet in person the great names in our profession. Here we picked up news of current and future expeditions, as well as unpublished new data fresh from the field. Graduate fellowships for field work were practically nonexistent in those days (there are precious few of them now), so getting on a field expedition—any field expedition—was an achievement. But there were far fewer students of anthropology then, and I honestly believe it was easier to find field work than it is now. Also, unlike most graduate students nowadays (do I sound very old?), we were delighted to

Bill Andrews and Indian at Sabbiche, Yucatán, 1934

serve anywhere, any time, without salary—just for expenses—deeming ourselves fortunate to get field experience on any terms.

To get back to the Peabody steps. I was standing there with A. V. Kidder,
chairman of the Division of Historical Research of Carnegie Institution, who
had taken me with him to his excavations at Pecos, New Mexico, when I was
a college freshman seven years before, had persuaded me to go to Harvard
graduate school, and had placed me on my first Carnegie expedition to
Uaxactún in 1934. We were discussing my plans for Coahuila, when Samuel
K. Lothrop joined us. He was in the process of writing a report on a fine
collection of jade, pottery, and gold, owned by Father Rossbach of Chichicastenango, Guatemala, and said to have come from some stone slab tombs
near Zacualpa, a small village in the remote Quiché highlands. Lothrop had
visited Zacualpa briefly and had taken some photographs of the site where
the tombs had been opened. At that time little was known of Guatemala
highland archaeology. There had been isolated excavations here and there,
but no one knew as yet how these floating bodies of information fitted together. Mary Butler had analyzed and reconstructed one of the pioneering
chronological sequences of pottery for a subregion: materials from a series
of tombs in the Alta Verapaz. Lothrop himself had excavated on Lake
Atitlán in the western highlands, and his publication on the Zacualpa tomb

Bill Andrews at Kabah, 1934

offerings was nearing completion. He was enthusiastic about their significance, and when he heard that I was going to Coahuila he remarked that
investigations at Zacualpa would be much more important and why did I
not go there instead. I looked at my boss, Dr. Kidder, and asked him why
not. Kidder puffed away at his pipe a few moments—always unhurried, apparently never ruffled, surely never pressured by impertinent young graduate
students—and then said, calmly, "Sure. Go ahead." In less than five minutes
I had moved my plans thirteen hundred miles southward. Instead of the
happy-go-lucky prospect of simply joining an organized expedition as field
assistant, I was faced with running my first excavation in a foreign land, outfitting it, hiring the labor, getting the permits—for that matter finding the
place, which was at that time merely a one-sentence footnote in a book as
yet unpublished. I followed Lothrop into the museum to look at his map and
see where Zacualpa was anyway. He gave me the two snapshots he had taken
at the ruins, and said I could probably find the tombs by lining up features
of the landscape with trees and cliffs that showed in the photographs. And
that was it. What do I do next? Buy a pick and shovel? Five picks and shovels?
Or twenty? Do they sell wheelbarrows in Guatemala? I talk to the minister
of hacienda, with my country Spanish? Where was that Zacualpa again?

My budget for the entire operation was $1,600. And remember, if you
spend it all, you will have to walk home.

It was not as bad a prospect as it sounds. I had been to Guatemala twice,
and I knew conditions in the highlands reasonably well from my ethno-
graphic work there the year before. I had learned a fair amount of Spanish,
and although I could not discuss economic theory with a professor at San
Carlos University, I did have the earthy vocabulary for life in the sticks; and
I had served under two masters of field excavations: A. V. Kidder and
Ledyard Smith. Zacualpa was as nearly ideal an environment as one could
order. It was, in 1935, almost completely isolated. The roads to it were ter-
rifying—in fact, I understand that now, thirty years later, they are still forbidding—but the climate was delightful. The ruins were in La Vega, an
almost treeless valley 5,000 feet above sea level between high, pine-forested
plateaus, with a plentiful water supply from the shallow river that etched a
sinuous moat from fifty to sixty feet wide between its old valley floor and
sheer volcanic tuff cliffs towering over its northern banks. The days were
sunny and temperate, the nights frigid. The town of Zacualpa was only two
miles from the ruins, and my cook, María, and I went to market there every
Sunday to buy food and minor supplies, to pick up mail, and to pay respects
to the governor-appointed mayor. The town was far enough from the ruins
to discourage visitors, but the small boys of Zacualpa begged me to ride them
to La Vega after every trip to town and were glad enough to walk the two
miles back in return for the experience.

In the Guatemala highlands, each Indian village has its own costume. All
the women and girls from one place dress almost exactly alike, and so do the

men and boys; an expert in such matters, passing groups of natives along the road, can tell at once where they are from. The Zacualpa costume was, I thought, particularly appealing. The women wore a red blouse or *huipil* with fine white and yellow stripes and embroidery on the shoulders, a shawl of the same cloth, a dark blue skirt that hung from the waist to about halfway between knee and ankle, and a triangular *tzute* or head kerchief with tasseled corners which they often knotted over silver coins. The men's costume included the local gray wool skirt or apron worn throughout the Quiché area, white trousers, and a red belt or sash with embroidered animals. The men also carried a brown and white checkered knitted or crocheted bag and usually also a small cylindrical basket for the wool which they spun into yarn when they were not carrying a burden or otherwise occupied. When two men stopped to chat on the road, their hands were frequently busy with hand spindle and yarn, spinning the long-handled sticks, which were fitted through perforated clay or stone whorls—"flywheels"—and feeding the raw

Cuchumutanes Mountains, in the Guatemala highlands between Sacapulas and Nebaj.

yarn into the whirling top. Women, on the other hand, did all the weaving on simple two-bar hand looms, one end attached to a tree or house timber, the other fastened by a rope around the woman's waist or buttocks; as the weaver knelt at her work, she could adjust the tension on the loom by leaning slightly forward or backward.

I rented a dirt-floored, windowless, adobe hut within easy walking distance of the ruins; my only neighbors were Indians and a few ladino-Indian families who farmed corn and sugar cane in the valley. I brought an excellent cook with me from Guatemala City, and she cheerfully prepared fine meals, kept house, and did all my laundry in the nearby river. I will have more to say of María when I tell of my return to the highlands twelve years later. She was a wonderful and astonishing character. Although at age twenty-five I considered her a rather old woman, she came back with me to Guatemala City "slightly pregnant" by one of my married workmen, a circumstance that provided my Carnegie friends in the city with what seemed to me endless sly, barbed, tasteless, and completely unjust innuendoes.

I said that the valley was almost treeless. Actually, most of the Indian huts stood in little clusters of fruit trees: guava, orange, lime, mango, banana, plantain, guineo, and avocado—we had a fine orange tree by our house. María could obtain eggs, fruit, and many vegetables from our neighbors during the week, enabling us to limit to a minimum our visits to town—always made at risk to life, limb, and aged pickup truck, over a somewhat enlarged cow path that crossed the Río de la Vega at one point without benefit of bridge. The most exciting part of the trip to town was when our vehicle careened down the muddy slopes we had cut in either bank, sputtered across the river sending up sheets of water on windshield and side windows, and roared up the opposite bank to dry security again. Above the noise of motor and flying water one could hear the delighted screams of my little passengers, the Zacualpa *pantojos*, who thought I was doing them a favor to give them a ride to La Vega but who actually served a very useful function—that of ballast—over a road that bounded the vehicle up and down, shudderingly sideways and back, unless it was properly loaded.

Tropical flint corn, the staple crop in the valley, was planted according to the rains, theoretically, but since the land was usually so wet, no great harm was done if the rains arrived later than usual. The Indians plowed with one ox drawing a crude wooden single-handled plow, a small boy with goad walking in front to guide the animal. They plowed three times: in December (*romper*, to break), in January (*cruzar*, to cross), and in February (*terciar*, to "third"). After each plowing they crushed the larger clods of earth with a huge hoe. Early corn was planted in March, and harvested five or six months later, in August or September. Late *milpas* were planted in May, and harvested in October and November.

Although technically all Guatemala Indian antiquities were government property and by law subject to expropriation for purposes of excavation, I was anxious, in the interests of both justice and good will, to reimburse our landowners for whatever crops we might deprive them from planting because of our digging. All but the very steepest, biggest mounds were regularly put under cultivation if the ox and plowman could manage to negotiate the slopes successfully. Most of our excavations took place on one man's property, an absentee landlord who lived in Zacualpa, and a mortal political enemy of the mayor or, as he was called, the *intendente*. In an early conversation with this official, I had mentioned my intention of paying the owner. The mayor reacted almost violently. He reminded me of the law on this point, and said that we were not to pay the *dueño* one red centavo. I argued that the law merely said the government could expropriate archaeological land; it did not expressly forbid just reimbursement to the landowner. The *intendente* disagreed and remained very firm: by no means would he permit us to pay his rival. I asked the *intendente* to meet with me and the landowner to explain all this to the latter. The meeting was set for eleven in the morning at the *juzgado*. When I arrived (on time) the landowner was coming out, looking very disgruntled, and I was told that all was settled. I felt sure the dueño must believe that I had framed the whole thing with his enemy.

Later, however, I decided to risk an under-the-table payment, in a way

Chutix Tiox, Guatemala, a highland stronghold in the days of Columbus

that would protect me if it should come to light. Dr. and Mrs. Kidder visited me for a short time six weeks after my talk with the intendente. I rented, swept, washed down, and sprayed the adobe hut nearest mine, spread *petate* mats on the dirt floors, had a private latrine dug for them and enclosed it with a wall of corn stalks, and did all we could at least to duplicate my own crude but comfortable quarters. I then sent word to the property owner in town, inviting him out to La Vega for a drink one night to meet my boss. He rode out on horseback, doubtless expecting to get swindled out of some more land. After a couple of cognacs and small talk, I told him first that we were greatly disappointed over being prohibited by the mayor from paying him for the loss of his crop. I then asked him whether it was not approximately true that his land averaged two or at best three quintales (between two hundred and three hundred pounds) of corn to the *cuerda* (about one-tenth of an acre), and that this would have brought him $1.50 a *quintal,* or $4.50 in all. He nodded. I then told him that my great *jefe,* Doctor Profesor don Alfredo Kidder, was greatly appreciative of his position; although we could not legally pay him for the land, we wished to beg him to accept a token of our appreciation for his many other courtesies, with the request that in view of the circumstances he say nothing of this gift to anyone. Kidder then handed him an envelope containing $4.50 in cash. We had another couple of

Main acropolis, Chutix Tiox. Stone stairway leads to temple platforms

rounds of brandy, and the dueño left, a tall, thin, still dignified but surprised and pleased individual.

This was on a Thursday night. Sunday I went to market with María, and stopped in the mayor's office to pay my usual respects. There, sitting at the mayor's desk, was the new intendente, appointed the day before by the *jefe político* of the department of Quiché in an unexpected political shuffle. It was our landowner.

Saturday was always payday at Zacualpa. We made a ceremony of it, quitting work early in the afternoon and returning to my house, where the men waited in the yard while Ricardo Méndez (my foreman) and I drew up the payroll. They were called in one at a time and paid, the money being handed symbolically from me to the foreman to the barefooted laborer. One Saturday in mid-December Ricardo and I were in the hut working on the payroll. Suddenly I felt very dizzy; everything seemed to swim before my eyes. I was just about to tell Ricardo that I felt bad and would have to lie down for a moment, when María, who was outside talking to the men, shrieked, *"Temblor! Temblor!"* Sure enough, it was an earthquake—the strongest I had ever experienced. When the roof timbers began to creak, and bits of tiles dropped around us, Ricardo and I lost no time in getting outdoors. There were three strong quakes, with almost continuous tremors between. We stood in the yard and watched the entire house move in wavelike undulations. The Ford pickup truck rocked back and forth; I could even see its wheels turning. I was standing by a tub of water that we kept to wash potsherds in; the water splashed out on my shoes.

Then a great cloud of white dust rose from the base of the tuff cliffs across the river, and I knew there had been another landslide there. I ran in the house for my camera, but by the time I could reach an open view of the cliff the dust had thinned too much to show in a distant photograph. I now understood why that great sheer cliff stayed scarred with white instead of graying with the years.

By the middle of February, 1936, it was time to stop the excavations. After traveling all the way from the States; after providing the little expedition with everything from surveying instruments and photographic equipment to wheel barrows, picks, and shovels; after renting a house for more than four months, with a housekeeper-cook to make life easy; and after keeping a gang of fifteen men and their foreman busy all that time—my $1,600 was running out.

We had hundreds of cloth sacks filled with pottery, more than seven hundred objects of interest (jade figurines, carved bone figures, obsidian projectile points, stone bark beaters, hard greenstone celts, and so on) catalogued, a number of burials and cremations, and a full record of the rooms or terraces or strata from which they had come. These artifacts documented a long span of highland prehistory from the fifteenth century back to the early years of the Christian Era. But although we had probed deep under buildings and had sunk test pits in many places throughout the site, we had not yet found any remains of the earliest major period of Middle American archaeology: the Preclassic or Formative stage dating to centuries before the time of Christ. I wanted badly to fill in this ancient hiatus in our otherwise unbroken record, but had about decided that I would have to go home without doing so. Then came the surprise of the season.

Another thing I had not found in this ancient city was a good refuse dump: a place where broken pottery, tools, animal bones, and other garbage were tossed or swept when the plazas and temples were cleaned for ceremonies. These are usually difficult to find in a ceremonial center, just as they would be if someone a thousand years from now searched for a refuse dump at Rockefeller Center. At Uaxactún one had been found on the steep slopes of the Group A Acropolis; so it occurred to me that perhaps the Zacualpa Indians swept their trash over the precipitous edges of the Main Court where it dropped off to the river flowing far below. When I chose one of our workmen, Rumaldo, to go with me and explained to him what I wanted to do,

Workmen in exploratory trench under an ancient structure at Zacualpa

he told me of a place on the edge of the *barranca* where pottery vessels had washed out of the banks several years before and had tumbled down into the river. He led me to the spot; after clearing the loose stones and hundreds of potsherds along the edge of the steep bank, we began to cut a sheer face to see whether it was stratified there. We had to cut little ledges to stand on, because we were in constant danger of tumbling down the barranca. The drop of forty feet was so sheer that the large stones we dislodged fell into the river itself.

In an hour's digging we got a couple of hatfuls of sherds and two jade beads, but none of the whole vessels Rumaldo had promised. Next morning we returned with two more men—Ricardo, the caporal, and Manuel, a stupid lazy boy who kept his job by virtue of being Ricardo's cousin. My private name for him was Manuel the Mute. We dug for two hours with no results. Then Manuel—whom I shortly thereafter renamed Manuel the Magnificent —found a complete vessel, and by lunchtime four more. We had broken into an ancient cemetery, in which the burials had been in simple stone-slab cists apparently erected in gulleys that were eroding back from the barranca into the plaza, but were now buried two to six feet below the surface. The earth here was cement-hard, and the digging was slow and difficult. After lunch I called for reinforcements, and by day's end we had nine men working there, had found fifteen complete vessels, many big jade beads, and four large *camahuiles*, the greenstone or jade figurines found throughout the highlands.

Best of all, these burials dated to a period far older than anything we had yet found, extending our record of the site back to what we now estimate to be the five centuries immediately before Christ.

That same week an Indian making adobes only about three hundred yards from where we had been working all season uncovered a pottery vessel of this same period in sandy soil just under the surface. I left word for him to notify me if anything else turned up. That afternoon he sent word that more vessels were in sight. This second cache lay about ten feet away from the first one, again only a few inches below the ground. Four days later the Indian making adobes found still another cache of pottery, again about ten feet farther on; this one was associated with a jade bead and traces of human bone. In spite of our good fortune, I could not help but reflect bitterly that now that our time was up we were beginning to hit the jackpot everywhere.

I returned to Guatemala City on March 5. Dr. Kidder was there, excavating a pyramid just outside the city limits, at a site called Kaminaljuyú, once a huge metropolis as ancient highland cities go. There were several hundred mounds there, many of them large. At sundown, when they loomed big and dark in the fading light, their skyline was particularly awesome. Although a relatively small mound, the one under excavation contained several superimposed pyramids, each with a deep shaft grave in the courtyard in front; these tombs were lavishly stocked with archaeological treasures the likes of which I had never seen. Zacualpa had seemed big to me when I was there, but I really felt like a country boy when I saw the burials at Kaminaljuyú.

I tarried in Guatemala City several days, luxuriating in city comforts, seeing a movie almost every night, and consuming ice cream sodas by the dozen. One evening when we were alone at dinner, Mrs. Kidder began asking me rather strange questions in a most hesitant manner. Was I very anxious to get home to the States? Had I promised my family I would return in March? Was I tired and fed up after months of virtual isolation at Zacualpa? Eventually she got around to the point. The Kaminaljuyú excavation had become far more complex than Kidder had anticipated; the royal tombs and their amazing contents were more than both of them could cope with. Kidder would like me to stay and help, but he refused to ask me at the end of a long, hard season of my own. Mrs. Kidder said she had taken it on herself to sound me out. As if there were any question of what I would do! Enthralled, I was at work the next morning.

This was archaeology de luxe. Kidder and I arose early and breakfasted alone in the fine pension dining room. Then we strolled to the front door, where a taxi and driver waited to take us to the digging! The pension cook had prepared a picnic lunch for us, which we ate at the site, often finding a bottle of sauterne in the hamper. After work, back to the pension in style, a hot shower, cocktails, for dinner the best food in the city, and afterward the movies. We were really a little ashamed of ourselves, but we told each other that one could not buck fate.

Restoration drawing of a pyramid at Kaminaljuyú, Guatemala

From A. V. Kidder, J. D. Jennings, and E. M. Shook, *Excavations at Kaminaljuyu, Guatemala.*

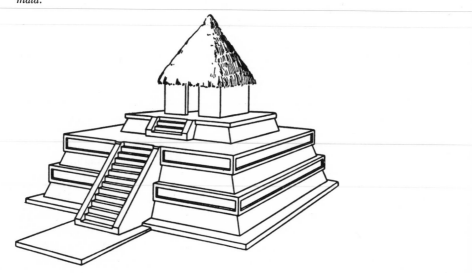

Kaminaljuyú spanned a considerable time in Guatemala prehistory, but these particular tombs were of the Early Classic period, about the fourth to seventh centuries A.D. J. Eric S. Thompson and others had noted the close resemblance between certain Early Classic ceramics in this Maya area and those of Teotihuacán, the famous city of giant pyramids, elaborate temples, and "palaces" far to the northwest, near Mexico City. The Kaminaljuyú discoveries revealed that Teotihuacán influence in the Maya highlands was far greater than had been supposed. The contents of our tombs—and there were thirteen major shaft graves like the one I shall describe here—could have come almost intact straight from Mexico. Some of the finds were surely imported from the north. The carvings on a stone plaque and on a trophy skull were in typical Tajín-Totonac Mexican style.

Kidder was inclined toward the view that there was no mass migration of Teotihuacán Mexicans into the Guatemala highland; nor, on the other hand, was there a necessarily slow diffusion of culture from one area to the other. Instead, he thought it likely that a small group of warlike adventurers from the north conquered Kaminaljuyú and became overlords of the resident population. If so, this was one of a long series of Mexican conquests of the Maya; influences from Teotihuacán and, later, from Tula in Hidalgo, have been noted throughout the Maya area, from northern Yucatán (where Mexican Toltec invaders are actually depicted in the temple murals), to the Petén, British Honduras, the other southern lowlands, and the Guatemala highlands.

The burial furniture of the shaft graves was, as I said, lavish. From it one could only infer a highly opulent and autocratic ruling class of priest-kings and warriors. Certainly it was clear that at the death of one of these great personages, a barbarically splendid funeral was held; wives, concubines, or servants were sacrificed; and the deceased was provided with great treasures to accompany him to the next world. The tomb in which Mrs. Kidder and I began was a vertical shaft, roughly square in outline, measuring about eight or nine feet on a side; it was originally about seven feet deep, although it was now ten or twelve feet below the surface. It had once been lined with mats, roofed with timbers, and probably left unfilled for some time after the funeral; the bodies had decayed, slumped from their original sitting position to the floor, and had become covered with a thin layer of dark material, probably the disintegration of their own wrappings before the pit was filled. Kidder found that the stairway of a later structure was built over the tomb roof; when the roof later began to sag, it weakened the stairway, which had to be demolished and rebuilt for a subsequent structure.

Three individuals had been placed in the tomb. A middle-aged male, seated cross-legged and upright in the center of the tomb floor (before he slumped), was obviously the principal personage. The other two skeletons were of adolescents, presumably slaves or concubines sacrificed to accompany their master.

The central figure was lavishly adorned. He wore a necklace of fine, large

jade beads, a bracelet of twenty jade spangles on his left wrist, elaborately
carved jade earplugs, jade and copal ear ornaments, a jade pendant carved
to represent a crocodile, and a shell "horse collar" ornament. Two jade-
incrusted slate disks and jade mosaic sets lay directly under the skull. In his
lap was a pyrite-incrusted plaque, and underneath it a pair of spondylus
shells, containing a lump of unworked jade painted with cinnabar. Nine
stingray tails—with which the Maya are known to have mutilated themselves
in ritual bloodletting—also lay in the lap: they too were covered with cinnabar. There were also three bone awls—one made from the jaw of a puma.
Near the right knee were a second pyrite-incrusted plaque, shell and jade
ornaments, and several jaguar teeth and jaws.

The minor skeletons had far fewer funeral offerings. One wore shell disk
ear ornaments, and one had anklets or shin ornaments of scalloped shells.
The tomb was full of beautiful painted and modeled pottery, apparently
never used before the funeral and probably made specifically for it. There
were graceful little "cream pitchers," elegantly formed fish- and frog-effigy

Pottery incense burner in the form of an elaborately costumed drummer, from
tomb at Kaminaljuyú.

vessels, little "ivory ware" bowls, a fine double-spouted jar, two stuccoed and painted thin orange jars, and several black or orange ring-stand bowls and tripod cylindrical vases.

Obsidian flake blades, sequins, and mica disks were scattered about the tomb. In one place we found an alabaster double cup, carved from a single block of stone. Like all these tombs, this one also contained a stone mano and metate, on which the master's slaves or concubines could mill his corn in the afterworld. Two tortoise shells covered with ferric oxide paint lay in one corner. In many places we found areas of red, white, and black paint and stained areas or decomposed materials that were probably once fabrics, textiles, or skin robes. One such area was all that remained of a little "sack" containing magnetic iron powder.

I think most beginning archaeologists expect to experience a reasonable number of hardships and some physical discomfort in the field. Indeed, the probability of adventure is doubtless one of the attractions of the profession. What they are not prepared for, however—and I have seen several sturdy and brave young men almost ready to quit after being rudely initiated to this—

"Mr. Punch," pottery effigy vessel from tomb at Kaminaljuyú

are the maddening delays and the innumerable miles of red tape that one usually encounters before he can actually put a spade into the ground. Persons working in foreign countries are likely to blame this on the foreigners, but I have been just as frustrated by bureaucratic and personal obstructions here in the United States.

In scientific monographs and in official reports as well as in popular accounts of archaeological research, the archaeologist seems somehow from the beginning to be already at the site and all set to start digging. Or, at the very least, the mules are all packed and the expedition poised to take off into the jungle. Unfortunately, reaching either of these stages in an investigation is almost always the result of days, perhaps weeks, of the most unromantic activity, spent largely in the dull offices and halls of government buildings. Very few persons—Edwin M. Shook,* for one—have reported in any detail their difficulties of this nature. I feel that it is high time more of us did so, in order to warn the inexperienced that all archaeological activity does not glow

* "Tikal: Problems of a Field Director," in *Expedition*, vol. 4, no. 2 (Winter, 1962), pp. 11–26.

Pottery bowl buried under a giant cactus at Chutix Tiox. Ray Marino is in foreground.

perpetually with romance and adventure. I could document such experience with extracts from almost any of my diaries. What I reproduce here is by no means the worst; in fact, as I note in one entry, we were astonished at the speed with which we reached the field. If the reader finds the passages dull, that is partly my intention.

In 1947, I returned to Guatemala to fill in missing data from Zacualpa and, because the final or protohistoric period of highland archaeology was only sparsely represented there, to excavate at Utatlán, a Quiché city known to have flourished as late as Pedro de Alvarado's entry in 1524. Since my last work in Central America, I had directed an archaeological survey of northern Georgia for two years, had taught another two years at the University of North Carolina, and had moved to Tulane University in New Orleans in 1942. With me on the new expedition was a Tulane student, Ray Marino, who had taken some classes with me before the war and who had, like me, only recently returned from military service overseas. I could scarcely have chosen a better assistant. First of all—and he often accused me of picking him for this reason, not for the "A" he'd earned in my class—he was big (6 feet, 190 pounds) and strong as a young bull. More important, however, he was eternally good-natured and cheerful, and my frequent black moods of anger, frustration, and despair (during which he respectfully called me "Smiley") were difficult to maintain very long in his presence. When I went to Guatemala City for surgery in the middle of the season, he took over and ran the show for several weeks.

We finished packing in New Orleans at two o'clock on Tuesday morning, February 11, caught a brief nap, and were up at four again, to drive our loaded Jeep station wagon to Mobile, where the United Fruit Company's *Platano* was scheduled to sail at noon. She was delayed until the next night, giving us time to shop for odds and ends we had failed to get in New Orleans: a rear-view side mirror for the vehicle (it was so loaded you could not see out the back), another padlock, two pocket notebooks for expense accounts, a dozen clothespins to mend broken pottery, an old-fashioned can opener (the most difficult item of all to find), a second mosquito bar, a pint of five-per-cent DDT insecticide, a second inflatable air mattress, a machine screwdriver, some rubber cement, oil for our pistol, some mending cement, canned milk and other canned goods, chlorine tablets for unboiled water, and some glycerin and rose water. I wondered if we had overlooked this much more.

On Saturday, February 15, we arrived at Puerto Barrios about twelve-thirty. After immigration cleared us, I left Ray to supervise the unloading of the Jeep while I dealt with customs. Pío Porta, a cousin of one of our Tulane staff members, helped me immeasurably, guiding me from one office to another and from one warehouse to another, where he knew everyone. He saved me hours of time; this was important because everything closed early

Saturday, and we would have had to wait until Monday to finish and then take the Tuesday train to Guatemala City.

We got our hand luggage and three boxes cleared through customs and to the railroad station, and arranged for shipment of it all. I had no signed contract or permit yet in hand, and so we shipped the vehicle and its contents under seal to customs in Guatemala City.

Ray rescued the Jeep from the rough handling it was getting from the Barrios stevedores, and it escaped with two minor dents suffered as it came out of the ship's hold. He also locked it and refused to surrender the key to the numerous officials who claimed they had to "check the contents." Every Tomás, Ricardo, y Haraldo at the port wanted to get in that vehicle and see what he could lift. Ray had a simple formula for handling these situations: he simply put the keys in his pocket, jutted his large underslung jaw out a little farther while smiling amiably at one and all, and shook his head. We removed the side-view mirror and all the valve caps and locked them in, got the Jeep nailed down on the flatcar, and took the keys with us, above frantic protests that they were needed for "further handling," "inspections," and so on.

We registered at the Hotel Internacional, the same old ramshackle barn I had stopped at every trip since 1932, sent a telegram to our Guatemala agent, Mary Gueroult, saying that we would be there Sunday evening and asking her to save us a room at her parents' pension. Pío Porta joined us for drinks and dinner, but we declined an invitation to a fruit company dance that night —we were too bushed.

On Sunday, February 16, we were up at 5:45 and breakfasted. Who showed up at 6:30 but Pío Porta, bringing us the freight checks all made out, and three boys to carry our immense luggage. (We were carrying all our cameras and other breakables with us, in addition to our personal stuff.) He took us to the station and got all our baggage on the train while we bought tickets. Sunday is his one day off. Later I sent a bottle of Scotch to his house, with a note expressing our deepest gratitude, and I only hope he knows how heartfelt it was.

We arrived in Guatemala City at five forty-five in the afternoon. We assembled all our pieces of luggage; I called the baggage room, but our trunks had not come on this train. We dropped into bed at 8:30 P.M.

On Monday, we were up at 6:45, very rested. First we went to the station to see whether boxes or Jeep had arrived, but they had not. Then we had a tactics conference with our agent. She had already written the ministry of education requesting that our vehicle and supplies be admitted duty free, since the final signing of the contract by the president of the republic would take much time. She telephoned the ministry and asked for an audience, which was granted for Wednesday at three o'clock. They told her that they had sent the recommendation regarding the permit to the ministry of hacienda and crédito público. So we went there, and by a great stroke of luck were able to see the minister himself almost immediately. He was most co-operative and said he would issue the permit with a letter to the director of customs, to be ready at 9:00 the next morning. This was a major victory—I have seen this operation alone take a week.

Mary had already petitioned for and obtained a permit from the policía nacional for us to carry our .38 revolver and a hundred rounds of ammunition. The permit for ammunition was much more complicated, she said, than the one for the gun itself. In the meantime, we got the gun past customs at Barrios. We did not actually try to smuggle it in—that would have been fool-hardy—but it was deep in Ray's trunk, and if the official who opened the trunk saw it he made no objection.

Ray and I next called on Adolfo Molina, director of the Instituto Nacional de Antropología e Historia, which has direct control of our archaeological work in Guatemala. Molina was a pleasant young lawyer, and he promised to try to visit us in the field. Next we called at the Carnegie Institution offices to thank Bob Smith for bringing our signed contract down with him earlier from New Orleans. We also saw Ed Shook, just in from one dig and off again on another tomorrow, the artist Antonio Tejeda, and Kidder.

Ray and I then went to the Bank of London and cashed some traveler's checks, next to the cable office to register our MIDAMERES cable code address for Guatemala. Later in the evening we tried the railroad station again, but they disclaimed any knowledge of the boxes. We had to go there the next day and look for ourselves.

We shopped in the market and found two sturdy kitchen knives, just what we had wanted but could not find anywhere in New Orleans. The bargaining, as usual, started at one quetzal ($1.00) apiece; I offered fifty cents; he mentioned $1.75 for the two; I countered with $1.25; and we bought them for $1.40—everybody was satisfied. We went to Biener's, the photographic supply house, and left our 5 × 7 view camera to see if it could be repaired. The bulb was gone, the tube rotten, the shutter stuck, and the mouth pressure cylinder rusty. At another store we found three film packs for Ray's 2¼ × 3¼ camera.

I paid Mary Gueroult for three weeks' work as our agent. She had typed the nine copies of the contract, pushed it through the instituto and then the ministry of education, and had worked on the duty-free and pistol permits. She gave me carbons of the very flowerily worded legal-size petitions she had written to educación, hacienda, and policía nacional, together with all the succeeding correspondence.

Ed Shook had us to dinner at his house in the evening. At nine thirty we again dropped into bed like sacks of flour.

First of all on Tuesday, we went to the ministry of hacienda; after an hour's wait, we obtained the treasured duty-free permit. We telephoned customs and learned that the Jeep was there.

We then realized we would need drivers' licenses to drive it out, and also remembered we had not registered with the national police, which must be done within forty-eight hours of arrival in the city. So Ray and I went and registered, with much fingerprinting and photographing, then applied for driver's licenses, but were told that we must first buy our two hundred dollar bond, which meant of course that we had to go way back in town. Back we went and bought the bond (two dollars apiece), then returned to policía, but it was 11:45 and the medical examiner was not taking any more customers till afternoon. They told us, however, we could drive for two days on our Louisiana driver's permits.

We had lunch and rushed to customs, where obtaining the Jeep took most of the afternoon—thousands of papers, it seemed, to fill out, thousands of forms, revenue stamps to buy (at distant stores), fees to pay, come back for receipts and copies later. No, no, we must have them today. We would pay extra to expedite the matter. Every clerk was clamoring to have the Jeep's keys to "check the contents." Ray was clutching the keys and shaking his head with that jutting jaw and beatific but somehow deadly smile, while I rushed from office to office in a sort of Alice in Wonderland nightmare. Finally we rode out in triumph, the only casualty another slight dent in the Jeep where an oxcart backed into it in the warehouse.

By telephone the railroad station had been telling us that our boxes must have gone to the customs house. When we reached there and found them not, we had a bright idea: we persuaded a customs official to telephone the railroad station and let the two argue it out between them. This really cornered the railroad official, who could no longer say the boxes were "probably" at customs; so he made a new search, and finally admitted in a surprised voice that yes, the boxes were there after all.

Ray and I drove to the station in our hard-won Jeep and got the three boxes—another triumph. But there was not room in the Jeep for them; it was literally packed to the ceiling, fore and aft. We found a two-wheel mule cart to take them to the pension, while we crept along behind in our car. The illiterate mule driver could not read the street signs and became confused. Ray climbed in with him and rode the last half of the journey across town in the mule cart. As I rode behind them, I kept thinking of Ray's DFC which he earned flying fighter planes in North Africa; I racked my brain for a suitable award for this mission, but could think of none. We settled later for a bottle of fine tax-free American-made bottled-in-bond bourbon, which cost about half what it does at home.

Then we went to Tropical Radio and registered our code address with them—they were separate from the cable office. Again to Foto Biener, who said they could fix the camera.

In the meantime Mary Gueroult found a friend who would rent us his large garage for the Jeep and as a storeroom for supplies to be kept in the city, the pottery we would send back occasionally, and so on. Ray and I drove to his house, unloaded the Jeep, and put it up for the night.

After supper with Sam Lothrop, who was en route to Costa Rica for Peabody Museum of Harvard, Ray and I took stock of our progress. We were really days ahead of our anticipated schedule. We made a list of things we had to do before we could leave for the field; that took a little wind out of our sails, since it was formidable.

We devoted Wednesday morning to getting our driver's licenses. This involved filling out innumerable forms, going to a store for more revenue stamps, paying fees at the cashier's, and taking medical tests for eyesight, perspective judgment, co-ordination, and hearing. All these required long waits in separate lines. Equipped with licenses, we delivered a box we had brought to a friend in Guatemala, then shopped some more, buying, among other things, three varas of black cloth for photography.

Our appointment with the minister of education was first on the list in the afternoon. I paid him our respects and presented the *saludos* of the president of Tulane University, thanked him for his courtesies and help with the contract and especially for his writing the minister of hacienda about admitting our equipment duty-free. As we left, I asked him to write letters of introduction, together with instructions for co-operation, to the governors of the departments of Quiché, Chimaltenango, and Jutiapa, where we expected to work, and another letter "To Whom It May Concern." He promised to do this, and said the letters would be ready on Friday morning.

Then we called customs, who promised to return my hacienda papers and give me a copy of the minister's orders on Thursday. We continued our shopping, and bought compass dividers, paper plates, small hand pencil sharpeners, twine, labels, kerosene lamps, a saw, a geologist's pick, a 7.5-meter steel tape, two spring meter tapes, and a six-meter chain.

After supper I had a long talk with Kidder about our excavation plans and many other matters.

On Thursday, we went first to the customs house and got our hacienda papers from the administrador. He had to keep the originals, since they were addressed to him, but he had them all copied on a single officially stamped document, which is really more convenient than the original sheaf of many papers. We also got our receipt for the freight charges.

Next we went to the open market and looked for a large galvanized tub (to bathe in). We priced them here and there and found the asking price to be six dollars. One woman said five dollars; I said $2.50; and she, $4.50. We walked off for a while, but made it a point to come back to her stall. She asked whether we had found a tub, and we said no. Her *último precio* was now four dollars; I offered three dollars; finally I handed her $3.75, which she accepted. Ray looked at his former ivory tower professor with astonishment, disillusionment, and dismay.

Next we went to Biener's to have two pieces of ground glass and two spares cut for our cameras. We looked at tripods, which were too expensive, but were told they had some secondhand ones in the back. We bought a supply of postage stamps and immediately after lunch, went to Agencias Unidas for information on automobile insurance. We studied various policies and decided on the regular comprehensive coverage: liability and property damage, theft, and fire. The premium was high compared to those in the United States, but much of it would be refunded if we were there only five or six months.

We drove out to the army air base to inquire about getting our last inoculations; typhoid for Ray, and tetanus for me. We were told to go to the command post tomorrow and inquire there. We drove back to town, put up the car, and went to Biener's. They had repaired the 5 × 7 view camera, fitted several new parts, and put in a new tube and bulb. The ground glass was ready, and they had found the secondhand tripods. We made a quick trip back to the pension and returned with all our cameras and tilting tops to Biener's to find a tripod that would fit. This was complicated, because the cameras have one size screw (European) and the tripods and tilting tops another (American). We finally selected a good used tripod and two crowns which would take all three of our cameras. We had trouble getting a filter and filter holder for the 5 × 7, but a clerk sold us his personal ones on the condition we would offer them back to him in July if he could not find some to replace them. Our film was so fast that we needed filters, especially for the large camera, which operated on a bulb and had only one shutter speed—1/25 of a second.

On Friday, I went first to the ministry of education. They had not prepared the letters to the governors and told me to return at 4:00 P.M.

Ray and I drove around, asking about inoculations. We tried public health, but they had no tetanus serum. We went to the military attaché, who sent us to the Pan American Health Center. There the doctor said he had just received orders not to give any more shots, but he gave me some tetanus serum and sent us back to the army air base. There and at the dispensary we had our inoculations.

We looked everywhere for paper bags and finally found them at the biggest grocery store in town, where we bought three hundred large and two hundred small bags. After lunch I got a much-needed haircut and then went to the ministry of education. After a long wait, the letters were produced. That was the last major victory in the red-tape campaign.

Ray and I then went to the insurance office, where they had the policy ready for us. Now we were fully covered in Guatemala. We went again to Biener's to get the photographs we took to test our newly repaired camera. To our dismay, most of the pictures were light-struck. This was a blow, because at Tulane our cameras had been pronounced absolutely lightproof. Biener found the trouble—worn felt around the film-pack adapter—and promised to have it repaired by Saturday noon. We also gave them our 5 × 7 film holders, which must be loaded in total darkness, and asked them to load them for us.

I telephoned Tocsika Roach about our need for a cook, and she agreed to meet us at the pension at eleven tomorrow.

On Saturday, everything closed at noon; so we had to rush to get everything done. We filled the car with gas, bought an extra quart of oil to carry with us, and checked the tires. Ray went to Biener's and got the cameras and film holders. At the Carnegie Institution office, we ordered a hundred cloth bags made by a woman who works for the Carnegie secretary. We bought a German type of plug for our radio and an extension cord.

At eleven, I had met Mrs. Roach and talked to her for forty minutes. She would try to find us a cook. She planned to go to Joyabaj to look for some old furniture, and might see us.

Ray took the Jeep to Santa María, to get a closer view of the volcano and to test the vehicle on steep roads. He said that it barely made the grades although it was empty, and so we decided to reduce our equipment as much as possible.

In the evening, we had dinner with Barbara and Fernando Aldana.

On Sunday, immediately after breakfast, we began weeding out equipment we would not need until later.

We had dinner at Bob and Becky Smith's. We left early, and spent the rest of the day packing our own effects and loading the vehicle.

On Sunday, we packed our last items: ten pounds of sugar, which we heard was scarce in the hinterland, and some iodized salt (because of the prevalent goiter in the highlands).

We drove to Lake Atitlán via Mixco, Chimaltenango, Patzún, and Patcizía. We had lunch at Tzanjuyu with my old friend Franke. Then we drove to Sololá, Los Encuentros, Chichicastenango, San Sebastián Lemoa by its lovely little lake, and Santa Cruz Quiché. We first inspected the "hotel," but it was pretty bad: a bare yard with open latrines shielded only by boards. We inquired further, and found a pension that was much cleaner. We had dinner and went to bed.

On Tuesday we were up, shaved, dressed, breakfasted, and at the gobernación departamental by nine, when we had been told it opened. It was indeed open, but we found that the governor would not be there until eleven. So we drove out to the ruins of Utatlán, capital of the Quiché kingdom and a site we expected to test later, and spent an hour and a half there.

We were back at the governor's office promptly at eleven. He would arrive about eleven thirty, they said. I asked when he would leave for lunch; the answer was: twelve. We waited and waited. At eleven fifty-five, the governor walked up to the front entrance and everyone snapped to attention. His car, waiting for him there, warmed up. Someone scurried in and came running out with a small bag. The governor did not even go inside the building, but stepped in his car and was driven off. The captain of the guard told me that the governor had gone to the baths. "When will he be back?" "At two o'clock."

Ray was waiting in the park for me. Our helpless rage lasted through lunch and until two. We had broken speed records by getting out of Guatemala City in a week. We had driven all day over grueling roads to arrive here at night so that we could catch the governor early—passing up the joys of the luxurious tourist inns of Chichicastenango. We wanted to be on our way to Zacualpa—a really rough trip—before noon. Here it was two o'clock, and the governor had not even set foot in his office.

We returned to the plaza; as expected, the governor had not returned. The prediction was: "about two thirty." At three twenty-five he arrived, and I was the first to see him. By now I had worked up a first-class hate for him, and I was quite taken aback to find him a most pleasant and agreeable fellow—not at all like the pompous jefe político of Quiché when I was here on a similar mission in 1935—and extremely co-operative. At my request, he had his secretary prepare two letters, one to the alcalde of Zacualpa, another to the alcaldes of all towns in the department of Quiché in general. I told him of our plans as specifically as we knew them. He was most cordial and offered his further services in any way possible.

With the treasured letters I hurried back to the pension and waved them in Ray's face. He murmured, "Thank you, Lord!"—an expression he uses whenever our Jeep reaches the top of a particularly steep barranca and on similar victorious occasions. Although it was nearly four, we were so anxious to leave the pension and be on our way that we decided to pack the Jeep and take off.

We packed in exactly twenty-five minutes, leaving Quiché at four fifteen. The trip to Zacualpa took about two hours—it was a killer. In twelve years I had forgotten how bad the road was in spots and how steep the barrancas. But by taking the U-turns at the bottom in low gear, wide open, and somewhat in the style of dirt-track auto racing, we made them all right. Most cars are broken in at several thousand miles; our Jeep was shaken down and a hardened veteran at six hundred.

We passed through Chiché and then Chinique. In each town, people rushed to doors and windows to watch us lumber over the rough cobblestone streets. Children chased us for blocks, and the dogs went wild. Drivers headed their horses and mules into a wall, but even then the beasts pitched and whinnied.

At Zacualpa, which sees one bus and no other cars during a year, our reception was tumultuous. A throng hurried to the dirt plaza to see us, and scores of children swarmed around the Jeep, rubbed their hands wonderingly over its dust-caked red hood, and fiddled with the headlights and tires. I first looked up Ricardo Méndez, who had been my foreman twelve years earlier. He was astonished as I had never seen anyone before, and we exchanged a warm *doble abrazo*. He said that he had been to Guatemala City several years ago and had learned there that I was president of a great university in the United States. I let this one slide by, modestly. Anything for prestige is all to the good. If Tulane's President Harris shows up, I can always promote him to president of the United States.

There is no pension in Zacualpa, and of course no restaurant, but Ricardo recommended a neighbor who had an empty room. Then we called on the alcalde, who had been a minor village official in 1935 and remembered me. He offered his services and said he would send messages to the principal landowners in La Vega, the valley of the ruins.

It was now black dark—there are no electric lights in Zacualpa—and we had to find shelter for the Jeep: not from the weather, but from the bad little boys of town. Zacualpa has a healthy respect for these *pantojos,* and I well remember them from 1935. They would try to climb on my truck when it was going full speed. Wherever we stopped the Jeep, a swarm of them descended on it, picking at the tire valves, trying to remove the tail light and license, and working the front wheels back and forth. It never seemed to occur to anyone that a good whopping might help keep them under control. The mayor himself and many other old friends assured me that we must put the vehicle out of reach, *"que los pantojos no lo molestan."*

The alcalde recommended a place, so of necessity we had to go there. Ricardo stopped outside, because, he explained, he "never entered that house." Apparently Zacualpa was still, as it was twelve years earlier, a hotbed of rivalries, jealousies, and feuds. I went in and talked with a shrewish woman, who wanted to know how much we would pay. I said that was for her to decide. She said she had a cow and mules in the yard, and she would have to move them; besides, we would have to wait for her husband to return. I waited ten minutes, although I knew the husband was outside feigning indifference (prestige or status behavior in this countryside); indeed, the entire village knew exactly where we were every moment since we had arrived. So I now felt justified in returning to Ricardo and asking him to recommend another house. We then visited the only other house in town with a patio, and left the car there, locking the gates with an extra padlock. The señora was most cordial; when I offered to pay her for the car storage, she said it was not worth anything and we were welcome to use her yard.

We returned to our house and were served black beans, rice, tortillas, and coffee for the fifth time in as many starts since leaving Lake Atitlán. We choked them down and then, while a knot of curious natives stared unabashed through our window, we dejectedly unstrapped our army cots, set them up, inflated our air mattresses, brought out my blankets and Ray's sleeping bag, and fell into bed exhausted. Our first snores must have told the audience that the show was over.

On Wednesday after breakfast (yes—black beans, tortillas, eggs, and coffee) we called on the alcalde and got the letters he had promised. He gave us an Indian guide who spoke Spanish, and we set out for La Vega and the ruins. We had to leave the Jeep on the village side of the river; in twelve years the stream had eaten away about ten feet of bank where I used to ford it in my old pickup truck, and there was now a sheer vertical bank dropping straight down to the water, ten feet below. The Indian wanted to carry us across on his back (shades of Thomas Gage!), but we declined and waded the river ourselves.

The old road on the other side was absolutely impassable for a vehicle. That meant we would have to spend several days cutting and leveling so that the Jeep would get through. As we walked by the few huts in the valley, Indians came out and greeted me. They remembered my name—even some young men who had been children when I worked here twelve years ago.

We first saw Sarbelio Girón, who said the little hut I lived in before was not occupied. Then we visited Patrocinio Urizar, who had a somewhat cleaner and better unoccupied hut nearer the main ruins. We decided to live there, but the "road" was impassable between it and the other house. We spent at least an hour going over the terrain, deciding where to put a new road. It looked hopeless, but we were willing to gamble two days' work for six men at twenty-five cents apiece per day, the top prevailing wage in this area.

I hated to reject Sarbelio's house; so I explained to him on our way back why we needed the other one, and asked him to take charge of repairing that section of road. This would give him opportunity to include all his poor relatives on a paying job. He was delighted.

We next ran into Rumaldo, who had been my nearest neighbor (three hundred yards) and night watchman at the ruins in 1935. I knew I could trust him implicitly, and I put him in charge of cutting down the steep river banks where we would have to ford the stream. If all these projects were successful, Ray and I decided, we would quit archaeology and take up engineering.

Everybody—our landlady for one, and even Ricardo—wanted us to employ his sons, who were invariably "young but strong and big." Ricardo was employed and could not leave work to be my foreman again, but he urged that I name his son, who is "young, but strong and a good boy." Choosing foreman and laborers would be touchy. We wanted to stay in the good graces of some men in town, but we wanted to remain even more friendly with our neighbors in La Vega, since that is where we would live and work. Even there we would have to choose between several property owners. We decided that these preliminary road-building jobs, each under the direction of a different man, would give us a good idea of who was the best foreman, and whose relatives worked the best.

Since we needed two more picks and some other supplies, we drove to Joyabaj. The road was terrible, but our Jeep was now almost empty and it took the barrancas with ease. In Joyabaj, which incidentally Thomas Gage visited in the early seventeenth century, we found everything we lacked except gasoline: two picks (no handles, however), two kerosene lamps, four quart bottles of kerosene, two sacks of powdered lime for our La Vega latrine, a carton of matches, and two glass tumblers.

On the way back we stopped at a small terrace or mound we had spotted from the road, and picked up a bagful of good potsherds. Fifty yards up the road was another small eminence which planters had cut into; here we filled two large bags with sherds in a short time.

We returned to La Vega, again leaving the car on the road and wading the river, and walked about a mile with the picks to Patrocinio's house—he would need them the next day on the road work. Rumaldo told us that he was having trouble finding help for his riverbank work.

On Saturday, we completed all the road work and made the first test flight to our house. I piloted the Jeep over, and Ray brought it back.

After breakfast we learned that the owner of the land on the village side of the river had returned from a three-day horseback trip to Tecpán. We talked to him and arranged for cutting some of his fruit trees and transplanting some of his three-year-old coffee trees, so that we could cut the road through a corner of his property. Then we waded the river and made a note of all sections of the road that needed final touches. The rest of the morning we directed work on the final agonizing slope to our hut. We walked back to the river with Sarbelio, pointing out the places that needed

Uncovering stairway to platform at Zacualpa. Ray Marino at right

repairing, and waded the river to show him how and where to cut the last remaining section through the coffee trees. Later we drove into town and found our first mail from home—also the cloth bags from Guatemala City.

Then we went to the river for a real bath and to wash our dirty clothes. After lunch we returned to the river and directed the work on the ford. It was a big job, but the seven men cleaned it up by four in the afternoon. Sarbelio assured us that he had repaired the spots we had shown him, and had put stakes in to hold the tree trunk we had put in place to reinforce and widen our bridge over one gully. So Ray and I climbed in the Jeep and took off on the great test of our three-day engineering project. We crossed the river fairly easily, roared up the first big hill with power to spare, negotiated the gully bridge with about one inch leeway on each side, and then took on the second big sector of our road building, which we knew to be the most difficult. Here we had to ease down a steep slope, get a running start across big stones in a stream bed—but not fast enough to ruin the crossing there—then leap up the other side with the throttle wide open and in low gear, taking a ninety-degree turn halfway up. We made it, but after taking the sharp turn the Jeep jumped a couple of feet from one side of the road to the other and scared the daylights out of us.

Before starting back, I arranged Sarbelio's gang's payroll while Ray took the men to repair the section of road where the car almost left it. The gang thought they were through for the day, and Ray said that they were sullen when he told them to move a large quantity of dirt. He himself pitched in with a shovel, and that improved their mood. They cut the road down to a hard subsurface and banked it at the sharp turn.

Ray piloted the Jeep on the test run back in the other direction. He had no trouble on the first bad section. We stopped at Patrocinio's house and paid off his gang. The total cost of our new road—three days' work for twelve men and two foremen working from seven in the morning until five in the afternoon—was $9.75.

We set out again with Ray at the wheel. He crossed the bridge over the gully, where a few inches of misjudgment would have sent us over the side, went down the bad hill, negotiated the river successfully, but on the Zacualpa side the Jeep barely made it in low gear. We waded back to see what the trouble was, and decided there was too much soft sand on one side of the road. This would be difficult to correct, since there is no firm underfooting so close to the river and the road must be kept at a minimum tilt.

We stopped long enough to pay Vitalino for the corner of his land we cut through and then drove home.

On Monday, we spent the entire day moving into the hut in La Vega and putting finishing touches on the road and river crossing. We took a load of large, heavy, flat rocks and paved the river slopes on each side for several feet up the bank. Ray supervised this operation as well as the cutting away of the side of the bank at the sharp turn just below our house, where we still had trouble making the curve, maintaining speed, and staying on the road.

We made several trips between Zacualpa and La Vega, moving all our belongings. We paid our bill at the house in town; we were really glad to get out of there.

We splashed water on the hard-packed earthen floors and adobe walls of our house, sprayed it some with DDT solution, and built a set of rough plank shelves. Planks are scarce, and to rent these from Sarbelio cost us as as much as a couple of month's rent for the house itself, which was $1.50 a month. Our values here shifted rapidly to local scales. We laid down the woven mats we had bought at Zacualpa market on Sunday, and moved in our belongings. The latrine was nearly finished, lacking only the seat board and one wall of corn stalks. The workmen did not follow our instructions on this latrine job; almost everything they had done there had to be redone. But it was clean and neat, open to sky and sun, and sterile with good white lime—a thing of beauty and a joy forever after the nauseating *excusados* of Santa Cruz Quiché and Zacualpa.

I had explained politely to Sarbelio yesterday that we were glad to have neighbors watch us clean up the old house, but that from now on we would want some privacy—that was why we were leaving Zacualpa town. Would he please keep the children off our *corredor?* When we drove up that day a crowd had gathered, including several adults. They stood there, and stared, and sucked sugar cane noisily, and scattered orange peels everywhere. I found Sarbelio and told him that his family and neighbors were treating us like animals in a zoo; for six days we had eaten, dressed, brushed our teeth, worked, gone to bed, everything with a crowd watching us. Now they must treat us like their own neighbors. He shooed the crowd away, and they did not come back all day.

But while we were eating supper we looked up and saw two men standing and staring at us. I went to the door and said good evening politely. They said the same. Then I asked, "What do you want?" They just grinned and said, "Nothing." So I simply closed the door in their faces. I try to understand and adapt to cultural differences, but this is one I have never understood in rural Latin America. I realize that we are curiosities, but they should not treat us like freaks in a sideshow; if I looked in their window while they were undressing for bed, I would probably get a face full of buckshot. Shoot first and ask questions later is not completely passé in many places. If there is one custom I have learned in rural Yucatán and Guatemala, it is to approach a house slowly, deferentially, and knocking or calling well before reaching the door. Here in the highlands many houses enforce this custom with fierce black dogs, which keep you well at bay until the dueño appears. Yet nowhere in rural Latin America has this courtesy been reciprocated, until, as here in La Vega, we let it be known that we had suffered enough public examination.

The day ended perfectly after all our work and all our gripes. Ray cooked a superb supper, the likes of which we had not tasted for a long, long time. I went to Patrocinio's house, five hundred yards away, and bought lard, and he gave me a basket of oranges from his trees. While Ray was boiling water and preparing the meal, I drove to town and bought a small frying pan, a strainer, and two loaves of wonderful fresh bread. Coming home was the Jeep's first night flight over the new road; by now it knew every inch of the way, and there was no trouble.

We spent most of the evening unpacking footlockers. Ray turned on the battery-powered short-wave radio, and we had wonderful, wonderful United States music. For the first time Ray stayed awake more than two minutes after he went to bed; he lay on his cot for an hour, drinking in the music. This was the first expedition on which I had a radio, and I will never be without one again; the pleasure it gave us that night alone was worth its cost and the trouble of getting it here. We even heard President Truman speak and the first world news in three weeks. But it was that sweet, sweet music that really shed trouble and fatigue.

This account could go on and on. If the reader's patience has been taxed in a few minutes' reading, imagine ours when we lived it! We had arrived in Guatemala more than two weeks before this last entry, and we had only just moved into our permanent hut; excavations had not even been started,

The "Ugly Duckling" pot, Zacualpa

in spite of our being in a country that I knew well and in a valley where I was already known. Still, I considered seventeen days a speed record for getting ready to dig—far better than I had hoped for.

As a referee for some government and foundation grant award programs, I frequently read a proposal in which the applicant presents a schedule that allows him a day or two of preparation and survey in the country before beginning his excavations. This type of proposal immediately tells me that the applicant is wholly inexperienced in field work, and that he has had very bad advice or none at all.

One of our most interesting discoveries at Zacualpa was one of the most unpromising in first appearance. When we uncovered it, we were not at all impressed, since it was a very ordinary small clay jar. The top was broken and the lid had fallen inside the vessel, with earth tightly packed around it.

We laid this ugly duckling aside, postponing for several days the chore of cleaning out the dirt which, we supposed, caused it to be so heavy. Indeed, we were so little concerned with its value, that we left it outside in the yard until the following Sunday, "catch-up" day for such unpleasant tasks.

The next week end I removed the lid and the upper layers of dirt, pouring in a little water at a time to loosen the earth which had dried hard through the centuries. I was amazed to see a bright green stone near the top. I

washed it carefully; its surface was carved—eyes, nose, mouth, arms, hands crossed over breast.

Below it were more. With mounting excitement we cleaned nine stone figurines, ranging in size from eight inches to two inches tall, and all neatly arranged according to size. Under these strange small figures, with their inscrutable (and identical) features, were twenty-eight jade beads, graduated in size like matched pearls; a carved jade plaque; a pair of identically carved stone figurine-pendants; a delicate blade of obsidian volcanic glass; several polished stone objects of unknown use; and a clay back for an iron pyrite mosaic or mirror.

We hoped that this discovery would shed new light on a figurine cult that survived many centuries of prehistoric times. The Maya Quiché Indians, who live in this region today, are said to make a small stone figurine when a baby is born; they hide the figurine, which is not brought out again until the individual dies. It is not yet clear whether this is a survival of the original use to which these objects were put, or whether the little idols represent a particular god or group of gods. Someone has suggested, for example, that our nine figurines may represent the Nine Lords of the Night, who figured prominently in the Maya religious calendar.

We worked at Zacualpa longer than we had originally planned. The rainy season was drawing closer. Already the first showers were beginning to fall, and the Indians were planting corn—sure signs that the heavier rains would follow shortly.

We decided to move to our next objective, Utatlán, just at the nick of time. The night before our scheduled move, it rained heavily in the moun-

Stone figurines from the "Ugly Duckling" pot

tains. When we awakened the next morning, the Río de la Vega was in flood. We walked down to the banks and watched the raging torrent; we could not even wade the river, much less cross it in a car. Even worse, the flood had destroyed our river crossing; the banks we had worked so hard to grade and pave were again deep masses of mud.

After many hours of makeshift repairs the next morning we made it across to the far bank in our Jeep, but there the wheels began to dig in. Instead of stalling, which would have dug us hopelessly into the mud, Ray shifted immediately to reverse, backed full speed across the river and up the La Vega bank, got another start, and tried again. This startling operation shook us up considerably, to say the least; Natalia, our cook, began praying in a loud voice.

We had no better luck on the second attempt, but Ray managed to hold the car on the slopes while we unloaded about three hundred pounds of equipment. He then backed across the river a second time, roared forward again, and, with mud and water blacking out the windshield and sputtering in the motor, climbed the bank successfully.

Crossing the mountains between Zacualpa and Utatlán, I drove and Ray sat beside me with his door half open, poised with an armful of heavy bags of broken pottery. When the car would falter on a steep turn, Ray would jump out, relieving the load not only of his 190-odd pounds but also of the fifty or sixty pounds of pottery which he took with him when he jumped.

We rented a little adobe house at San Sebastián Lemoa, not far from the ruins of Utatlán. It overlooked a lovely lake, surrounded by gentle slopes where Indian women and children tended sheep. At the foot of a low pine ridge we went swimming every evening after work. A good road passed directly behind our house. This was indeed archaeology de luxe.

Our only annoyance at Lemoa was that of thieves. On the very first evening there, when Ray and I were both inside the hut working, someone crept up to the corredor and stole our prized electric railroad lantern. Repeated thefts thereafter taught us not to leave anything, no matter how trifling, outside at night. When we came back from one trip, we found that thieves had even torn down the woven mats which formed the walls of our outdoor latrine.

We reported these thefts promptly to the Indian mayor of Lemoa. He forwarded the reports to police headquarters at Santa Cruz Quiché. Two months later we received official acknowledgment, profusely stamped and sealed and notarized, with assurances that an investigation would be made if we would just sign certain other forms and return them to the capital of the department. We sent word back to drop the whole thing; we were leaving for the States in three days.

Utatlán, the ruin we were then investigating, was the capital of an ancient kingdom inhabited in prehistoric times by Indians called the Quiché, the ancestors of the present aborigines of this region. For generations before the

Spanish Conquest, the Quiché had warred bitterly with their neighbors. One of the rival tribes—the Cakchiquels—weakened by rebellions, fire, and plagues, was about to be crushed by the Quiché here at Utatlán. Sinacam, the Cakchiquel monarch, sent the Spaniards in Mexico an appeal for help, since he had heard of these strange invincible white men. Cortes immediately dispatched Pedro de Alvarado at the head of some Spanish troops and Indian allies.

After several unsuccessful attempts to defeat Alvarado in open battle, the Quiché determined to annihilate his forces through trickery. As he approached Utatlán, they invited him to enter the city peacefully and said that they wished to be friends and would recognize the king of Spain as their emperor.

But when Alvarado reached Utatlán and saw, as he later put it, that this was "a very strong and dangerous place, that more resembles a robber stronghold than a city," he became suspicious. Utatlán is truly a fortress city; it is surrounded on all sides by precipitous ravines, in many places more than a thousand feet deep. Alvarado is said to have learned that the Indians planned to cut off the only two escape exits from the city, set it afire, and cut his forces to pieces in the narrow walled streets where horsemen would be at a disadvantage.

Alvarado therefore dispatched a patrol to secure the exit causeways. He then withdrew his force to the open plain opposite the city stronghold. Using tactics of counterdeceit, he invited the Indian leaders to his camp, took them

San Sebastián Lemoa, Guatemala

captive, obtained a confession from them, and burned them alive. In his report he also states that he "sent to burn the town and destroy it."

At Utatlán we sank nine large test pits in different parts of the ruins. In the main section of the city we found at least two earlier periods of construction. The inner buildings were beautifully preserved, having been protected from weathering by the outer layers.

We were particularly interested in two of our pits, which revealed clay-walled rooms grouped in large "apartment house" units covering about half an acre and subdivided by narrow alley ways; this was doubtlessly part of the great palace described by an early Spanish chronicler.

In one of the rooms of an earlier palace under this one, we found a clay wall with a mural painted in brilliant colors, still vivid after at least four and a half centuries. It depicted a blue lake with yellow shells, covered by an ornamented canopy, with a much-plumed green snake winding above it. In trash dumps over the sides of the steep ravines we found thousands of broken vessels, animal bones left from cooking, and stone and bone and copper tools and weapons.

Work at Utatlán was often trying, because the people who lived nearby were convinced that the ruins contained great treasures of gold and jewels. Frequently, when we returned to work in the morning, we found that vandals had been in our pits, ruining our careful stratigraphic studies and ruthlessly destroying architectural features to find out what was underneath.

Once when Ray and I were on a trip, a drunk came to the door and demanded money of our cook, Natalia. She said sure, wait a minute, and went inside the house. She came out brandishing a machete and made for the tramp, apparently with murderous intent. He departed running, as the Latins say.

Perhaps because occurrences like this began to tell on her nerves, Natalia finally tendered her resignation. We were glad to grant this, for several reasons. Although no sniveling coward, as the above incident shows, Natalia was not particularly resourceful in other ways. When Ray and I wanted something special to eat, we had to hunt it ourselves; Natalia gave up too easily. Furthermore, she took an inordinately sympathetic interest in stray flea-bitten dogs, and our house gradually became a mecca for these highly undesirable animals. Again, Natalia was what you might call a drab character; her total vocabulary seemed to be *sí, señor* and *no, señor*. Although this is usually considered a sterling attribute for a servant, Ray and I had reached the stage where we would have welcomed even an occasional comment on the weather from her after so many months. And finally, I had learned recently that María, who had worked for me twelve years before, was again available.

María, a part-Indian woman of perhaps fifty-five years of age, was a wonderful character. She was everything that Natalia was not: gay, talkative, lusty-languaged, resourceful—and she hated all dogs. Although she never intruded on our privacy, she was fun to have around the house. When the hot work in the excavations made us moody and tired, María was always good for a laugh.

As for resourcefulness, nothing seemed to occur to her to be impossible. The first day she came, we noticed her down at the lakeside, busying herself with a strange assortment of forked poles, sticks, vines, hammer, and nails. By evening, without saying anything to anyone, she had built a little wharf out into the water, complete with side benches and other devices which enabled her to wash dishes and clothes in the clearer, deeper water without getting her feet muddy or wet. How she sank the necessary stakes in the lake bed and got the whole diabolical contraption to hang together is still beyond me. It did not, however, surprise María; she never even mentioned the accomplishment to us.

María took entertaining seriously. At Lemoa we were closer to Santa Cruz and Chichicastenango, and so we occasionally had guests. What banquets! Ray, who had helped Natalia plan our meals, would sometimes ask María what was on the menu for a coming dinner party. She would name a meat, a salad, and a few vegetables. If Ray suggested a substitute, María always agreed respectfully; but when we sat down to dinner, in came not only what Ray had ordered, but also what María had thought we should have in the first place, plus a few dishes she knew were my favorites, plus a few more she had thought up since talking to us. Both we and our guests would sit there bug-eyed while María calmly made numerous trips in and out, bringing an armful of platters each trip. Her idea of a dinner party was not so much a well selected menu as a shoot-the-works one.

It was now raining hard, and further digging at Utatlán was out of the question. We settled down at Lemoa to divide our time between writing up our pottery, to reduce the great bulk that would have to be moved to Guatemala City, and visiting various ancient sites in this general area.

Two sites were only a mile or so from our house. We walked to them, made sketch maps and photographs, and took surface collections for later study. The first, which we named Pacho, consisted of four mounds facing a small court. A stone idol stood in front of one mound. These structures are still used as places of native worship. Kneeling on ground strewn with pine needles, the Indians burn incense here and say half-Christian, half-pagan prayers.

We named the other site Nimpokom, "Mean Old Man," because the Indian owner of the property and his woman clearly did not want us meddling. He knew only a few words of Spanish, and so we could not explain that our intentions were honorable. He kept muttering and pointing to the largest mound. "It's mine. It's mine. No place for you here." He went into his house and brought out a machete, and his woman seized a formidable club; the two of them proceeded to patrol the mound, following us around but keeping between us and the large prehistoric structure.

It was perhaps rude of me to stay, but having come this far I was not willing to leave without a surface collection. We tried to show him what we were picking up from the ground, and told him that it was work for the government, but he did not understand at all. He kept repeating his motto: "It's mine. No place for you here." Ray and I managed to stay about twenty minutes, circling the structure and its belligerent defenders at a fairly safe distance, until we obtained an adequate sample of surface potsherds.

While we were at Lemoa, Ray obtained mules and a guide and rode the long precipitous trail over the mountains to San Andrés Sajcabaja. He visited Pantzac, one of the six or seven ruins within a few miles of this isolated town. On his return to Chinique, where he had rented the mules, Ray was startled to learn that his guide had been released from jail for a few days to make this trip with him.

Back at Lemoa the weeks clicked by, as the great stacks of cloth bags bulging with pottery fragments were gradually emptied and their contents recorded. We were of no mind to carry this great weight of material over the ten-thousand-foot Chichoy Pass when we moved. What we finally carried back to Guatemala City was the cream of the crop, the finest pottery specimens of each type. It was a queer sensation to see the tangible fruits of many months of excavating assembled on a few tables in the National Museum of Guatemala. The tons of materials we originally dug from the accumulated debris of more than seventeen centuries had been boiled down to recorded form on a sheaf of papers about a foot thick and a file of several hundred photographs and drawings.

ONE

•

Guillelmo Dupaix 1805

An Austrian Dragoon Goes to Palenque

[Two of the earliest archaeological explorers of Maya ruins were army officers. One was Antonio del Río, a captain of artillery, who visited the now
famous ruins of Palenque, in Chiapas, Mexico, in 1787. The other was
Guillelmo Dupaix, a retired officer of Austrian dragoons, who was commissioned by Charles IV of Spain to survey the antiquities of Mexico. Dupaix
left us a detailed account of his investigations between 1805 and 1807, published many years later, from which I have translated some anecdotes below.

[Charles Farcy, who wrote a preface to the 1844 edition of these reports,
said that Dupaix was a simple, truthful man, who made no pretense at being
a scholar, although he was better versed in history and archaeology than
most of his fellow countrymen of the time. "He restricts himself," wrote
Farcy, "to recounting, without pomp and without grandiloquence, the discoveries which he made during the course of his expeditions. . . . His report
is almost a travel journal . . . told with prudence devoid of exaggeration, and
with a simple good-heartedness, full of interest for those who seek the truth."
H. E. D. Pollock noted in 1940 that although Dupaix's descriptions were
none too accurate, still for the times they were encouraging for their attention to building materials and methods of construction. The real value of the
work, said Pollock, lies in the accompanying drawings by Castañeda, which,
although interpretive and impressionistic, were "the first of Maya architecture to be published, and the only ones known at that time with the exception
of the unpublished Bernasconi and lost del Rio copies."

[Dupaix, accompanied by the artist Luciano Castañeda, arrived in Mexico

The following selections from Dupaix have been translated by the present editor
from Guillelmo Dupaix, *Antiquités Mexicaines* (Paris, 1834).

71

on January 5, 1805. He visited Puebla, Tepeyacan, Tehuacan, then Orizaba, Chapulco, and Zongolican, recording all along the way the ancient ruins, sculptures, and other relics that he encountered.]

The village of Zongolican is twelve leagues south of Orizaba, and one reaches it via Tequilla, a village of native Indians, via some undulating hills, winding over steep roads to the capital, which is situated at about the center of this sierra, in a deep valley, somewhat circular and crowned by large elevated rocks. The streams enter it in falls and cascades, and almost immediately drain off into various gulleys. . . .

We left this head-village after a stay of eight days, forced on us by the bad weather, and we were going to sleep at a tobacco hacienda of Rocha, situated a day's journey from San Sebastian. We were going to eat there, but an unfortunate accident occurred, for on the narrow road, cut into the slope of the main mountain, and on the edge of a precipice which dropped into a deep chasm, the rider behind me suddenly fell backwards, together with his horse, and both disappeared. The rider was able to get loose from the horse by grasping the branches of trees, and he escaped with his life, not without some bruises. The animal was rolling over and over, making a noise like a great flood of water, thrashing about and breaking everything that checked the speed and violence of his fall; until he happened to come up against some very sturdy trees which stopped his further flight. Finally, after immense labor, and with the help of the Indians who were following me, armed with levers, machetes, axes, and lariats, it was possible to haul him up from above, without any damage to the animal other than some wounds which did not hinder him from resuming the journey.

That same day, in the afternoon along toward dusk, the artist's horse, trying to avoid a mudhole, got too close to the treacherous edge of the road, where the thick foliage concealed a great precipice below; he lost his footing and fell. The rider had the presence of mind to throw himself over the side into the quagmire, but his mount did not stop until he reached the very bottom of this chasm. The rider had to go on foot for a league back to the hacienda, and put the authorities of the nearby village, in which we had dined, in charge of recovering the horse—if there was any life left in him—which they did and brought him in at night, without incident. As for the artist, he got off safe and sound, if thoroughly frightened.

[It was on his third expedition, begun in December, 1807, that Dupaix visited Palenque, which had been discovered only sixty-one years before, but was already (as it has been ever since) a mecca of archaeologists. With him again was an artist—as well as a secretary and some soldiers from the Mexican regiment of dragoons. The party went first to Puebla, where Dupaix had learned of various archaeological remains that he wanted to investigate.]

To carry out this project, I requested pack mules for the following morning, but since they were not provided until pretty late in the day, and our day's journey was to Tecalle, seven leagues from Puebla, we would not arrive there until late at night. But impatience drove me on alone, and in the black dark I got lost, and not finding anyone to ask the way of, I found myself in the harsh necessity of groping about in the dark, stumbling over rugged terrain and rough ravines, until God chose to guide me and take me out of this gloomy labyrinth to the very edge of the village, where there very shortly awaited me a not very pleasant adventure. At the first hut I could find, I asked an Indian girl for directions to a road or street that would take me to the municipal headquarters. Her laconic response was to retreat hastily into her dwelling and close the door. I went on to the next house, and in order to enter it or its enclosure I had to dismount and leave my horse outside. As soon as an Indian man and woman who answered my knock saw me, the man fled and the woman shut herself up in the little house, and in this manner we conversed, I with my questions and they with their answers.

First I must explain that there were roaming about this region some robbers disguised some as soldiers, others as priests or friars, and with these as my antecedents the Indians did me the honor of considering me one of their confederates. Thus it was, that on taking leave of this house, quite vexed, I looked for my horse and could not find it, and in all this uncertainty I had no idea what had happened, when all of a sudden and stealthily some thirty Indians attacked me. The first thing they did was to take away my sword and tie me hand and foot, and each of them vied with the others in pulling the ropes tight on each side of me, as though they meant to quarter me, and then they carried me, hoisted in the air, as if in triumph or apotheosis. In this critical situation, and not at all made for this mode of travel, I kept crying, "*Hombres! Hijos!* Look, I am a captain and I am asking where the municipal center is!" But they were deaf as rocks, until, by divine Providence, there appeared an old Indian, seeming more rational than that throng of irrationals, and spoke to them in their language; at that they threw me down and each of them disappeared, leaving me alone with the old man, who accompanied me to the municipal center, where my group, very worried indeed, was waiting for me. Afterward there appeared my sword and my horse. In a little while the Governor of the Republic arrived, to whom I made bitter complaints about his Indians' offenses to me, and, in a way, to take vengeance on them, I clapped him with my right hand, with all the force of which I was capable, a sharp slap in the face. The reply which he gave me was, "God's will be done," which disarmed me and I was sorry that I had done it. By chance the subdelegate was not there and came the following morning, having left in his place a representative, who managed for the moment to provide for our needs. The following day this subdelegate regretted what had happened to me, and gave me all the satisfaction to be had within his power;

he jailed the guilty parties, which, for Indians, is a most painful punishment —but it was only just, in view of the blows they gave me, as well as having partly broken my sword. And thus concluded this doleful adventure.

Finally having finished a full examination of these ruins [at Tepexe el Viejo], I returned to the village of Ocotzingo determined to undertake the route to Palenque.

Palenque is situated some eight arduous days' journey over some roads (if you can call them that—some narrow rugged trails that wind around the mountains and precipices), sometimes on muleback, sometimes afoot, or in a litter or hammock. One is obliged in certain places to cross bridges, or more accurately, some badly placed or badly balanced tree branches, and pass through lands covered with forests, deserted and depopulated. One has to sleep always outdoors except for some few villages and camps.

To carry our loads and hammocks we took with us some thirty to forty strong and vigorous Indians. Finally, having experienced during this long and arduous journey every kind of discomfort, we arrived safely, by divine grace, at the village of Palenque Nuevo, principal goal of this third royal expedition. . . .

As soon as the rainy season ended, I moved with great eagerness to the celebrated ruins, inappropriately called Palenque Viejo, for the name is a new one, subsequently given this site by the Spaniards; when its primitive

Masonry bridge at Palenque. Dupaix (1807) evidently described the scene to an artist.

From G. Dupaix, *Antiquités Americaines.*

inhabitants disappeared, they took with them its real name. The only thing left to us from this most ancient nation is the sad skeleton of its fine arts which have never been revived.

The ruins lie two leagues southeast of the village. It appears that they built this city on the high slopes of a pass in the steep mountains, so that in unforeseen events they would find a safe retreat. Besides its usefulness, they knew how to take advantage of the beauty which this eminence provides, embellished by the leafy foliage of luxuriant vegetation. Water, that universally useful element, circulates here with a murmur pleasant to both ear and eye, a pure and crystal clear liquid flowing through narrow ravines adorned with simple and fragrant wild flowers. Similar sites favored by nature cannot be deprived of living things, and this is borne out by the great number of animals—quadrupeds and birds, large and small—which delight in reproducing their species in these peaceful solitudes.

Satisfied of contemplating this fortunate region, I turned my attention to investigating its architectural works, and I began with the largest edifice. . . . In the ruins, in a flat place from which the Indians cleared away the forest, and which in ancient times formed a plaza in front of the great monument, and in order to have it, in that season, more at our disposition and within view of the excavations, I had some huts built, made of poles and covered entirely with fronds very similar to those of the banana, for we needed these as protection from sun, rain, and animals.

Masonry bridge at Palenque
Photograph by A. P. Maudslay in 1880.
From *Biologia Centrali-Americana: Archaeology,* vol. iv.

Having finished our investigation of these most ancient relics worthy of much fame, I resolved at last, and with some regret, to leave this site so favored by nature and art, to make my way to Tabasco, and in five days of travel, three by land and two by navigable rivers, we arrived at Villa-Hermosa. As soon as I jumped ashore, I went to present my passports and other credentials to the acting governor of Santa-Maria; although he was fully satisfied, as was only just, the people were not, at least in their appearance, and they began to make ugly faces at me, forming a false judgment about my person, for they considered me French, although I am an Austrian by origin and birth. The same thing happened, as I have already stated, in Ciudad Real.

If my legs had not been painful from sores resulting from the stings of various poisonous insects, I would have mounted my horse at once and de-

Interior of temple room, Yaxchilán
Photograph by Teobert Maler, 1898.
From *Researches in the Central Portion of the Usumatsintla Valley*, 1901. Copyright 1901 by Peabody Museum of American Archaeology and Ethnology, Harvard University. Courtesy of Peabody Museum of Harvard University.

parted, but now I was determined to abandon travel by land and transfer to water, and thus it was that I embarked in a canoe, made of two logs, on the majestic river which today they call the Tabasco, formerly the Grijalva and the Banderas. Due to certain mishaps, we were nine days on its waters, and at last disembarked on the wide sandbars near the ocean, at the mouth of the Alvarado. Our sea voyage was short and happy.

Another adventure, and it was the third and last—thank God!—was awaiting me in this village of mulattoes and fishermen. As soon as the acting governor—a captain of militia and an old acquaintance—learned of our arrival, he came to receive me at the banks of the river, and assigned me lodging, granting me every assistance for my needs. We were with him all day, peaceful and happy to find ourselves in the land of Mexico (or belonging to its viceroyship). But this pleasure was ephemeral, and was disturbed before dusk. A European ringleader, a butter and wine merchant by profession, standing in front of a handful of drunken muleteers, all armed with machetes, tried to attack my lodging, under the pretext that I was French. On hearing the tumult, there came at once the governor, the priest, the lieutenant of police, and the officers of the lancers, to save us. This lazy vagabond requested, in the name of the people, that my leather trunks and those of the artist be inspected, in spite of my passports, etc., having been publicly declared to the satisfaction of these gentlemen—which they proceeded to carry out most rudely. Finally the police lieutenant, in company with these officials, took the trunks to his house to inspect fully the papers and drawings they contained. As a result of this momentary junta, at two o'clock in the morning they dispatched a messenger posthaste on horseback with part of my papers to the governor of Vera-Cruz, in the meantime placing me under guard of twenty-four men with their lieutenant of lancers, to wait for the instructions from the governor. The following day before dawn I was escorted by an official and four lancers, and as a prisoner—without knowing why—to the artillery barracks. The next day this official summoned me and gave me an honorific reception, and saw fit to give me a certain satisfaction, then set me at liberty and offered me some soldiers to help me as far as Jalapa. It so happened that there arrived a party of dragoons from Mexico and I availed myself of them as an escort to Puebla. There the governor decided, for the safety of our persons and our baggage, to give me two provincial dragoons as far as the capital, where we arrived without incident, praised be the Lord!

• •

TWO

John L. Stephens 1839

Death Robed in Terror

[The man who first awakened widespread American and English interest in the Maya ruins of Central America was John Lloyd Stephens, a New York lawyer and world traveler, whose book on Arabia and the Holy Land had become a best seller in 1837. Stephens, always seeking new lands to explore, was fascinated by some dramatic accounts of almost unbelievable discoveries of ancient stone cities in Mexico, Honduras, and Guatemala early in the nineteenth century. He found a kindred soul in the gifted English architect and draftsman Frederick Catherwood, who shared Stephens' interest in antiquities and readily agreed to accompany him on an expedition of Central American exploration.

[In the fall of 1839, Stephens and Catherwood landed at Belize, the capital of the colony of British Honduras, and then proceeded by coastwise steamer to Puenta Gorda, thence up the beautiful tropical Río Dulce to Lake Izabal, where they began the long overland journey across the Mico Mountains toward their first destination, the ruins of Copán. This trip was to give them their first experience with the tropical rain forests, rugged mountain ranges, and baked deserts of Central America. Earlier I described El Oriente of 1934, the scorched semi-arid "Wild East" of Guatemala and adjacent Honduras, where the heat reduced women's costumes to a skirt as they wrapped (and smoked) cigars in front of their adobe huts. A century earlier, Stephens passed through the same land. A typical proper, conservative gentleman of

The selections from Stephens are, in the order quoted below, from the following works. John Lloyd Stephens, *Incidents of Travel in Central America, Chiapas, and Yucatan* (New York: Harper & Bros., 1841): Vol. I, pp. 54–59, 101–5; Vol. II, pp. 359–61, 371–73. John Lloyd Stephens, *Incidents of Travel in Yucatan* (New York: Harper & Bros., 1843): Vol. I, pp. 107–18; Vol. II, pp. 98–99.

the time, he seems to have been shocked most of all, at first, by this "careless" dress of the natives. When he and his party reached the Motagua River,
they crossed in a canoe, after their mules had been driven reluctantly to swim
the rapid current to the far bank.]

During all this time we sat in the canoe, with the hot sun beating upon
our heads. For the last two hours we had suffered excessively from heat; our
clothes were saturated with perspiration and stiff with mud, and we looked
forward almost with rapture to a bath in the Motagua and a change of
linen. We landed, and walked up to the house in which we were to pass the
night. It was plastered and whitewashed, and adorned with streaks of red in
the shape of festoons; and in front was a fence made of long reeds, six inches
in diameter, split into two; altogether the appearance was favourable. To
our great vexation, our luggage had gone on to a rancho three leagues beyond. Our muleteers refused to go any farther. We were unpleasantly situated, but we did not care to leave so soon the Motagua river. Our host told
us that his house and all that he had were at our disposal: but he could give
us nothing to eat; and, telling Augustin to ransack the village, we returned
to the river. Everywhere the current was too rapid for a quiet bath. Calling
our canoe man, we returned to the opposite side, and in a few minutes were
enjoying an ablution, the luxury of which can only be appreciated by those
who, like us, had crossed the Mico Mountain without throwing away their
clothes.

There was an enjoyment in this bath greater even than that of cooling our
heated bodies. It was the moment of a golden sunset. We stood up to our
necks in water clear as crystal, and calm as that of some diminutive lake, at
the margin of a channel along which the stream was rushing with arrowy
speed. On each side were mountains several thousand feet high, with their
tops illuminated by the setting sun; on a point above us was a palm-leafed
hut, and before it a naked Indian sat looking at us; while flocks of parrots,
with brilliant plumage, almost in thousands, were flying over our heads,
catching up our words, and filling the air with their noisy mockings. It was
one of those beautiful scenes that so rarely occur in human life, almost realizing dreams. Old as we were, we might have become poetic, but that Augustin came down to the opposite bank, and, with a cry that rose above the
chattering of parrots and the loud murmur of the river, called us to supper.

We had one moment of agony when we returned to our clothes. They lay
extended upon the bank, emblems of men who had seen better days. The
setting sun, which shed over all a soft and mellow lustre, laid bare the seams
of mud and dirt, and made them hideous. We had but one alternative, and
that was to go without them. But, as this seemed to be trenching upon the
proprieties of life, we picked them up and put them on reluctant. I am not
sure, however, but that we made an unnecessary sacrifice of personal comfort. The proprieties of life are matters of conventional usage. Our host was a

don; and when we presented our letter he received us with great dignity in a single garment, loose, white, and very laconic, not quite reaching his knees. The dress of his wife was no less easy; somewhat in the style of the old-fashioned shortgown and petticoat, only the shortgown and whatever else is usually worn under it were wanting, and their place supplied by a string of beads, with a large cross at the end. A dozen men and half-grown boys, naked except the small covering formed by rolling the trousers up and down in the manner I have mentioned, were lounging about the house; and women and girls in such extremes of undress, that a string of beads seemed quite a covering for modesty.

Mr. C. and I were in a rather awkward predicament for the night. The general reception-room contained three beds, made of strips of cowhide interlaced. The don occupied one; he had not much undressing to do, but what little he had, he did by pulling off his shirt. Another bed was at the foot of my hammock. I was dozing, when I opened my eyes, and saw a girl about seventeen sitting sideway upon it, smoking a cigar. She had a piece of striped cotton cloth tied around her waist, and falling below her knees; the rest of her dress was the same which Nature bestows alike upon the belle of fashionable life and the poorest girl; in other words, it was the same as that of the don's wife, with the exception of the string of beads. At first I thought it was something I had conjured up in a dream; and as I waked up perhaps I raised my head, for she gave a few quick puffs of her cigar, drew a cotton sheet over her head and shoulders, and lay down to sleep. I endeavoured to do the same. I called to mind the proverb, that "travelling makes strange bedfellows." I had slept pellmell with Greeks, Turks, and Arabs. I was beginning a journey in a new country; it was my duty to conform to the customs of the people; to be prepared for the worst, and submit with resignation to whatever might befall me.

As guests, it was pleasant to feel that the family made no strangers of us. The wife of the don retired with the same ceremonies. Several times during the night we were waked by the clicking of flint and steel, and saw one of our neighbours lighting a cigar. At daylight the wife of the don was enjoying her morning slumber. While I was dressing she bade me good-morning, removed the cotton covering from her shoulders, and arose dressed for the day.

[After days of rough travel and some dangerous adventures, Stephens and Catherwood reached the Copán River and had their first glimpse of all that remained of a major masonry structure of the ancient Maya.]

The massive stone structures before us had little the air of belonging to a city, the intrenchment of which could be broken down by the charge of a single horseman. At this place the river was not fordable; we returned to our mules, mounted, and rode to another part of the bank, a short distance above. The stream was wide, and in some places deep, rapid, and with a broken and stony bottom. Fording it, we rode along the bank by a footpath encumbered with undergrowth, which Jose opened by cutting away the branches, until we came to the foot of the wall, where we again dismounted and tied our mules.

The wall was of cut stone, well laid, and in a good state of preservation. We ascended by large stone steps, in some places perfect, and in others thrown down by trees which had grown up between the crevices, and reached a terrace, the form of which it was impossible to make out, from the density of the forest in which it was enveloped. Our guide cleared a way with his machete, and we passed, as it lay half buried in the earth, a large fragment of stone elaborately sculptured, and came to the angle of a structure with steps on the sides, in form and appearance, so far as the trees would enable us to make it out, like the sides of a pyramid. Diverging from the base, and working our way through the thick woods, we came upon a square stone column, about fourteen feet high and three feet on each side, sculptured in very bold relief, and on all four of the sides, from the base to the top. The front was the figure of a man curiously and richly dressed, and the face, evidently a portrait, solemn, stern, and well fitted to excite terror. The back was of a different design, unlike anything we had ever seen before,

Copán River, with ruined acropolis on far side
Photograph by A. P. Maudslay, 1890.
From *Biologia Centrali-Americana: Archaeology,* vol. i.

and the sides were covered with hieroglyphics. This our guide called an "Idol;" and before it, at a distance of three feet, was a large block of stone, also sculptured with figures and emblematical devices, which he called an altar. The sight of this unexpected monument put at rest at once and forever, in our minds, all uncertainty in regard to the character of American antiquities, and gave us the assurance that the objects we were in search of

Carved stela, Copán
Drawing by Frederick Catherwood, 1839.
From John Lloyd Stephens, *Incidents of Travel in Central America, Chiapas, and Yucatan.*

were interesting, not only as the remains of an unknown people, but as works of art, proving, like newly-discovered historical records, that the people who once occupied the Continent of America were not savages. With an interest perhaps stronger than we had ever felt in wandering among the ruins of Egypt, we followed our guide, who, sometimes missing his way, with a constant and vigorous use of his machete, conducted us through the thick forest, among half-buried fragments, to fourteen monuments of the same character and appearance, some with more elegant designs, and some in workmanship equal to the finest monuments of the Egyptians; one displaced from its pedestal by enormous roots; another locked in the close embrace of branches of trees, and almost lifted out of the earth; another hurled to the ground, and bound down by huge vines and creepers; and one standing, with its altar before it, in a grove of trees which grew around it, seemingly to shade and shroud it as a sacred thing; in the solemn stillness of the woods, it seemed a divinity mourning over a fallen people. The only sounds that disturbed the quiet of this buried city were the noise of monkeys moving among the tops of the trees, and the cracking of dry branches broken by their weight. They moved over our heads in long and swift processions, forty or fifty at a time, some with little ones wound in their long arms, walking out to the end of boughs, and holding on with their hind feet or a curl of the tail, sprang to a branch of the next tree, and, with a noise like a current of wind, passed on into the depths of the forest. It was the first time we had seen these mockeries of humanity, and, with the strange monuments around us, they seemed like wandering spirits of the departed race guarding the ruins of their former habitations.

We returned to the base of the pyramidal structure, and ascended by regular stone steps, in some places forced apart by bushes and saplings, and in others thrown down by the growth of large trees, while some remained entire. In parts they were ornamented with sculptured figures and rows of death's heads. Climbing over the ruined top, we reached a terrace overgrown with trees, and, crossing it, descended by stone steps into an area so covered with trees that at first we could not make out its form, but which, on clearing the way with the machete, we ascertained to be a square, and with steps on all the sides almost as perfect as those of the Roman amphitheatre. The steps were ornamented with sculpture, and on the south side, about half way up, forced out of its place by roots, was a colossal head, evidently a portrait. We ascended these steps, and reached a broad terrace a hundred feet high, overlooking the river, and supported by the wall which we had seen from the opposite bank. The whole terrace was covered with trees, and even at this height from the ground were two gigantic Ceibas, or wild cotton trees of India, above twenty feet in circumference, extending their half-naked roots fifty or a hundred feet around, binding down the ruins, and shading them with their wide-spreading branches. We sat down on the very edge of the wall, and strove in vain to penetrate the mystery by which we were sur-

rounded. Who were the people that built this city? In the ruined cities of
Egypt, even in the long-lost Petra, the stranger knows the story of the people
whose vestiges are around him. America, say historians, was peopled by
savages; but savages never reared these structures, savages never carved
these stones. We asked the Indians who made them, and their dull answer
was "Quien sabe?" "who knows?"

There were no associations connected with the place; none of those stirring recollections which hallow Rome, Athens, and

"The world's great mistress on the Egyptian plain;"

but architecture, sculpture, and painting, all the arts which embellish life,
had flourished in this overgrown forest; orators, warriors, and statesmen,
beauty, ambition, and glory, had lived and passed away, and none knew that

Buried stela, Copán
Drawing by Frederick Catherwood.
From John Lloyd Stephens, *Incidents of Travel in Central America, Chiapas, and Yucatan.*

such things had been, or could tell of their past existence. Books, the records of knowledge, are silent on this theme. The city was desolate. No remnant of this race hangs round the ruins, with traditions handed down from father to son, and from generation to generation. It lay before us like a shattered bark in the midst of the ocean, her masts gone, her name effaced, her crew perished, and none to tell whence she came, to whom she belonged, how long on her voyage, or what caused her destruction; her lost people to be traced only by some fancied resemblance in the construction of the vessel, and, perhaps, never to be known at all. The place where we sat, was it a citadel from which an unknown people had sounded the trumpet of war? or a temple for the worship of the God of peace? or did the inhabitants worship the idols made with their own hands, and offer sacrifices on the stones before them? All was mystery, dark, impenetrable mystery, and every circumstance increased it. In Egypt the colossal skeletons of gigantic temples stand in the unwatered sands in all the nakedness of desolation; here an immense forest shrouded the ruins, hiding them from sight, heightening the impression and moral effect, and giving an intensity and almost wildness to the interest.

[The years that Stephens spent in the most remote parts of Central America never inured him to certain customs and attitudes he considered barbarous and repugnant. Many of these had to do with the treatment of the dead, which, to a North American, seemed particularly unfeeling and callous. Two of these incidents occurred on his trip to and from Palenque, the second great ruined city that he had wanted to visit in this land.]

The next day again was Sunday. It was my third Sunday in the village, and again it was emphatically a day of rest. In the afternoon a mournful interruption was given to the stillness of the place by the funeral of a young Indian girl, once the pride and beauty of the village, whose portrait Mr. Waldeck had taken to embellish his intended work on Palenque. Her career, as oftens happens with beauty in higher life, was short, brilliant, and unhappy. She had married a young Indian, who abandoned her and went to another village. Ignorant, innocent, and unconscious of wrong, she was persuaded to marry another, drooped, and died. The funeral procession passed our door. The corpse was borne on a rude bier, without coffin, in a white cotton dress, with a shawl over the head, and followed by a slender procession of women and children only. I walked beside it, and heard one of them say, "bueno Christiano, to attend the funeral of a poor woman." The bier was set down beside the grave, and in lifting the body from it the head turned on one side, and the hands dropped; the grave was too short, and as the dead was laid within the legs were drawn up. Her face was thin and wasted, but the mouth had a sweetness of expression which seemed to express that she had died with a smile of forgiveness for him who had injured her. I could not turn my eyes from her placid but grief-worn countenance, and so touching was its expression that I could almost have shed tears. Young, beautiful, simple, and innocent, abandoned and dead, with not a mourner at her grave. All seemed to think that she was better dead; she was poor, and could not maintain herself. The men went away, and the women and children with their hands scraped the earth upon the body. It was covered up gradually and slowly; the feet stuck out, and then all was buried but the face. A small piece of muddy earth fell upon one of the eyes, and another on her sweetly smiling mouth, changing the whole expression in a moment; death was now robed with terror. The women stopped to comment upon the change; the dirt fell so as to cover the whole face except the nose, and for two or three moments this alone was visible. Another brush covered this, and the girl was buried. The reader will excuse me. I am sorry to say that if she had been ugly, I should, perhaps, have regarded it as an every-day case of a wife neglected by her husband; but her sweet face speaking from the grave created an impression which even yet is hardly effaced. . . .

Go where we will, to the uttermost parts of the earth, we are sure to meet one acquaintance. Death is always with us. In the afternoon was the funeral of a child. The procession consisted of eight or ten grown persons, and as many boys and girls. The sexton carried the child in his arms, dressed in white, with a wreath of flowers around its head. All were huddled around the sexton, walking together; the father and mother with him; and even more than in Costa Rica I remarked, not only an absence of solemnity, but cheerfulness and actual gayety, from the same happy conviction that the child had gone to a better world. I happened to be in the church as they approached, more like a wedding than a burial party. The floor of the church was earthen, and the grave was dug inside, because, as the sexton told me, the father was rich and could afford to pay for it, and the father seemed pleased and proud that he could give his child such a burial-place. The sexton laid the child in the grave, folded its little hands across its breast, placing there a small rude cross, covered it over with eight or ten inches of earth, and then got into the grave and stamped it down with his feet. He then got out and threw in more, and, going outside of the church, brought back a pounder, being a log of wood about four feet long and ten inches in diameter, like the rammer used among us by paviors, and again taking his place in the grave, threw up the pounder to the full swing of his arm, and brought it down with all his strength over the head of the child. My blood ran cold. As he threw it up a second time I caught his arm and remonstrated with him, but he said that they always did so with those buried inside the church; that the earth must be all put back, and the floor of the church made even. My remonstrances seemed only to give him more strength and spirit. The sweat rolled down his body, and when perfectly tired with pounding he stepped out of the grave. But this was nothing. More earth was thrown in, and the father laid down his hat, stepped into the grave, and the pounder was handed to him. I saw him throw it up twice and bring it down with a dead, heavy noise. I never beheld a more brutal and disgusting scene. The child's body must have been crushed to atoms.

Toward evening the moschetoes began their operations. Pawling and Juan planted sticks in the ground outside the convent, and spread sheets over them for nets; but the rain came on and drove them within, and we passed another wretched night. It may be asked how the inhabitants live. I cannot answer. They seemed to suffer as much as we, but at home they could have conveniences which we could not carry in traveling. Pawling suffered so much, and heard such dreadful accounts of what we would meet with below, that, in a spirit of impetuosity and irritation, he resolved not to continue any further. From the difficulty and uncertainty of communications, however, I strongly apprehended that in such case all the schemes in which he was concerned must fall through and be abandoned, as I was not willing to incur the expense of sending materials, subject to delays and uncertainties, unless in special charge, and once more he changed his purpose.

I had but one leave-taking, and that was a trying one. I was to bid farewell to my noble macho. He had carried me more than two thousand miles, over the worst roads that mule ever travelled. He stood tied to the door of the convent; saw the luggage, and even his own saddle, carried away by hand, seemed to have a presentiment that something unusual was going on. I had often been solicited to sell him, but no money could have tempted me. He was in poorer condition than when we reached Palenque. Deprived of corn and exposed to the dreadful rains, he was worse than when worked hard and fed well every day, and in his drooping state seemed to reproach me for going away and leaving him forlorn. I threw my arms around his neck; his eyes had a mournful expression, and at that moment he forgot the angry prick of the spur. I laid aside the memory of a toss from his back and ineffectual attempts to repeat it, and we remembered only mutual kind offices and good-fellowship. Tried and faithful companion, where are you now? I left him, with two others, tied at the door of the convent, to be taken by the sexton to the prefect at Palenque, there to recover from the debilitating influence of the early rains, and to roam on rich pasture-grounds, untouched by bridle or spur, until I should return to mount him again.

[In their first travels in Latin America, Stephens and Catherwood were able to visit Yucatán only briefly, but they were so intrigued with this region, its people, and its antiquities, that they resolved to return to explore it more thoroughly as soon as opportunity offered. In 1840, about a year after their return to the United States, they were back in Mérida, capital of Yucatán, this time accompanied by a medical friend, Doctor Cabot.]

Secluded as Merida is, and seldom visited by strangers, the fame of new discoveries in science is slow in reaching it, and the new operation of Mons. Guerin for the cure of strabismus had not been heard of. In private intercourse we had spoken of this operation, and, in order to make it known, and extend its benefits, Doctor Cabot had offered to perform it in Merida. The Merida people have generally fine eyes, but, either because our attention was particularly directed to it, or that it is really the case, there seemed to be more squinting eyes, or biscos, as they are called, than are usually seen in any one town, and in Merida, as in some other places, this is not esteemed a beauty; but, either from want of confidence in a stranger, or a cheap estimation of the qualifications of a medico who asked no pay for his services, the doctor's philanthropic purposes were not appreciated. At least, no one cared to be the first; and as the doctor had no sample of his skill with him, no subject offered.

We had fixed the day for our departure; and the evening but one before, a direct overture was made to the doctor to perform the operation. The subject was a boy, and the application in his behalf was made by a gentleman who formed one of a circle in which we were in the habit of visiting, and whom we were all happy to have it in our power to serve.

The time was fixed at ten o'clock the next day. After breakfast our sala was put in order for the reception of company, and the doctor for the first time looked to his instruments. He had some misgivings. They were of very fine workmanship, made in Paris, most sensitive to the influence of atmosphere, and in that climate it was almost impossible to preserve anything metallic from rust. The doctor had packed the case among his clothing in the middle of his trunk, and had taken every possible precaution, but, as usual upon such occasions, the most important instrument had rusted at the point, and in that state was utterly useless. There was no cutler in the place, nor any other person competent to touch it. Mr. Catherwood, however, brought out an old razor hone, and between them they worked off the rust.

At ten o'clock the doctor's subject made his appearance. He was the son of a widow lady of very respectable family, about fourteen years old, but small of stature, and presenting even to the most casual glance the stamp of a little gentleman. He had large black eyes, but, unluckily, their expression was very much injured by an inward squint. With the light heart of boyhood, however, he seemed indifferent to his personal appearance, and came, as he said, because his mother told him to do so. His handsome person, and modest and engaging manners, gave us immediately a strong interest in his favour. He was accompanied by the gentleman who had spoken of bringing him, Dr. Bado, a Guatimalian educated in Paris, the oldest and principal physician of Merida, and by several friends of the family, whom we did not know.

Preparations were commenced immediately. The first movement was to bring out a long table near the window; then to spread upon it a mattress and pillow, and upon these to spread the boy. Until the actual moment of operating, the precise character of this new business had not presented itself to my mind, and altogether it opened by no means so favourably as Daguerreotype practice.

Not aiming to be technical, but desiring to give the reader the benefit of such scraps of learning as I pick up in my travels, modern science has discovered that the eye is retained in its orbit by six muscles, which pull it up and down, inward and outward, and that the undue contraction of either of these muscles produces that obliquity called squinting, which was once supposed to proceed from convulsions in childhood, or other unknown causes. The cure discovered is the cutting of the contracted muscle, by means of which the eye falls immediately into its proper place. This muscle lies under the surface; and, as it is necessary to pass through a membrane of the eye, the cutting cannot be done with a broadaxe or a handsaw. In fact, it requires a knowledge of the anatomy of the eye, manual dexterity, fine instruments, and Mr. Catherwood and myself for assistants.

Our patient remained perfectly quiet, with his little hands folded across his breast; but while the knife was cutting through the muscle he gave one groan, so piteous and heart-rending, that it sent into the next room all who were not immediately engaged. But before the sound of the groan had died away the operation was over, and the boy rose with his eye bleeding, but perfectly straight. A bandage was tied over it, and, with a few directions for its treatment, amid the congratulations and praises of all present, and wearing the same smile with which he had entered, the little fellow walked off to his mother.

The news of this wonder spread rapidly, and before night Dr. Cabot had numerous and pressing applications, among which was one from a gentleman whom we were all desirous to oblige, and who had this defect in both eyes.

On his account we determined to postpone our departure another day; and, in furtherance of his original purpose, Dr. Cabot mentioned that he would perform the operation upon all who chose to offer. We certainly took no trouble to spread this notice, but the next morning, when we returned from breakfast, there was a gathering of squint-eyed boys around the door, who, with their friends and backers, made a formidable appearance, and almost obstructed our entrance. As soon as the door opened there was a rush inside; and as some of these slanting eyes might not be able to distinguish between meum and tuum, we were obliged to help their proprietors out into the street again.

At ten o'clock the big table was drawn up to the window, and the mattress and pillow were spread upon it, but there was such a gathering around the window that we had to hang up a sheet before it. Invitations had been given to Dr. Bado and Dr. Munoz, and all physicians who chose to come, and having met the governor in the evening, I had asked him to be present. These all honoured us with their company, together with a number of self-invited persons, who had introduced themselves, and could not well be turned out, making quite a crowded room.

The first who presented himself was a stout lad about nineteen or twenty, whom we had never seen or heard of before. Who he was or where he came from we did not know, but he was a bisco of the worst kind, and seemed able-bodied enough to undergo anything in the way of surgery. As soon as the doctor began to cut the muscle, however, our strapping patient gave signs of restlessness; and all at once, with an actual bellow, he jerked his head on one side, carried away the doctor's hook, and shut his eye upon it with a sort of lockjaw grip, as if determined it should never be drawn out. How my hook got out I have no idea; fortunately, the doctor let his go, or the lad's eye would have been scratched out. As it was, there he sat with the bandage slipped above one eye, and the other closed upon the hook, the handle of which stood out straight. Probably at that moment he would have been willing to sacrifice pride of personal appearance, keep his squint, and go through life with his eye shut, the hook in it, and the handle sticking out; but the instrument was too valuable to be lost. And it was interesting and instructive to notice the difference between the equanimity of one who had a hook in his eye, and that of lookers-on who had not. All the spectators upbraided him with his cowardice and want of heart, and after a round of reproof to which he could make no answer, he opened his eye and let out the hook. But he had made a bad business of it. A few seconds longer, and the operation would have been completed. As it was the whole work had to be repeated. As the muscle was again lifted under the knife, I thought I saw a glare in the eyeball that gave token of another fling of the head, but the lad was fairly browbeaten into quiet; and, to the great satisfaction of all, with a double share of blackness and blood, and with very little sympathy from any one, but with his eye straight, he descended from the table. Outside he was received with a loud shout by the boys, and we never heard of him again.

The room was now full of people, and, being already disgusted with the practice of surgery, I sincerely hoped that this exhibition would cure all others of a wish to undergo the operation, but a little Mestizo boy, about ten years old, who had been present all the time, crept through the crowd, and, reaching the table, squinted up at us without speaking, his crisscross expression telling us very plainly what he wanted. He had on the usual Mestizo dress of cotton shirt and drawers and straw hat, and seemed so young, simple, and innocent, that we did not consider him capable of judging for himself. We told him he must not be operated on, but he answered in a decided though modest tone, "Yo quiero, yo quiero," "I wish it, I wish it." We inquired if there was any one present who had any authority over him, and a man whom we had not noticed before, dressed, like him, in shirt and drawers, stepped forward and said he was the boy's father; he had brought him there himself on purpose, and begged Doctor Cabot to proceed. By his father's directions, the little fellow attempted to climb up on the table, but his legs were too short, and he had to be lifted up. His eye was bandaged, and his head placed upon the pillow. He folded his hands across his breast, turned his eye, did in all things exactly as he was directed, and in half a minute the operation was finished. I do not believe that he changed his position a hair's breadth or moved a muscle. It was an extraordinary instance of fortitude. The spectators were all admiration, and, amid universal congratulation, he was lifted from the table, his eye bound up, and, without a word, but with the spirit of a little hero, he took his father's hand and went away.

At this time, amid a press of applicants, a gentleman came to inform us that a young lady was waiting her turn. This gave us an excuse for clearing the room, and we requested all except the medical gentlemen and the immediate friends to favour us with their absence. Such was the strange curiosity these people had for seeing a most disagreeable spectacle, that they were very slow in going away, and some slipped into the other rooms and the yard, but we ferreted them out, and got the room somewhat to ourselves.

The young lady was accompanied by her mother. She was full of hesitation and fears, anxious to be relieved, but doubting her ability to endure the pain, and the moment she saw the instruments, her courage entirely forsook her. Doctor Cabot discouraged all who had any distrust of their own fortitude, and, to my mingled joy and regret, she went away.

The next in order was the gentleman on whose account we had postponed our departure. He was the oldest general in the Mexican service, but for two years an exile in Merida. By the late revolution, which placed Santa Ana in power, his party was uppermost; and he had strong claims upon our good feelings, for, in a former expatriation from Mexico, he had served as volunteer aid to General Jackson at the battle of New-Orleans. This gentleman had an inward squint in both eyes, which, however, instead of being a defect, gave character to his face; but his sight was injured by it, and this Doctor Cabot thought might be improved. The first eye was cut quickly and successfully, and while the bloody orb was rolling in its socket, the same operation was performed upon the other. In this however, fearing that the eye might be drawn too far in the opposite direction, the doctor had not thought it advisable to cut the muscle entirely through, and, on examining it, he was not satisfied with the appearance. The general again laid his head upon the pillow, and the operation was repeated, making three times in rapid succession. Altogether, it was a trying thing, and I felt immensely happy when it was over. With his eyes all right and both bandaged, we carried him to a caleza in waiting, where, to the great amusement of the vagabond boys, he took his seat on the footboard, with his back to the horse, and it was some time before we could get him right.

In the meantime the young lady had returned with her mother. She could not bear to lose the opportunity, and though unable to make up her mind to undergo the operation, she could not keep away. She was about eighteen, of lively imagination, picturing pleasure or pain in the strongest colours, and with a smile ever ready to chase away the tear. At one moment she roused herself to the effort, and the next, calling herself coward, fell into her mother's arms, while her mother cheered and encouraged her, representing to her, with that confidence allowed before medical men, the advantage it would give her in the eyes of our sex. Her eyes were large, full, and round, and with the tear glistening in them, the defect was hardly visible; in fact, all that they wanted was to be made to roll in the right direction.

I have given the reader a faint picture of Daguerreotype practice with young ladies, but this was altogether another thing, and it was very different from having to deal with boys or men. It is easy enough to spread out a boy upon a table, but not so with a young lady; so, too, it is easy enough to tie a bandage around a boy's head, but vastly different among combs and curls, and long hair done up behind. As the principal assistant of Doctor Cabot, this complicated business devolved upon me; and having, with the help of her mother, accomplished it, I laid her head upon the pillow as carefully as if it had been my own property. In all the previous cases I had found it necessary, in order to steady my hand, to lean my elbow on the table, and my wrist on the forehead of the patient. I did the same with her, and, if I know myself, I never gazed into any eyes as I did into that young lady's one eye in particular. When the doctor drew out the instrument, I certainly could have taken her in my arms, but her imagination had been too powerful; her eyes closed, a slight shudder seized her, and she fainted. That passed off, and she rose with her eyes all right. A young gentleman was in attendance to escort her to her home, and the smile had again returned to her cheek as he told her that now her lover would not know her.

This case had occupied a great deal of time; the doctor's labours were doubled by the want of regular surgical aid, he was fatigued with the excitement, and I was worn out; my head was actually swimming with visions of bleeding and mutilated eyes, and I almost felt doubtful about my own. The repetition of the operations had not accustomed me to them; indeed, the last was more painful to me than the first, and I felt willing to abandon forever the practice of surgery. Doctor Cabot had explained the modus operandi fully to the medical gentlemen, had offered to procure them instruments, and considering the thing fairly introduced into the country, we determined to stop. But this was not so easy; the crowd out of doors had their opinion on the subject; the biscos considered that we were treating them outrageously, and became as clamorous as a mob in a western city about to administer Lynch law. One would not be kept back. He was a strapping youth, with cast enough in his eye to carry everything before him and had probably been taunted all his life by merciless schoolboys. Forcing himself inside, with his hands in his pockets, he said that he had the money to pay for it, and would not be put off. We were obliged to apologize, and, with a little wish to bring him down, gave him some hope that he should be attended to on our return to Merida.

The news of these successes flew like wild-fire, and a great sensation was created throughout the city. All evening Doctor Cabot was besieged with applications, and I could but think how fleeting is this world's fame! At first my arrival in the country had been fairly trumpeted in the newspapers; for a little while Mr. Catherwood had thrown me in the shade with the Daguerreotype, and now all our glories were swallowed up by Doctor Cabot's cure of strabismus. Nevertheless, his fame was reflected upon us. All the afternoon squint-eyed boys were passing up and down the street, throwing slanting glances in at the door, and toward evening, as Mr. Catherwood and I were walking to the plaza, we were hailed by some vagabond urchins with the obstreperous shout, "There go the men who cure the biscos."

[Stephens, the perfect gentleman, the urbane conservative, who was careful to express every emotion most delicately, occasionally admitted, even in print, that he was not unaware of a pretty face or an attractive figure among the young mestiza ladies of Yucatán. He attended a dance in Ticul.]

To sustain the fancy character, the only dance was that of the toros. A vaquero stood up, and each Mestiza was called out in order. This dance, as we had seen it among the Indians, was extremely uninteresting, and required a movement of the body, a fling of the arms, and a snapping of the fingers, which were at least inelegant; but with las Mestizas of Ticul it was all graceful and pleasing, and there was something particularly winning in the snapping of the fingers. There were no dashing beauties, and not one who seemed to have any idea of being a belle; but all exhibited a mildness, softness, and amiability of expression that created a feeling of promiscuous tenderness. Sitting at ease in an arm-chair, after my sojourn in Indian ranchos, I was particularly alive to these influences. And there was such a charm about that Mestiza dress. It was so clean, simple, and loose, leaving

"Every beauty free
To sink or swell as Nature pleases."

The ball broke up too soon, when I was but beginning to reap the fruit of my hard day's work. There was an irruption of servants to carry home the chairs, and in half an hour, except along a line of tables in front of the audiencia, the village was still. For a little while, in my quiet chamber at the convent, the gentle figures of las Mestizas still haunted me, but, worn down by the fatigues of the day, I very soon forgot them.

• • •

THREE

Arthur Morelet 1846

Lost in the Rain Forest

[Arthur Morelet, whom E. George Squier described as "a French gentle-man of leisure and extensive scientific acquirements," was another of the early explorers of Central America. His account of his travels, first published in France as *Voyage dans l'Amerique Centrale, l'Ile de Cuba, et l'Yucatan,* and the collections of animals, reptiles, insects, and plants which he took back with him to Paris reflect his wide interests. I have chosen from his writings (translated into English by Mrs. M. F. Squier in 1871) those which tell chiefly of his explorations at Palenque, mecca of most of the archaeological explorers of that time as well as the present.

[Morelet landed in the city of Campeche, then Yucatán's second largest city, on its west coast facing the Gulf of Mexico. There he prepared for his expedition into the interior, exchanging his trunks for boxes that could be loaded on mule back, abandoning every article not necessary for the trip, and buying a hammock and drugs. He then secured passage for the Island of Carmen off the southern shores of the gulf. His companion was named Morin, whom Morelet described as "half-sailor, half valet, with the advantage of two years' experience in these countries." From Carmen they proceeded by canoe to the mouth of the Palizada River, an eastern outlet of the Usumacinta, one of the largest waterways of Central America.]

Vegetation assumes a more and more interesting appearance as one ad-vances towards the interior. Great willows with trailing branches, gigantic bamboos, beautiful *cyperaceae* or sedges resembling the papyrus, aquatic palm-trees with their slender stems, the cecropia with its immense leaves—all unite in ornamenting both banks of the river. Besides these, masses of

The selections from Morelet are, in the order quoted below, from C. A. Morelet, *Travels in Central America* (New York: Leypoldt, Holt, & Williams, 1871), pp. 50–54, 65–81, 99–108, 345–52.

verdure, spangled with bunches of violet flowers, prodigious white tree trunks, and vines slender and delicate as the rigging of a ship, continually present themselves to the eye. I observed among other beautiful trees, the *jahuacte* palm, with its graceful branches bending over the water. Its fruit is acidulous, and of the shape and size of an acorn. It is much sought for by children, and is not without its appeal to the traveller. A great variety of birds enjoy their existence in peace in these solitudes. Among them is the ibis with its brilliant plumage, the *aramus* with its ringing voice, and the blue prophyrio called by the inhabitants *gallo de Montezuma* (Montezuma's chicken). The king-fisher, with its ringed neck, is also found here, of much larger size than with us. It flutters continually over the water, while the falcon, uttering piercing shrieks, plunges suddenly into the river, rises perpendicularly with its prey, and then whirls itself upwards high in the air, until almost lost to the view. In contrast with these pleasant sights, we fancied that we discerned numerous alligators, motionlessly watching us from the shores of the little coves of the river—but then it was almost impossible to distinguish these amphibious monsters from the uprooted trunks of trees, which the river had covered with its slimy sediment. Reposing on the deck, wrapped in my cloak, I enjoyed with rapture a view truly enchanting from its novelty, and sufficiently exciting to make up for the lack of associations. During the whole of my journey, these pleasurable emotions continued; my interest and curiosity were constantly excited, for I was travelling towards the Unexplored and Unknown; and always excepting the impression produced by my first view of the New World, I must say that the scenes on the Usumasinta, by their melancholy grandeur, and primitive poetry, have left the most profound and lasting impressions on my mind.

Toward evening we reached a low piece of ground, surrounded by pools of water, called the Island of Birds, but which should have borne the name of Paradise of Mosquitos. As soon as the boat was secured, every one commenced making preparations for the night, by putting up a kind of square tent, made from a few yards of muslin. These tents are in general use in this country. Once inside of them, (and the operation of entering must be performed with great rapidity), every aperture is closed by tucking the ample folds of the muslin under the mat which serves as a bed. I was not so much of a novice as to be totally unprovided with some protection of this kind, for I had purchased in France a mosquito net, which, according to the representations of the vender, was of the newest and best variety. But I was soon convinced that the inventor of my net had never travelled on the Usumasinta! Hardly had I introduced myself, with the utmost adroitness and caution, under my gauze curtain, than the enemy, guided by his unfailing instincts, contrived to effect an entrance into my sanctuary. I heard with terror his familiar hum, and any lingering doubts as to the reality of his presence were soon dispelled by hundreds of bites all over my person. Vainly did I endeavor, by every possible device, to expel my persecutors. Finally, abandoning the attempt in no very amiable frame of mind, I vacated the place, wishing alike the net and its inventor to the devil! I went out, but the buzzing noise of mosquitos seemed to resound all along the banks; the air was thick with them; and I verily believe they were sufficiently numerous to have hidden even the sun from view! The hours passed tediously enough, in vain efforts to do battle against the myriads of my invisible enemies. I contemplated with indifference the nocturnal aspect of the landscape—the great shadows thrown on the water, and the phosphorescent light emitted by the fire-flies! The partisans of final causes will doubtless find some satisfactory manner of explaining the mosquito's mission and utility. For myself, after having, during that whole night, reflected on the subject, I was forced to admit that I could arrive at no conclusion, implying a useful or ornamental purpose in the creation of this most pestilent of insects!

The morning finally broke, and I had the satisfaction of rousing every one from his slumbers. Soon after, we embarked. The weather had cleared up and was delightful, but the wind was not strong, and as we proceeded slowly, I was enabled to do a little quiet shooting from the deck of our boat. Don Pancho kindly steered it so as to receive the game as it fell, not because he shared my ambition to advance the interests of natural science, but because he saw an augmentation of our supply of provisions in every bird added to my collection. In truth, our fare was anything but sumptuous. Mouldy biscuits, *tassajo*, and black beans formed our repasts so constantly and so usually, that I found myself frequently sighing for the shark's flesh of Campeachy. Toward the middle of the day, we reached the farm of San Geronimito, where we saw a large quantity of dye-woods piled up on the bank awaiting transportation to the Lagoon. Flowing into the Usumasinta at this point, is the *Rio Viejo,* which encircles a vast territory, intersected by lagoons, called the island of San *Isidro*. The fall of the land is here so trifling and indecisive, that the *Rio Viejo* describes three quarters of a circle, and in one place runs for near two leagues in an entirely opposite direction from its general course, as if in doubt which route to follow in order to reach the ocean.

As we approached the town of *Palizada,* the river became narrower and more rapid; the forests were more open, and the eye was enabled to wander at will over the undulating bosoms of the savannas, illuminated by the rays of the setting sun, where quiet seemed to reign supreme. . . .

It was ten o'clock at night, when a group of coca trees, in this part of the world a sure sign of human habitations, rising over the forest, gave notice that the village of Palizada was near at hand. Directly we discerned lights, and a confused mass of objects moving about in the darkness, and soon after we reached the landing place of the town, after a journey of fifty-four hours from Carmen. We had travelled upward of eighteen leagues, in accomplishing a distance of not more than seven, in a direct line. The hour was rather late to seek for shelter; fortunately, however one of our passengers was a resident here, and relieved our embarrassment on this score by placing his dwelling at our service. Hammocks were soon hung up, and each of us took one and slept with real satisfaction until morning. Hospitality does not involve great trouble or responsibility under the tropics, where, with two nails and a few yards of cotton cloth, the host is always prepared to receive and entertain his visitors!

At the end of a week, after laying in a supply of provisions, consisting of biscuits, rice, and salt-meat, I had my baggage placed on board of a *cayuco,* and started for the ruins of Palenque, distant thirty-five leagues. During the dry season this distance can be lessened by travelling directly across the country; but when the waters are high, it is safer to sail up to the village of *Las Playas,* from whence there is a tolerable road to the town of *Santo Domingo,* two leagues distant from the ancient city.

I observed, after leaving Palizada, that the Usumasinta began to change its appearance, and that on both banks there were occasional cultivated fields, with little houses scattered here and there. At one of these we stopped to procure mangos, water-melons, and *pozol.* The Indians never set out on any expedition without a supply of pozol. This is maize made into a kind of paste, sweetened with sugar to suit the taste, and when mixed with water serves at once for food and drink. It is, at the same time, the most economical and portable kind of provision for a journey.*

We poled along very slowly, until our boatmen, whom no encouragement

---

* Here I may repeat what has never failed to receive mention among all travellers in these countries, namely, that the *maize* or Indian corn constitutes the principal article of food of the people. It is most used in the form of *tortillas.* These are made by removing the outer husk of the kernels by soaking them in strong alkali; afterwards the grain is carefully washed in cold water, ground fine with a stone roller, on a concave grinding-stone, and then, in the form of a fine paste, flattened out in thin cakes, and baked rapidly on earthen platters, placed over a hot fire. The name *totoposte* is given to a kind of cake made of the same maize-paste with the tortilla, but it is thinner, only baked on one side, and then allowed to become completely dry and crisp. It has the same relation to the *tortilla* that the biscuit of commerce has to bread, and like that is specially used by travellers and sailors. The *tamal* is also made of maize, prepared as above described, mixed with pork chopped fine, tomatoes, pepper, and other unctuous and savory ingredients, which after being thoroughly cooked together, are divided into small portions of a pound each, and finally enveloped in the husks of maize, equally for preservation and ease of transport. Sometime fowls, fish, and even vegetables and comfits are used among the ingredients instead of pork. But in addition to these substantial preparations, the maize enters into various nourishing beverages, such as *tiste,* made of parched maize ground up with sugar, cinnamon, and cacao, and, when drunk, mixed with water; the *atolé,* a kind of porridge made of the young maize while yet soft, etc. Without the maize and the plaintain the population of tropical America could not exist.

could stimulate to greater speed, perceived a *cayuco* which had started from Palizada half-an-hour before our own, and which the curves in the river had hitherto concealed from our view. This acted as a charm in overcoming their apathy; they determined by a common impulse to pass by the boat ahead, which, however, was manned by sailors equally determined not to be beaten. An exciting race was consequently kept up all the day, much to our satisfaction. Voyaging in these canoes is not without its danger, when the bow oarsman is careless, or when his head or his vision is affected by alcohol. The depth of the water obliges the navigator to keep close to the shores, which are full of roots, scraggy tree-trunks, and vegetable *debris* embedded in the mud. The most perfect equilibrium has therefore to be maintained, for the *cayuco* is only a hollow trunk of a tree, narrow, light and unsteady. The river is deep, and its steep banks are slimy and infested by alligators. To fall overboard is consequently most disagreeable as well as dangerous. So, what with dread of being upset, warfare against troublesome flies by day, and still more troublesome mosquitos by night, the voyager here is not without his excitements, albeit not of the pleasantest kind.

At eight leagues from Palizada, after sending off a large outlet in a northeastern direction, the Usumasinta assumes its proper name. From this point the country again becomes wild in appearance; all traces of civilization disappear, and the stream, which is here double its former width, flows majestically through an unbroken avenue of gigantic trees. We were now nearing the confines of Yucatan; the left shore was already in the territory of

Bridge over swamp, El Petén. Forked stakes driven into the bajo floor support a single-pole balance walkway.

Tabasco. On approaching this wooded region, we heard for the first time the *alüates,* or red monkeys, which fill the forests night and morning with their fearful cries. It was sundown when we anchored in a little sheltered creek, where, on the top of a steep bank, we discerned a poor hut, to which we made our way, and where we obtained all we could expect or hope for in such a spot—shelter, fire, and water. This place is called *Ortega.*

While Morin was occupied in preparing supper, I shouldered my gun, and, crossing the little clearing back of the hut, entered the forest. But how am I to describe the spectacle which there greeted my enraptured sight? From the first step I took, I fancied myself on enchanted ground. I was surrounded by palm trees, a strange and monstrous vegetation, vines trailing in every direction in the wildest disorder, old branches of trees covered with bulbous plants, like so many aerial gardens—in a word, I found myself in a scene of splendor, richness, and diversity, exceeding in its beauty the wildest dreams of the most vivid imagination! A few stray gleams of sunshine streaming through the foliage revealed all this beauty immediately before me, but beyond was a profound darkness, impenetrable even to the sun. I stopped, bewildered and dazzled, like one who in a dark night suddenly sees a meteor flash before his eyes. I was so ecstatically absorbed, that I did not even feel the bites of mosquitos which swarmed around me! But as the shades of evening were falling, I feared to pursue my walk farther, standing always in wholesome dread of serpents and wild animals.

I had taken but a few steps backwards, towards the skirts of the forest, when a species of fig fell at my feet. In stooping to pick it up, what was my surprise to find it rapidly followed by others, some of which struck me in their descent. There was not the least breath of air to stir the trees, and the figs were far from being sufficiently ripe to have fallen from maturity. I looked up and fancied that I perceived a black form perfectly motionless, but partially concealed by the foliage. I could not feel satisfied to leave my doubts unsolved, so discharged my gun at the object, which immediately fell, then caught itself, fell a little lower, caught itself again, and finally disappeared in the thicket. I had seen sufficient to convince me that it was a monkey of the *alüate* variety. At the report of my gun, half-a-dozen black, grinning visages suddenly made their appearance through the branches, and then as suddenly disappeared. I was probably right in firing; yet I could not help regretting the severity of the reproof I had administered, and I left the battle-field without further disturbing these poor children of the wilderness.

On quitting the forest, I stopped to contemplate the imposing appearance presented at this hour by the Usumasinta. It seemed to be a vast basin, in which the weary waters took their rest, before following the current which slowly drew them towards the Gulf. The silence was profound, and heightened rather than disturbed by the distant howls of the alüates. The shadows deepened rapidly as the sun declined, and when it sank at last beneath the horizon, darkness seemed to fall like a veil over the earth. The river was here and there bright under the lingering beams, but these soon paled away, leaving the land and water to the sombre embraces of the night.

On my return to the hut, I was almost suffocated by the smoke from the smouldering brands which our boatmen had piled together as a preventive against mosquitos. Seated near the fire, they devoured a heron, which we had killed in the morning, with no other seasoning than green peppers; while Morin put the finishing touch to some mysterious dish of his own composition. Fortunately I was hungry, for there was little before me to provoke an appetite. When our meal was concluded, and every one had lighted his cigar, I questioned our host touching his solitary existence. His family consisted of a wife and two young children; his furniture of a couple of hammocks, a mat, and a few cooking-utensils. His gun, fishing-line, and a small cultivated field near by supplied him with provisions; when he had an abundance of these, he exchanged the surplus for such useful articles as the boatmen, who occasionally landed here, happened to bring with them. He had never been further away from this spot than to Palizada, and had no desire to exchange his solitary life and frugal independence for the excitement and sweets of civilization. "Porque?" Why? he exclaimed interrogatively, when I asked him if he would not like to see the great ocean, and the ships and people of other lands. "Porque? soy contento!" Why; am I not content? Nor was he alone in his philosophy; hundreds like him live and die in a like manner, without passing or seeking to pass beyond the congenial solitudes of the familiar wilds where their fathers lived and died before them.

Hardly had he finished his simple history, when a cry from the banks of the river startled us all, it was so like a human scream, a single one, but full of agony. We glanced anxiously at each other, and then all hurried off toward the spot from whence it seemed to proceed. But the thick growth of the bamboos retarded our steps, and the night moreover was very dark; we listened anxiously but could hear nothing; the murmuring of the river and the buzzing of insects were the only sounds which fell on our ears. Perhaps some wayworn traveller, belated on these dangerous shores, had fallen a prey to wild animals? We shouted, but without awakening even an echo; and finally wended our way back to the hut, with hearts full of the saddest reflections.

This incident rendered our host somewhat more communicative, and he related to us many of the dangers attendant on his mode of life. Jaguars frequently prowled about his dwelling; alligators often approached it, hoping in the darkness to secure a choice morsel in his dogs or his chickens; while venomous reptiles glided familiarly over his very doorsill. These details interested but did not entertain us; since we knew that we were to pass the night just outside the hut, in an open shed. I loaded my gun, and had a large fire built on the side of the shed next to the forest. But our worst enemy, the implacable mosquito, despised our defences. I was especially singled out as his victim here, as I had been before at the *Isla de Pajaros*. In vain I had my mosquito-bar sewed to the mat which served as my bed; the precaution was idle, and only resulted to my disadvantage. Those of my readers who have ever been under the tropics, will pardon me should I repeat myself. The valiant Cortez himself grumbled bitterly about the mosquitos which he found here, and even the great battles in which he was engaged could not efface the recollection of his struggles against these despicable little enemies.* It was only nine o'clock, so I had ample time for meditation. The moon was shining full upon the river; nothing could surpass the splendor of the night. But the calm and religious repose of the scene was rudely disturbed by the howls of the alüates which throng the banks of Usumasinta, and every night keep up a horrible chorus, so loud and sustained as to drown all other noises. No traveller ever heard the cry of this animal for the first time except with a choking sense of alarm; and no experience can reconcile him to it. I heard it every night for weeks, but it never failed to send a chill to my extremities, and I shudder now as I recall it. What with the alüates and mosquitos, the reader may be sure I got but little sleep at Ortega, and experienced a malicious pleasure in rousing up Morin and our companions, with the first glow of morning, and hurrying our departure.

Sunrise, in these wilds, is always welcomed with a choral hymn from the throats of its feathered inhabitants, in which all join without regard to the melody of their voices. Loudest and most discordant in the concert is the *penelope,* known in this country under the imitative name of *chachalaca,* which scrambles among the branches and flutters from tree-top to tree-top in a thorough gale of excitement and exuberant spirits—a tempting mark alike for the sportsman and the epicure.

As we moved up the river, I could not forbear instituting a general comparison between the forests here and our own, from which they differ not more in detail than in their distant aspects. Unlike ours, they do not round in uniform masses with waving outlines, but appear traced against the sky in a broken and often fantastic line. Here are tall apexes, curiously scant in their foliage, skeleton giants of the forest, and close by, in sharp contrast, a series of huge parasols of verdure, supported on stems so light that they seem to be suspended in the air by an invisible support. But most imposing in size, and richest in foliage, the *cantemon* is the real monarch of the woods. The very sky seems to rest on its majestic crown. We passed under one of these colossi, from the branches of which depended a little city of the oriole or hanging birds' nests, so high in the air that the eye failed to detect the threads by which they were supported. In these aerial retreats this bright little member of the *passeres* family is safe from every terrestrial enemy; only the hawk or the falcon can reach him there. Among the flowering trees which

---

* "Los mosquitos que lo picavan de dia como de noche, que á lo que despues le oia decir, tenia con ellos tan malas noches, que estaba la cabeca sin sentido de no dormir."—B. Diaz, *Hist. Verdad,* c. 181.

thronged the banks of the river, I observed the *inga,* which sprinkled our boat with its silvery and fragrant flowers as we swept beneath it.*

Night, under the tropics, seems less a period of repose than the midday hours. When the sun reaches the zenith, as if by common accord, the breezes subside, the leaves droop, the birds retire to the coolest recesses of the forest, and man himself relapses into a sympathetic silence. Perhaps it was then that I most enjoyed the strange and rich variety and novelty of the scenes around me. In a half-lethargic state I would lie back in the boat, and let the landscape float before my half-closed eyes, until gradually I would seem to lose my identity and become part of the scene itself, and absorbed in its mysterious embrace. Then I would drop off in slumber as dreamless and profound as if I had never known existence, nor shared the hopes and fears of human life.

The thermometer, during these noon-day calms, often marked as high as 88° of Fahrenheit in the shade and 104° in the sun. At such times our progress was slow, and we often stopped under the shadow of some overhanging tree and indulged in a general *siesta.*

Towards evening we reached a new offshoot of the Usumasinta, flowing towards the north, and called *Rio Chico.* The point of divergence was marked by a promontory of some elevation, supporting an inhabited hut almost buried in the thick foliage. Here we stopped for the night. A fire was lighted, and our stock of provisions brought up from the boat—that is to say, such scant supply as our fishing and shooting during the day had afforded us. With these and a few *tortillas* obtained in exchange for tobacco, we made up our meal. The occupants of the hut watched its preparation and disappearance, with that silent and distrustful curiosity which the presence of a foreigner seems always to inspire in the secluded inhabitants of these countries, and which neither kindness nor long acquaintanceship is successful in overcoming.

Hardly had we finished our repast when we were startled by the sudden barking of dogs in the neighborhood of the hut. In countries like this, such sounds have a sinister significance. Our host leaped up, listened a moment, and then seizing his gun rushed outside. "Es un tigre!" he exclaimed, as he disappeared through the doorway. We instinctively armed ourselves with such weapons as were at hand, and followed. The night was intensely dark, for the moon had not yet risen; but the youngest son of our host, lighting a torch, courageously took the lead, and guided us toward the nearest thicket, whence the sounds which we had heard seemed to proceed.

By the aid of a *machete* we soon effected a clearing, when we discovered one of the dogs of our host stretched on the ground fearfully lacerated. At the sound of his master's voice the poor animal endeavored to rise, turned a dying glance towards the woods beyond, made an ineffectual effort to bark, and

* A singular and undescribed species, called *bits* by the Indians. The fruit is siliquose, like the tamarind, and ripens in August.

fell down dead. His back had been broken by the paw of the jaguar, which had escaped into the depths of the forest. It was useless to attempt pursuit, so we retraced our steps with a feeling of mingled disappointment and relief; while the Indian set fire to the thicket without reflecting that he was thereby endangering the safety of his own hut. The bamboos blazed and crackled like straw, and the fire spread for a considerable distance. As it shot up in spires and shed its fitful glare on the forest, we fancied that we saw myriads of frightful shapes starting out from the darkness, and then retreating again in demoniac glee. But fortunately the hut of the Indian, our refuge for the night, escaped the conflagration.

I had hoped to obtain here the rest of which I was so greatly in need, and early sought repose. The hut contained but one room, divided into several compartments by mosquito nets, resembling the steerage berths of a ship. A gun, two *machetes*, a few earthen and wooden vessels, and a scant supply of provisions suspended from the rafters, constituted all the movable effects of the inhabitants; but, on the other hand, their landed property was considerable, for it was without bounds! In a corner some brands were burning, sending out a dense smoke, which was intended to be a preventive against mosquitos. But notwithstanding this precaution, which rendered the atmosphere hot and almost intolerable, these pests came in by thousands, with the freedom of the wind, through every crevice of the hut! The imprecations of our host, who tossed about restlessly in his hammock, and who was continually making efforts to destroy his persecutors by slapping violently the exposed parts of his person, proved to me that the epidermis of the Indians is not more impervious than our own!

At last, my efforts to get asleep proving fruitless, I got up and left the abominable den in which we were imprisoned. Pedrito, the oldest son of our host, a youth of fourteen or fifteen years, with whom I had struck up a little acquaintance after the alarm of the jaguar, seemed equally restless, and followed me to the banks of the river. The present of a cigar disposed him to be confidential, and I soon put him entirely at his ease by questioning him on subjects with which he was familiar; that is to say, about the productions of the country, the animals infesting the forests, and the occupations of his family. He spoke Spanish very well, and as he appeared intelligent and communicative for an Indian, I took pleasure in drawing him out. At the end of half an hour we became great friends; he in turn questioning me, and listening without distrust to my replies. Suddenly he interrupted me in the middle of a sentence, by pointing to a grove which we overlooked from the high point where we were seated. "Hark, señor!" he exclaimed; "did you not hear something?"

"I fancied that I heard the moan of some wild animal," was my reply.

"It is not an animal," he rejoined in a mysterious tone, placing his forefinger on his lips. A few notes in a louder key proved the truth of his assertion.

"Then it is a bird, I suppose?"

He did not reply, but bent over the promontory and with neck stretched forward, and listening ear, seemed absorbed in profoundest contemplation. When, however, I repeated my inquiry, he answered in a low voice, that he now saw the bird in the bushes.

The interest which he evidently felt, communicated itself to me, as I was convinced that the bird which could thus arrest his attention must be both curious and rare. "Do not move," I said, rising quietly, "I will go for my gun." But Pedrito, without uttering a word, motioned me not to leave.

I should have disturbed myself unnecessarily had I done so, for at that moment the bird, as if suspecting my design, flew out of the grove toward the opposite shore, where his voice became confounded with the murmur of the river.

"Well!" I said, "now that it is gone, you will at least tell me its name?"

"It is a *buho,* señor," replied Pedrito, with animation. "Of course you have heard of the *buho.*"*

"In truth, I fancied it was a bird of that species; but had this one any peculiar merit?"

Pedrito raised his eyes timidly to mine, and I imagined that I discovered in his glance a shade of doubt or distrust, which I hastened to dissipate by the offer of another cigar.

"Do you not know, señor," he replied, carefully putting away his present, "do you not know that the *buho* has miraculous powers; he can make his master rich, cure him of sickness, and win for him the heart of the woman he loves?"

"Indeed!" I rejoined, "I was ignorant of all this; come, explain the whole matter to me, so that I may profit by your knowledge, should I ever be able to get this wonderful bird!"

Thus encouraged, the young Indian proceeded to tell me all that he knew of the *buho.* He enjoined, in case I ever became its fortunate possessor, to give it every care and attention, since its death, if the result of negligence, would be sure to be followed by the greatest misfortunes. He added, that to obtain one without injuring it, required such a combination of fortunate circumstances, that with all his anxiety to possess a *buho,* he had never succeeded in securing one.

These details interested me, in spite of their childishness, reminding me of an ancient superstition mentioned by the old Spanish historians. The Indians of Honduras, according to Herrara, had the art of evoking the evil spirit, who appeared to them in the form of a quadruped or bird, with which they entered into such intimate relations that the death of the one was

* A species of owl, called *tecolote* by the Indians.

invariably followed by the immediate death of the other.* It was substantially the same superstition which I encountered on the banks of the Usumasinta, making allowance for the modifications it had undergone during the lapse of ages. When Pedrito had concluded his recital, I inquired whence he derived such valuable information. He mentioned the name of one of his uncles residing at *Jonuta*, as his authority. "But," I inquired smilingly, "in solitudes like these, where are the maidens to be found for your birds to charm?"

As he was about to reply, a bright light suddenly flashed on the water, and on looking in the direction of the hut we saw its occupants moving about with torches in their hands, and at the same moment we heard a confused murmur like that from a camp surprised by an enemy. Thinking that the jaguar had again made his appearance, we hastened back, but before we could reach the hut Pedrito's father called out to us to stop. We obeyed, full of apprehension and unable to understand the mysterious injunction. Suddenly the young Indian, all of whose faculties had been on the alert, seized my arm and in a tremulous voice exclaimed, "Do not move; it is a serpent!"

"If it be only a serpent," was my rejoinder, "this stick is sufficient for our defense."

"No, no!" he exclaimed, holding me back, "it is the *nahuyaca;* and the *nahuyaca* never forgives!"

There was a moment of suspense, during which every eye searched the ground in order to discover the reptile. Morin proved to be most fortunate, and a shot from his gun broke its back and enabled us to capture it with ease. The Indians regarded it without moving a muscle, or saying a word. But I was delighted beyond measure with the lucky chance which had thus thrown in my way so fine a specimen of this singular and most dreaded of vipers, of which I then supposed we had no accounts except the very imperfect ones left us by the early conquerors. I found out, however, on my return to France, that it had been described briefly by Lacépède, under the name of *vipera Brasiliana,* from a specimen in the Museum. Later, the traveller Spix brought another specimen with him from Brazil, from which M. Schlegel, in his *Essai sur la Physionomie des Serpents,* drew most of the information which we possess concerning it. He gave it the name of *jararaca.* In Brazil, where they are very numerous, they are of different colors, which has led to some confusion in their description. All of those which I saw during my travels were precisely alike, and seemed to me very similar to the *bothrops surucucu* of Spix. Resembling the rattlesnake in shape and color, its back is ornamented with a longitudinal series of brown spots of trapezoidal shape, relieved by a bright yellow border; its belly is also yellow; its

---

* Herrara, Dec. iv. 1. viii. c. 4. See also Torquemada, who asserts positively that, "Viniendo á los ageüros que tenian, digo que eran sin cuento; creian en aves nocturnos, especialmente en el *Buho* y en los mochuelos, etc."—*Monarchia Ind.,* t. ii., 1. vi, c. 48.

head triangular and flat; and its angular body is endowed with great muscular strength—features which identify it as one of the most deadly of reptiles. The one killed by Morin was nearly two yards in length.*

The fangs of the *jararaca*, slender, long, and capable of being raised considerably by the movement of the maxillars, on penetrating the skin only produce two scarcely perceptible punctures whence escape a few drops of blood, but the wounded part tumefies very rapidly. The absorption of the poison by the blood manifests itself in a general prostration of the system, a burning thirst, retching, and by other symptoms which I have before mentioned. Livid spots soon appear around the wound, forerunners of a gangrene, which spreads rapidly over the whole person, and, sooner or later, ends in death.

There is no security in external or internal remedies against the *jararaca's* bite, for up to the present time no specific has been found for its cure. The only proper course to pursue is carefully to wash the wound, and by tight ligatures above and below it, prevent the virus from infecting the blood. The part should then be scarified or cupped, if possible, and cauterized. In a word, it is necessary to neutralize a poison the effects of which it is impossible to contend against. Sudorifics, administered in large doses, complete a course of treatment which one can easily adopt for himself. A traveller, and above all a naturalist, should never move about in these countries unprovided for an emergency of this kind; for safety depends on celerity, and the slightest delay may be followed by fatal results.

In the morning we left this dangerous locality. We had, however, added to our company a dog, which proved to be a most useful acquisition. Fida had short, coarse hair, was of reddish color, and marked like a zebra; her ears were erect, her snout delicate, and altogether she resembled the greyhound in shape, only that she was rather more compact. She was, doubtless, of European extraction; but the breed had evidently been long acclimated under the tropics. She was, perhaps, a descendant (who knows?) of that famous greyhound left on the island of Carmen during the expedition of Grijalva. This dog of ours was, moreover, courageous in the extreme, and full of a rare intelligence, which careful training finally developed to a wonderful degree. I was fortunate enough, but not without great trouble, to carry her with me to France, where, unhappily, her primitive elegance of shape gradually disappeared under the enervating influences of repose and civilization. I would have liked much to take little Pedrito with me also, for the

* The discovery of this species of *trigonocephalus* in Central America fills up a chasm in the geographical range of the reptile. It is found in the *tr. atrox* L. in Guiana; in the *tr. lanceolatus* Opp. in Martinique and Santa Lucia; and finally in the *tr. cenchris* Sch. in the southern States of the American Union. These dangerous ophidians are therefore spread all over the inter-tropical portions of the New World, from South Carolina to Brazil. They have not yet been found either in Europe or in Africa.

young Indian interested me greatly, but his father refused his consent; not unwisely, as I have often thought since.

We diverged from the Usumasinta, to enter the *Rio Chico,* which, in turn, was abandoned three leagues farther on, for the *Chiquito,* a muddy channel, narrow and stagnant, which communicates with the Lagoon of *Catasaja.* This unfrequented region seemed to me wilder than any we had yet traversed. Monkeys clustering among the vines, clambered to the very tops of the trees on our approach, in the utmost agitation and alarm. Tapirs, roused from their slumbers, rushed from us in terror, dashing through the forest, regardless of obstructions. Great lizards loosened their hold on the branches of the trees, and fell trembling into the mud; and numberless iguanas, green, purple and brown, scrambled along the banks of the stream, and vanished in their holes. We killed a number; one in particular was of great size and peculiar color, which I considered worthy of preservation; but unfortunately he was so much mutilated by shot, that I reluctantly consigned him to our cook. At one point, perched on the top of a ceiba tree, which time had stripped of its foliage, we perceived the king of the vultures (*Sarcoramphus papa* of Lin.,) a fine bird of black and white plumage, whose head and neck, during the season of mating, are brilliant with the most exquisite colors. He manifested no alarm on our approach, and we did not attempt to molest him. In view of these immense forests of lofty trees, the haunts of wild beasts, strange birds and unknown reptiles, shrouded with vines hanging in festoons from the branches or trailing like serpents along the ground, with the sinister, sad waters of the river in front, so silent that no sound save that of the plunge of the alligator in their depths reached the ear: in view of all these, I experienced a nervous excitement, which kept my imagination in constant activity. Every instant I looked for some new and startling incident, or some strange and marvellous spectacle. As we advanced, the forest by degrees seemed to lose all signs of life; there was a death-like silence; no wind, no current, and the declining rays of the sun glistened on the dead waters as on a mirror of brass. Our oarsmen appeared prostrated, while Morin and myself, bathed in perspiration, reclined listlessly on the deck of the *cayuco.* Nevertheless, the dreariness of the forest was occasionally relieved by the *jolocin,* a tree of great size, bearing immense pink flowers, which blossom before the leaves make their appearance. About three in the afternoon, we reached the Lagoon of *Catasaja,* a broad sheet of water, surrounded by forests. The mountain of Palenque now became visible, describing a perfect trapezium against the horizon. An hour later, we landed in the province of Chiapa, after having sailed twenty-six leagues from the town of Palizada.

[In Las Playas, their next stop, Morelet and his companion procured guides and animals for the journey to Palenque. At the ruins they cleared away the rubbish around the Palace group and made their residence in the lower story, which opened directly on the forest. They constructed a rude fireplace and kitchen, used a broad polished stone as a table, and arranged their beds in the subterranean chambers.]

We passed a fortnight in the solitudes of Palenque, the remembrance of which will never be effaced from my memory. We hunted, we spread snares for wild animals, we collected plants, shells and butterflies, of which there were infinite varieties, without ever becoming weary of admiring the beauties of nature, or of wandering among the ruins which have kept the secret of their origin so well. Morin, whose intelligence was undeveloped, here began to perceive new worlds opening before him, and to take great interest in the study of natural history. He carefully put by a store of *cocuyos*,* or fireflies, which he determined to take with him to France, imagining that the phosphorescent eyes of these insects would always continue bright!

The mornings here were delightful. Humming birds darted among the vines which twined themselves around the walls of the old palace, while green and purple dragon-flies darted about in rapid and capricious flight. The gnats, at the same time, emerged in clouds from the depths of the under-growth; the woodpecker commenced his ringing stroke on the trunks of decaying trees, and the whole forest became full of the sights and sounds of life and motion. But at midday everything became again silent and motion-less; all animation seemed suspended beneath the ardor of the solar rays,

---

* *Elater noctilucus* Fabr.

Ruins of Palenque
From Arthur Morelet, *Travels in Central America.*

notwithstanding the impenetrable mass of verdure which arched over all; and only the monotonous murmur of the river, which flows at the foot of the ruins, broke the death-like silence.

When night fell, however, the ruins appeared to be enchanted, and I can well conceive that the superstitious terrors of the Indians would prevent their remaining here in the darkness. They imagine that the place is haunted by the spirits of its early occupants; that by moonlight the bas-reliefs become invested with life, and that the warriors step out of their stone frames and stalk through the sombre galleries. . . . For my own part, although without fear of these nocturnal visitors, there were times when I could not avoid some little superstitious emotion. Tiny, winged lamps seemed floating in the atmosphere, first with the brilliancy of a spark, then with a fugitive brightness which lost itself in a train of light; at the same time undefinable sounds seemed to proceed from all parts of the woods—not terrific like those which startled me on the banks of the Usumasinta, but soft and sweet like the music of birds, and as mysterious as the accents of an unknown tongue. I seemed to detect life in all things around me; the plants, the trees, the old walls themselves, appeared imbued with its spirit, and to speak a language of their own. My ears listened with rapt attention to this strange harmony, and my eyes questioned the darkness, but in vain, to discover the beings who thus manifested their existence. Now it was like the silvery tinkle of a little bell, or a plaintive voice calling in the distance, then a rustling sound, and next a sob from the interior of the ruins. Again, it was like a thousand gentle whispers, a thousand little cadences, celebrating, in a universal concert, the coolness and magnificence of the night. At one time I surprised a frog on the staircase, whose croakings had mystified us, from its resemblance to the barking of a dog. Even Fida had been equally deceived with ourselves, and during our first night in the ruins had kept up a reciprocal chorus with the inhabitant of the stream.

Our mode of life was very regular. As soon as daylight began to disappear, we lighted a great fire under the peristyle. Morin then prepared supper, and we did not retire until sleep weighed down our eyelids. Seated on the ruined staircase, we enjoyed to the fullest extent the cool evening air, fragrant from the forest, thinking over, the while, the events of the day or contemplating silently the evolutions of phosphorescent insects. Sometimes a sudden breath of wind would cause the tall trees to tremble, and make our fire blaze up more brightly. The shadows would move about as if endowed with life; our dog would drowsily raise her head, and we would listen and wait, full of that kind of nervous suspense which accompanies the expectation of something to come, one knows not what. And when, at a later hour, we left the gallery for our subterranean bed-chamber, the dying embers of our fire would cast a red glare down the steep stairway leading to the forest, and on the neighboring vegetation, causing the darkness beyond to appear all the more profound, and to throw out in greater distinctness the little insect lights which glittered like stars on its ebon bosom. Altogether, the place was one of solemn beauty, heightened by the solitude and seclusion, and appealing with double force to the educated mind from its mysterious associations.

One day, I heard in the neighborhood some notes which arrested my attention; they were clear, limpid, and full of cadence, such as those produced by a musical box. As singing birds are rare in this part of the country, I concluded that these sounds proceeded from a wonderful variety of which the Indians had spoken to me, and which, according to their traditions, is only to be found in places where there are ruins. I shouldered my gun with the liveliest satisfaction, and started in pursuit of the unseen musician. After listening a few moments, I found that the aerial voice proceeded from the banks of the stream. I slid down the embankment towards it with the greatest precaution; but the bird had already changed his position, and was singing on a neighboring hill, which I ascended without feeling in the least discouraged. From the hill, as the note seemed to recede, I went down into the valley beyond, paying little attention to the new scenery which surrounded me. I left behind me the tumuli and *debris* which usually served us as landmarks, following from thicket to thicket, from glade to glade, the object of my ardent wishes. Frequently his notes seemed just above my head, sounding distinct and loud like a song of triumph. I gradually became imbued with that feverish anxiety so common to hunters, and still more so among naturalists. I searched for the bird on every branch, and frequently believed myself so close to him that my piece was raised to fire, when his note, sounding far away, would confound but not discourage me. Finally his song seemed to recede farther and farther, until only a feeble echo reached my ear. At last even this ceased, leaving me alone, and bewildered in the dense forest. At first I experienced no feeling of apprehension. I remained quiet, and listened for some time, until I found there was no longer any hope, and that the provoking bird with his siren song had indeed disappeared. Then I mechanically retraced my steps, wending my way, as I supposed, in the direction whence I had come. I continued on my course for a while without anxiety, diverted as I was by the varieties of plants and insects which I encountered in my path. After a while, however, I observed that the path was altogether strange and unfamiliar. The forest was free from undergrowth, the ground broken, and immense trees, with pyramidal trunks and widespreading arms, shadowed over a multitude of dwarf palms of the height of our fern trees. I became alarmed and hurriedly ascended a high point of ground near by and looked anxiously in all directions; but I saw nothing except the foliage of the great forest, and heard nothing but the beating of my own heart. With sudden energy and in alarm, I made an effort to climb to the top of a tree. Alas! after I had succeeded in doing so, I was terrified in the extreme to find only an ocean of verdure before my eyes, which appeared to extend to the very horizon, and seemed limitless.

I descended and shouted for my companion. But finding this unavailing, I seated myself at the foot of a tree and pressing my hands against my head endeavored to devise some means of escape from my dreadful situation; but I could not concentrate my thoughts. All my faculties seemed paralyzed, the blood appeared to rush to my head, and I was morally incapable of a single effort. The position of a man lost in a wilderness is cruelly dramatic, and can only be appreciated by one who has himself endured the agony of mind which it entails. I know not how long my mental faculties continued prostrated; but after a time I rose full of the worst forebodings, yet with a fixed plan of action. There was no fear of darkness overtaking me for several hours, which would afford ample time for me to retrace my steps. This I set about doing in the following manner. I selected the spot where I was standing as a point of departure, and determined, happen what might, never to lose sight of it for a moment. A colossal tree, the bark of which I whitened, and some stones which I piled up at its base, marked the spot and rendered it visible at a distance. My purpose was now to walk in a right line in every direction from this central point, until I encountered some sign of the ancient city.

Persuaded as I was that I had strayed to the eastward of the ruins, I walked, as I supposed, in that direction, marking as I went certain trees, and breaking down the branches around me, to indicate my course. After several attempts to fix my direction, I reached a piece of swampy ground covered with *arums* and *scitamineae.* There were no longer any ligneous plants to be seen, and fancying that I had reached the confines of the wood, I crossed the marsh, where the broken stalks preserved the traces of my footsteps. I now beheld with pleasure the azure roof of the firmament, which seemed to smile on me while affording me free air and light. But I advanced in vain; no change was perceptible in the surrounding objects; there was only the same waving vegetation, the same lustrous leaves, large as those of the bananna tree, filling up the space with their wild luxuriance, and shutting the horizon from view. Finding here nothing that I remembered having seen before, I thought it useless to proceed in this direction, and sadly retraced my steps. As I reached the outskirts of the forest, a clear, musical, and sonorous note rang through its depths, like the ironical voice of an evil spirit. My feelings, on hearing this unexpected call, I can never forget. I know not what superstitious idea crossed my mind, and caused the blood to rush hurriedly through my veins; but I determined not to be misled a second time, but continued my course without even thinking of using my gun against the invisible bird which seemed to make a trial of its power over me by awakening, at different points, the echoes of its delusive melody.

With some difficulty I regained my starting point. Far from being discouraged by the want of success attending my first effort, I found myself more calm and collected than before. Reflection had strengthened my courage, by giving me confidence in the success of the plan which I had adopted. The ruins could not possibly be very far distant, and I should certainly reach them in the morning, if I failed in doing so today. Animated by new hopes of success, I directed my steps towards the north, not forgetting, however, to take the proper precaution for ensuring my return, if necessary. The forest in this direction was on rising ground, thickly covered with dead leaves. I successively traversed several hills separated by narrow valleys, in which reigned the profoundest silence. The undergrowth soon commenced, and rapidly became more and more dense. I was only able to make my way with the greatest effort through the maze of branches and vines which obstructed my progress. My brow was wet with perspiration, my face and hands were covered with blood, but no obstacle could turn me from my course. A single thought absorbed my faculties, and my only fear was that of losing the thread which was to guide me. At last I succeeded in escaping from this almost impenetrable thicket, and saw before me a steep hill less thickly covered with vegetation. In ascending this I made a misstep and suffered a fall. At the moment I paid but little attention to this incident, but it subsequently appeared that a sharp point of rock had penetrated my right knee, reaching to the bone, and bruising it in such a manner as afterwards to occasion me the greatest pain and annoyance.

From the high point which I now succeeded in reaching, I could see nothing around me which wore a familiar look. Daylight was beginning to fade; there was nothing left for me to do but to retrace my steps, and make up my mind to remain at my station patiently until morning. My courage, however, was beginning to flag. The rapidly increasing darkness, the prospects of a night of anxiety, an intolerable thirst, the silence of these woods, the disappointment which had thus far attended my efforts—all these contributed to sadden and discourage me. After I had repassed the thickets which obstructed the valley, I found, to my consternation, that either from want of care or absence of mind, I was again lost! A deathlike shudder passed over me; the perspiration started from every pore, and my very breath seemed suspended. These painful sensations, however, did not at all resemble the feeling of stupor which overwhelmed me when, for the first time, I became conscious of my terrible situation. I still retained my presence of mind, and was able to deliberate on the course which I should pursue.

It was unsafe to stay in the thicket, on account of the reptiles and wild beasts which infested it, and I therefore, ascended the hill which I had just left, but in another direction, when I discovered through the trees another eminence, which, by its isolated situation and conical shape, particularly arrested my attention. I advanced towards it, and found that the stones scattered around its foot seemed to bear the traces of human industry, although defaced by age. They had evidently formed part of some ancient structure which time had levelled to the ground. I will not attempt to describe the surprise, the joy and the gratitude which swelled my heart at this unexpected discovery. I fell upon my knees, and from the depths of my soul thanked God for lending me his protecting aid, at the very moment when I began to doubt his clemency! This done, I proceeded on my way.

Great caution was necessary. The tumulus before me was probably connected with other ruins, but nevertheless it was unfamiliar to my eyes. I resolved therefore to pursue the plan I had previously adopted, that is to say to explore the country around, but always adopting some point as a centre. I had advanced but a short distance, when new remains encouraged me to keep on in the same direction. I soon came to another small hillock, the top of which was covered with ruins. Their shape and style were becoming insensibly familiar to me, and without exactly taking in their details, which the darkness was rapidly veiling, I instinctively felt that they were not strangers. It was thus, link by link, that I succeeded in reuniting the chain which I had so imprudently broken. By the time the last ray of daylight had faded, I reached the southern front of the Palace worn out with fatigue, bruised, and bleeding—but I had acquired valuable experience for the future. Morin, in his anxiety for me, had forgotten to prepare supper, and as a

Temple at Palenque
Photograph by Kahlo.

crowning misfortune, Fido, disgusted with so long a fast, devoured greedily the collection of birds and insects which had cost me so dear.

I have described this adventure in detail, in order to convey an impression of the dangers which a stranger incurs in traversing the forests of the new world. As to the wonderful bird, the immediate cause of my misfortune, I never heard its note again; I have even forgotten the tradition concerning it which was told me on the banks of the Usumasinta. On the following morning I made some amends for my ill success in hunting it, by killing a superb *hocco* (*crax alector,* L.) the first large specimen of the gallinae which we had thus far seen. Birds of this species under the tropics, take the place of the turkey, which is a native of colder climes.

The ruins of Palenque, during the fine season, are resorted to as a place of enjoyment by the fashionables of Santo Domingo, who establish themselves there, with their families, to the great damage of the monuments, which bear many sad traces of their sojourns. They suspend their hammocks under the shade of the majestic trees, and swing in them indolently, listening to the murmur of the streams, and regaling themselves meanwhile with the shell-fish which are found here in great abundance. It is a specimen of *melanie,* in taste resembling our periwinkles. The Indians consider them very dainty morsels, and always lay in a store of them whenever an opportunity offers. I have often admiringly watched their dexterity in extracting the mollusc from his testaceous covering. While walking along they strike two of them together with such precision and force, that in spite of the hardness of their shells the ends of both are broken, and their contents extracted and swallowed without a moment's loss of time. The shell of the *melanie* makes excellent lime, which is the only kind used in the vicinity. It is probable that it entered largely into the composition of the stucco used for the edifices of the ancient city.

It was with great regret that we left this spot; and I am almost ashamed to confess the vulgar consideration which induced us to hasten our departure. Our stock of rice and black beans, to which we had been reduced for two days, finally began to give out! There was no game to be had, and the forest yielded no fruit; our only resource against hunger was the shell-fish of the stream; famine therefore forced us to desert the ruins, and return to the village. The sun was already up when we descended the steps of the old Palace for the last time. Echo repeated the same sounds which had greeted us every morning on our awakening. The sonorous tap of the woodpecker was audible on the hollow trees; the humming-bird buzzed along the cornices, while large blue butterflies flitted past the deserted peristyle. . . . I bade adieu to all these companions, who had served to enliven our solitary existence; gave one parting glance at the ruins and then plunged into the dark and almost pathless forest.

[Reading these tales of adventure in the wilderness and the long descriptions of the antiquities that enticed them into months of lonely travel, one might well gain the impression that these travelers were intellectuals who gave little or no thought to the opposite sex, or, if they did, that a sense of delicacy prevented them from admitting it in print. But this was not always true. As we have seen, even the dignified John L. Stephens dropped an observation here and there that showed he was not unappreciative of a pretty female face and a comely figure. The French writers, particularly, were less inhibited in this respect. Morelet, for example, visiting Cobán in the Alta Verapaz, a region long inhabited by German colonizers and coffee planters who introduced a strong European strain in the Indian population there, describes what he called a "love episode" in his travels.]

Now that I am about to close my chapter on Coban—the quiet and delightful spot where some of the happiest hours of my life were spent—I feel a strange longing to take the reader, who has followed me thus far, into my confidence, and I cannot resist the flood of memories which are welling up from the depths of my heart. Facts often present a better picture of the moral aspects of a country than the longest homilies. I scarcely dare invoke this consideration, and yet I will not reject it, if you, oh reader! be willing to admit its value.

I occupied a neat little house in the town of Coban, in the midst of a garden filled with coffee, orange and pimiento trees, which, during the day, afforded a delightful shade, and in the evening gave out a delicious perfume of cloves. This little house belonged to a family composed of three sisters and a brother, who lived opposite in a larger dwelling, separated from the others by one of those avenues of trees which I have already described. They were called Indians; why, I do not know. Perhaps because of the kindly relations which they kept up with the aborigines, whose language they spoke with the utmost fluency. But a certain delicacy of shape, fine, silken hair, and an intelligence well cultivated, denoted, particularly in the women, that they were not pure Indians, but had an infusion of foreign blood.

The most perfect harmony existed in this family. The eldest sister was perhaps thirty-five years of age. Active and industrious, she divided her time between domestic duties and devotional exercises. She attended to the business matters of the little family, while the young brother cultivated a piece of land, situated a short distance up the mountain, for their common use.

The second sister was a girl of about twenty-eight years, rather pleasing in appearance, although inclining to *embonpoint*. She was of a gentle, amiable disposition, and, from choice, had resolved upon a life of celibacy. She attended more especially to the household duties, and in the fulfilment of her task displayed a spirit of method, order and neatness rarely met with in Spanish countries. The youngest, Juana, was about sixteen years of age, and did not in any particular resemble the elder sisters. She displayed a strange mixture of indifference and vivacity, of curiosity and carelessness, of wildness, cultivation and delicacy, proceeding evidently from a mixed ancestry. In her the Indian element certainly predominated. Her face usually wore an expression of melancholy, but when gay and animated all the blood of the tropics seemed coursing through her veins.

Juana's intelligence appeared to be less flexible and less developed than that of her sisters. With her, instinct was all powerful. Her principal charm consisted in her ingenuous nature, which betrayed her slightest emotions with spontaneous vivacity. I was on terms of intimacy with the family, and observed with the greater interest the little incidents which threw out, in bold relief, this innocent nature, inasmuch as I had so long been deprived of the delights of domestic life.

The young girl, in her turn, was not insensible to the unusual movement which our arrival occasioned. The presence of two strangers in quest of novelty had effectually broken in upon the quiet monotony of her existence. Less industrious than her sisters, whose almost maternal tenderness excused her idleness, she spent most of her time in our society. Our collections, our effects, our daily occupations, were so many novelties appealing to her curiosity. She enquired about all things without attaching importance to any. Her nature was a most impressible one, but she was so changeable and so impulsive that nothing left any very deep traces on her mind. I doubted whether she was capable of loving; she was certainly in perfect ignorance of the mysteries of the human heart and the realities of life. Seated in careless grace under the myrtles of the garden, her head resting upon her hand, her tresses unbound, and reaching almost to the ground, she would follow, for whole hours, the movements of my pencil without the slightest symptom of weariness; but hardly was the drawing finished before she would snatch it from me, and bound away like a fawn, to show it to her sisters and enjoy their surprise and admiration.

After Juana had become my almost constant companion, life wore for me a new aspect. Her presence invested the minutest objects with a certain charm; it was the ray of sunlight which gives warmth and soul to the picture. To correct her ideas, reply to her questions, and develop her intelligence, became my favorite occupation. I was surprised at not having previously remarked the harmonious accents of her voice, the beauty of her hair, the flexibility of her waist, the air of picturesque grace which pervaded her whole person. I had at first looked upon her only as a simple child; had she already become a dangerous woman? A wise man would not have hesitated; he would have escaped from the fascination without stopping to fathom its mystery. Alas! I must, in all humility, confess that such an idea never entered my mind!

Obeying her natural impulses, and seeming unconscious of the existence elsewhere of social distinctions and conventionalities, Juana kept me in a constant state of perplexity. Sometimes I thought that she loved me, but at others this notion vanished. A look of indifference, some trivial action, or a symptom of coldness, dissipated the illusion. The pain which I then felt was greatly softened by a generous impulse of my heart. After all, what were my intentions in regard to her? Should I bring trouble and shame upon this family, in which I had been so hospitably welcomed? Should I not rather fly from the spot while it was yet time? I decided upon taking my departure, yet day after day I lingered, quaffing still deeper the delicious poison of her presence.

One morning the young girl rapped at my door, bringing with her a superb bouquet, which she had just gathered in the garden, to make up for the loss of some flowers which I had dropped the day previous in fording a stream. It would have been an act of ingratitude, to have explained to her the particular interest which I felt in the simple field flowers which I had lost. "This," said she, "is the *vergonzosa*. See, *señor* how sensitive it is! I have scarcely touched it, and yet it is already shrivelled up!" She showed me a sensitive plant, the leaves of which, one after another, had contracted under the touch of her fingers. "This one," she continued, "we call the passion flower; here are the spear, the nails, and the crown of thorns; it weeps every Good Friday," she added, with a pretty air of mystery, "at the hour when our Saviour expired." "As to that," I interrupted, smiling, "I am a little dubious about it!" "You do not believe me, then? Well, ask my sister, Teresa!" Then suddenly changing her tone and manner, "It is really true, *señor*, that you intend to leave us, as Morin affirmed last night?" At this unexpected enquiry, I was somewhat startled, and did not answer. Putting down her bouquet, and taking my hand within her own, she continued, with an affectionate expression which I had never before seen upon her face, "Are you not content here? Why will you go to Guatemala?" And her lustrous dark eyes were turned on me with a glance which thrilled my very soul.

Alas! how fragile a thing is virtue. I had long been vibrating between the hopes and fears of success, and had determined upon remaining silent; yet here, at the first temptation, my secret was about to be divulged. The trial was a severe one; the attitude of Juana, the emotion of her voice, her look in which I read a prayer, all intoxicated and subdued me, and gliding my arm around her waist, I exclaimed,

"In the name of Heaven, Juana, may I hope that you love me?"

"Oh yes, you may well believe that I do," she answered unhesitatingly.

"And you wish me to remain at Coban?"

"Of course I do," she said, bending her head until her ebon tresses grazed my cheek, "at least you will not go until after my marriage?"

Her words fell with a chill on my heart. Mechanically, I withdrew my arm from her waist, and my hand disengaged itself from her clasp. The young girl cast on me a look of astonishment, not unmixed with anxiety, yet she was evidently ignorant of the blow she had dealt.

"What is the matter, *señor?*" she exclaimed, in a voice made tremulous by apprehension.

I made no answer. My tender illusions were rudely dispelled. I rose, opened the window, and took a few steps, incapable of a single coherent thought or expression. At last, by a painful effort I recovered my self-possession, reseated myself and decided upon my course of action.

"Then you are about to marry, Juana?"

"Yes, *señor,*" she replied, lowering her eyes with an air of instinctive delicacy.

"When is the ceremony to take place?"

"In about a month, *señor:* my brother Fabricio will not be at liberty until the harvest is over."

"But you are not about to marry your brother, I suppose?"

"Oh, *señor!*" and a hearty laugh betrayed her pearl-like teeth. "Fabricio and I are to be married on the same day."

"Well, and who is your betrothed?" I inquired, assuming an air of indifference.

"My betrothed, *señor?* Why, have you not heard of Don Santiago Correntes?"

"He is certainly not a very ardent lover," I could not help observing, "for I do not once remember having seen him at your house."

"This is not surprising," she rejoined hastily, "since he has been at Salama these two months."

"And you love this young man, Juana?"

"*Señor?*"

"I understand. As for him, of course he cannot but love you?"

"Certainly, *señor,* since he wishes to marry me."

"Well then, all is for the best."

I opened a case, and drew from it a coral necklace, which I threw around her neck. "Here Juana, is my marriage gift, for on the day of your wedding I shall be far away. Be happy, dear child," I added, pressing a kiss on her forehead, "and sometimes remember the poor traveller in your prayers."

And here perhaps the indulgent reader will permit me to anticipate events, and give the sequel of the little love episode of Juana and the Stranger. A month after leaving Coban, and having, in the meantime, reached Guatemala, I was one day surprised in my garden by an apparition, having the lank figure and all the peculiar lineaments of my ancient fellow-traveller, honest Diego de la Cueva, who had accompanied me through the forest between Tenosique and Peten, and who was reported to me at the latter place, as having died, in the odor of sanctity, at the village of Sacluc. I was speechless with astonishment as the familiar figure approached me. It advanced with a dignified step and ceremonious manner, bearing in one hand a hat, and in the other a little bundle.

"I perceive that you are surprised, Señor *caballero*," observed the apparition, as it paused in front of me, "and this is an evident sign that your worship has not forgotten me."

"And is that really *you*, Don Diego, and are you sure you are of this world?" I exclaimed, as soon as I had recovered my powers of utterance.

"At your service, *caballero!*" he responded, with a grave and respectful bow. "I was myself for a long time in doubt on the subject."

On hearing these words, which carried conviction with them, I approached Don Diego, gave him the benefit of a close inspection, and congratulated him as befitted the occasion. I then begged him to gratify my curiosity, touching his adventures since we parted, while awaiting the preparation of the dinner to which I invited him. "I have no monkey to offer you," I added smiling, "but I hope that you will be able to make a meal without it."

"Would to heaven, your worship," he replied, with a deep-drawn sigh, "would to heaven that I had met with even a monkey on the infernal road over which I have just travelled! I should not then so often have had cause to regret the excellent fare I enjoyed while journeying in your company."

The compliment appeared to me exaggerated, but perhaps he was sincere. We seated ourselves in the shade. Diego put down his bundle, asked for some tobacco, rolled up a *cigarette* and commenced the recital of his adventures, or, perhaps I should say, misfortunes. He had long lain at death's door, in the village of Sacluc, where I had left him, but his good constitution finally triumphed over the disease. As soon as he was convalescent, he started after us, but when he reached Flores, he found that we had left that town five days before. The corregidor, on learning his history, kindly gave him shelter, until the departure of the courier for Guatemala, with whom he made the journey. He ended his narrative by imitating the cry of the *hocco,* of which he had made a careful study on the way.

Morin here joined us, and his astonishment was scarcely less than mine. Diego repeated his adventures to him, while I glanced over a letter from the corregidor, in which, even through the ceremonious forms of Spanish politeness, there was much that was kind and genuine. Our ancient travelling companion having reached Coban, without once getting off our track, had soon discovered the house which we had occupied during our stay. He regretted being unable to pass more than one day there, for the hospitality of the ladies was such as to efface from his mind even the agreeable recollections of Flores.

At this stage of his story, Don Diego thought it requisite to assume an air of mystery, which brought a smile to my lips. And when I enquired if he had any message for me, he opened his vest and displayed a bag of blue cloth suspended around his neck like an amulet. This bag contained a letter, which he ceremoniously presented to me, and of which the following is a literal translation:

"SEÑOR AND FRIEND:

"Since your departure we have had a great grief. God has taken to himself the soul of poor Santiago. He rests in peace at Salama. If you still love Juana, come to her as soon as you receive this. In five days you can be in Coban, and oh! how happy I shall be to see you! Fabricio will accompany you to the *sierra,* where he has seen some beautiful green birds. My sister has been saving seeds for you, and I have collected some beautiful shells from the garden hedge. May Heaven ever watch over you!

"JUANA."

FOUR

● ● ● ●

E. George Squier 1849-1877

Idols, Mummies, and Robbers

[E. George Squier is my favorite archaeological writer of the early period of exploration in Latin America, and I am tempted to say that he is my favorite of them all—early and modern—except that it is difficult to make comparative judgments when almost a century separates two authors. One does not have to share all his typical eighteenth-century social or political values to realize that most of his accounts are accurate and, for the period, objective and scholarly. They are at the same time lively and humorous, and highly revealing of the author's personality. They reflect his joy of life in general, and his intense interest in all aspects of Latin American life and culture, both ancient and modern. They reveal his tremendous energy and will to finish whatever he started, no matter how great the obstacles. His sense of humor and its spontaneous, unforced, unobtrusive expression in his writings, I find delightful. His narratives move swiftly; the persons in them are sharply and, one feels, accurately characterized. His descriptions of the landscape are vivid and stirring.

[Squier was actively engaged in archaeological investigations most of his adult life. As a young man he explored the ancient monuments of New York State and of the Mississippi valley, and later, as chargé d'affaires of the United States to the republics of Central America, he had ample opportunity to travel widely in that area and to satisfy his curiosity regarding its

The selections from Squier are, in the order quoted below, from the following works. E. G. Squier, *Nicaragua: Its People, Scenery, Monuments, and the Proposed Interoceanic Canal* (New York: Appleton, 1852), Vol. II, pp. 35–56. Copyright 1851 by E. G. Squier. Reprinted with permission of Appleton-Century-Crofts. E. George Squier, *Peru: Incidents of Travel and Exploration in the Land of the Incas* (New York: Holt, 1877), pp. 6–7, 62–63, 72–81, 91–97, 325–36, 340–46, 366–68, 371–75, 550–54, 561–67.

pre-Columbian remains. In 1849, he sailed from New York, accompanied by the artist James McDonough. Keeping meticulous journals, he was able to write a detailed account of his travels, and our first quotations are from the two volumes resulting from this work, *Nicaragua: Its People, Scenery, Monuments, and the Proposed Interoceanic Canal.*

[In December, Squier, McDonough, and a servant set forth on an expedition to carry out Squier's long-cherished wish to investigate the antiquities reported to exist near Granada and on the islands of Lake Nicaragua. After recording many stone sculptures in the Masaya area, they rode to Granada, where an American doctor friend of Squier's joined them.]

Dec. 2, 1849.—This afternoon we prevailed upon Pedro—who, with his six stout sailors, had been drunk for a week, but were now sober and anxious to lay in a new supply of reals for another debauch—to take us over to the little island of Pensacola, almost within cannon-shot of the old castle of Granada. A young fellow, whilom a sailor, but now in the Dr.'s service, on half-pay, as honorary man of all-work, averred that upon this island were *"piedras antiguas"* of great size, but nearly buried in the earth. It seemed strange that in all our inquiries concerning antiquities, of the padres and licenciados, indeed of the "best informed" citizens of Granada, we had not heard of the existence of these monuments. The Dr. was not a little skeptical, but experience had taught me that more information, upon these matters, was to be gathered from the bare-footed *mozos* than from the black-robed priests, and I was obstinate in my determination to visit Pensacola.

It was late when we started, but in less than an hour we leaped ashore upon the island. It is one of the "out-liers" of the labyrinth of small islands which internal fires long ago thrust up from the depths of the lake, around the base of the volcano of Momobacho; and its shores are lined with immense rocks, black and blistered by the heat which accompanied the ancient disruptions of which they are the evidences. In some places they are piled up in rough and frowning heaps, half shrouded by the luxuriant vines which nature trails over them, as if to disguise her own deformities. In the island of Pensacola these rocks constitute a semi-circular ridge, nearly enclosing a level space of rich soil,—a kind of amphitheatre, looking towards the west, the prospect extending beyond the beach of Granada to the ragged hills and volcanic peaks around the lake of Managua. Upon a little elevation, within this natural temple, stood an abandoned cane hut, almost hidden by a forest of luxuriant plantains, which covered the entire area with a dense shadow, here and there pierced by a ray of sunlight, falling like molten gold through narrow openings in the leafy roof.

No sooner had we landed, than our men dispersed themselves in search of the monuments, and we followed. We were not long kept in suspense; a shout of *"aqui, aqui,"* "here, here," from the Dr.'s man announced that they were found. We hurried to his side. He was right; we could distinctly make out two great blocks of stone, nearly hidden in the soil. The parts exposed, though frayed by storms, and having clearly suffered from violence, nevertheless bore evidences of having been elaborately sculptured. A demand was made for the machetes of the men; and we were not long in removing enough of the earth to discover that the supposed blocks were large and well-proportioned statues, of superior workmanship and of larger size than any which we had yet encountered. The discovery was an exciting one, and the Indian sailors were scarcely less interested than ourselves. They crouched around the figures, and speculated earnestly concerning their origin. They finally seemed to agree that the larger of the two was no other than "Montezuma." It is a singular fact that the name and fame of the last of the Aztec emperors is cherished by all the Indian remnants from the banks of the Gila to the shores of Lake Nicaragua. Like the Pecos of New Mexico, some of the Indians of Nicaragua still indulge the belief that Montezuma will some day return, and reëstablish his ancient empire.

I was convinced that there were other monuments here, but the sun was going down, and having resolved to return the next day, I gave up the search,—not, however, without engaging Pedro to be ready, with men and tools, to return at sunrise the next morning.

Pedro, for a miracle, was true to his word (probably because he had no money wherewith to get drunk); and the dew was fresh on the leaves, the parrots chattered vociferously, and the waves toyed cheerfully with the black basaltic rocks, as we leaped ashore a second time on Pensacola. The boat was moored, coffee speedily made and despatched, and then Pedro's crew stripped themselves naked, and made other formidable preparations for disinterring the idols. But the preparations were more formidable than the execution. They commenced very well, but long before the figures were exposed to view, they were all smitten with a desire to hunt up others,—a plausible pretext for skulking away and stretching themselves on the ground beneath the plantains. I was at one time left wholly alone; even Pedro had disappeared; but the rascals came tumbling together again when I proclaimed that the "aguardiente" was circulating. By dint of alternate persuasions and threats, we finally succeeded in getting the smaller of the two figures completely uncovered. It had evidently been purposely buried, for one of the arms had been broken in its fall into the pit which had been previously dug to receive it, and the face had been bruised and mutilated. In this way the early Catholic zealots had endeavored to destroy the superstitious attachment of the aborigines to their monuments. It was, however, satisfactory to reflect that the figures were probably, on the whole, better preserved by their long interment than if they had been suffered to remain above ground. The next difficulty was to raise the prostrate figure; but after much preparation, propping, lifting, and vociferation, we succeeded in standing it up against the side of the hole which we had dug, in such a position that my artist could proceed with his sketch. It represented a human male figure, of massive proportions, seated upon a square pedestal, its head slightly bent forward, and its hands resting on its thighs. Above the face rose a heavy and monstrous representation of the head of an animal, below which could be traced the folds of a serpent, the fierce head of which was sculptured, open-mouthed and with life-like accuracy, by the side of the face of the figure. The whole combination was elaborate and striking.

The stone from which the figure here described was cut, is a hard sand-stone, of a reddish color; but the sculpture is bold, and the limbs, unlike those of the monoliths of Copan, are detached so far as could be done with safety, and are cut with a freedom which I have observed in no other statuary works of the American aborigines.

To enable M. to make a drawing of the monument just disclosed, and to relieve him from the annoyance of our men, I deferred proceeding with the exhumation of the remaining one until he had finished, and therefore summoned all hands to search the island for others,—stimulating their activity by the splendid offer of a reward of four reals (equivalent to two days' wages) to any one who should make a discovery. I also joined in the search, but after wandering all over the little island, I came to the conclusion that, if there were others, of which I had little doubt, they had been successfully buried, and were past finding out, or else had been broken up and removed. So I seated myself philosophically upon a rock, and watched an army of black ants, which were defiling past, as if making a tour of the island. They formed a solid column from five to six inches wide, and marched straight on, turning neither to the right hand nor to the left, pertinaciously surmounting every obstacle which interposed. I watched them for more than half an hour, but their number seemed undiminished; thousands upon thousands hurried past, until finally, attracted by curiosity, I rose and followed the line, in order to discover the destination of the procession,—if it were an invasion, a migration, or a simple pleasure excursion. At a short distance, and under the cover of some bushes, the column mounted what appeared to be simply a large, round stone, passed over it, and continued its march.

The stone attracted my attention, and on observing it more closely, I perceived traces of sculpture. I summoned my men, and after a two hours' trial of patience and temper, I succeeded in raising from its bed of centuries another idol of massive proportions, but differing entirely from the others, and possessing an extraordinary and forbidding aspect. The lower half had been broken off, and could not be found; what remained was simply the bust and head. The latter was disproportionately great; the eyes were large, round, and staring; the ears broad and long; and from the widely-distended mouth, the lower jaw of which was forced down by the hands of the figure, projected a tongue which reached to the breast, giving to the whole an unnatural and horrible expression. As it stood in the pit, with its monstrous head rising above the ground, with its fixed stony gaze, it seemed like some gray monster just emerging from the depths of the earth, at the bidding of the wizard-priest of an unholy religion. My men stood back, and more than one crossed himself as he muttered to his neighbor, "*es el diablo!*" "it is the devil!" I readily comprehended the awe with which it might be regarded by the devotees of the ancient religion, when the bloody priest daubed the lapping tongue with the yet palpitating hearts of his human victims!

It was long past noon before we commenced the task of raising the largest and by far the most interesting idol to an erect position. This was no easy undertaking. The stone, although not more than nine feet high, measured ten feet in circumference, and was of great weight. We were but eleven men all told; Pedro said it was useless to try, we might turn it over, but nothing more. Still I was determined it should be raised, not only for the purpose of observing its effect in that position, but because I was convinced that the under side must exhibit more clearly the finer details of the sculpture than the upper, which had been partially exposed above the ground. I gave each man a prodigious dram of *aguardiente*, which inspired corresponding courage, and after procuring an additional number of stout levers and props, we proceeded to raise the recumbent mass. Our progress was slow and difficult, the sweat rolled in streams down the glossy skins of our sailors, who—thanks to the ardiente—worked with more vigor than I thought them capable of exerting. The aguardiente was worth more than gold to me that day. The men shouted and cheered, and cried, "*arriba con la niña!*" "up with the baby!" But before we got it half raised, a thunder-storm, the approach of which had escaped our notice in the excitement, came upon us, as only a tropical thunder-storm knows how to come. I beat a retreat, dripping with perspiration, into the deserted hut; while the men sat coolly down and took the pelting,—they were used to it! The storm passed in due time, but the ground was saturated, and the feet sank deeply in the soft, sticky mass around the "niña." Still, in order to save another visit in force the next day, I determined not to relinquish the task we had begun. But the difficulties were now augmented, and it was only after the most extraordinary exertions, at imminent danger of crushed limbs, that we succeeded in our object. With bleeding hands, and completely bedaubed with mud, I had at last the satisfaction to lead off in a "*Viva por la niña antigua!*"—"Hurrah for the old baby!" I am not quite sure but I took a drop of the aguardiente myself, while the shower was passing. Pedro and his crew responded by a "*Vivan los Americanos del Norte!*" which, being interpreted, meant that they "wouldn't object to another drink." This was given of course, whereupon Pedro insinuated that "*Los Americanos son diablos!*"—"The Americans are devils;" which remark, however, Pedro meant as a compliment. The figure, when erect, was truly grand. It represented a man with massive limbs, and broad, prominent chest, in a stooping or rather crouching posture, his hands resting on his thighs, just above the knees. Above his head rose the monstrous head and jaws of some animal; its fore paws were placed one upon each shoulder, and the hind ones upon the hands of the statue, as if binding them to the thighs. It might be intended, it probably was intended, to represent an alligator or some mythological or fabulous animal. Its back was covered with carved plates, like rough mail. The whole rose from a broad, square pedestal. The carving, as in the other figure, was bold and free. I never have seen a statue which conveyed so forcibly the idea of power and strength; it was a study for a Samson under the gates of Gaza, or an Atlas supporting the world. The face was mutilated and disfigured, but it still seemed to wear an expression of sternness, if not severity, which added greatly to the effect of the whole. The finer details of workmanship around the head had suffered much; and from the more decided marks of violence which the entire statue exhibits, it seems probable that it was an especial object of regard to the aborigines, and of corresponding hate to the early Christian zealots.

The sun came out brightly after the rain, and although wet and weary, and not insensible to the comforts of dry clothes and the seductions of a hammock, I could hardly tear myself away from these remarkable monuments—overturned perhaps by the hands of Gil Gonzalez himself, at the time when, in the language of the chronicler, "the great cazique Nicaragua consented to be baptized, together with nine thousand of his subjects, and thus the country became converted." "The great idols in his sumptuous temples," continues the historian, "were thrown down, and the cross set up in their

The bongo *La Carlota*

From E. G. Squier, *Nicaragua: Its People, Scenery, and Monuments*, 1852. Copyright 1851 by E. G. Squier. Courtesy of Appleton-Century.

stead." The same authority assures us that "Nicaragua was a chief of great good wit, and though the Spanish captain was a discreet man, it puzzled him much to explain to Nicaragua why it was that so few men as the Spaniards coveted so much gold."

M. returned the next day and completed his drawings, while I busied myself in preparing for a voyage to the great uninhabited island of Zapatero.

The T.'s had volunteered one of their *bongos*, one of the largest and most comfortable on the lake; and as most of this kind of unique craft are only gigantic canoes, hollowed from a single trunk of the cebia, and quite as well fitted, and just as much disposed, to sail upon their sides or bottom up as any other way, it was a gratification to know that "La Carlota" had been built with something of a keel, by a foreign shipwright, and that the prospect of being upset in the first blow was thereby diminished from three chances in four, to one in two. The voyager who has sailed on the restless lake of Nicaragua in gusty weather, with bungling sailors, can well comprehend the satisfaction with which we contemplated "La Carlota," as she rocked gracefully at her moorings, off the old castle on the shore. She was perhaps sixty feet long, and her *chopa* was capable of accommodating four or five persons with lodgings,—something in the pickled mackerel order, it is true, but not uncomfortably, in the moderated views of comfort which the traveller in Central America soon comes to entertain. In front of the *chopa* were ten benches, for as many oarsmen, and places for setting up the masts, in case the winds should permit of their use. "La Carlota," withal, was painted on the outside, and had a figure head; indeed, take her all in all, she looked a frigate among the numerous strange pit-pans, piraguas, and other anomalous and nameless water-craft around her. Thus far all was well. The next thing was to get a crew together; but this devolved upon the junior Mr. T. After two days of exertion, for there was a great conjunction of *fiestas* at the time, they were enlisted and duly paid,—everybody expects pay in advance in Central America! A fixed number of reals were counted out for the commissary department, and the patron, Juan, solemnly promised to be ready to set sail the next morning at sunrise for the island of *Zapatero*, the "Shoemaker," where Manuel, who was to go along as a guide, assured us there were many *frailes*, friars, some kneeling, others sitting, and still others standing erect, or reclining as if in death, besides many other wonderful and curious things, among which was a deep salt lake.

The Dr. and myself completed our arrangements over night. After breakfast the next morning, which had been fixed for our departure, I proposed to go down to the lake, supposing that as Juan had promised to be ready by sunrise, we might possibly succeed in getting off by nine or ten o'clock at the furthest. The Dr., however, protested that it was useless to go down so early,—"he was not going to broil in the sun, on the open beach, all the forenoon, not he;" and he comforted us with the assurance that he had lived in the country ten years, and that if we got off before the middle of the afternoon, we might perform any surgical operation we pleased upon either one of his legs! My time was limited, and these vexatious delays almost worried me into a fever. At eleven o'clock, however, I prevailed upon the Dr., much against his will, and amidst his earnest protestations that he "knew the people, and that it was no kind of use," to go down to the shore. There swung our bongo, precisely as we had left it the day before, and not a soul on board! The shore was covered with groups of half-naked women, seated just at the edge of the water, engaged in an operation here called *washing*, which consisted in dipping the articles in the water, and placing them on a rough stone, and beating them violently with a club, to the utter demolition of everything in the shape of buttons! Groups of children were paddling in little pools, or playing in the sand; sailors just arrived were landing their cargoes, carrying the bales on their shoulders through the breakers, and depositing them in creaking carts; here and there a horseman pranced along under the shadow of the trees on the shore; and amongst all, imperturbable buzzards in black, and long-legged cranes in white, walked about with prescriptive freedom! Altogether it was a singular mixture of civilized and savage life, and one not likely to be forgotten by the observant traveller.

I was, however, in no mood to enjoy the scene,—and the Dr.'s "I told you so!" as he quietly seated himself on a log in the shade, was cruelly provoking. After diligent search, we found two of our crew, with only a cloth wrapped around their loins, lying flat on the sands, their faces covered with their sombreros, and the hot sun beating down upon their naked bodies,—perfect pictures of the intensest laziness. "Where is the patron?" They simply lifted their hats, and responded, "Quien sabe?" "Who knows?" The eternal "Quien sabe," and uttered without so much as an attempt to rise! This was unendurable; I gave them each an emphatic kick in the ribs with my rough travelling boots, and brought them to their feet in an instant, with a deprecatory exclamation of "*Señor!*" One was despatched to hunt up the others among the pulperias of the town, with emphatic threats of great bodily harm, if the delinquents were not produced within a given time. The second one, a strapping Mestizo, who still rubbed his side with a lugubrious expression of face, was ordered to deposit himself within short range of my formidable-looking "Colt," with an injunction not to move unless ordered. Directly, another recreant was discovered, doing the agreeable to a plump coffee-colored washing-girl,—nothing chary of her charms, as may be inferred from the fact that excepting a cloth, none of the largest, thrown over her lap, she was *au naturel*. He too was ordered to take up his position beside the other prisoner, which he did with a bad grace, but greatly to the pretended satisfaction of the coffee-colored girl, who said that he was "*malo*," bad, and deserved all sorts of ill. "A woman is naturally a coquette, whether in a white skin or black," philosophized the Dr.; "that yellow thing don't mean what she says. I'll wager they have just agreed to get married, or what is the same thing in these countries."

It was high noon long before we got our vagrant crew under our batteries; and conscious of their delinquencies, and not a little in awe of our pistol butts, they really exerted themselves in getting the boat ready. Half a dozen naked fellows plunged into the surf, their black bodies alternately appearing and disappearing in the waves, and towed the "Carlota" close in shore, under the lee of the old castle. The sails, our provisions, blankets, etc., were placed on board, and then we mounted on the shoulders of the strongest, and were duly deposited on the quarter-deck. The bells of the city chimed two o'clock, as we swept outside of the fort into the rough water. It was all the men could do to overcome the swell, and the sweeps bent under their vigorous strokes. Once in deep water, the waves were less violent, but they had the long, majestic roll of the ocean. Here every oarsman pulled off his breeches, his only garment, deposited his sombrero in the bottom of the boat, and lighted a cigar; they were now in full uniform, and pulled sturdily at the oars. Juan, the patron, drew off his breeches also, but, by way of maintaining the dignity of the quarter-deck, or out of respect to his passengers, he kept on his shirt, a flaming red check, and none of the longest, which, as he bestrode the tiller, fluttered famously in the wind.

One hour's hard pulling, and we were among the islands. Here the water was still and glassy, while the waves dashed and chafed with a sullen roar against the iron shores of the outer rank, as if anxious to invade the quiet of the inner recesses,—those narrow, verdure-arched channels, broad, crystal-floored vistas, and cool, shady nooks in which graceful canoes were here and there moored.

Perhaps a more singular group of islets cannot be found in the wide world. As I have before said, they are all of volcanic origin, generally conical in shape, and seldom exceeding three or four acres in area. All are covered with a cloak of verdure, but nature is not always successful in hiding the black rocks which start out in places, as if in disdain of all concealment, and look frowningly down on the clear water, giving an air of wildness to the otherwise soft and quiet scenery of the islands. Trailing over these rocks, and dropping in festoons from the overhanging trees, their long pliant tendrils floating in the waves, are innumerable vines, with bright and fragrant flowers of red and yellow, mingled with the inverted cone of the "gloria de Nicaragua," with its overpowering odor, with strange and nameless fruits, forming an evergreen roof, so close that even a tropical sun cannot penetrate. Many of these islands have patches of cultivated ground, and on such, generally crowning their summits, relieved by a dense green background of plantains, and surrounded by kingly palms, and the papaya with its golden fruit, are the picturesque cane huts of the inhabitants. Groups of naked, swarthy children in front,—a winding path leading beneath the great trees down to the water's edge,—an arbor-like, miniature harbor, with a canoe lashed to the shore,—a woman naked to the waist, with a purple skirt of true Tyrian dye, for the famous murex is found on the Pacific shores of Nicaragua, her long, black, glossy hair falling over neck and breast, and reaching almost to her knees,—a flock of noisy parrots in a congressional squabble among the trees,—a swarm of parroquets scarcely less noisy,—a pair of vociferating macaws like floating fragments of a rainbow in the air,—inquisitive monkeys hanging among the vines,—active iguanas scrambling up the banks,—long-necked and long-legged cranes in deep soliloquy at the edge of the water, their white bodies standing out in strong relief against a background of rock and verdure,—a canoe glancing rapidly and noiselessly across a vista of water,—all this, with a golden sky above, the purple sides of the volcano of Momobacho overshadowing us, and the distant shores of Chontales molten in the slanting sunlight—these were some of the elements of the scenery of the islands,—elements constantly shifting, and forming new and pleasing combinations. Seated upon the roof of the chopa, I forgot in contemplating the changing scenery the annoyances of the morning, and felt almost disposed to ask the pardon of the marineros whom I had treated so unceremoniously.

Our men, for we were now in the cool shadow of the mountain, pulled bravely at the oars, chanting a song which seems to be eminently popular amongst all classes of the people. I could not catch the whole of it, but it commenced:

> "Memorias dolorosas
> De mi traidor amante,
> Huye de mi un instante
> Haced lo por piedad."

At the end of each stanza they gave a sharp pull at the sweeps, and shouted "*hoo-pah!*"—a freak which seemed to entertain them highly, although we "couldn't exactly see the point of it." It was nearly sunset when we arrived at Manuel's islands; for though Manuel went with us as a guide, at the rate of three reals per day, he had, nevertheless, a house in town, not to mention a couple of islands, upon one of which was his country-seat, and upon the other his plantain walk and fruitery. His country-seat consisted of a cane hut; but he proudly pointed out to us a heap of new tiles and a pile of poles, and said he meant one day to have a *palacio* on Santa Rosa, for so he called his island. I did not envy him his prospective palace, but Santa Rosa was a gem. Its outer shore, fronting the turbulent water, was lined with immense rocks, within which was a barrier of large trees, draped over with vines, and completely sheltering Manuel's hut from the winds and storms of the lake. Upon the inner side was a little, crescent-shaped harbor, in which our bongo rocked lazily to and fro. A couple of tall cocoa trees, a cluster of sugar-canes, and a few broad-leaved plants at the water's edge, gave a tropical aspect to the islet, which looked to me, in the subdued half-light of the evening, as a very paradise for a recluse.

Juan proposed to stay here for the night, as the wind was now too violent to permit us to venture outside of the islands; besides, our improvident men had yet to lay in their supply of plantains—the staff of life to the inhabitants of Central America. A little boat was accordingly despatched to a neighboring island, for these indispensable articles, while the remainder of the crew made supper for themselves. A single kettle, their machetes, and fingers were their only service, but it was an effective one, and they made themselves as merry as if there was nothing in the wide world left to wish for. For ourselves, a cup of coffee and a cut of cold chicken sufficed.

The moon was nearly at her full, and the transition from day to night was so gradual as hardly to be perceived. Rosy clouds hung long in the west, changing slowly to deep purple and grey; but when the dominion of the moon came on, they lighted up again with a silver radiance. A mass, like a half transparent robe, rolled itself around the summit of the volcano; the verdure of the island looked dense and heavy upon one side, while the other was light, and relieved by glancing trunks and branches. Deep shadows fell on water, with shining strips of silver between, and excepting the chafing of the lake upon the outer shores, and the prolonged moan of the howling monkey, there was not a sound to disturb the silence. It is true our men talked long, but it was in a low tone, as if they feared to disturb the general quiet. They finally stretched themselves on their benches, and my companions wrapped themselves in their blankets and composed themselves for the night. I did so also, but I could not sleep; it was not the holy calm of the scene—the remembrance of dear friends, or those dearer than friends—it was no sentimental revery, no pressure of official cares, that kept me awake that night,—but it was "las pulgas," *the fleas* from Manuel's Santa Rosa! They seemed to swarm in my clothing. I waited in vain for them to get their fill and be quiet, but they were insatiable, and almost maddened me. I got out upon the pineta, and there, under the virgin moon, carefully removed every article of my apparel, and lashed and beat it angrily over the sides, in the hope of shaking off the vipers. The irritation which they had caused was unendurable, and, overcoming all dread of alligators and fever, I got over the side, and cooled myself in the water. I did not go beneath the chopa again, but wrapped my blankets around me, and coiled myself on the pineta.

I had just fallen into a doze, when I was awakened by the clattering of oars, and found Juan, with his flaming, fluttering shirt, standing over me at the rudder. It was about two o'clock, and as the wind had abated a little, our patron seized upon the opportunity to run down to Zapatero. He had no notion, in which I agreed with him, of attempting the trip with a light boat, in the midst of the fierce northers which prevail at this season of the year. I had been a little nervous about the business from the start, for I had spent one night upon this lake which I am not likely to forget,—and had exacted a promise from the men to load in stones, at the islands, by way of ballast. They made a show of compliance, and next morning I succeeded in finding some twenty-five or thirty small stones deposited near the first mast, weighing in all, perhaps, two hundred pounds!

A short spell at the oars, and we were outside of the island. A broad bay stretched dimly inwards towards the city of Nicaragua; and directly before us, at the distance of twenty miles, rose the high, irregular island of Zapatero; beyond which a stationary mass of silvery clouds showed the position of the majestic volcanic cones of the great island of Ometepec. The wind was still strong and the waves high, and the boat tumbled about with an unsteady motion. Amidst a great deal of confusion the sails were raised—sails large enough for an Indiaman, for the marineros of Lake Nicaragua consider that everything depends on the size of the canvas. The "Carlota" was schooner-rigged, and no sooner was she brought to the wind, than her sails filled, and she literally bounded forward like a race-horse. She heeled over until her guards touched the water, precipitating the Dr., who insisted on remaining within the chopa, from one side to the other, amidst guns, books, blankets, pistols, bottles, and all the et ceteras of a semi-pleasure excursion. But, as I have said, he was a philosopher, swore a little, rubbed his shins, and braced himself crosswise. I remained outside, and hung tightly to the upper guards. The lull, if it can be so called, under which we had started, was only temporary. Before we had accomplished a tenth of the distance to the island, the wind came on to blow with all its original violence. The waters fairly boiled around us, and hissed and foamed beneath our stern. I cried to Juan, who was struggling at the rudder, to take in sail, for the canvas almost touched the water, and seemed really bursting with the strain, but he responded "too late," and braced himself with his shoulder against the tiller, holding with both hands to the guards. I expected every moment that we would go over,—but on, onward, we seemed actually to fly. The outlines of Zapatero grew every moment more distinct, and little islands before undistinguished came into view. As we neared them, the wind lulled again, and we breathed freer when we dashed under the lee of the little island of Chancha, and threw out our anchor close to the shore. "Holy Mary," said Juan, as he wiped the sweat from his forehead, "the devils are out in the lake to-night!" We had made upwards of twenty miles in less than two hours.

I crept within the chopa, where the Dr. was rubbing his bruises with brandy, and slept until aroused by the loud barking of dogs. The sun was up; we were close to a little patch of cleared land, upon one side of which, halfhidden among the trees, was a single hut. The owner, his wife, his children, and his dogs, were down on the shores, and all seemed equally curious to know the object of our sudden visit. Juan frightened them with an account of a terrible revolution, how he was flying from the dangers of the main, and advised the islander to keep a sharp look-out for his safety. The Dr., however, delivered the poor man from his rising fears, and ordered Juan to put on his shirt and pull across the channel to Zapatero. An inviting, calm harbor was before us, but we were separated from it by a channel five hundred yards broad, through which the compressed wind forced the waters of the lake with the utmost violence. It seemed as if a great and angry river was rushing with irresistible fury past us. A high, rocky, projecting point of Zapatero in part intercepted the current below us, against which the water dashed with a force like that of the ocean, throwing the spray many feet up its rocky sides. The men hesitated in starting, but finally braced themselves in their seats, and pushed into the stream. The first shock swept us resistlessly before it, but the men pulled with all their force, under a volley of shouts from Juan, who threw up his arms and stamped on his little quarter-deck like a madman. It was his way of giving encouragement. The struggle was long and severe, and we were once so near the rocks that the recoiling spray fell on our heads; but we finally succeeded in reaching the little, sheltered bay of which I have spoken, and, amidst the screams of the thousand waterfowls which we disturbed, glided into a snug little harbor, beneath a spreading tree, the bow of our boat resting on the sandy shore. "Here at last," cried M., and bounded ashore. I seized a pistol and sword, and followed, and leaving the Dr. and the men to prepare coffee and breakfast, started in company with Manuel to see the *"frailes."* Manuel was armed with a double-barrelled gun, for this island has no inhabitants, and is proverbial for the number of its wild animals, which find a fit home in its lonely fastnesses. I carried a first-class Colt in one hand, and a short, heavy, two-edged Roman sword in the other, as well for defence as for cutting away the limbs, vines, and bushes which impede every step in a tropical forest. Manuel said it was but a few squares to the *"frailes,"* but we walked on and on, through patches of forest and over narrow savannahs, covered with coarse, high, and tangled grass, until I got tired. Manuel looked puzzled; he did not seem to recognize the land-marks. When he had been there before, it was in the midst of the dry season, and the withered grass and underbrush, stripped of leaves, afforded no obstruction to the view. Still he kept on, but my enthusiasm, between an empty stomach and a long walk, was fast giving place to violent wrath towards Manuel, when suddenly that worthy dropped his gun, and uttering a scream, leaped high in the air, and turning, dashed past me with the speed of an antelope. I cocked my pistol, and stood on my guard, expecting that nothing less than a tiger would confront me. But I was spared the excitement of an adventure, and nothing making its appearance, I turned to look for Manuel. He was rolling in the grass like one possessed, and rubbing his feet and bare legs with a most rueful expression of face. He had trodden on a bees' nest, and as he had taken off his breeches, to avoid soiling them, before starting, I "improved" the occasion to lecture him on the impropriety of such practices on the part of a Christian, a householder, and the father of a family. I was astonished, I said, that he, a gentleman past the middle age of life, the owner of two islands, should make such a heathen of himself as to go without his breeches. And as I have heard the special interposition of Providence urged on no more important occasions than this, at home, I felt authorized in assuring him that it was clearly a signal mark of Divine displeasure. Manuel appeared to be much edified, and as I was better protected than himself, he prevailed upon me to recover his gun, whereupon, taking another path, we pushed ahead.

After toiling for a long time, we came suddenly upon the edge of an ancient crater of great depth, at the bottom of which was a lake of yellowish green, or *sulphurous* color, the water of which Manuel assured me was salt. This is probably the fact, but I question much if any human being ever ventured down its rocky and precipitous sides. Manuel now seemed to recognize his position, and turning sharp to the left, we soon came to a broad, level area, covered with immense trees, and with a thick undergrowth of grass and bushes. There were here some large, irregular mounds composed of stones, which I soon discovered were artificial. Around these Manuel said the *frailes* were scattered, and he commenced cutting right and left with his machete.

Stone sculptures, Zapatero, Nicaragua

From E. G. Squier, *Nicaragua: Its People, Scenery, and Monuments.* Copyright 1851 by E. G. Squier. Courtesy of Appleton-Century.

I followed his example, and had not proceeded more than five steps, when I came upon an elaborately sculptured statue, still standing erect. It was about the size of the smaller one discovered at Pensacola, but was less injured, and the face had a mild and benignant aspect. It seemed to smile on me as I tore aside the bushes which covered it, and appeared almost ready to speak. In clearing further, but a few feet distant, I found another fallen figure. From Manuel's shouts I knew that he had discovered others, and I felt assured that many more would reward a systematic investigation—and such I meant to make.

I was now anxious to return to the boat, so as to bring my entire force on the ground; and calling to Manuel, I started. Either Manuel took me a shorter path than we came, or else I was somewhat excited and didn't mind distances; at any rate, we were there before I expected. The sailors listened curiously to our story, and Juan, like Pedro before him, whispered that *"los Americanos son diablos."* He had lived, man and boy, for more than forty years within sight of the island, and had many times been blockaded by bad weather in the very harbor where we now were, and yet he had never seen, nor ever so much as heard that there were *"frailes"* there!

During our absence, a weather-bound canoe, with Indians from Ometepec, discovering our boat, had put in beside us. They were loaded with fruit for Granada, and "walked into" our good graces by liberal donations of *papayas, marañons, oranges, pomegranates, zapotes,* etc. They were small but well-built men, with more angular features than the Indians of Leon, and betraying a different stock. It will be seen, as we proceed, that they are of Mexican origin. All had their heads closely shaved, with the exception of a narrow fringe of hair around the forehead, extending from one ear to the other—a practice which has become very general among the people. I admired their well-formed limbs, and thought how serviceable half-a-dozen such stout fellows would be amongst the monuments, and incontinently invited them to accompany us, which invitation they accepted, much to my satisfaction.

Leaving a couple of men to watch the boats, I marshalled my forces, and set out for the *"frailes."* We mustered twenty-four strong, a force which I assured myself was sufficient to set up once more the fallen divinities, and possibly to remove some of them. As we went along, we cleared a good path, which, before we left, began to have the appearance of a highway.

While M. commenced drawing the monument which still stood erect, I proceeded with the men to clear away the bushes and set up the others. I knew well that the only way to accomplish anything was to keep up the first excitement, which I did by liberal dispensations of aguardiente—the necessities of the case admitted of no alternative. The first monument which claimed our attention was a well-cut figure, seated crouching on the top of a high, ornamented pedestal. The hands were crossed below the knees, the head bent forward, and the eyes widely opened, as if gazing upon some object upon the ground before it. A mass of stone rose from between the shoulders, having the appearance of a conical cap when viewed from the front. It was cut with great boldness and freedom, from a block of basalt, and had suffered very little from the lapse of time.

A hole was dug to receive the lower end, ropes were fastened around it, our whole force was disposed to the best advantage, and at a given signal, I had the satisfaction of seeing the figure rise slowly and safely to its original position. No sooner was it secured in place, than our sailors gave a great shout, and forming a double ring around it, commenced an outrageous dance, in the pauses of which they made the old woods ring again with their favorite *"hoo-pah!"* I did not like to have my *ardiente* effervesce in this manner, for I knew the excitement, once cooled, could not be revived; so I broke into the circle, and dragging out Juan by main force, led him to the next monument, which Manuel called "El Cañon," the Cannon.

It was a massive, cylindrical block of stone, about as long and twice as

Stone sculptures, Zapatero, Nicaragua

From E. G. Squier, *Nicaragua: Its People, Scenery, and Monuments.* Copyright 1851 by E. G. Squier. Courtesy of Appleton-Century.

thick as the twin brother of the famous "peace-maker," now in the Brooklyn navy-yard. It was encircled by raised bands, elaborately ornamented; and upon the top was the lower half of a small and neatly cut figure. In the front of the pedestal were two niches, deeply sunk, and regular in form, connected by a groove. They were evidently symbolical. Notwithstanding the excitement of the men, they looked dubiously upon this heavy mass of sculpture; but I opened another bottle of aguardiente, and taking one of the levers myself, told them to lay hold. A hole was dug, as in the former case, but we could only raise the stone by degrees, by means of thick levers. After much labor, by alternate lifting and blocking, we got it at an angle of forty-five degrees, and there it appeared determined to stay. We passed ropes around the adjacent trees, and placed *falls* above it, and when all was ready, and every man at his post, I gave the signal for a *coup de main*. The ropes creaked and tightened, every muscle swelled, but the figure did not move. It was a critical moment; the men wavered; I leaped to the ropes, and shouted at the top of my voice, "*Arriba! arriba! viva Centro America!*" The men seemed to catch new spirit; there was another and simultaneous effort, —the mass yielded; "*poco mas, muchachos!*" "a little more, boys!" and up it went, slowly, but up, up, until, tottering dangerously, it settled into its place and was secured. The men were silent for a moment, as if astonished at their own success, and then broke out in another paroxysm of ardiente and excitement. But this time each man danced on his own account, and strove to outdo his neighbor in wild gesticulation. I interfered, but they surrounded me, instead of the figure, and danced more madly than before, amidst "vivas" for North America. But the dance ended with my patience,—luckily not before. By a judicious use of aguardiente, I managed to keep up their spirits, and by four o'clock in the afternoon, we had all the monuments we could find, ten in number, securely raised and ready for the draughtsman. Besides these, we afterwards succeeded in discovering a number of others,—amounting in all to fifteen perfect, or nearly perfect ones, besides some fragments.

The men, exhausted with fatigue, disposed themselves in groups around the statues, or stretched their bodies at length amongst the bushes. Wearied myself, but with the complacency of a father contemplating his children, and without yet venturing to speculate upon our singular discoveries, I seated myself upon a broad, flat stone, artificially hollowed in the centre, and gave rein to fancy. The bushes were cleared away, and I could easily make out the positions of the ruined *teocalli*, and take in the whole plan of the great aboriginal temple. Over all now towered immense trees, shrouded in long robes of grey moss, which hung in masses from every limb, and swayed solemnly in the wind. I almost fancied them in mourning for the departed glories of the place. In fact, a kind of superstitious feeling, little in consonance with the severity of philosophical investigation, began to creep over me. Upon one side were steep cliffs, against which the waters of the lake chafed with a subdued roar, and upon the other was the deep, extinct crater, with its black sides and sulphurous lake; it was in truth a weird place, not unfittingly chosen by the aboriginal priesthood as the theatre of their strange and gloomy rites. While engaged in these fanciful reveries, I stretched myself, almost unconsciously, upon the stone where I was sitting. My limbs fell into place as if the stone had been made to receive them,—my head was thrown back, and my breast raised; a second, and the thought flashed across my mind with startling force—*"the stone of sacrifice!"* I know not whether it was the scene, or the current of my thoughts, perhaps both, but I leaped up with a feeling half of alarm. I observed the stone more closely; it was a rude block altered by art, and had beyond question been used as a stone of sacrifice. I afterwards found two others, clearly designed for the same purpose, but they had been broken.

[For the next twenty years Squier maintained a lively interest in Central American culture, both ancient and modern, publishing several books, shorter monographs, and articles on the antiquities, ethnology, historical documents, linguistics, and contemporary sociopolitical life of Nicaragua, Honduras, and El Salvador. At this stage in his life he began to lose his eyesight, owing, he was told, to "undue exposure and protracted over-exertion." His doctors told him that he must choose between absolute mental rest and total blindness. In the hope of improvement through a change of scene and occupation, he accepted an appointment as commissioner of the United States to Peru, charged with the settlement of the conflicting claims between the two countries.

[When he had concluded his official duties he began an archaeological exploration of Peru and Bolivia, which, during a year and a half, carried him to many of the ruins that have since become famous but were then scarcely known to the outside world: such sites as Chimu, Pachacamac, Tiahuanaco, Ollantaytambo, Pisac, and ruins in the Santa, Nepeña, Casma, Chillon, Rimac, Cañete, Pisco, and Arica valleys. He spent some time on Lake Titicaca, almost 13,000 feet high in the Bolivian Andes. Of this immense and varied area, he wrote in part as follows.]

In no part of the world does nature assume grander, more imposing, or more varied forms. Deserts as bare and repulsive as those of Sahara alternate with valleys as rich and luxuriant as those of Italy. Lofty mountains, crowned with eternal snow, lift high their rugged sides over broad, bleak *punas,* or tablelands, themselves more elevated than the summits of the White Mountains or of the Alleghanies. Rivers, taking their rise among melting snows, precipitate themselves through deep and rocky gorges into the Pacific, or wind, with swift but gentler current, among the majestic but broken Andes, to swell the flood of the Amazon. There are lakes, ranking in size with those that feed the St. Lawrence, whose surfaces lie almost level with the summit of Mont Blanc; and they are the centres of great terrestrial basins, with river systems of their own, and having no outlet to the sea.

The two great mountain ranges which determine the physical aspect of
the South American continent attain their maximum of bulk, and have their
most decided features in what was the Inca Empire. . . . There is . . . a narrow but often interrupted strip of land between the Cordillera and the sea,
which, however, from Guayaquil southward is throughout as desert as the
flanks of the mountains themselves are bare and repulsive. A waste of sand
and rock, it is the domain of death and silence—a silence only broken by the
screams of water-birds and the howls of the sea-lions that throng its frayed
and forbidding shore.

Bold men were the *conquistadores*, who coasted slowly along these arid
shores in face of the prevailing south wind and against the great Antarctic
current. Nothing short of an absorbing love of adventure, and a consuming
and quenchless avarice, could have prevented them from putting down
their helms and flying shudderingly from the Great Desolation before them.

[During his residence in Lima, Squier visited the ruins of Pachacamac,
about twenty miles south of the capital, on the right bank of the Río Lurin,
overlooking the sea.]

We started from Chorillos, where we had spent the night, by sunrise, prepared for a stay of several days. Our route lay to the southward, over the
dusty Pisco road, and we were soon out of sight of the gardens and cultivated fields of the Rimac Valley, riding over barren and sandy hills, and
plains none the less sandy and barren. The sun became scorchingly hot long
before we obtained our first view of the green valley of Lurin, and the sparkling waters of the river of the same name, which flow to the southward, and
in sight of the celebrated ruins that we had come to visit, and which we
found without any difficulty. They cover wholly, or in part, four considerable hills of regularly stratified but somewhat distorted argillaceous slate,
the strata varying from two inches to a foot in thickness, breaking readily
into rectangular blocks, which were used by the old builders for the foundations of the walls, and to a great extent worked into the structures themselves. The site of the ruins is most forbidding in aspect, and is a waste of
sand, which has been drifted into and over a large portion of the buildings
within the outer walls, some of which have been completely buried.

The desert extends northward to the valley of the Rimac, and inland to
the mountains, that rise, naked and barren, in the distance. In contrast to
these are the green and fertile little valley of Lurin on the south, and the
blue waters of the Pacific on the west, with its picturesque rocky islands,
against which the waves chafe with a ceaseless roar, and over which constantly hovers a cloud of sea-birds. The ruins consist of large adobe bricks,
and the stones already mentioned. Some of the walls are in a fair state of
preservation, considering the heavy and frequent shocks of earthquakes to

which they are exposed on this coast; but, owing to the absence of rain and frost, they have suffered little from the effects of the weather.

Pachacamac is one of the most notable spots in Peru, for here, as we are told by the old chroniclers, was the sacred city of the natives of the coast, before their conquest by the Incas. Here was the shrine of Pachacamac, their chief divinity, and here also the Incas erected a vast Temple of the Sun, and a house of the Virgins of the Sun, side by side with the temple of Pachacamac, whose worship they were too politic to suppress, but which they rather sought to undermine, and in the end merge in that of their own tutelary divinity. The name Pachacamac signifies "He who animates the universe," "The Creator of the world." . . .

In ancient times, Pachacamac was the Mecca of South America; and the worship of the Creator of the World, originally pure, invested the temple with such sanctity that pilgrims resorted to it from the most distant tribes, and were permitted to pass unmolested through the tribes with which they might happen to be at war. Of course, around both the ancient and the modern temple there gradually sprung up a large town, occupied by priests and servitors, and containing *tambos,* or inns, for the pilgrims. But the desert has encroached on the old city, and buried a large part of it, with a portion of its walls, under the drifting sands. Nothing can exceed the bare and desolate aspect of the ruins, which are as still and lifeless as those of Palmyra. No living thing is to be seen, except, perhaps, a solitary condor circling above the crumbling temple; nor sound heard, except the pulsations of the great Pacific breaking at the foot of the eminence on which the temple stood.

It is a place of death, not alone in its silence and sterility, but as the burial-place of tens of thousands of the ancient dead. In Pachacamac, the ground around the temple seems to have been a vast cemetery. Dig almost anywhere in the dry, nitrous sand, and you will come upon what are loosely called *mummies,* but which are the desiccated bodies of the ancient dead. Dig deeper, and you will probably find a second stratum of relics of poor humanity; and deeper still, a third, showing how great was the concourse of people, and how eager the desire to find a resting-place in consecrated ground.

Most of the mummies are found in little vaults, or chambers of adobes, roofed with sticks, or canes, and a layer of rushes, and of a size to contain from one to four and five bodies. These are invariably placed in a sitting posture, with the head resting on the knees, around which the arms are clasped, or with the head resting on the outspread palms, and the elbows on the knees, enveloped in wrappings of various kinds. Sometimes they are enveloped in inner wrappings of fine cotton cloth, and then in blankets of various colors and designs, made from the wool of the vicuña and the alpaca, with ornaments of gold and silver on the corpse, and vases of elegant design by its side. But oftener the cerements are coarse, the ornaments scant and mean, indicating that of old, as now, the mass of mankind was as poor in death as impoverished in life. Fortunately for our knowledge of the people of the past ages, who never attained to a written language, they were accustomed to bury with their dead the things they most regarded in life, and from these we may deduce something of their modes of living, and gain some idea of their religious notions and beliefs. In fact, the interment of articles of any kind with the dead is a clear proof of a belief in the doctrine of a future state, the theory being that the articles thus buried would be useful to their possessor in another world.

To ascertain something more about the ancient inhabitants of Pachacamac than could be inferred from their monuments, I explored a number of their graves, during my ten days' visit there. I shall not try to give the general results of my inquiries, but will record what I found in a single tomb, which will illustrate how a family, not rich, nor yet of the poorest, lived in Pachacamac.

I shall assume that the family occupying this tomb lived in what may be called "an apartment," or one of the tenement-houses in the ancient city, which were, in some respects, better than ours. They were of but one story, and had no narrow, dark, common passages, but all the apartments opened around a spacious central court. Some of these tenements were composed of but a single room. This family probably had three: a large one, about fifteen feet square; a small sleeping-room, with a raised bank of earth at one end; and another smaller room, or kitchen, with niches in the walls to receive

Peruvian mummies
From E. G. Squier, *Peru: Incidents of Travel and Exploration in the Land of the Incas.*

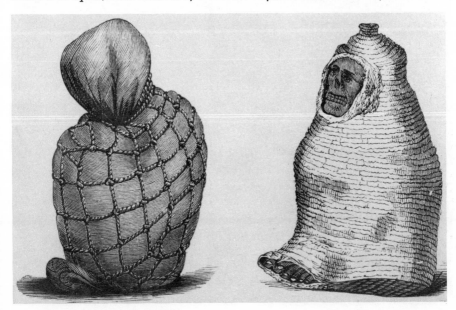

utensils, and with vases sunk in the earth to contain maize, beans, etc., that seem to have been leading articles of food. The plan is of such a dwelling. The implements, utensils, ornaments, and stores have disappeared; but we find many of them in the family tomb in the neighborhood of the temple.

This particular tomb was one of the second stratum of graves, and was, therefore, neither of the earliest nor latest date. It was walled with adobes, was about four feet square by three feet deep, and contained five bodies: one, of a man of middle age; another, of a full-grown woman; a third, of a girl about fourteen years old; a fourth, of a boy some years younger; and the fifth, of an infant. The little one was placed between father and mother: the boy was by the side of the man; the girl, by the side of the woman. All were enveloped in a braided net-work or sack of rushes, or coarse grass, bound closely around the bodies by cords of the same material.

Under the outer wrapper of braided reeds of the man was another of stout, plain cotton cloth, fastened with a variegated cord of llama wool. Next came an envelope of cotton cloth of finer texture, which, when removed, disclosed the body, shrunken and dried hard, of the color of mahogany, but well preserved. The hair was long, and slightly reddish, perhaps from the effects

left, Pattern of cotton shroud
From E. G. Squier, *Peru: Incidents of Travel and Exploration in the Land of the Incas.*
right, Ancient spindle
From E. G. Squier, *Peru: Incidents of Travel and Exploration in the Land of the Incas.*

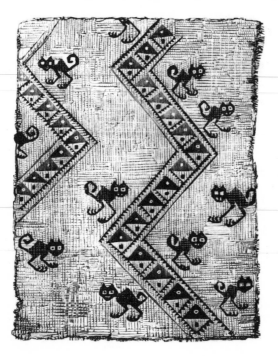

of the nitre in the soil. Passing around the neck, and carefully folded on the knees, on which the head rested, was a net of the twisted fibre of the agave, a plant not found on the coast. The threads were as fine as the finest used by our fishermen, and the meshes were neatly knotted, precisely after the fashion of to-day. This seems to indicate that he had been a fisherman—a conclusion further sustained by finding, wrapped up in a cloth, between his feet some fishing-lines of various sizes, some copper hooks, barbed like ours, and some copper sinkers. Under each armpit was a roll of white alpaca wool, and behind the calf of each leg a few thick, short ears of variegated maize. A small, thin piece of copper had been placed in the mouth, corresponding, perhaps, with the *óbolos* which the ancient Greeks put into the mouths of their dead, as a fee for Charon. This was all discovered belonging exclusively to the fisherman, except that, suspended by a thread around the neck, was a pair of bronze tweezers, probably for plucking out the beard.

The wife, beneath the same coarse outer wrapping of braided reeds, was

top left, Wallet, folded
From E. G. Squier, *Peru: Incidents of Travel and Exploration in the Land of the Incas.*
bottom left, Wallet, unfolded
From E. G. Squier, *Peru: Incidents of Travel and Exploration in the Land of the Incas.*
right, Spool of thread
From E. G. Squier, *Peru: Incidents of Travel and Exploration in the Land of the Incas.*

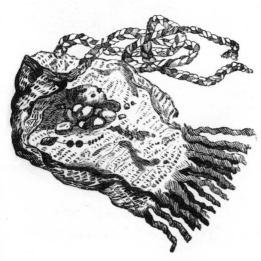

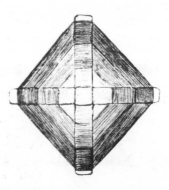

enveloped in a blanket of alpaca wool finely spun, woven in the style known as "three-ply," in two colors—a soft chestnut-brown and a pure white. . . .

Below this was a sheet of fine cotton cloth, with sixty-two threads of warp and woof to the inch. It had a diamond-shaped pattern, formed by very elaborate lines of ornament, inside of which, or in the spaces themselves, were representatives of monkeys, which seemed to be following each other as up and down stairs.

Beneath this was a rather coarsely woven, but yet soft and flexible, cotton cloth, twenty yards or more in length, wrapped in many folds around the body of the woman, which was in a similar condition, as regards preservation, to that of her husband. Her long hair was less changed by the salts of the soil than that of her husband, and was black, and in some places lustrous. In one hand she held a comb, made by setting what I took to be the bony parts—the rays—of fishes' fins in a slip of the hard, woody part of the dwarf-palm-tree, into which they were not only tightly cemented, but firmly bound. In her other hand were the remains of a fan, with a cane handle, from the

left, Knitting utensils
From E. G. Squier, *Peru: Incidents of Travel and Exploration in the Land of the Incas.*
top right, Skein of thread
From E. G. Squier, *Peru: Incidents of Travel and Exploration in the Land of the Incas.*
bottom right, Toilet articles
From E. G. Squier, *Peru: Incidents of Travel and Exploration in the Land of the Incas.*

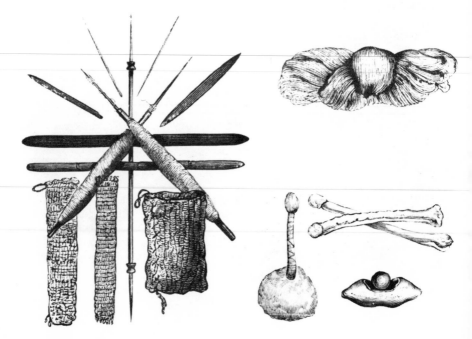

upper points of which radiated the faded feathers of parrots and humming-birds.

Around her neck was a triple necklace of shells, dim in color, and exfoliating layer after layer when exposed to light and air. Resting between her body and bent-up knees were several small domestic implements, among them an ancient spindle for spinning cotton, half covered with spun thread, which connected with a mass of the raw cotton. This simple spinning apparatus consisted of a section of the stalk of the quinoa, half as large as the little finger, and eight inches long, its lower end fitted through a whirl-bob

bottom center, Netting instrument
From E. G. Squier, *Peru: Incidents of Travel and Exploration in the Land of the Incas.*
left, Dried parrot
From E. G. Squier, *Peru: Incidents of Travel and Exploration in the Land of the Incas.*
top center, Boy's sling
From E. G. Squier, *Peru: Incidents of Travel and Exploration in the Land of the Incas.*
right, Infant's burial net
From E. G. Squier, *Peru: Incidents of Travel and Exploration in the Land of the Incas.*

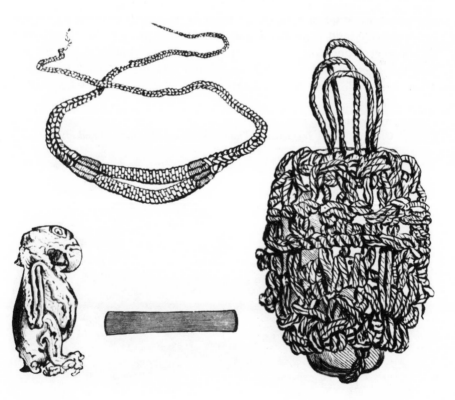

of stone, to give it momentum when set in motion by a twirl of the forefinger and thumb grasping a point of hard wood stuck in the upper end of the spindle. The contrivance is precisely the same as that in universal use by the Indian women of the present day. Only I have seen a small lime, lemon, or potato with a quinoa stalk stuck through it, instead of the ancient stone or earthen whirl-bob.

One of the most interesting articles found with the woman was a kind of wallet, composed of two pieces of thick cotton cloth of different colors, ten inches long by five broad, the lower end of each terminating in a fringe, and the upper end at each corner in a long braid, the braids of both being again braided together. These cloths, placed together, were carefully folded up and tied by the braids. The packet contained some kernels of the large lupin, sometimes called "Lima beans"; a few pods of cotton, gathered before maturity, the husks being still on; some fragments of an ornament of thin silver; and two little thin disks of the same material, three-tenths of an inch in diameter, each pierced with a small hole near its edge, too minute for ornament apparently, and possibly used as a coin; also some tiny beads of chalcedony, scarcely an eight of an inch in diameter.

The body of the girl was peculiar in position, having been seated on a kind of work-box of braided reeds, with a cover hinged on one side, and shutting down and fastening on the other. It was about eighteen inches long, fourteen wide, and eight deep, and contained a greater variety of articles than I ever found together in any grave of the aborigines. There were grouped together things childish, and things showing approach to maturity. There were rude specimens of knitting, with places showing where stitches

Pottery from Pachacamac
From E. G. Squier, *Peru: Incidents of Travel and Exploration in the Land of the Incas.*

had been dropped; mites of spindles and implements for weaving, and braids of thread of irregular thickness, kept as if for sake of contrast with others larger and nicely wound, with a finer and more even thread. There were skeins and spools of thread; the spools being composed of two splints placed across each other at right angles, and the thread wound "in and out" between them. There were strips of cloth, some wide, some narrow, and some of two and even three colors. There were pouches, plain and variegated, of different sizes, and all woven or knit without a seam. There were needles of bone and of bronze; a comb, a little bronze knife, and some other articles; a fan, smaller than that of the mother, was also stored away in the box.

There were several sections of the hollow bones of some bird, carefully stopped by a wad of cotton, and containing pigments of various colors. I assumed at first that they were intended for dyes of the various cotton textures we had discovered; but I became doubtful when I found a curious contrivance, made of the finest cotton, evidently used as a "dab" for applying the colors to the face. By the side of these novel cosmetic boxes was a contrivance for rubbing or grinding the pigments to the requisite fineness for use. It was a small oblong stone, with a cup-shaped hollow on the upper side, in which fits a little round stone ball, answering the purpose of a pestle. There was also a substitute for a mirror, composed of a piece of iron pyrites resembling the half of an egg, with the plane side highly polished. Among all these many curious things, I dare say, none was prized in life more than a little crushed ornament of gold, evidently intended to represent a butterfly,

Ruins of Cajamarquilla
From E. G. Squier, *Peru: Incidents of Travel and Exploration in the Land of the Incas.*

but so thin and delicate that it came to pieces and lost its form when we attempted to handle it. There was also a netting instrument of hard wood, not unlike those now in use in making nets.

The envelopes of the mummy of the girl were similar to those that enshrouded her mother. Her hair was braided and plaited around the forehead, encircling which, also, was a cincture of white cloth, ornamented with little silver spangles; a thin narrow bracelet of the same metal still hung on the shrunken arm, and between her feet was the dried body of a parrot, doubtless her pet in life, brought perhaps from the distant Amazonian valleys.

There was nothing of special interest surrounding the body of the boy; but bound tightly around his forehead was his sling, finely braided from cotton threads.

The body of the infant, a girl, had been embedded in the fleece of the alpaca, then wrapped in fine cotton cloth, and placed in a strangely braided sack of rushes, with handles or loops at each end, as if for carrying it. The only article found with this body was a sea-shell containing pebbles, the orifice closed with a hard pitch-like substance. It was the child's rattle.

Besides the bodies, there were a number of utensils, and other articles in the vault; among them half a dozen earthen jars, pans, and pots of various sizes and ordinary form. One or two were still incrusted with the soot of the fires over which they had been used. Every one contained something. One was filled with ground-nuts familiar to us as pea-nuts; another with maize, etc., all except the latter in a carbonized condition.

Besides these articles, there were also some others, illustrating the religious notions of the occupants of the ancient tomb, and affording us scant but, as far as they go, certain ideas of the ancient faith and worship.

Subterranean vaults, Cajamarquilla
From E. G. Squier, *Peru: Incidents of Travel and Exploration in the Land of the Incas.*

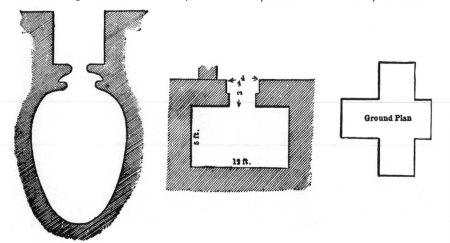

Some four or five leagues from Lima, following up the valley of the river Rimac, is a side valley, an amphitheatre among the hills, containing several important haciendas, of which those of Huachipa and La Niverea are the principal. This valley is watered by a large *azequia,* deriving its supply from the river higher up, and which dates from the time of the Incas. The water, however, cannot, or could not, be carried, under the hydraulic system of the ancients, sufficiently high up on the flanks of the hills to irrigate the whole of this subsidiary and remarkably fertile valley. Its upper or higher part, therefore—an extent of several square miles—like all the rest of Peru where not irrigated, is an arid area, without vegetation of any kind; while the lower or irrigated part is covered with luxuriant grain fields and meadows.

On this plain, and covering nearly a square league, are the remains of an ancient town, now known as the ruins of Cajamarquilla. These consist of three great groups of buildings on and around the central masses, with streets passing between them. It would be impossible to describe this complicated maze of massive adobe walls, most of them still standing, albeit much shattered by centuries of earthquakes, or to convey an idea of the pyramidal edifices, rising stage on stage, with terraces and broad flights of steps leading to their summits. It is enough to say that many of the buildings of the ruined city, the history of which is lost even to tradition, are complicated structures, their apartments connecting by blind and narrow passages, and containing many curious subterranean vaults or granaries, which consisted of excavations made in the hard ground, of various shapes and sizes. Some were round, like a vase or jar, and again others were square. They are called *ollas,* or *tinajas* (vases, or jars), and were no doubt intended for the storage of household supplies. The plans . . . will afford a better idea of their construction than can be given by words.

The privacy of these rooms was insured by walls in front of the doors. The door-ways are all low, and vary in form, a few of which are given in the engraving. There are no windows in the dwellings, and the roofs are flat.

Doorways
From E. G. Squier, *Peru: Incidents of Travel and Exploration in the Land of the Incas.*

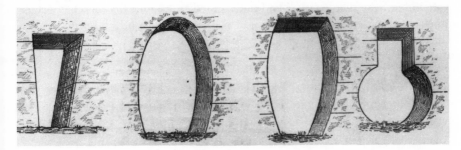

No traces of gables are to be seen. In many there was an earthen elevation or daïs, and they seem to have been supplied with suitable closets. Among these edifices an army might conceal itself; and, in fact, these ruins have several times been made the refuge of bands of robbers and vagabonds, so as to require, on one occasion, a full regiment of soldiers to hunt them out and expel them.

I had gone to the hacienda of La Niverea, at the invitation of its proprietor, Don Pablo, who was also the owner of the waste lands occupied by the ruins, for the purpose of making a thorough investigation of them. I was accompanied by a friend, who was both draughtsman and photographer, and we intended to spend a week there, and bring away such plans and views as would give a clear notion of the singular and undescribed remains of the ancient city. We found at the hacienda a detachment of troops from Lima, a lieutenant and some five-and-twenty men, who seemed to be in no hurry to leave the comfortable foraging afforded by Don Pablo's well-cultivated hacienda, with its acre or two of vineyard, now purple with such grapes as are found nowhere in the world except Peru.

We commenced operations among the ruins the very day of our arrival, assisted by a couple of Chinese laborers, kindly lent us by our host. We went to our work early, and returned late, our interest deepening with every hour's investigation. On the second day, the lieutenant and his squad left, alleging that the *ladrones* had been heard from over the mountains, in the valley of Chillon, whither they went "to persecute them." I suspected that the "persecutors" of the robbers had got some hint of their approach to La Niverea, and, either from fear or through complicity, had determined to give them a clear field.

On our third day among the ruins, my companions succumbed to the heat and glare of the sun reflected from the bare walls, and returned to the hacienda with many symptoms of fever, leaving me with but one assistant, A-tau, a Chinese, who could neither speak nor understand more than half a dozen Spanish words; but who, nevertheless, I had little difficulty in making comprehend all that I required in the way of aiding me in my survey. He carried the measuring-line and stakes, and myself the compass and note-book.

Having long before recognized the utter impossibility of making a complete plan of the whole city, I had determined to run out the most important streets, and make a detailed survey of a section sufficiently large to convey a clear notion of the whole. I ran my lines on the walls, which are in general broad and firm enough to permit one to walk along their tops. We had proceeded on a single, slightly deviating course for nearly half a mile, past the principal pyramidal pile among the ruins, and nearly to their centre, and were silently intent on our work, when, being in advance, I was startled in every nerve by the sudden apparition of three men leaping suddenly to their feet from the earthen floor of one of the smaller rooms, where they had been comfortably reclining on a heap of *piliones* and *ponchos*. They were armed, and their hands were on their weapons in a moment. I gave the universal salutation of the mountaineers, *"Dios y paz"* (God and peace), which was responded to in like manner.

It was Rossi Arci himself, the "Robber of the Ruins," and his companions, whom I had surprised. I knew that I was in for it, so I made a bold advance by clambering down the broken wall, with outstretched hand, which was accepted reluctantly. I soon found that I was suspected of being a Government agent, making a plan of the ruins for official use. I knew there was no time for trifling, and that a fearless manner was my only guarantee of safety. I offered him my flask, which he declined, saying, "After you," and for reasons afterwards obvious, I commenced. My excellent friend paid profound respects to the flask when passed to him; and, as I handed him one of my cards, and he read the name with the appendage, *"Comisionado de los Estados Unidos,"* he said, "Bien [good]; pardon me," and lifted his sombrero. He followed the explanation of my plans with apparent interest, but I fear he was not exactly the man to appreciate archaeology. One fellow of the party had encountered me some months previous at the ruins of Amacavilca, and had seen the great range of my wonderful breech-loading rifle, and gave a pretty high notion of the efficiency of that weapon. The robber wished to possess himself of so valuable an addition to his armory, and immediately made me an offer of one hundred Bolivian dollars, adding, slowly, "When I get them; for, señor, we really are not rich." I, however, declined the generous offer; but I promised to send him a few bottles of *italia,* such as I had with me. As we parted, he said, "You may come back to-morrow to your nonsense [*tonterías*] without fear; and I will send a reliable man for the rifle. *Adios, amigo!"* I sent A-tau to carry the bottles, which he did with great reluctance. It was after dark when he returned, grossly intoxicated. It seems that my friend Rossi Arci had insisted on my drinking first, not from motives of courtesy, but to assure himself that there had been no poisons artfully dissolved in the tempting *italia;* and when he got hold of A-tau's bottles, the Celestial wretch was compelled to drink a third of each to give assurance that a similar "doctoring" had not taken place at the hacienda. Between fright and an overdose of brandy, I lost my assistant next day, and Don Pablo a laborer for a week.

Four weeks afterwards, a swollen and disfigured corpse was exposed in the Grand Plaza of Lima. It was that of Rossi Arci. He had made a bold attack on a Government guard of about a hundred soldiers, who were conveying a remittance of coin, at a place noted in the annals of Peruvian brigandage as Rio Seco, about half-way between Lima and Cerro de Pasco. The fight lasted some hours, and frequently swayed in his favor; and it is not impossible that he would have captured the booty had he not received a severe wound in the groin, which compelled him to retire, and of which he died the next day. His last request was to be buried in the bottom of an *azequia,* so that his body might not fall into the hands of the authorities. His request was complied with; but one of his followers gave himself up, and purchased clemency by revealing the secret of the brigand's grave. A commission was sent to verify the statements of Arci's follower, and the decaying body was identified and brought to Lima amid the rejoicings of the people. The commander of the *remisa* was promoted, and a general feeling of relief pervaded the community.

Immediately on our arrival in Copacabana, the commandante had sent an Indian with an order to the alcaldes of the island of Titicaca to have a balsa in readiness for us on the following day at the embarcadero of Yampupata, four leagues distant. We started for that point at noon, with the intention of reaching the island the same night. The road descends abruptly from the rocky eminence on which the town is built into a beautiful level amphi-theatre two miles broad, and curves around the head of a bay that here projects into the land between two high and rugged capes. The water toyed and sparkled among the pebbles on the shore, and along it a troop of lively plover was racing in eager search for the minute mollusks drifted up by the waves, with the advance and recession of which their line kept a waver-ing cadence. Past the little plain is what in Peru is called a *ladera;* in other words, the road runs high up along the face of the steep, and in many places absolutely perpendicular, headlands that overhang the lake, and be-comes a mere goat's path, narrow and rugged, half worn, half cut, in the rock.

But neither the difficulty nor the danger of the path could wholly with-draw our attention from the hundreds of wide and wonderful views that burst on our sight at every bend and turning. The bold, bare peninsulas; the bluff, panoramic headlands behind which the lake stole in, through many a rent in their rocky palisade, and spread out in broad and placid bays; the islands equally abrupt and bold and bare; the ruddy bulk of the sacred island of Titicaca; the distant shores of Bolivia, with their silver cincture of the Andes; the blue waters and sparkling waves, with almost every other element of the beautiful and impressive—went to make up the kaleidoscopic scenes of the afternoon, and, with the cloudless sky, bright sunlight, and bracing air, to inspire us with a sense of elevation and repose inconsistent with the babbling of waters, the rustle of leaves, and the murmurs of men.

Beyond the *ladera* we came once more to the pebbly shore of the lake; then, climbing the steep neck of a rocky peninsula, and skirting the culti-vated slopes of a gentle declivity, between walls of stone enclosing fields of ocas, which, newly dug, shone like carnelians on the gray earth, we de-scended to the embarcadero of Yampupata, which is now, as it probably always was, the point of embarkation. Here is a sandy beach between rocky promontories, and a tambo of stone, windowless, and with but a single opening into its bare interior, black with smoke, floored with ashes, and sending forth indescribable and offensive odors. There was no balsa to convey us to the island, which lay, glowing in the evening sun, temptingly before us, and appearing, through the moistureless air, as if scarcely at rifle-shot distance. We hurried to a group of huts clustered round a little church a mile to our left, but most of the population were absent in Copacabana or at work in the oca fields; and we learned little from the blind, the halt, and the deaf that remained behind, except that balsas would come for us from the island. Through our glasses we could discover a number of these moored in little rock-girt coves and indentations of its shores, but there was nobody near them, nor any signs of life whatever. In vain, as night fell, we lighted fierce and ephemeral fires of quenua stalks; our signals were unanswered, and we were obliged to dispose ourselves for the night in the cold and gloomy tambo, a rough stone hut, filthy beyond expression, standing close to the shore.

I was up at daylight, and went down to the shore, where the lake-weed was matted together with ice, and where a group of Indian women were shiveringly awaiting the arrival of a balsa which I discerned just paddling out from under the shadow of the island. Although apparently so near, the balsa was several hours in crossing the strait, and it was ten o'clock before it ranged up along-side and under the protection of some rocks to the left of the tambo. It was small, water-soaked, and its highest part elevated only a few inches above the water. The Indian women endeavored to get aboard, but a personage in a poncho, and evidently in authority (for he carried a tasselled cane), forbade them. He approached us, hat in hand, with the usual salutation of "*Tat-tai Viracocha*," and announced himself as *curaca* of Titicaca, at our service. Berrios declined to embark on the balsa, which, to start with, was a ticklish craft, and with H—, myself, the alcalde, and the two boatman, barely kept afloat.

Sailing in a balsa is by no means the perfection of navigation, nor is the craft itself one likely to inspire high confidence. It is simply a float or raft, made up of bundles of reeds, tied together, fagot-like, in the middle of which the voyager poises himself on his knees, while the Indian *marineros* stand, one at each extremity, where they spread their feet apart, and, with small and rather crooked poles for oars, strike the water right and left, and thus slowly and laboriously propel the balsa in the required direction. Of course this action gives the craft a rocking, rolling motion, and makes the passenger feel very much as if he were afloat on a mammoth cigar, pre-disposed to turn over on the slightest pretext. Then, if the water be a little rough, a movement takes place which probably is unequalled in bringing on the pleasant sensation of sea-sickness. Some of the balsas, however, are large, with sides built up like guards, which can be rigged with a sail for running before the wind, and are capable of carrying as many as sixty people.

Leaving behind the little *playa*, or beach, our Indian boatmen pushed along under a steep, rocky cliff, until they reached the point where the strait between the main-land and the island is narrowest. The water at the foot of the cliff is very deep, but wonderfully transparent, and we could trace the plunge downwards of the precipitous limestone buttresses until our brains grew dizzy. We were more than two hours in propelling the balsa across the strait, a distance which an ordinary oarsman in a White-hall boat would get over in fifteen minutes, and landed on the island under the lee of a projecting ledge of rocks, full in view of the Palace of the Incas and the terraces surrounding it, half a mile to our right.

I do not think I shall find a better place than this for saying a few words about Lake Titicaca, which was for many weeks a conspicuous feature in our landscape, and which is, in many respects, the most extraordinary and interesting body of water in the world. It is a long, irregular oval in shape, with one-fifth of its area at its southern extremity cut nearly off by the opposing peninsulas of Tiquina and Copacabana. Its greatest length is about 120 miles, and its greatest width between 50 and 60 miles. Its mean level is 12,488 feet above the sea. With a line of 100 fathoms I failed to reach bottom, at a distance of a mile to the eastward of the island of Titicaca. The eastern, or Bolivian, shore is abrupt, the mountains on that side pressing down boldly into the water. The western and southern shores, however, are comparatively low and level, the water shallow and grown up with reeds and rushes, among which myriads of water-fowls find shelter and support.

The lake is deep, and never freezes over, but ice forms near its shores and where the water is shallow. In fact, it exercises a very important influence on the climate of this high, cold, and desolate region. Its waters, at least during the winter months, are from ten to twelve degrees of Fahrenheit warmer than the atmosphere. The islands and peninsulas feel this influence most perceptibly, and I found barley, pease, and maize, the latter, however, small and not prolific, ripening on these, while they did not mature on what may be called the main-land. The prevailing winds are from the north-east, and they often blow with great force, rendering navigation on the frail balsas, always slow and difficult, exceedingly dangerous. The lake has several considerable bays, of which those of Puno, Huancané, and Achacache are the principal. It has also eight considerable habitable islands, viz.: Amantené, Taqueli, Soto, Titicaca, Coati, Campanario, To-quaré, and Aputo. Of these the largest is that of Titicaca, on which we have just landed; high and bare, rugged in outline as ragged in surface, six miles long by between three and four in width.

This is the sacred island of Peru.[*] To it the Incas traced their origin, and

* "It is called sacred," says Pedro Cieza de Leon, "because of a ridiculous story that there was no light for many days, when the sun rose resplendent out of the island; and hence they built here a temple to its glory, which was held in great veneration, and had virgins and priests belonging to it, with mighty treasures."

to this day it is held by their descendants in profound veneration. According to tradition, Manco Capac and his wife and sister, Mama Ocllo, children of the Sun, and commissioned by that luminary, started hence on their errand of beneficence to reduce under government and to instruct in religion and the arts the savage tribes that occupied the country. Manco Capac bore a golden rod, and was instructed to travel northwards until he reached the spot where the rod should sink into the ground, and there fix the seat of his empire. He obeyed the behest, travelled slowly along the western shore of the lake, through the broad, level *puna* lands, up the valley of the Pucura, to the lake of La Raya, where the basin of Titicaca ends, and whence the waters of the river Vilcanota start on their course to swell the Amazon. He advanced down the valley of that river until he reached the spot where Cuzco now stands, when the golden rod disappeared. Here he fixed his seat, and here in time rose the City of the Sun, the capital of the Inca empire.

The most reliable of the chroniclers, Garcilasso, tells us that besides building a temple on the island of Titicaca the Incas sought in all ways to ennoble it, as being the spot where their ancestors, descending from heaven, first planted their feet. They levelled its asperities as far as possible, removing rocks and building terraces, which they covered with rich earth brought from afar, in order that maize might be grown, which, from the cold, might not be otherwise cultivated. The yield was small, but the ears were regarded as sacred, and were distributed among the temples and convents of the empire, one year to one, and the next to another, so that each might have the advantage of a portion of the grain which was brought, as it were, from heaven. This was sown in the gardens of the temples of the Sun, and of the convents of the virgins, and the yield was again distributed among the people of the various provinces. Some grains were scattered among the stores in the public granaries, as sacred things which would augment and preserve from corruption the food of the people. And, such was the superstition, every Indian who had in his store-house a single grain of this maize, or any other grain grown in the sacred island, could never lack bread during his life-time.

The etymology of the name of the island, which has been extended to the lake, is not clear. It has been variously derived from *titi*, signifying "tiger," or "wild-cat," and *kaka*, "rock" or mountain crest: so that it would signify "Tiger Rock," or "Rock of the Tiger," perhaps from some fancied resemblance of the island, or some part of it, to that animal when seen from a distance. The tradition insists, however, that formerly a tiger, or puma, was seen at night on the crest of Titicaca, which carried a great carbuncle or ruby in its head that flashed its light far and wide over the lake, through all the extent of the Collao. Another derivative is from *titi*, "lead" or "tin," and *kaka*, "rock" or "crest," as before; *i.e.*, the "Mountain of Tin." There seems to be no good reason for this characterization, as there are no traces of metal in the island.

Upon this island, the traditional birthplace of the Incas, are still the remains of a temple of the Sun, a convent of priests, a royal palace, and other vestiges of Inca civilization. Not far distant is the island of Coati, which was sacred to the Moon, the wife and sister of the Sun, on which stands the famous palace of the Virgins of the Sun, built around two shrines dedicated to the Sun and the Moon respectively, and which is one of the best-preserved as well as one of the most remarkable remains of aboriginal architecture on this continent. The island of Soto was the Isle of Penitence, to which the Incas of the ruling race were wont to resort for fasting and humiliation, and it has also many remains of ancient architecture.

Two alcaldes of the island, residing in the little village of Challa, were waiting on the rocks to receive us, which they did with uncovered heads and the usual salutation. They told us that they had mules ready for us beyond the rocks, up and through which we clambered by a steep and narrow path, worn in the stone by the feet of myriads of pilgrims. This leads to a platform 73 feet long and 45 broad, faced with rough stones carefully laid and reached by a flight of steps. Above this is another platform, ascended in like manner, on the farther side of which are the remains

Niche in ruins at landing, Island of Titicaca
From E. G. Squier, *Peru: Incidents of Travel and Exploration in the Land of the Incas.*

of two rectangular buildings, each 35 feet long by 27 feet broad, with a narrow passage between them.

The front of each building is much ruined, but is relieved by reëntering niches of true Inca type, and characteristic of Inca architecture. Midway from the passage between the buildings, which is only thirty inches wide, doors open into each edifice, which is composed of but a single room. The farther sides of these have niches corresponding with those of the exterior. Opposite them, and designed apparently more for use than ornament, are two lesser and plain niches, like closets sunk in the wall. If there were any windows, they were in the upper portions of the walls, now fallen. Both buildings are of blue limestone, roughly cut, and laid in a tough clay. They were probably stuccoed.

The purpose of these structures, or rather this structure, is pretty well indicated by the early writers,* who tell us that the pilgrims to the sacred island and its shrines were not allowed to land on its soil without undergoing certain preliminary fasts, penitences, and purifications in Copacabana; and after landing on the island they had to pass through certain "portals," the first of which was called *Pumapunco,* or Door of the Puma, where was a priest of the Sun to receive confession of their sins and admit expiation. The next portal was called *Kentipunco,* because it was adorned with the plumage of the bird *kenti,* where other ceremonies had to be performed. The third was called *Pillcopunco,* or the Gate of Hope, after passing which the pilgrim might continue his journey to the sacred rock of the island, and make his adorations. But he could not approach the spot within two hundred paces. Only special priests of exceptional sanctity were allowed to tread the consecrated soil around it.

We can readily conceive that the structure under notice was in some way connected with these rites, and how the pilgrim, on disembarking, was conducted from one terrace to another, and finally made to pass, as through a portal, between the two buildings of which we still find the remains. In the island of Coati, and in many of the approaches to edifices known to have been temples, we find corresponding buildings, which probably answered a similar purpose.

On the side of the hill overlooking the landing-place, still called Pumapunco, are terraces, with traces of buildings, which Calancha and some of the chroniclers imagine to have been parts of a fortification; but I incline to the belief that they were residences of the priests and *balseros,* or attendants on the landing-place.

After making a rapid plan of these remains, we mounted our mules, and, with an alcalde trotting along in front of us and another behind, we started

---

* We find it thus recorded by the Padre Ramos in his history of the "Sanctuary of Copacabana," of which church he was a priest, at a period when the traditions of the natives were comparatively fresh and uncorrupted.

for the holy *kaka*, or rock, of Manco, and the convent of the ancient priests, at the opposite end of the island. The path skirts the flanks of the abrupt hills forming the island, apparently on the line of an ancient road supported by terraces of large stones, at an elevation of between two and three hundred feet above the lake, the shores of which are precipitous. At the distance of half a mile from the landing, we passed a fine ruin called the Palace of the Inca, and farther on passed also the Bath of the Incas, in a beautiful, protected amphitheatre, irrigated by springs, yellow with ripening barley, and full of shrubs and flowers. Here the path turns to the right over the crest of the island, two thousand feet high, and runs along dizzy eminences, from which, far down, may be discerned little sheltered *ensenadas,* or bays, almost land-locked, where there is a poor thatched hut or two, a balsa riding at her moorings or dragged up to dry on the shore, a few quenua-trees, and whence comes up the sole music of the Sierra, the bark—half yelp, half snarl—of the ill-conditioned, base-tempered, but faithful dogs of the country. Sometimes our course was on one side of the crest, and sometimes on the other, so that we had alternating views of the Peruvian and Bolivian shores of the lake, and of the bays and promontories of the island.

At almost the very northern end of the island, at its most repulsive and unpromising part, where there is neither inhabitant nor trace of culture, where the soil is rocky and bare, and the cliffs ragged and broken—high up, where the fret of the waves of the lake is scarcely heard, and where the eye ranges over the broad blue waters from one mountain barrier to the other, from the glittering crests of the Andes to those of the Cordillera, is the spot most celebrated and most sacred of Peru. Here is the rock on which it was believed no bird would light or animal venture, on which no human being dared to place his foot; whence the sun rose to dispel the primal vapors and illume the world; which was plated all over with gold and silver, and covered, except on occasions of the most solemn festivals, with a veil of cloth of richest color and material; which sheltered the favorite children of the Sun, and the pontiff, priest, and king who founded the Inca empire.*

The sun had set, casting a fleeting crimson glow on the snows of Illampu, which was followed by a deadly, bluish pallor, and it was beginning to be dark before we got through with our investigation of the rock of Manco Capac. We had arranged to pass the night at the little hacienda of the

---

* Calancha and Ramos report, on the authority of the oldest and best-informed Indians of their day, that "the whole concavity of the rock was covered with plates of gold and silver, and that in its various hollows different offerings were placed, according to the festival or the occasion. The offerings were gold, silver, shells, feathers, and rich cloth of *cumibi.* The entire rock was covered with a rich mantle of this cloth—the finest and most gorgeous in colors of any ever seen in the empire."

Pila, or Fountain, of the Incas, and retraced our path thither slowly and with difficulty. The hacienda consisted of three small buildings, occupying as many sides of a court. One of these was a kitchen and dormitory, another was a kind of granary or store-house, and in the third was an apartment reserved for the proprietor of the hacienda, a resident of Puno, when he visited the island. The room was neatly whitewashed, the floor was matted, and there were two real chairs from Connecticut, and a table that might be touched without toppling over, and used without falling into pieces. The alcaldes who had us in charge attended faithfully to our wants, and served us in person with chupe, ocas, and eggs. Their authority over the people of the hacienda seemed absolute.

The night was bitterly cold, and we had no covering except our saddle-cloths, having declined the use of some sheepskins, which the alcaldes would have taken from the poor people of the establishment. A sheepskin, or the skin of the vicuña, spread on the mud floor of his hut, is the only bed of the Indian from one year's end to the other. It is always filthy, and frequently full of vermin. Before going to bed we went out into the frosty, starry night, and were surprised to see fires blazing on the topmost peak of the island, on the crest of Coati, and on the headland of Copacabana. Others, many of them hardly discernible in the distance, were also burning on the peninsula of Tiquina and on the bluff Bolivian shores of the lake, their red light darting like golden lances over the water. Our first impression was that some mysterious signalling was going on, connected, perhaps, with our visit. We ascertained, however, that this was the Eve of St. John, which is celebrated in this way throughout the Sierra. On that night fires blaze on the hill-tops in all the inhabited districts of Peru and Bolivia, from the desert of Atacama to the equator.

We were up early, and for the first time ate our chupe with satisfaction, for it was hot. We found the houses of the hacienda seated in the saddle of a ridge projecting into the lake, and terminating in a natural mound or eminence, rounded with great regularity by art, and terraced from the very edge of the water up to its top by concentric walls of stone. Traces of a building, like a belvedere or summer-house, were conspicuous at its summit, from which a fine view of the lake, its islands, and the distant nevados is commanded. At the foot of this eminence, on both sides, are little bays with sandy beaches, that on the right pushing inland towards the terraced Garden of the Incas. Here is the most sheltered nook of the island, and the terraces are covered with barley in the ear, just changing from green to golden, and as we zigzag down we come to patches of pease and little squares of maize, with stalks scarcely three feet high and ears not longer than one's finger, but closely covered with compact vitreous grains.

We go down, down, until we get where we hear the pleasant plash and gurgle of waters; there is an oppressive odor of fading flowers; and in a few minutes we stand before the Pila of the Incas. We are midway down the sloping valley, amidst terraces geometrically laid out and supported by walls of cut stone, niched according to Inca taste, and here forming three sides of a quadrangle, in which there is a pool, forty feet long, ten wide, and five deep, paved with worked stones. Into this pour four *chorros,* or jets of water, each of the size of a man's arm, from openings cut in the stones behind. Over the walls around it droop the tendrils of vines and the stems of plants that are slowly yielding to the frost, and, what with odors, and the tinkle and patter of the water, one might imagine himself in the court of the Alhambra, where the fountains murmur of the Moors, just as the Pila of the Incas tells its inarticulate tale of a race departed, and to whose taste and poetry it bears melodious witness. The water comes through subterranean passages from sources now unknown, and never diminishes in volume. It flows to-day as freely as when the Incas resorted here and cut the steep hill-sides into terraces, bringing the earth to fill them—so runs the legend—all the way from the Valley of Yucay, or Vale of Imperial Delights, four hundred miles distant. However that may be, this is the garden *par excellence* of the Collao, testifying equally to the taste, enterprise, and skill of those who created it in spite of the most rigorous of climes and most ungrateful of soils. Below this reservoir the water is conducted from terrace to terrace until it is finally discharged into the lake.

Pila, or fountain, of the Incas, Titicaca
From E. G. Squier, *Peru: Incidents of Travel and Exploration in the Land of the Incas.*

Half-way from the Garden of the Incas to the embarcadero, standing on a natural shelf or terrace overlooking the lake, but much smoothed by art, is *El Palacio del Inca*, the Palace (so called) of the Inca, to which I have already made a brief reference. Its site is beautiful. On either side are terraces, some of them niched, and supporting small dependent structures, while the steep hill behind, which bends around it like a half-moon, is also terraced in graceful curves, each defined, not alone by its stone facing, but by a vigorous growth of the shrub that yields the Flor del Inca, which blossoms here all the year round.

The building is rectangular, 51 by 44 feet, and two stories high. The front on the lake is ornamented or relieved on the lower story by four high niches, the two central ones being door-ways. On each side are three niches, the central one also forming a door-way. It is divided into twelve small rooms, of varying sizes, and connected with each other. There are altogether four sets of rooms, two groups of two each, and two of four each. These rooms are about thirteen feet high, their walls inclining slightly inwards, while their ceiling is formed by flat, overlapping stones, laid with great regularity. Every room has its niches, some small and plain, others large and elaborate. The inner as well as the exterior walls were stuccoed with a fine, tenacious clay, possibly mixed with some adhesive substance, and painted. Some patches of this stucco still remain, and indicate that the building was originally yellow, while the inner parts and mouldings of the door-ways and niches were of different shades of red.

The second story does not at all correspond in plan with the first. Its entrance is at the rear, on a level with a terrace extending back to the hill, and spreading out in a noble walk faced with a niched wall, and supporting some minor buildings, or "summer-houses," now greatly ruined. It appears to have had no direct connection with the ground story by stairs or otherwise. The rooms, which are also more or less ornamented with niches, are separated by walls much less massive than those below, and do not seem to have been arched as those are, but to have been roofed with thatch, as were most of the structures of the Incas. The central part of the front of the second story was not enclosed, although probably roofed, but formed an esplanade, 22 feet long and 10 broad, flanked by rooms opening on it.

Two niches, raised just enough to afford easy seats, appear in the wall at the back of the esplanade, whence may be commanded one of the finest and most extensive views in the world. The waves of the lake break at your very feet. To the right is the high and diversified peninsula of Copacabana; in the centre of the view, the island of Coati, consecrated to the Moon, as was Titicaca to the Sun; and to the right, the gleaming Illampu, its white mantle reflected in the waters that spread out like a sea in front. The design of this esplanade is too obvious to admit of doubt, and indicates that the builders were not deficient in taste, or insensible to the grand and beautiful in nature.

Tradition assigns the construction of this palace to the Inca, Tupac Yupanqui, who also built the Temple of the Moon and the Convent of the Virgins dedicated to her service in the island of Coati. He built it—so runs the legend—that during his visits he might always have before him the seat and shrine of the Inti-coya, the sister and wife of his parent, the Sun.

During our stay on the island of Coati we used our photographic tent as our sleeping-quarters; but the splendid moonlight was too attractive to allow us to withdraw to such close quarters, and we remained out far in the night, till the chilling breezes from the snowy Andes sent us, shivering, to our couches.

Three days were devoted to the interesting ruins on this island, and they were marked by one of the few accidents that befell me during my exploration. I had completed my surveys on the third day; and, mounted upon a fragment of wall still rising some ten feet from the ground, I was taking my last look of the island and the lake, when the ancient structure yielded to my weight, and I fell, bringing a mass of ruins with and upon me. I was so much cut and bruised, especially in my right thigh and leg, that I fainted. Recovering consciousness, I endeavored in vain to extricate myself; then, seeing some Indians busied preparing chuño not more than a hundred yards from where I lay, I called to them as loudly as I could; but they would not or could not hear me. All then depended on my own efforts. Removing stones with great difficulty, one by one, I at length succeeded in freeing myself, and scrambled to my feet in great pain. I was able to stand and could walk, though in exquisite suffering. The camp was at least a mile and a half away; but I started for it, and when, with great effort, I reached my companions, it was only to pass the night in intense distress.

The next morning we made sail for Titicaca; but, owing to head winds, the voyage was long and tedious, consuming the whole day. Leaving Professor Raimondi to sketch the Palace of the Inca, which I had explored on my former visit, I climbed the hill to the hacienda, and there passed a most uncomfortable night. The next day I again renewed my inquiries for the Temple of the Sun but with equally unsatisfactory result. No one seemed to possess the slightest knowledge in regard to it. Failing thus to obtain information, I resolved to begin my labors by examining personally a ruined building at the extreme point of the island, to which some of the natives referred me as the largest ruins they knew. Looking into Calancha's work, I found that, on the authority of Ramos, he actully placed the Temple of the Sun in that spot. With no guide but Calancha's not very definite statements, and the fact that the landing-place of the Incas was a bay called Kintipuca, I skirted the eastern flank of the island, following an ancient winding road for nearly a mile, where I found extensive remains, reputed to be those of the temple I was so anxious to find.

Garcilasso says of this structure that it was only comparable with that of Cuzco, although the remains, as we shall see, are far from justifying the remark of the Inca chronicler. He affirms, on the strength of reports current in his time, that it was plated over with gold, and that all the provinces of the empire made offerings to it every year, of gold, silver, and precious stones, in recognition of the great blessings which in this same island the Sun had conferred on the human race. He adds, on the authority of Blas Valera, that the precious metals which had accumulated in the temple, apart from all that was necessary for making the utensils used in its service, would have built another temple, of like dimensions, from its foundation upwards; but that all of this vast treasure was thrown into the lake when news came of the arrival of the Spaniards.

After thoroughly exploring the ruins of the sacred island, we took a moment when everything seemed to be favorable, and launched the *Natividad* for Puno; but we no sooner got from under the lee of the island than the wind shifted, drove us at right angles to our proper course, and soon increased to a gale, while waves like those of the ocean broke over our little craft. We were tossed and driven before the storm, heartily sick and sore, till the moon rose and the wind subsided somewhat. The next day was not more favorable. Again the gale sprung up, and we pitched and tossed on the waves, seeing storms break on the lake in all directions, while snow set in, with bitter cold. Puno we could not make; we were driven completely across the lake, and when night fell we found ourselves in a little bay just above that of Escoma. Here we thankfully anchored, and began to study our position.

Pentland's map dotted down some ruins in this vicinity, and, as the wind was still unfavorable, I resolved to remain for a day and examine them. I found some large stone chulpas of comparatively rude construction, one of them standing on a ledge overlooking the valley of Escoma. It is remarkable as containing two separate chambers, each with a separate entrance, one above the other, the upper one roughly vaulted. The chambers had been long since rifled by treasure-hunters, and at the time of my visit nothing remained in them except some crumbling skeletons and broken pottery. From the site of this monument, on the other side of the valley, may be seen one of the ancient *pucaras,* or hill forts, consisting of a series of five concentric terraces and stone-walls surrounding a conical eminence of great regularity of form.

The wind at last condescended to favor us, and in our frail vessel we embarked once again for Puno; but, after a blinding storm of snow and sleet of more than twenty-four hours' duration, and in which we could but just keep the *Natividad* afloat by assiduous bailing, a reaction came, and we had pleasant weather, but no wind. We lay becalmed for five days, during which we exhausted all our stores, and for two days were without food of any kind. I hope that that voyage of discovery may be of some use to the world, for I certainly shall undertake no more in an open boat, on a stormy lake, two miles above the level of the sea, with the thermometer perversely inclined to zero.

Our friends in Puno had become greatly concerned on account of our long absence; in fact, they had given us up; and when we were observed working across the bay, they hastened down to the little mole, and received us with a cordial welcome.

After our expedition I "assisted" at a grand "function," a patriotic Festival of Flags, I should call it, symbolical of a union of all the republics against monarchical intervention in America. I signed an *acto* on the occasion; and, what was more, carried an American flag, which the young ladies of the Colejio had improvised for the occasion, getting the number of the stripes wrong, and the azure field a world too little, but making up for all in the size and weight of the staff. But that was not the worst. We had to go through a mass and a benediction of the *banderas* in the chill cathedral, with many genuflections and much kneeling on the cold stones, besides enduring a speech from the prefect afterwards, with heads uncovered, in the frosty air. To the American flag had been given the post of honor, with those of Chili and Mexico on either hand. And as, by a remarkable and unprecedented coincidence, two young American engineers had arrived in Puno, so that the Yankee element mustered four strong, and in part recognition of the high honor given to the United States on the occasion of the

Balsa navigation on Lake Titicaca
From E. G. Squier, *Peru: Incidents of Travel and Exploration in the Land of the Incas.*

"function," Mr. T—— determined that the Glorious Fourth, then close at hand, should be celebrated by a dinner, and "with all the honors."

And it was so celebrated. The brass six-pounder of the place was fired, a gun for each State, at sunrise; the bells were pealed at noon; a mass was performed in the cathedral at two o'clock; the garrison was paraded as an escort to the American flag, which was carried in triumph through the streets; and, altogether, Puno held high holiday on the 4th of that July. Even the morose Aymarás seemed to relent, and a few of the more volatile Quichuas were seen to smile. It was the grand *fiesta* of St. Jonathan, and Chicha could be had gratis in the plaza.

The severe hurt received among the ruins of Coati, and a fever super-induced by exposure on the lake, kept me from taking an active part in an entertainment and ball given in our honor, which were shared in cordially, and with genuine sympathy, by all the people of Puno who had ever heard of the United States, constituting the most respectable, but by no means the most numerous, class. I regretted this, as it prevented me from witnessing an incident which, while it illustrates some things in Peru, is not to be taken as characteristic of the whole people.

It must be premised that in the smaller towns of Spanish America the populace invite themselves to witness, if not exactly to participate in, any social gathering that may take place. The style of buildings around a court entered by a single great door-way precludes much exclusiveness, even if it were attempted. The court of Mr. T——'s house was consequently filled, not alone while dinner was going on, but afterwards; and policy, as well as regard for custom, would have induced him to be extremely liberal of solids as well as liquids to the "outsiders." Most of these left when the invited and presumably more respectable guests departed; but a few inveterates, who had got a taste of genuine cognac, persisted in remaining, in hope of another drink. The great door was closed at midnight, and merely the wicket left open—a hint to leave which only two or three of the self-invited guests or spectators failed to understand. Finally, all had departed except a stalwart mestizo, who wore a long and ample cloak, and lingered and chatted, and chatted and lingered, until Mr. T——, imagining that all he wanted was brandy, gave him half a bottle, and, gently crowding him towards the wicket, said,

"Now, my friend, it is past two o'clock. I am very tired; and really you must go!"

"Open the door," responded the man with the cloak.

"Surely you can go out by the wicket. Why should I open the door?"

"To let me out."

This was too much, and our host, in a fit of irritation, gave the persistent intruder a push. Staggering, he dropped a lady's parlor-chair that he had concealed under his cloak, darted through the wicket, and disappeared in the darkness.

We were fully two hours in ascending the steeps, and reaching the high mountain-circled plain in which stands the straggling town of Curahuasi, a well-watered village buried among the trees and shrubbery. Although more than eight thousand feet above the sea-level, we noticed several fields of sugar-cane near the village. We had no letters to Curahuasi, and went straight to the post-house, a squalid hut indeed, with but two rooms, one of which was kitchen and dormitory, shared equally by the family, dogs, hens, and guinea-pigs. The other, or guests' room, had a rickety table as its complement of furniture, and its mud floor was piled with rubbish of all descriptions, dust-covered and repulsive, showing that no one had occupied it for a long time.

Our men cleared a space wide enough for our beds, and here we awaited the arrival of H———. That he had not reached the *posta* did not surprise us, as it was still early, and it was not impossible that he had found some better stopping-place in the village. So we rambled out inquiring of every body we met whether he had been seen, but heard nothing of him. Night came, and we recklessly burned our last candle, and kept alternate watch for him in the street. It was past midnight before we gave up our expectations of his arrival, and went to bed, counting on seeing him early in the morning. Towards daylight, but while it was still dark, we were startled by a loud pounding at the door. Supposing that it proceeded from our missing companion, I rose hastily, struck a light, and removed the brace against the door, when the strangest figure entered that I ever saw in my life. It was that of a man, tall and skeleton-like. His limbs were bare and deeply scarred, and his long, tangled hair was bleached by sun and weather. Beneath his left arm he carried a miscellaneous collection of sticks, bones, pieces of rope, and other rubbish, and in his right hand a long and gnarled stick. Altogether, with his deeply sunken eyes and parchment skin, he might have passed for one of Macbeth's witches, and was not a pleasant object for one to encounter when just awaking from sleep. I perceived at once that he was insane, but, as insane men have disagreeable freaks, I was not sorry to find that my friends were also awake and at my side. Our visitor, however, showed no violence, but commenced talking rapidly and incoherently.

We thought for a while that he intended to communicate something to us about H———, but we could extract nothing coherent from him. He seemed to comprehend that we were foreigners, and repeated frequently the word "*Ingleses*" (Englishmen). We gave him the fragments of our supper, and he left. Next day we ascertained that he was a Spaniard, who had been at one time largely engaged in mining in the vicinity, but had become completely demented some years ago in consequence of death in his family and financial troubles.

Morning brought no news of the missing artist. We climbed the hills back of the town in a vain effort to discover some approaching figure in the direction whence he was expected. At ten o'clock, after great difficulty, we succeeded in finding the syndic, and in despatching Indian couriers to Huay-narimac, where H———— had proposed to cross the river, with instructions to scour the banks as far as they could be followed, and to explore every hut on the way. Another courier was sent back to Bellavista, to ascertain if, failing in his attempt, he had returned thither.

It was useless for my friends to remain waiting in our wretched quarters, and it was arranged that they should leave at noon, and wait for me in Abancay, nine leagues distant. I passed the day anxiously, my apprehensions increasing hourly; and when some of the couriers returned at night without bringing any news of our missing friend, I felt deep alarm. The night, in the filthy little *posta*, was long and dreary, and my feelings were in no degree soothed by the circumstance that my servant, Ignacio, had improved the idle day in getting dead-drunk.

Morning came, and still no intelligence. By ten o'clock the Indians had all come in, having failed to obtain the slightest news or trace of the missing man, and the belief was reluctantly forced upon me that he had been swept down by the current of the river into the deep cañon through which it flows, and where it would be impossible to follow, even with boats. The syndic agreed with me that I could do no more; and, arranging with him to send a courier to me at Abancay, if he succeeded in obtaining any information as to the fate of our friend, I determined to start for that place, and enlist the power of the sub-prefect in making further investigations. I found myself almost powerless in Curahuasi, even with the aid of the syndic, and could excite no kind of interest among the stolid and sullen Indians, in the object of my solicitude.

At Abancay the sub-prefect took up the matter with zeal, and issued imperative orders to all the authorities within his jurisdiction to spare no efforts to ascertain the fate of the missing artist. We remained for several days in Abancay; but, hearing nothing relating to the lost man, we were compelled to pursue our journey over the mountains to the coast, in the full conviction that the worst had happened.

Some time after my return to the United States, I received the following letter from Professor Raimondi, who had been my fellow-voyager in the open-boat exploration of Lake Titicaca. It is dated from Cuzco:

"As regards our friend, Mr. H————, I have received the most extraordinary story. It seems that he did swim the Apurimac in safety, and, finding the water pleasant, under the great heat of the valley, he placed his clothes on a rock overhanging the stream, and amused himself by taking a longer bath. Unfortunately, a sudden gust of wind tumbled his bundle of clothing, containing also his shoes, into the river. His efforts to recover it were fruitless, and, after receiving several severe bruises among the rocks in the attempt, he was glad to get ashore again, naked as our father Adam. Here, on the arid, treeless bank, among sharp rocks, spiny cactuses, and thorny acacias, under a fervid sun, and swarmed all over by venomous sand-flies, he commenced his search for some inhabited place. His feet, however, soon became cut up by the sharp stones, and his person blistered by the heat. His only relief consisted in throwing water from time to time over his body, until night, with its dews, came on, and sheltered his nakedness. The heat in the close *quebrada* of the Apurimac, although intense by day, gives place to rather severe cold after sundown, and Mr. H———, to protect himself from this, was obliged to dig a bed in the warm sand, where he passed the night. The next day he resumed his painful journey, but night again came on without his being able to reach any human habitation. For three whole days he wandered about in this primitive condition, without nourishment of any kind. His feet were cut in pieces, and his body raw with the heat, bites of insects, and the scratches of shrubbery. Finally he reached a wretched hut, but his miseries did not end here.

"It should be premised that this *quebrada* is notorious for its insalubrity. Fever here reigns supreme, and has inspired the few Indians who live here with the greatest dread. Having little conception of things not material, they have come to give even to diseases a physical form, and the fever is embodied in a human figure. Consequently, when Mr. H——— approached the hut, its occupants imagined that the dreaded fever had made its palpable appearance. Some of them fled in terror; but others, more valiant, caught up stones wherewith to attack and drive off the horrible apparition, so that he had a narrow escape with his life. After much delay and trouble, the fears of the Indians were allayed, and the sufferer was admitted to such shelter and food as the wretched hut could afford. Here he was subsequently found by the men in search of him, taken to Curahuasi, and thence to Abancay, where he was hospitably treated. It was, however, some months before he became able to move about. I venture the prediction that he will never again flinch from the imaginary dangers of the swinging bridges of Peru."

As I have said, I never saw H——— after our parting at the Hacienda Bellavista; but many months after my return to the United States, he forwarded to me from Lima many drawings and sketches which he had made after our separation.

We recruited a week at Ayacucho before starting over the Despoblado intervening between this ancient and historical town and the coast—a region in no place less than fourteen thousand, and generally not less than eighteen thousand, feet above the sea. The journey is a long, tedious, and exhaustive one, and for several days after leaving Ayacucho lies over the broad, lofty mountain billow, distinguished from the Andes proper by the name of the Cordillera de la Costa. There are neither towns nor refuges, except caverns, in this cold, arid, desolate region—no wood, and, for long distances, neither grass nor water. To be overtaken here by storms, or to have your animals succumb to fatigue or the dreaded *soroche,* involves, as its least consequence, great suffering, and often loss of life, as the thousands of skeletons and desiccated bodies of men and animals scattered over the savage *punas* and among the lofty passes of the mountains too plainly suggest to the adventurous traveller.

For five days we struggled over the bleak hills and barren plains, through a savage scenery which only the pencil of Doré could depict, with no shelter except such as our little photographic tent afforded, and without food, except such as we carried with us, or was afforded by the flesh of a few biscachas, vicuñas, and huanacos, the only animals to be found here. The rainy season was commencing, and the bitter winds howled in our ears, and drove the sand, like needles, into our tumid faces, while the snow flurried around the high, rugged peaks that lifted their splintered crests on every hand.

On the sixth day after leaving Ayacucho, our arriero halted us on the brow of a tremendous ravine, up the walls of which we had scrambled for two weary hours, with imminent peril to life and limb. It was only two o'clock; and although the animals drooped their heads and breathed heavily—for we were nearly sixteen thousand feet above the sea—I felt impatient at the halt, especially as I saw that he had commenced unloading the mules with the evident intent of going into camp.

"Why," I asked, "are we stopping at this hour?"

The artist and the Indians
From E. G. Squier, *Peru: Incidents of Travel and Exploration in the Land of the Incas.*

He did not answer in words, but waved his hand in the direction of the vast, open, but most dreary and desolate broken plain, that seemed to spread out interminably before us. A plain without a blade of grass or sign of life, bare, bleak, and looking as if furrowed by the searching winds that had swept out every grain of sand from between the jagged edges of the rocks that projected, like decaying fangs, above its surface. "But we have got to cross it—why not now?"

"*No hay agua—nada!*" (There is no water—nothing).

We succeeded, however, in carrying our point. Our arriero, with unconcealed disgust and some muttered words in Quichua, which we did not understand, but which were significant enough, repacked the animals and started them off, at a rapid pace, over the rough and repulsive *puna*.

How he kept our already weary animals at the tremendous pace across the *puna* that he did, I do not know. I only know that we had a brief race on the edge of the plain after a wounded vicuña, and that we halted only once or twice to bag a stray biscacha. Yet, long before dark, we could barely detect our baggage-animals, looking like ants in the distance. C——— had gone on with them. As it grew darker we changed our saddles, and took a bearing upon our friends before they were out of sight.

It was well that we did so; for a minute afterward they had disappeared behind a swell in the land. I had been riding "El Nevado" all the day, leaving my mule to run free, while D——— had left "Napoleon" to do the same—the free animals running with their halters fastened to our cruppers. But as this was a rather unnecessary precaution, and, when moving rapidly, an obstruction, we packed the slaughtered vicuña and biscachas on the liberated animals, and cast them loose, and then started at a round pace to overhaul our train. "El Nevado" and his companion fell a little behind, but not to such a distance as to alarm us, especially as we soon struck the trail. Sometimes we lost sight of our followers behind some inequality of the ground, but always discovered them pacing after us when we ascended the swells of the land.

It was getting dark, and we could with difficulty make out the track, at best but lightly marked in the flinty soil. Our chief guides were the white skeletons of animals that had succumbed, and had been left by the side of the path as prey for the condors.

We did not doubt that "El Nevado" would follow us, especially as his foster-brother was ahead. As soon as it became absolutely dark, we slackened our pace, and peered ahead to discover our companions, and behind to discern our horses, but equally without result. All trace of our road disappeared. We dismounted, and literally felt our way. I resorted to the Indian expedient of putting my ear to the ground, to detect the step of man or animal, but in vain. There was but one thing left to do; so I fired a round from my rifle. A second or so afterwards a faint response, so faint that we thought it an exhausted echo, seemed to rise from some place deep down to our left.

I fired another round, and we listened intently. A moment more, and a faint report struggled up, as from the bottom of a well.

We found that our arriero had plunged into a ravine that might be called an abyss, because there was a little water there, a few tufts of coarse ichu grass, and, what was of no little importance, some heaps of vicuña dung, which answered for fuel. D——— and myself, after a sumptuous supper of charqui and coffee, scrambled up to the plain again in a vain search for our missing animals. We went to bed (if stretching one's self on the bare ground may be called going to bed) under hopeful assurance from our arriero that the *bestias* would find us before morning.

Morning came, raw and damp, and the animals had not made their appearance. While breakfast was preparing, D——— and myself climbed the steep sides of the ravine again, only wondering how we ever got up or down in the dark.

We mounted the rocks and ranged our glasses around the horizon, in vain effort to discover the animals. Scrambling down again, we instructed the train to push ahead, unburdened ourselves of our *alforjas* and water-proof over-garments, retaining only our pistols: in short, put ourselves in light-marching order, and, telling our friends that we would overtake them before night, started off again to scour the plain in search of "El Nevado" and his errant companion.

We rode for two hours, back over the dreary plain, looking for the trail of our missing animals, and were about giving them up, when we came suddenly upon their tracks. It was past noon, but to give up now, on the very threshold of success, was not to be thought of a second time. Up, up for half a mile, where foot of man or horse had perhaps never gone before, to the rough crest of a rocky peak that seemed to dominate the forest of similar eminences around it, and which broke off in an absolute precipice on the other side.

We followed a narrow, lightly worn path, the merest trace in the steep declivities of the barren hills, winding out and in, now around the heads of lateral ravines, and then down into the dry, stony beds of torrents. Suddenly, on turning a sharp bend, some object started from the path in front, and began with deer-like fleetness to ascend the mountain. It only needed a second glance to perceive that the object was an Indian dressed in vicuña skins, and with a head-dress of flossy alpaca, which drooped behind him in the form of the conventional fool's cap. We shouted for him to stop, but he paid no attention to our command, until D——— threw up the loose dirt a few yards in advance of him with a bullet from his revolver. Then he came down, meekly enough, holding his alpaca cap in both trembling hands.

We reassured him as well as we could, and were delighted that he knew a few words of Spanish, in virtue of which we made out that the stray animals were just around a projecting ledge in another *barranca*. He led the way, and, after a tough scramble, we came in sight of a poor hut of stones sunk in the earth, with the exception of its conical roof of ichu grass, and hardly distinguishable from the hard and barren soil. On the instant "Napoleon" set up a shrill, interrogative neigh, which was responded to by an affirmative winnow from "El Nevado," safely tethered behind the Indian hut, whose occupants, an unkempt woman with two equally unkempt children, suddenly projected their heads, like rabbits, from a low orifice at the base of the hut, and as suddenly withdrew them.

The Indian, who was the shepherd of some llama and alpaca flocks that found a scanty support in a neighboring valley, had encountered the animals that morning, struggling on the blind path to his hut, and had tethered them there, not knowing what else to do with them. We found that his wages were eight dollars a year, and his means of support such llamas and alpacas as might die, and a little quinoa that he was able to cultivate in a distant *quebrada*. The vicuña and biscachas that he had found still strapped on the backs of our mules were a bountiful and unexpected addition to his scanty stores; and I have no doubt he had already made sacrifice of a quid of coca to the Indian god corresponding to the genius of Good Fortune. We rewarded our new acquaintance as we were able, and he undertook to guide us back to the trail we had left, a good league and a half distant.

We recovered our horses, but we nearly lost our lives. It was late in the afternoon when we struck out again on the horrible waste which we had traversed twice before. The sky was sullen and threatening, and every portent was of cold and storm. The prospect was not provocative of conversation; and we urged our animals, which seemed to comprehend the situation, at the top of their powers over the stony *puna*. Directly rain began to fall, changing rapidly to sleet, which fell in blinding sheets, and froze on our garments. Every indication of the trail soon disappeared, and an icy waste spread around us as far as we could see. To stand still was to freeze; to go on was to wander off in an unknown desert.

We gave ourselves up to the guidance of our horses, "Napoleon" heroically leading the way. On, on we trudged, the icy crust crackling under our tread, until it became pitch-dark, when we discovered, by the zigzagging course and downward plunge of our animals, that we were descending rapidly. They ultimately stopped, and we supposed that we had reached the place of our previous night's bivouac. But by the light of a twisted roll of paper, ignited by the solitary match that had escaped being wetted in D——'s pocket, we found that we were in a ravine full of great rocks, and that the animals were at a dead fault as to how to get on farther. They huddled close to us, and we stood leaning on their rimy necks all that long and dreary night—oh, how long and dreary!—until the sun struggled through the clouds, surcharged with snow, and thawed our stiff, unyielding garments. It was nearly noon before we could find the trail, which we followed until late in the afternoon, when we were met by an Indian, carrying charqui and bread, one of several messengers whom C——— had sent back from his camp under the friendly rock which our arriero described with grim irony as the "Posada de San Antonio." We found C——— in great distress on account of our absence. He had kept awake all night, and had repeatedly fired his gun to guide us to camp.

We were now upon the banks of a small rivulet, the source of the river Pisco, and from a high point, the highest in the Western Cordilleras, caught our first view of the Pacific. The descent was now very rapid, and in a few hours we were among some fine alfalfa estates. At 7 P.M. we reached the estate of La Quinya, where we were hospitably permitted to sleep in the corridor.

The next day, at an early hour, we arrived in Pisco, after experiencing an earthquake in the morning, which lasted a few seconds, and to which I have already referred. We were thirty days in making the journey from Cuzco to Pisco, which includes five days' stoppage at Ayacucho. At Pisco we met the welcome letters and papers from home.

After two years, spent in exploring the country, during which we crossed and recrossed the Cordillera and the Andes, from the Pacific to the Amazonian rivers, sleeping in rude Indian huts or on bleak *punas,* in the open air, in hot valleys, or among eternal snows, gathering with eager zeal all classes of facts relating to the country, its people, its present and its past, I found myself surrounded with my trophies of travel, on the deck of a steamer in the harbor of Callao, homeward-bound, brown in color and firm in muscle.

FIVE

Désiré Charnay 1858-1882

The Two Discoverers of Yaxchilán

[The "love episode" of Arthur Morelet in Guatemala was presented earlier. Another French archaeological explorer of the nineteenth century who possessed a roving eye for more than antiquities was Désiré Charnay, whose *Ancient Cities of the New World* in more than one passage dwells on the beauty and charms of the young women he encountered during his extensive travels in Mexico and Central America. Charnay was particularly smitten with the Indian girls of Yucatán, and he was never too occupied with his accounts of Maya ruins and the countryside to neglect an appreciative remark on the physical attractions of some maiden that caught his eye. The following anecdote, for example, is inserted in a chapter on Chichén Itzá, its art, architecture, and Toltec connections (which, incidentally, he was one of the first to recognize).]

Our excursions in these impenetrable woods, our ascents and descents of the pyramid, the arduous work attending the taking of squeezes, made our life very harassing; it could have been more easily borne had we been able to sleep, but the scorching days were succeeded by icy-cold nights, which kept us awake, so that we rose in the morning more unrefreshed and more tired than when we turned in for the night.

Some compensation we had in our walks round the pyramid, beguiling the time we could not sleep with a cigar, contemplating the fine starry nights and sometimes the lunar rainbows so rarely seen; or we watched the broad shadow of the pyramid cast athwart the white haze shrouding the plain,

The selections from Charnay are, in the order quoted below, from Désiré Charnay, *The Ancient Cities of the New World* (New York: Harper & Bros., 1888), pp. 346–48, 372–74, 424–36.

fringed by an immense brilliant corona, which seemed to float in space. Never had I gazed on anything so curious and fantastic as this terrestrial halo; and if the ancient worshippers of Cukulcan ever witnessed the phenomenon, they must have deemed it little short of miraculous.

We were still without a cook; for Julian was so atrociously bad that I kept him at the squeezes, taking the cooking ourselves in turn, which wasted much valuable time. One evening, after everybody had gone to rest, I was sitting alone writing my impressions, my head full of the ruins and the people who inhabited them. I suddenly looked up, to see standing before me a lovely maiden more like an apparition than a mortal being. Was this the shade of a Maya princess who had returned to the scenes of her former life, conjured up by my imagination? Meanwhile the beauteous figure stood looking and smiling at me. I was amazed, speechless, hardly daring to break the spell, when a third figure stood out from the dark entrance, in whom I recognised the commandant of Pisté.

"You are surprised at our visit," he said.

"Rather, especially at this hour, and in such a night."

Désiré Charnay
From Désiré Charnay, *Ancient Cities of the New World.*

"Time is of no account when you wish to serve a friend; I heard that you required a cook, I brought you mine, that's all."

"A cook!" I ejaculated to myself. What a fall! my Indian princess a cook! I looked at her again, and I could not believe so much youth and beauty were put to such menial occupation. I wondered at the commandant's self-abnegation. I was somewhat embarrassed, nevertheless, as to where I should put her. I called up Julian to prepare a bed for her, but as he was not easily roused, I had time to reflect that with a hundred men about me, El Castillo was no fitting place for a young girl. I was profuse in my acknowledgments to the commandant, observing that as nothing was ready, it would perhaps be better to put off her coming for a day or two, apologising for the trouble they had taken in coming through the woods and having to climb the pyramid in such a pitch-dark night. He knew what I meant. I slipped a coin in the girl's hand, as she held a bottle towards me. "Drink," said the officer; "it is Josepha's present to you." I did so, while Josepha merely put her lips to

Chichanchob (Casa Colorada, Red House) Chichén Itzá
From Désiré Charnay, *Ancient Cities of the New World.*

the bottle. We shook hands, and my two visitors disappeared in the night. The draught was *Staventum*, a strong spirit,* which made me light-headed, and in a fit of somnambulism I wandered about, spouting poetry at the top of my voice, on the very edge of the pyramid, whence I was fortunately removed, without any further result than to awake the next day with a splitting headache. Our long-expected cook arrived at last, and she was so old, and such a fright, that it relieved me of all fear on her account.

[Later, en route to the ruins of Kabah and Uxmal, Charnay reached the hacienda of Uayalceh, one of the vast plantations with a pretentious house surrounded by cloisters that reflected the enormous wealth of henequen planters of the time. In a cool, open cloister of this impressive establishment, he was served breakfast, "washed down with a bottle of Spanish wine and a delicious cup of coffee," and then resumed his march, reaching Sacalun late in the afternoon, where he stopped to rest the hot, panting mules.]

It was formerly a place of some importance; but its chief attraction lies in its cenoté, 65 feet deep. Steps with a balustrade lead to the surface of the water, while the great stalactites which hang down from the vault and almost meet the stalagmites rising from the ground, form an imposing and weird scene. Yet it was here that I experienced the most charming adventure that I met in the whole course of my travels; and, although two-and-twenty years have elapsed, the dear, sweet remembrance of that day is as fresh as ever.

I was on my way to Uxmal, when through some egregious stupidity of the driver I was obliged to put up here for the night. There was of course no inn, and I found a bed at a poor widow's, who took in casual travellers like myself. The accommodation was of the scantiest: a hammock, a small table, a chair or two, was all the furniture of a room which was at the same time the kitchen, the parlour, and the sleeping chamber. The widow apologised for having nothing better to offer, but it was easy to guess from her noble manners and appearance, that she had known better days. I watched my dinner being prepared; the table neatly laid, everything so scrupulously clean, that I could have found it in my heart to be indulgent had the cooking been execrable, but all was as good and nice as would have satisfied the most fastidious palate. Two lovely maidens helped their mother and served at table; my eyes sought the younger, whose transparent skin, pearly teeth, hair of raven wing's blackness, magnificent, languid eyes, fairy-like form moving over the ground with an indescribable undulating movement, moved me body and soul every time she gazed in my direction. Her look of innocence and simplicity added to the charm which seemed to emanate from her

* Editor's note: Charnay here refers to Xtabentun, a sticky sweet liqueur still made in Yucatán.

whole person, accepting with child-like pleasure my open admiration, while a soft blush spread over her countenance as she met my enraptured gaze. Their story was this:

The hacienda had been burnt down, her husband massacred, and she had been obliged to fly with her little ones to escape a worse fate, to find on their return the place a heap of ruins. She told of their lone, joyless life, of a still darker future, and tears coursed down her cheeks furrowed by care and privations rather than age.

I was young, impulsive, I wished I were rich. Why should I not . . . In a moment, ancient monuments, the world, my possible career, all was forgotten in face of these tearful countenances and their undeserved misfortune. Why not accept the love, the happiness, which were offered to me? And how delightful to relieve their misery, to feel that a whole family would be made happy and comfortable by me and through me! All this and a great deal more I expressed, and was amply repaid by the angelic smile of the young girl, and the mother's grateful acknowledgments. Night, however, brought calm to my disturbed imagination, and I resolved on a speedy flight, as the only means of escape from a too fascinating but dangerous position. The next day I announced my departure, and I never saw her again. And now, after so many years, I was back in the same place again. I sought the house, to find that my youthful love-dream was no longer here, but had gone to live somewhere in a large city. I came away sad at heart, disappointed; yet better so. In two-and-twenty years, Time, in all probability, had not spared her, more than he had me.

[Like Morelet, Charnay traveled southward to Campeche and the Usumacinta, where he had heard of the discovery, twelve years before, of an as yet scientifically unreported ruined city. At Tenosique he procured men, mules, and horses, the last in such "wretched condition" on their return from a long trip in the Petén of northern Guatemala that they required a week of rest before they could undertake another arduous journey into the jungle.]

To reach the ruins, a space of some five leagues of forest will have to be cleared on the right side of the river, which will take us opposite the ruins, but a canoe must likewise be made to ferry us across. For this purpose I despatch some men in advance, while we fill up the weary time of waiting by trying to catch some fish. Curiously enough, a number of sea-fish is found here in the Usumacinta, 100 miles from its mouth; and when swollen by rain it brings from distant Guatemala large quantities of lobsters, together with pumice stones.

We set out on the 15th of March, 1882, and are soon in a tangle of wood and beset with obstacles of every kind; while the mules get unloaded, go astray, tarry in green pastures, and are altogether very troublesome.

We have left behind us the low marshy level, and are nearing the Cordillera, bearing to the south-east on the Peten road. The forest seems absolutely interminable with magnificent cedar and palm-trees, over 100 feet high, the trunks of which almost disappear under flowering lianas, while the broad-leaved Palmyra palms commingle with Brazil wood, and form boundless domes of verdure. It would be pleasant enough could one get used to being eaten up by mosquitoes and garrapatas. The stations where we encamp, although not possessed even of a hut, are carefully marked in the maps for the benefit of muleteers; they are always on rising ground, in the vicinity of water and ramon for the animals, their staple food on the march. Our day's journey has told already on them; the men disperse to cut down ramon. Julian is putting up our camp-beds, while cook is busy with our supper, which usually consists of a kind of Scotch broth, made of dried meat, rice, and black beans, a round of biscuit, and a cup of coffee, except on days when our larder has been replenished on the way by a wild duck, a peccari, and sometimes a monkey!

In the evening the men grouped round the fire, indulge in a social weed, while recounting adventures more or less authentic, then we all retire behind our mosquito curtains and rest our weary limbs on soft green leaves. Our slumbers are often interrupted by the roar of the wild beast, the plaintive cries of nocturnal birds, and howling monkeys. We rise before daybreak, and what with breakfast, saddling and loading our animals, the sun is high on the horizon before we can continue our journey. No incident breaks the wearisome monotony of our progress, but towards noon I notice to our right traces of buildings, vast esplanades, the stone edges of which are still intact, whilst the guide says that towards the valley of S. Pedro, to our left, are entire monuments still standing—the town of Izancanac, perhaps. Indeed, the whole country is covered with ruins, to study which a lifetime were not too long.

The region is full of the memory of the conqueror. He must have travelled this very road on his march to Honduras. It was in these woods that, under pretext of a conspiracy, he caused Guatemozin to be executed. The young Aztec prince displayed the intrepid spirit of his better days; he reproached Cortez for his want of faith, protesting the while his innocence. A tardy monument has just been raised to the upholder of Indian independence in that Tenochtitlan which he defended as long as there was stone upon stone, whilst not even a bust marks the presence of his murderer.

The region we now traverse, covered with immense forests, was cultivated and inhabited before the Conquest; great cities rose in this trackless labyrinth, the vestiges of which have been noticed by us, whilst frequent mention of them is found in various authors. On this route Cortez saw "a great city," with strong buildings of stone on the summits of mounds, just as at the present day. . . .

Meanwhile our journey becomes more and more harassing; we have been obliged to leave one of the horses and a mule to the jaguars, and not to overload the others, Lucian and I ride in turn the only remaining horse. We cross the Arroyo Yalchilan* on the Guatemala border, not far from Locen, and leaving the Peten road, we steer to the south-east-south, on the path cleared by our men, and encamp on the bank of the running stream in which we lave our dust-travelled limbs.

The next day we climb the range of hills which divide us from the upper Usumacinta, and which are almost impassable for loaded animals. The sharp stones destroy the leather of our boots, and cut the mules' feet to pieces, while we are in danger of being lost down the ravines and precipices. The better to ease the mules' backs, we leave here such provisions as we shall not require, for game will not be wanting on our way, and everything will be safe until we return. A scaffolding supported on poles fixed to the ground is made, on which wine, biscuit, salt meat, and beans are deposited.

Here we encamp for the night—the sixth since we left Tenosiqué—and the next day we begin the ascent of Mirador and Aguila; the latter, although not more than 1,300 to 1,400 feet in height, is exceedingly steep and arduous. We meet an old montero, Don P. Mora, who left his native village three months since, and is living in the Sierra with two Indians, whose business is to mark mahogany trees ready for the market. Don Pépé had built himself a hut on the Chotal river; he shoots whatever comes within the range of his

* It is urged that Yalchilan should be written either Xalchilan or Jalchilan, *x* and *j* being convertible letters having a strong aspirate; but as doctors are not agreed, the name is suffered to stand as in the text.

Don Pepe Mora, Chotal River, Chiapas, Mexico
From Désiré Charnay, *Ancient Cities of the New World.*

muzzle, for the support of himself and his companions. The poor old fellow is reduced to a deplorable state by marsh fever; he volunteers some valuable hints, which I repay with a glass of wine and a few cigars.

Some hours more and we reach the broad level, and set up our tents on the Chotal, a tributary of the Usumacinta. The forest round is teeming with life; parrots and aras fill the air with their shrill cries, yellow-crested hoccos* move silently among the higher branches, while howling monkeys peer inquisitively at us, and herds of wild boars rush madly past us. We are in the country of the Lacandones; here and there traces of cultivation are still visible, and huts which have been abandoned on the approach of timber merchants, plainly show that they were inhabited not long ago. We raise our "camp," *en route* for the Yalchilan Pass, and arrive in the evening on the right bank of the Usumacinta.

Paso Yalchilan is a geographical point, meaning any given place on the right bank of the Usumacinta, dividing Mexico from Guatemala. We reached it so late that we had barely time to unload our animals and get them some fodder before the night set in. But now I discovered that the mule carrying the material for our squeezes had lagged behind; but it was too dark, the men declared, to go hunting for him in the insecure forest, next morning would be time enough. In the night we were rather startled by cries of "Al tigre! al tigre!" (the tiger). It turned out to be only a jaguar, but it served

* The Hocco, or Powise (*Crox alector*), is a bird nearly the size of a turkey, and much prized for its delicate flesh.—TRANSL.

Encampment at Paso Yaxchilán, Chiapas, Mexico
From Désiré Charnay, *Ancient Cities of the New World.*

to remind us to keep a fire burning. The next day some of the men set to work at our cabins, whilst others went in quest of the wretched mule, which they found almost dead with fatigue and want of food. They also brought to the general larder a nice young boar, which was received with joyful shouts, immediately cut up, roasted, and eaten at our midday meal down to the last morsel.

Our shots brought the canoeros I had sent in advance to construct a canoe. My inquiries as to the work done were met with the unsatisfactory answer that nothing was finished; they had been unlucky in the choice of timber, etc. I immediately set out to see how it was, and to my great annoyance I found that hardly any progress had been made. In fact, the men had taken it mighty easy, had lived like lords on the supplies I had given them, varying their fare with fish from the river and game from the forest; causing me a delay which might ruin my expedition, for our supplies would not last out if this was the way they went to work. I was returning with head downcast, looking at the broad river, here over 500 feet across, pondering on the distance which divided me from the goal of my expedition, when I spied ahead of us a boat manned by a Lacandon, who on perceiving us veered quickly round. Fortunately one of our men spoke Maya; he hailed the man, promising him a great reward if he would steer towards us. He came to our encampment, and when I heard that he was a chief, I showed him the presents I had brought, telling him they would be his and any of his people's he should bring to me. We learnt that he had two more canoes he was willing to let us have for a consideration, and I congratulated myself on being able to attain my end so easily.

Usumacinta River at Paso Yaxchilán
From Désiré Charnay, *Ancient Cities of the New World.*

We were now waiting with some impatience for the cayucoes, when a large canoe manned by three white men loomed in the distance; a horrible suspicion flashed across my mind, that they were men belonging to another expedition, who had forestalled me. The canoe came near, and I learnt that they had been on a foray expedition among the Lacandones, but had been unable to obtain anything except a few tomatoes, and were now returning to the ruins to join their master, Don Alvaredo, and that their provisions were running very short.

"Have you another canoe?" I inquired.

"Yes, much larger than this."

"Look here, my good fellows, take my card to your master with my compliments, together with half a wild pig, salt meat, rice, biscuits, and in return ask him to lend me his large canoe, which these men I send with you will bring."

The strangers rowed away, and I began to prepare for the next day's expedition, in which Lucian and six men would accompany me, leaving the rest behind to take care of our heavy luggage under the superintendence of Julian. But in the morning early I had a severe attack of malaria, which

Structure 33, Yaxchilán
From Désiré Charnay, *Ancient Cities of the New World.*

threatened at one time to delay our journey. A few hours' rest, however, and a good dose of quinine, restored me sufficiently to allow my setting out for the long-sought, long wished-for ruins, which we reached in three hours, landing near an enormous pile of stones—a kind of votive pillar—rising on the left bank of the river, which has withstood the buffeting of the waters for several centuries. This stone mound was described to me at Tenosiqué, as having formed part of an old bridge which spanned the river at this point. But what we know of the natives' method of building makes this supposition impossible, for the river is too broad, and on the other hand, had a bridge formerly stood here, remains would be found either on the opposite side or in the bed of the river. There is very little doubt that for all the purposes of daily life, the inhabitants of this city used "canoas" just as they do now.

We had made but a short way among the ruins lying in every direction, when we were met by Don Alvaredo, whose fair looks and elastic step showed him to be an Englishman. We shook hands; he knew my name, he told me his: Alfred Maudslay, Esq., from London; and as my looks betrayed the inward annoyance I felt:

"It's all right," he said; "there is no reason why you should look so distressed. My having had the start of you was a mere chance, as it would have been mere chance had it been the other way. You need have no fear on my account, for I am only an amateur, travelling for pleasure. With you the case of course is different. But I do not intend to publish anything. Come, I have had a place got ready; and as for the ruins I make them over to you. You can name the town, claim to have discovered it, in fact do what you please. I shall not interfere with you in any way, and you may even dispense with mentioning my name if you so please."

I was deeply touched with his kind manner, and I am only too charmed to share with him the glory of having explored this city. We lived and worked together like two brothers, and we parted the best friends in the world.

SIX

Alfred P. Maudslay 1882

In the Village of the Savage Dogs

[Sir Alfred Percival Maudslay, the British archaeologist who so generously shared with Charnay the honor of exploring Menché, now called Yaxchilán, was born in 1850 and died in 1931. Immediately after graduation, with "a great desire to see a tropical forest," he went to the West Indies, Panama, and Guatemala. Later he visited Iceland, and served five years as a colonial administrator in Fiji, the latter assignment resulting in a book called *Life in the Pacific Fifty Years Ago.*

[Maudslay's first trip to Central America was the first of seven. None of his professional writings, and very few of the pages of his one popular book, written with his wife, mention the terrific hardships of travel in those days. As Alfred M. Tozzer noted in an obituary of Maudslay, the search for chicle had not yet begun in the Guatemalan lowlands, scene of so many of Maudslay's travels; hence there were few trails through the bush, and these very poor. The photographic record of his investigations is masterful, especially when we consider the unwieldy, bulky equipment he had to carry with him and the lack of any cooling agencies for water and of ready-mixed developing chemicals that are standard today in any darkroom. "Maudslay's indefatigable labors, covering many years in an adverse environment," wrote Sylvanus G. Morley in 1920, "easily constitute the most important contribution to Maya archaeology."

[Maudslay was another of the early travelers who met and described the primitive Lacandón Indians of Chiapas. In March, 1882, he started, in company with the manager of a mahogany cutting company, on an expedition

The quotation from Maudslay is from A. C. and A. P. Maudslay, *A Glimpse at Guatemala* (London: John Murray, 1899), pp. 236–38.

down the Río de la Pasión to explore the ruins of Yaxchilán—or, as he and some others called them, Menché—which had been described for the first time by a European only the year before. At the Paso Real, Maudslay was fortunate to obtain as guide one of the canoemen who had accompanied the previous expedition.]

Three days later I parted company with Mr. Schulte near the mouth of the Rio Lacandon, where he was about to establish a new "Monteria." The banks of the river here begin to lose their monotonous appearance, and for the first time since leaving the Paso Real we caught sight of some hills in the distance. At midday we entered a gorge about a league in length, where the river flows between high rocky and wooded banks and in some places the stream narrowed to a width of forty feet. The current was not very swift, but the surface of the water moved in great oily-looking swirls which seemed to indicate a great depth. Below the narrows the river widens very considerably and the current becomes much more rapid, and great care had to be taken in guiding the canoes so as to avoid the numerous rocks and snags. This day we travelled about thirty miles below the Boca del Cerro and then camped for the night. Several times during the day we had seen traces of the Lacandones, "Jicaques" or "Caribes" as my men called them (the untamed Indians who inhabit the forests between Chiapas and Peten), and while stopping to examine one of their canoes, which we found hauled up on a sand-spit, its owner, accompanied by a woman and child, came out of the forest to meet us. The man was an uncouth-looking fellow, with sturdy limbs, long black hair, very strongly-marked features, prominent nose, thick lips, and complexion about the tint of that of my half-caste canoemen. He was clothed in a single long brown garment of roughly-woven material, which looked like sacking, splashed over with blots of some red dye. The man showed no signs of fear and readily entered into conversation with one of my men who spoke the Maya language; but the woman kept at a distance, and I could not get a good look at her.

Later in the day we landed to visit a "caribal," or Indian village, which my guide told me stood somewhere near the river-bank. There was no trace of it, however, near the river, so we followed a narrow path into the forest marked by two jaguars' skulls stuck on poles, and here and there by some sticks laid across the track, over which the Indians had probably dragged their small canoes. About two miles distant from the river we found three houses standing in a clearing near the bank of a small stream. A woman came out to meet us, and received us most courteously, asking us to rest in a small shed. Her dress was a single sack-like garment similar to that worn by the man whom we had met earlier in the day; her straight black hair fell loose over her shoulders, and round her neck hung strings of brown seeds interspersed with beads and silver coins, dollars and half-dollars, which she said were obtained in Tabasco. Two other women came out of their houses to greet us, and they told us that all the men were away hunting for wild cacao in the forest and would not return for five days. The walls of the houses were very low, but in other respects they resembled the ordinary ranchos of the civilized Indians. I asked if I might look into one of them, but my mozos strongly advised me not to make the attempt, as the numerous howling dogs shut up inside were very savage, and were sure to attack me.

The clearing round the houses was planted with maize, plaintains, chillies, tobacco, gourds, tomatoes, calabash-trees, and cotton. We exchanged a little salt for some plaintains, yams, and tomatoes without any haggling, and the women agreed to make me some totoposte which I was to send for in a few days, and one of them, pointing to a silver dollar on her necklace, said that they wanted a coin like that in payment. I was surprised

A. P. Maudslay and Maya stela, Copán

From A. P. Maudslay, *Biologia Centrali-Americana: Archaeology*, vol. i.

to find the women so pleasant-mannered and free from the dull shyness which characterizes the civilized Indians. On my return up the river some days later I again visited this "caribal," and was received with equal courtesy by the men, who had then returned from the forest, to whom I repeated my request to see the inside of one of their houses; however, a very rapid glance was sufficient to satisfy my curiosity, for as soon as I showed myself at the half-open door seven or eight dogs tied to the wall-posts nearly brought down the house in their efforts to get at me, and two of them were with difficulty prevented by the women from breaking the cords which held them. Some especial significance must attach to the wearing of the brown-seed necklaces, for no offers which I could make would induce either man or women to part with one of them. I was much impressed by the striking likeness which the features of the elder man, who appeared to be the leader of the village, bore to those carved in stone at Palenque and Menché. The extremely sloping forehead was not quite so noticeable in the younger men, and it may be that the custom of binding back the forehead in infancy, which undoubtedly obtained amongst the ancients, is being now abandoned. These people still use bows and stone-tipped arrows, which they carry with them wrapped in a sheet of bark.

To return to my journey to Menché. After visiting the "caribal" we continued our course down-stream and camped for the night on the right

Structure 30, Yaxchilán

Photograph by Teobert Maler, 1898. From *Researches in the Central Portion of the Usumatsintla Valley,* 1901. Copyright 1901 by Peabody Museum of American Archaeology and Ethnology, Harvard University. Courtesy of Peabody Museum of Harvard University.

bank of the river; the next morning an hour's paddle with the very rapid current brought us in sight of a mound of stones piled up on the left bank of the river, which we had been told marked the site of the ruins. On the 18th March, the day of my arrival, the water in the river was so low that the mound stood high and dry; but from the colour and marks on the stones it appears as though the average height of the water were two or three feet from the top of the mound. We soon scrambled up the rough river-bank, and began to cut our way through the undergrowth in search of the ancient buildings, which we found to be raised on a succession of terraces to a height of over 250 feet with slopes faced with well-laid masonry or formed into flights of steps. . . .

The house or temple which I chose for a dwelling-place . . . is a long narrow structure, measuring on the outside 73 feet long by 17 feet broad. There are three doorways giving access to the single chamber, which is divided up into a number of recesses by interior buttress-walls. In the middle recess we found a cross-legged figure of heroic size, reminding me of the seated figure on the great Turtle of Quirigua; the head with its head-dress of grotesque masks and feather-work was broken off and lying beside it. There appears to have been some sort of canopy of ornamental plaster-work above the recess, which had fallen down and lay in a confused heap of dust and fragments around the figure. When I first entered the house there must have been over a hundred pieces of rough pottery . . . strewn on the floor and clustered around the stone figure. Many of these pots contained half-burnt copal, and from the positions in which we found them it is evident that they must have been placed in the house within recent years, probably by the Lacandones, who still, I am told, hold the place in reverence. In this house, and in most of the other buildings still standing, stone lintels span the doorways, many of them elaborately carved on the underside.

•• ————

Teobert Maler 1895-1900

To Lake Pethá and Beyond

[Phillips Russell called Teobert Maler "the soldier of fortune and of Maximilian, who came to Mexico with the French invaders, drifted to Yucatan, and eventually allowed his entire being to be dissolved by contact with Maya art and archaeology, just as insects are dissolved in the cups contained in the bodies of certain carnivorous plants. Even in poverty he used his gifts as an artist to make reproductions of Maya relics, and became much sought after by museums. He soon lost interest in mundane actualities, quarrelled with his friends, withdrew into a broody solitude in which he dreamed of magnificent temples as yet unrevealed, and finally died of the fever which consumed his imagination as well as his flesh."

[Louis J. Halle, Jr., described him as follows:

["Maler . . . was an Austrian archaeologist and a character. For a number of years, about the turn of the century, he was almost continuously engaged in exploring the territory from British Honduras through the Usumacinta drainage. His reports, which occupy several folio volumes of the 'Peabody

The Russell quotation is from Phillips Russell, *Red Tiger: Adventures in Yucatan and Mexico* (New York: Brentano's Publishers), p. 145. Copyright 1929 by Brentano's, Inc. Reprinted by permission of Curtis Brown, Inc. The Halle quotation is from Louis J. Halle, Jr., *River of Ruins* (New York: Henry Holt and Company, 1941), pp. 151–52. Copyright 1941 by Louis J. Halle, Jr. Reprinted with permission of Holt, Rinehart and Winston, Inc.

The selections from Maler are, in the order quoted below, from Teobert Maler, *Researches in the Central Portion of the Usumatsintla Valley* (Cambridge, Mass.: Peabody Museum of American Archaeology and Ethnology, Harvard University, "Memoirs," Vol. II, 1901–1903), pp. 24–30, 31–39, 100–101, 105, 109–13, 198–203. Copyright 1901–1902 by Peabody Museum of American Archaeology and Ethnology, Harvard University. Reprinted by permission of the publisher.

Museum Memoirs,' are a strange mixture of archaeological measurements (a passion for taking measurements is sometimes the chief qualification of an archaeologist) and adventure-narrative written in a curiously innocent style. The man, in his writings, shows himself alternately a dryasdust pedant and a romantic schoolboy. He is also unmistakably a child of his age and, as such, more easily contemptuous of native shortcomings than we. Of the inhabitants of the Usumacinta region he writes: 'It is long since a respectable, stationary population inhabited these fruitful shores, and the dubious elements sunk in sloth, filth, and every possible vice, whose miserable habitations are met with here and there, are constantly shifting since they acquire no fixed property rights.' No fixed property rights! There, buttoned up to the chin in its own legality, speaks the 19th century. The institution of private property having no formally documented standing on these fruitful shores, the natives are, of necessity, dubious elements, not respectable! One gathers that nothing but properly notarized title-deeds will ever rescue them from 'every possible vice.' O Age of Law Triumphant! Yet Teobert Maler was something of a

Teobert Maler
From Teobert Maler, *Impresiones de Viaje a las Ruinas de Cobá y Chichen Itzá.*

hero. Those measurements of his, which are, in most cases, the only detailed archaeological knowledge available on the region, were made at the cost of such hard living as few civilized men could endure for a like period, and with a pertinacity (also proper to the age) that never acknowledged defeat.

["Maler's last report, the one on Tikal, was issued by the Peabody Museum in 1911 under embarrassing handicaps. Its author, once more in his native Austria, had broken off all correspondence with the museum to the extent, even, of not sending plans and measurements necessary to the completion of the volume or correcting the proof. I do not know that he has ever been heard from since, and by now, after thirty years of silence, he has probably gone to his grave. But his ghost, I venture to think, still battles against the raging waters of the Usumacinta, still overcomes fearsome odds to take measurements that will no longer find their way to any human eye. One tangible relic is left in Petén. On the walls of the ruined palace at Tikal, among other bits of vandalism, I found scratched into the smooth plaster that neat, almost feminine signature so familiar from his published maps, together with a date: *Teoberto Maler* 1895."

[In 1898, after exploring the route from Chinikahá to the ruins of Palenque, Maler returned to his headquarters at Tenosique, to organize a second expedition—"this time for the exclusive purpose of rediscovering the long since forgotten Lake of Pethá." Having engaged new men and procured fresh provisions, he went again to La Reforma and picked up his equipment stored there. Then, although it was late in August and "the rainy season had set in full force, the forest paths were soaked, and all the rivers and brooks were swollen," he crossed the Chinikahá River and took the narrow forest trail inland, three days later reaching Las Tinieblas, the last outpost of the lumber companies operating in this area.]

Tinieblas is occasionally visited by neighboring Lacantuns, who sell to the employees beautiful bows and arrows, rare birds and other articles; and yet none of the people here had the least idea where the Lake of Pethá was situated or how the Indian settlements could be reached.

As was my custom, I closely questioned the men here whether in their search for trees or in hunting, they had ever found ruins. They declared unanimously that they had never seen a trace of ruins in the neighboring forests.

Mr. Guillen arrived on the 31st of August, and all the details of our projected expedition were discussed most thoroughly with him. As I was fully prepared, we were able to leave Tinieblas on the next day (September 1st). Our saddle and pack animals were, of course, left behind. There were six of us in all. We took with us only a small camera (9 × 12 cm.) and the most necessary provisions. In addition we were all armed.

Following a forest path, we came once more to the camino de los Tzendales and to the halting-place San Antonio, where a large galeron invited repose; but as this San Antonio is barely two leagues from Tinieblas, we continued our march and pitched our tent near a small brook about a league from El Espejito. On the road we met some men with a train of mules coming from Tzendales. They were also carrying with them some bound mozos, who had committed a horrible double murder at Tzendales.

At an early hour on September 2nd we reached the halting-place El Espejito, about four leagues from San Antonio. Here we decided to abandon the road to Tzendales, and turning to the right, we pushed forward into the forest in a southerly or southeasterly direction. Soon we had to ford a not insignificant tributary of the Chocolhá, and in doing so we took advantage of the lime-rock formations of the river bed at this spot. A few steps beyond we found to our great joy an Indian trail which led in exactly the same direction which we had intended to take. Convinced that this trail must lead somewhere, we followed it for two leagues over hills and ravines, coming finally to a pass on the upper Chocolhá (right bank), where, from all appearances, the Lacantuns were accustomed to cross the river.

At this spot the river, flowing over a great bed of lime rock, forms a small waterfall only about one and one-half metres high. In the dry season the Indians probably cross the river by walking on this ledge, but at present the river was so high that such a proceeding was out of the question. In the mean time we encamped on a terrace on the hither side, erecting a small palmleaf hut for the night. Then we felled several small trees of light wood, which we cut into six long pieces and fastened them firmly together by means of tough vines, *bejucos* (climbing plants). Having finished our small raft, we decided to attempt a crossing a little below the waterfall, at a place where the river forms large, deep pools. One of my most skilful men, provided with a long pole and a large roll of bejucos, boldly leaped on to the raft and safely reached the other bank. The improvised bejuco rope was now firmly fastened to either shore.

I had bidden the man search carefully on the opposite bank to see whether the Indians had not concealed a small boat somewhere among the trees projecting into the water. Hardly had he touched the opposite bank when his joyful shout announced that he had found a fine new cayuco. He unfastened the boat, got into it, and brought it to our bank, abandoning the now useless raft to float down the river.

The cayuco had very recently been made from a *caoba* tree. We tied it firmly to a tree, lest it should be torn away during the night by the chance swelling of the stream. The finding of this cayuco was the second piece of good fortune that befell us on our expedition to Pethá.

There was now nothing further to do, and we cooked a fine *Craz rubra,* which we had killed on the way. It invariably rained at night.

On the morning of September 3d, after crossing and recrossing the river three times, the passage over the Chocolhá was completed. The little Indian boat was now fastened as securely as possible to the left bank, so that it might serve us on our return. At a distance of only two hundred paces from our crossing-place, we saw a well-built open champa, and a smaller one near by for cooking. Several pottery cooking-utensils lay around, and at a short distance we saw the clearing where the caoba had been felled and the cayuco had been made. Numerous hunter's trails ran in all directions from the hut, which was very confusing to us, but, true to our purpose to move always in a southerly or southeasterly direction, we chose the path which seemed to correspond best to that direction. The sequel proved that we had made a wise choice. We marched on uninterruptedly, crossing numerous brooks and also on the left a large tributary of the Chocolhá. The region became wilder and more mountainous, but we followed the path closely uphill and downhill, though it was often hardly discernible, convinced that it must lead somewhere. Towards noon, as we were already very tired, we made a short halt for rest and food. Then we pushed on again in spite of heavy showers of rain which drenched us to the skin. Finally we came to a small milpa established in the midst of the forest. This was the first sign that we were near an Indian settlement. The rain ceased. We proceeded cautiously. Descending the last declivity, suddenly a silvery expanse of water gleamed between the dark branches of the trees. A few steps further down, the path ended at the waters of the Lake of Pethá. Where the path ended three cayucos were fastened to the trees, and the oars belonging to them were found hidden in the branches. This was the third piece of good luck that had befallen us on our romantic expedition to Pethá. Indeed, of what advantage would it have been to us to have reached the lake without boats to navigate it! Fearing rain in the night, we went promptly to work to erect a large champa close to the water, covering it as well as we could with palm-leaves and pieces of cloth. We also slung from tree to tree the hammocks which we had brought with us, and soon in grateful repose forgot the hardships of the day.

The distance from Chocolhá to the northern border of the Lake of Pethá was probably only five or six leagues, but as the Indian trail was very much overgrown, we had frequently to use our machetes to make our way through. It was near the close of the day. All was in order. I revelled in the enjoyment of the glorious panorama afforded by the lake, which here forms a large almost circular basin more than two kilometres in diameter. On the distant southern shore, opposite our camping-place, we saw quite a large waterfall plunging into the lake, the sound of which reached us from the distance. Low mountain ranges bordered the southern shore, and in the background towered the mighty crests of the Sierra Madre in what we supposed to be the direction of Ocotzinco.

Suddenly my men who were employed in cooking informed me that a cayuco was passing near the distant southern shore. I attentively looked in that direction, and just as the cayuco passed in front of the waterfall, I distinctly saw its black silhouette with two men standing erect thrown into bold relief against the white background. Soon after the cayuco vanished into one of the coves in that vicinity, the position of which we impressed upon our memories. This was our first sight of human beings, but the Indians on their part had not noticed us. I had the two best cayucos cleaned and all the seams very carefully calked with clay. The necessary oars—*canaletes,* as they are called here—were also made ready, and on Sunday, September 4th, we rowed for the first time on the lake in our small barks so fortunately acquired. There were only two men in each, while two remained in the camp.

However lazy and shiftless the men of Tenosique may be in other respects, they display great aptitude on the water. It seems indeed as if rowing were the only occupation which they do not object to, for they perform all other labor with the greatest reluctance.

We crossed the lake in the direction of the waterfall, where we had seen the small boat disappear. We found at the right of the waterfall a small inlet hidden among the trees, to the bank of which several cayucos were fastened. We secured our boats here and followed a rather rocky trail inland. After travelling for about half an hour we came to a large milpa in which bananas, *papayos,* and sugar-cane were growing, in addition to very tall maize. At the end of the milpa we saw a group of houses, which we approached; but no one came to meet us, and there was no barking of dogs. The stillness of death prevailed on all sides. We entered the houses. There were two large ones intended for the main dwellings, which were surrounded by several small huts, which served for kitchens, sleeping-rooms, and shelters for small domestic animals. All were made entirely of poles roofed over with palmleaves. The two main houses and the adjacent huts were filled with household implements of every description, and gave a very complete idea of what the present Maya-Lacantun industry can produce in the way of articles for household use. Such an opportunity of examining all at once the entire domestic establishment, even to the slightest details, of this remarkable people, seemed to me not likely to occur again. I therefore at once set to work to examine everything, even the smallest object, directing my attention particularly to finding utensils that should display drawings which might be regarded as writing, since my many friends in Europe and America are especially interested in this particular question. Many cooking-utensils and water-jars, *cazuelas y cántaros,* lay scattered around on the floor of the huts and also on the ground outside. Everything was in great disorder, as if the inhabitants had suddenly forsaken their possessions. The cooking-vessels and pots resembled in shape those of the Indians of Yucatan and Tabasco, and were of dark gray-brown clay. The water-jars, *cántaros,* were of superior workmanship and were made of lighter, whitish-gray clay, and, strange to say, all were of the strongly bulging shape, which is generally considered peculiar to Spanish-African jars. Many had two handles near the neck, but some had only one handle and a small projecting animal head served the purpose of the other. Aside from the animal heads, none of this pottery had

any designs whatever. There was a large grinding-stone, *metlatl*, on a platform which rested on pegs, and several smaller ones stood near by. Several
large nets, which were filled with *calabaza* bowls, *xicalli*, for drinking *potzol*
and *balché*, hung on the rafters of the main houses; some of these were
adorned with pretty incised designs, but there was nothing of a hieroglyphic
character. The smoke had colored these vessels a beautiful dark-brown.
From the rafters also hung bundles of tobacco leaves, which were most carefully wrapped in banana leaves. My men could not resist the temptation of
taking a few of these for their own use. Several bows and arrows and other
small trifles lay on the timbers at the base of the roof or hung on the vertical
poles of the walls. In various gourds which I examined I found tree-resin,

left, Calabash drinking vessel

From Teobert Maler, *Researches in the Central Portion of the Usumatsintla Valley*, 1901.
Copyright 1901 by Peabody Museum of American Archaeology and Ethnology, Harvard
University. Courtesy of Peabody Museum of Harvard University.

top right, Incised design on calabash drinking vessel

From Teobert Maler, *Researches in the Central Portion of the Usumatsintla Valley*, 1901.
Copyright 1901 by Peabody Museum of American Archaeology and Ethnology, Harvard
University. Courtesy of Peabody Museum of Harvard University.

bottom right, Incised design on calabash drinking vessel

From Teobert Maler, *Researches in the Central Portion of the Usumatsintla Valley*, 1901.
Copyright 1901 by Peabody Museum of American Archaeology and Ethnology, Harvard
University. Courtesy of Peabody Museum of Harvard University.

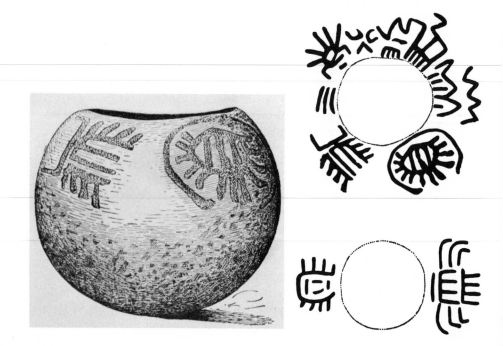

wax, aromatic herbs, seed-corn, lime, points of flint for arrows, and even alligator teeth, which were probably intended for the necklaces of the women, etc. Small spindles with cotton threads, small wooden spoons, tufts of feathers, and skulls of peccaries, deer, and apes were also stuck between the poles. There were even some billets of pitch-pine, *ocotl*, which must have been brought from a distance, for there are no pine-trees in the neighborhood of Pethá. In one of the small open huts hung a large gourd, which served for a beehive. It had a small hole on one side through which the bees passed in and out. My attention was attracted by some bird-cages, prettily plaited of a fine kind of bejuco, pear-shaped and having little trap-doors, and also by other baskets of simple but pretty shape. Of the different skins of small mammals, a yellowish one with brown spots seemed to me especially interesting, inasmuch as I had no knowledge of the little creature to which it belonged. Against the wall of the largest hut there was a wide board resting on pegs, which held a dozen of those well-known incense vessels each of which has the face of a god in front. The majority of these were much larger than those which I had once found in the temples of Yaxchilan, but were less graceful and so completely covered with copal, *chapopotl*, burned quite black, that their shape was hardly recognizable. Knowing how unwilling the Lacantuns are that a stranger should approach their gods, I improved this

Pottery incense burner

From Teobert Maler, *Researches in the Central Portion of the Usumatsintla Valley*, 1901. Copyright 1901 by Peabody Museum of American Archaeology and Ethnology, Harvard University. Courtesy of Peabody Museum of Harvard University.

opportunity to take the incense vessels for a moment out of the dark hut, and because they were so black, directly into the sunlight, in order to photograph them with my camera before we should be surprised by Indians who might come this way. When I had photographed them, I quickly put the vessels back in their places. Luxuriantly tall maize surrounded the huts, but there was a space left in which bloomed the beautiful yellow *Simpalxochitl* and the *Espuelas*—red dotted with white. There was also a little bed of *Yerba buena.*

Having thoroughly explored the huts, we intended to continue our journey in the hope of finding inhabited dwellings; but unfortunately the paths branched off in such a manner and were so ill-defined that we were puzzled which way to turn. We therefore decided to return to our camping-place, but not without taking a small supply of young maize ears, *elotl,* which, when boiled with salt, are an agreeable vegetable. As payment we left a mirror and a red silk handkerchief by the incense vessels. And as we crossed a large ant hill of yellow earth, I made several distinct impressions upon it with my shoes, thinking that if the Indians should come this way they would doubtless notice that strangers had been here and wished to have intercourse with them. Once more embarked in our frail crafts, we visited the waterfall and slowly rowed past the small islands in this part of the lake, to our camp, where those guarding it had in the mean time somewhat improved the huts and cooked our evening meal.

On September 5th we undertook a thorough exploration of the lake in all directions. This time taking the right hand, that is, following the northern shore, we came to a canal overhung by trees, through which we pushed our way as well as we could. It led to an extremely picturesque, large western basin, a long narrow arm of which branches off in a northwesterly direction. This part of the lake is also surrounded on all sides by mountains. The most beautiful vegetation extends close to the water's edge, while in several places perpendicular cliffs rise to a height of twenty to thirty metres. We rowed all round this extension, especially examining the cliffs to see if they might not display pictorial representations of some kind. The indigenous vegetation developed on these often fantastically piled up rocks is of special interest. Many of the rarest orchids, bromelia- and agave-varieties, which are seldom met with elsewhere, were here just now at the height of their gorgeous bloom. After the exploration of this extension, we passed back into the transverse arm, which is also diversified by cliffs and islets, in order directly to enter a larger western or southwestern extension, which we likewise explored to its end. I had brought my little camera with me to take small views of the most beautiful spots, although convinced that it is impossible for photography alone to convey an adequate idea of the incomparable, ever-varying beauty of these sheets of water set in vegetation untouched by the hand of man. Small flocks of black aquatic birds, which my men called *cuervos de agua* (water-ravens), were stirred up here and there by the approach of our cayucos. Strange to say, we did not see a single duck or other species of water-fowl. Probably the birds stay away during the rainy season, because the lake has no beach; but I think it probable that ducks, herons, and pelicans frequent the lake in the dry season when the water has fallen perhaps full five metres and large portions of the shore are above water. We found the water very deep everywhere, and therefore used only oars and never poles. Returning from the southwest arm, we skirted the southern shore and the inlets on that side, and came to an exceedingly beautiful southern passage, which led back to the main or large eastern basin. Along this passage—on our left as we passed through—we again saw great cliffs rising perpendicularly from the water. These we also investigated in the hope of finding pictorial representations, and to our great joy we discovered three separate large pictures. . . .

After we had passed through the strait of the picture-rocks, with its poetic beauty, we turned into a bay on the southern shore where a second waterfall, shaded by tall trees, plunges foaming over the rocks into the lake. Then—as night was already approaching—we crossed the large eastern basin to our camp on the northern shore, where in the mean time our meal had been prepared, and we soon resigned ourselves to calm repose. The fact that we had explored this glorious lake even to its remotest corner without the aid of the Indians and without arousing the suspicion of these people, usually so crafty, and that, in addition, we had made use of their own cayucos, was a source of great astonishment to us. It seemed like a dream!

The entire length of the lake from the eastern margin of its large round basin to the extreme end of its western ramifications we estimated at six or seven kilometres. The diameter of the round basin, to which its name Pet-há = *Agua circular*, refers, may be two kilometres, while the width of the western arms varies from two hundred to four hundred metres. We found the water of such great depth everywhere that steamships could easily sail on this lake, probably even in the dry season, when the water doubtless falls about five metres.

In the forenoon of September 6th we went again to the *Roca de las Pinturas*. I took some tracing paper with me in order to make a tracing of the well-preserved black drawings. A large *kommehen* (wood-destroying insect larvae) nest, which was attached to the cliff below the drawing, we cut to pieces with our machetes. Having thus cleared the drawing, I fastened over it with small pieces of wax a large sheet of the transparent paper, and standing on a projecting rock, as best I could, I proceeded to make the tracing. Scarcely had I finished this somewhat trying task when my men told me that an Indian boat was coming toward us. I told the men to quietly await its arrival. I should have preferred not to encounter the Indians at the picture rocks, but there was not time to go elsewhere, and therefore I seated myself on the projecting rock to wait for the cayuco, which was not within my circle of vision. Suddenly the cayuco came around the rocks, and our friendly calls soon brought it alongside of our own. In it were a man, his wife, an infant, and two older children. Hardly had the man noticed that I was standing directly under the picture on the rock than, exhibiting signs of extreme terror, he called out to me in broken Spanish, "No hombre—quítate de ahí—es mi santo—es el Cristo-María de nosotros—cuidado hombre—te come el tigre—vámonos hombre—por eso mucho agua por el mal corazon de mi santo—por eso muy crecidos los rios y la laguna—vámonos—vámonos."

I pacified the man as well as I could, assuring him that we too held this "saint" in great veneration, and had brought him a small offering, so that he would grant us fine weather and abundant maize. After this I stepped into my cayuco, gave my hand to the man and asked his name. Chankin,—*chichan*, abbreviated *chan* (*tšitsan*, *tšan*) = small; *kin* (*k'in*) = sun, priest,— he answered. Then I explained to him that we had come to see the lake and to visit his countrymen who were living in its vicinity, and also that we would like to purchase a few pretty things as well as food of them, for which purpose we had brought with us useful articles; knives, fish-hooks, handkerchiefs, mirrors, and salt, of which they never have a sufficient supply. On telling him that in our search for their dwellings we had come across a large group of houses full of all kinds of utensils, but without inmates, Chankin replied that the houses were those of his brother who died recently. And what did he die of? "Quien sabe, Señor?—Por el mal corazon de su santo," the man answered angrily.

Chankin, who had learned a little Spanish in his frequent intercourse with the neighboring monterías, was a robust man in middle life, and was dressed in a shirt-like garment of coarse cotton. Long raven-black hair surrounded his beardless face, which was of a genuine Indian cast. His wife was of smaller frame, and was also dressed in cotton; her face and arms were badly bitten by flies. A fine set of bow and arrows wrapped in bark lay on the bottom of the cayuco. I asked the Indian to sell them to me, which he did for two pesos.

We rowed now to the landing-place on the south shore, where we fastened the boats. I was firmly resolved not to lose sight of the man at any price, for otherwise we might forever miss the opportunity of coming in contact with the Indian settlements of Pethá.

Chankin first took a path to the large waterfall. The river, which was very full at this season, rushed with tremendous force downward over terraced rocks into the lake. Our Indian took his way unconcernedly through the midst of this mass of water. I had had a stout walking-stick cut for myself, and there was nothing for me to do but to follow the man or to stay behind. Bracing myself firmly with my staff against the rocks, I too walked through the waterfall in extreme danger of being hurled into the foaming depths by the impetus of the rushing water. Taking off their shoes, three of my men followed very reluctantly. We then went on over desperately rough trails, soon reaching the same river (as I have reason to suppose) at a spot where it was spanned by the long and thick trunk of a tree, which at this time was about eighty centimetres below the surface of the water. At this place the river was several metres deep and impassable; so our Indian went straight over the smooth tree-trunk, in doing which the prehensile power of his toes was of great advantage to him. By the aid of a long pole in one hand and a shorter staff in the other, I succeeded with extreme difficulty in crossing. My men also made their way across by the aid of poles. Soon we had to cross the river for a third time, and again on the long and thick trunk of a tree, which this time, by way of variety, was suspended high above the water. We also successfully passed through this third and last Orphean ordeal to which Chankin subjected us.

On our way, however, between the first and second tree-bridges, we had caught glimpses among the trees on our right of "the dead brother's" large milpa, and I told my grumbling men that we should under no conditions go back over the frightful path by which Chankin had brought us, but that on our return we would clear a path to this milpa and then return to our landing-place by the trail we already knew.

After crossing the river for the third time, the path improved. We might have travelled about an hour, when we heard the barking of dogs and the hollow sound of conch-shells, *Strombus gigas*, with which the Indians greeted our arrival. The forest opened. We entered a milpa of tall and luxuriant maize, and from its group of huts Chankin's brother-in-law, *el suegro*, named *Māx* (*mās*) came to meet us surrounded by other Indians, including women and children. I saluted Māx, and explained my purpose in coming, while Chankin reported to him in Maya all the circumstances under which he had found us, so that I had no doubt that Chankin had been despatched to reconnoitre, purposely taking with him his wife and little children to cover his intentions.

Māx was not at all overjoyed at our arrival, but resigned himself to the inevitable. He promised us provisions—maize bread, *potsol, māxcal,* etc.—for the next day, when I was to visit him again with my men. For the present I found myself compelled to return as quickly as possible to the camp, as the day was near its end and we were threatened with a downpour of rain. We therefore took our leave, and lost no time in reaching the nearest tree-bridge. We notched the slippery surface of the trunk with our machetes, so that this passage lost much of its peril. Then, after reaching the point which brought us in line with the dead brother's milpa, we cut our way directly through the forest and without much difficulty reached the abandoned group of huts. Before we continued our journey, however, I permitted my men to take an abundant supply of ears of maize, bananas, and sugar-cane to punish the fellow who had dragged us over waterfalls and tree-trunks to his *suegro*.

Amid a light shower of rain we reached the landing-place. The last rays of sun disappearing behind the mountains lighted us as we rowed over the mirror-like surface of the beautiful lake to our camp, where those who had been left behind had spent the day not without anxiety on our account. Of course my companions never wearied of recounting to their comrades all the experiences of this day. Each one considered himself a hero.

On the next day (September 7th), leaving but a single man to guard the camp, we all crossed the lake to visit Māx and his associates. We intended to take our noon meal there, in order to have leisure to observe the habits and customs of the Indians and to take some small photographs. After crossing the tree bridge we succeeded in killing a black crax.

As we neared the huts we heard the hollow, somewhat weird sound of the conch-shells with which Māx and his associates celebrated our coming. I

Lacandón Indians

Photographed by Teobert Maler, 1898. From *Researches in the Central Portion of the Usumatsintla Valley*, 1901. Copyright 1901 by Peabody Museum of Harvard University. Courtesy of Peabody Museum of Harvard University.

greeted Mäx and the assembled Indians cordially, explaining to them that we would like to spend the day with them, and as we had shot a *kambul,* would they lend us a vessel in which to cook it? Upon this one of the women brought us a large pot, and my men began to prepare the bird.

Then I told the Indians that I had brought them a few presents, articles which might be useful to them in their remote forests, and I at once proceeded to distribute the salt among the men who were present. Each one received a gourd-bowl full. I also gave each man a large knife and several kinds of fish-hooks. As for the women and girls, they received gay silk and cotton kerchiefs, as well as silver ear-pendants and pretty mirrors.

Although this people, so simple in its wants, is incapable of genuine joy, a certain feeling of general satisfaction, nevertheless, became evident among them. Meanwhile I had set up the small camera in order to take a few photographs before this pleasant mood should vanish. As my brightly varnished camera with its brass mountings was a pretty sight when set up on its slender tripod, the people were not at all frightened by this magic box. I succeeded in taking several photographs, which in spite of their small size (9 × 12 cm.) gave a distinct picture of the features and dress of the men, women, and children.

The men wear an ample shirt-like garment, of strong, somewhat coarse cotton material, which reaches down to the calves of their legs; but on their hunting expeditions or on journeys they wear a garment of extra-coarse fleecy material. The women wear an undergarment which reaches from the hips down over the calves of their legs, and the shirt-like upper garment falls over this. Each woman is adorned with a thick bunch of necklaces or rather strings of seeds. They are made of hard, usually black, seeds mixed with cylindrical bones, teeth, small snail-shells, or whatever else they can obtain.

The uncut hair of the men falls about their faces, which sometimes gives them a wild and leonine aspect. The women part their hair in the middle, exactly like European women, and at the end of the braid they fasten a tuft

Lacandón bow (*top*) and arrows

From Teobert Maler, *Researches in the Central Portion of the Usumatsintla Valley,* 1901. Copyright 1901 by Peabody Museum of American Archaeology and Ethnology, Harvard University. Courtesy of Peabody Museum of Harvard University.

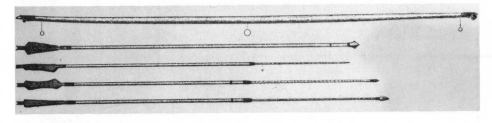

of gay bird-feathers, wings, and breasts. All the women have their ear-lobes
pierced; so they could delightedly insert the ear-rings (of English manufac-
ture) themselves or confidingly allow me to insert them. Neither men nor
women seemed to wear shoes of any kind.

Māx's premises consisted of a large main hut, where he lived with his
wives and children. This was surrounded by four smaller, half-open huts,
some intended for cooking, and some for the accommodation of guests, and
one was devoted exclusively to the incense vessels with faces of gods.

Here also was an abundance of cooking-vessels and implements of every
sort, and the inmates had hammocks made of agave cord for sleeping at
night and also for resting by day. The hammocks of the Lacantuns are very
different from those which are used elsewhere in Mexico. They do not consist of mesh-work, but a system of cross cords holds the lengthwise cords
together. They are also shorter than the Mexican ones, but are broad enough.
The people do not make their things for sale, but only for their own use, so
that it was utterly impossible for me to obtain one of their very prettily made
hammocks.

The wooden implement with which the women weave the cotton cloth,
la manta, is also interesting. An old woman was at work on a piece of material, and I wanted to buy the implement together with the partly finished
web, but she obstinately refused to sell it. The women, however, gave me
some of their seed necklaces as mementos, and I requested the men to bring a
few of their beautifully made bows and arrows to my camp, promising to
pay well for them.

The bows are usually made of *guayacan,* or *xibé,* or else of *chicozapote.*
The length of the men's bows varies from one hundred and fifty to one hundred and seventy centimetres, that of the larger boys from one hundred and
twenty-five to one hundred and thirty-five centimetres. All the bows are
thicker towards the middle and taper very much toward the ends. Each end
is firmly wound with a small cord, which is covered with resin, but the horns
themselves are left free to receive the end loops of the bow-string, which is
made of an agave cord, the windings of the small cord preventing the string
from slipping when the bow is drawn. The bows are apparently straight, but
on closer examination they are found to be very slightly curved. In using one
of these bows, the rule must be followed of drawing the bow not—as one
would be inclined to do—in the direction of the curve, in which case it would
very easily break, but always in the opposite direction, that is to say, on the
side of the outward curve (convex side). The Indians usually hold the bow
horizontally before shooting, and only at the moment of aiming and of
shooting is it placed in a perpendicular position. The arrows are only a little
shorter than the bow. They are of different kinds, according to the game to
be shot, but all, excepting the bird bolts, have this in common: the forward
part, corresponding to about a third of the length of the arrow, consists of a
cylindrical or a square rod of hard wood, which is deeply inserted in the

reed shaft, *carrizo* or *caña brava*, and firmly lashed at the place of insertion and also at the invisible lower end. The reed shaft, which forms two-thirds of the length of the arrow, has at its butt the notch for receiving the string, and on both sides of the notch there is a feather, which is firmly bound at its upper and lower ends to the shaft, with twine smeared with black resin. If too broad, the feathers are cut out about the centre. The little hard-wood rods simply end in sharp points, which suffice for killing fish and small birds, or else flint-heads, varying in size, are inserted, and these are also firmly lashed at the place of insertion with cords covered as usual with black gum. The arrows, which are intended for killing monkeys, have the forward piece of hard wood deeply barbed, so that the animal cannot shake off or pull out the arrow. Lastly, the arrows which are intended to stun a bird only for the time being, so that it can be caught unhurt, have a little conical piece of wood in place of a flint head.

The bow is bound up with the arrows, and the bundle is protected by a covering of bark (*majahua,* as it is called in Tabasco) which is usually stripped from young ceiba-trees. The art of cleaving flint into thin layers has been preserved up to the present day by this secluded little nation. It appears that in some cases the cleaving is facilitated by previously heating the stone red-hot, but this is not always done. The cleaving is effected by means of a piece of deer-horn, especially prepared for this purpose, and by means of this elastic medium the blow of the mallet is transferred to the edge of the stone. The layers thus obtained then receive the desired shape and an edge, by means of a piece of an old knife (now made of iron). Inasmuch as the Indians also find many discarded bottles in the abandoned monterías, they use the glass of these bottles in place of flint. They make the arrow-points of this broken glass, which does not admit of cleaving.

Package of flint flakes from which arrow points were made

From Teobert Maler, *Researches in the Central Portion of the Usumatsintla Valley,* 1901. Copyright 1901 by Peabody Museum of American Archaeology and Ethnology, Harvard University. Courtesy of Peabody Museum of Harvard University.

Flint flakes

From Teobert Maler, *Researches in the Central Portion of the Usumatsintla Valley,* 1901. Copyright 1901 by Peabody Museum of American Archaeology and Ethnology, Harvard University. Courtesy of Peabody Museum of Harvard University.

There were only a few domestic animals to be seen on Mãx's premises. The only mammals were dogs, which are always tied up, and belong to the present modern breed. Among the birds I noticed the large green parrots with blue heads, which occur exclusively in these forests. They are therefore called *los loros de los Lacandones* or *loros palencanos*. There were also several specimens of a beautiful small *Coturnix* species, called *bolonchac*, confined in small bejuco cages.

It is hardly to be expected that a remnant of those ancient breeds of dogs —*Techichi, Xoloitscuintli, Itscuintepotsotli*—should still be preserved among the Lacantuns. All the lumbermen who had come in contact with these Indians had seen only dogs of the same breed as those found everywhere in Mexico.

Hoping to throw light upon the still more important question as to the kind of pictorial representations still made by these Indians and whether they are of a hieroglyphic character, I looked about me very carefully in Mãx's huts, but of course without exciting the suspicion of the people. I regret to say that nothing bearing upon this matter could be found. The fact that the Indians of Pethá live so scattered that each family is about one league (or an hour's journey) from the other adds much to the difficulty of solving this question. It would be necessary to ascertain whether these people are anywhere grouped in villages, for in that case there would be more prospect of obtaining specimens of drawings.

In the mean time my men had deliciously prepared the crax, and the women supplied us with the necessary tortillas, which, made of new maize and half roasted, were especially palatable. At my special request, which I had also made on the preceding evening, they brought us large gourds full of balché (*baltšé*), a refreshing beverage made from the bark of a tree.

While we were satisfying our hunger with this food and drinking with it the national drink, balché, the men, having adorned their heads with bands dyed pink with chacavanté, withdrew into the huts containing the incense-vessels, to pray. The prayer consisted of monotonous, unintelligible cries, its purpose doubtless being to entreat the gods not to regard with anger the reception of strangers, and to avert any evil consequences that might arise from our visit. The women took no part in this religious ceremony.

At last the time came for us to depart, and we accordingly took leave of Mãx and the other Indians. Before doing so, however, I administered to a young girl very ill with fever a small dose of quinine, which she took tearfully. To an older woman covered with ulcers (elephantiasis?) we could only recommend a draught which she could make herself of the sarsaparilla occurring in that region. With these exceptions the people were all in good health.

We remained four days more (September 8th, 9th, 10th, and 11th) on the shore of that beautiful lake, over whose waters we never grew weary of rowing. The Indians made us several visits, bringing us food and enabling us to buy of them several additional sets of their handsome bows and arrows.

Māx, whose name means "howling-monkey" (*Stentor niger*), was not a frank, kindly-disposed man. He very evidently exercised a certain repressing influence over the others, who showed much greater openness in their intercourse with us when Māx was not present, and willingly gave me all the information I desired.

I questioned the people very closely as to whether they knew of any ruins in the forests of this region. Unfortunately, absolute ignorance seemed to prevail among them in regard to the matter. Indeed, I had already convinced myself of the fact that cities built of stone had never existed in the neighborhood of Pethá.

[Maya archaeologists freely admit that most of the ancient ruins they "discover" in the jungle were shown to them by *chicleros*, the hard-bitten chicle bleeders who roam the rain forests seeking new stands of the sapodilla (*chicozapote*) tree, which yields the latex known to us in the form of chewing gum. A jungle settlement in Mexico named after this tree was visited by Maler in 1897.]

The chicozapote is the tree which exudes a thick white mass in the rainy season when large connecting V's are cut one above the other in its bark. This liquid is collected in a vessel placed at the lowest V, and when evaporated it forms the well-known chewing-gum, *tsictin, tsiktin,* Hispanicized *chicle*. The collectors are called *el chiclero, los chicleros,* and their temporary camp, *una chiclería.* The roundish fruit of this tree looks like a potato, the meat is yellowish brown and has a pleasant winey taste. The dark redbrown wood belongs to the best of the Mexican forests.

One of my men had told me that when roving formerly through these woods with collectors of tsapotl resin they had found the ruins of a large city situated not far from the now-abandoned montería of "El Chicozapote," which might perhaps yield something of interest on closer examination. As a result of this information, we started, carrying the absolutely necessary luggage, in the direction of the settlement of El Chicozapote. This place is midway between El Chile and Anaité, being about three leagues (about twelve and a half kilometres) from these two points. There had been heavy rains during the last nights. For almost the entire journey we had to wade laboriously through water and mire. Worn out and drenched, we finally reached El Chicozapote, and took up our quarters in one of the huts, where we were at least sheltered from the rain.

To my great sorrow I had in the last days contracted a bad fever, which now broke out with great violence. Abstaining from food for three days and taking heavy doses of quinine in coffee, I succeeded in breaking it up completely. In such desperate conditions—surrounded by people who are constantly dissatisfied and grumbling—it is necessary to lose no time in curing one's self, otherwise the case lasts for months and the system is much reduced. In spite of the fact that I was very weak I undertook the exploration of the ruined city. Pushing our way in a southeasterly direction through the forest for about one and a half kilometres from the huts of the montería we in fact came to a large ruined city, where many remnants of buildings covered the extremely hilly tract of land. All, of course, was hidden in the dark forest of high trees.

Searching the ruins in all directions we were unable to find a building standing erect, nor was there an esplanade with sacrificial altars and deity-stelae, since the hilly nature of the ground would not have been favorable for such. Finally, however, we came to a half-ruined building of two chambers in a row, and to my very great satisfaction all four entrances to these rooms had their respective lintels sculptured on the under side and two of them still displayed their original beautiful coloration. This was a fortunate and unexpected find which repaid us in some measure for the hardships we had endured.

[Maler visited Yaxchilán about fourteen years after Maudslay—about fifteen years after its first description by a European. He objected strongly to the name Menché by which Maudslay and others called the ruined city.]

The name of the river Yāxchilan was extended to the ruined city, which had no name at all. In order to be quite clear, people said: *las Ruinas situadas rio abajo de la desembocadura del afluente Yāxchilan.*

At present the name Anaité is well known far and near. It is applied to a small tributary stream on the left bank, to a station at its mouth, and to the much-feared rapids some distance below; also to a large inland lagoon, and to two smaller ruined towns. The traveller who wishes to visit the large ruined city may express himself thus: *las Ruinas arriba de la desembocadura del Arroyo de Anaité,* and he will everywhere be understood.

To these ruins certain scholars have of late applied the imposing name "Menché-tinamit"! I do not remember ever having met with it in the books of Remesal, Juarros, Villagutierre, and others. This name is half Maya and half Nahuatl. *Menché* is equivalent to *mehenché* = mehén-tšé = young forest (*mehén* = seed, young ones, off-shoots; *ché* = tree). *Tinamit* in the pure Mexican form is *tenamitl* = city. Hence *Mehenché-tenamitl* (mehentšé-tenamitl) = young forest-city.

If one were to meet wood-cutters or resin-gatherers in these wild forests, and to their question, *¿Adonde se va Usted Señor?* were to answer, *Yo me voy á Mehenché-tenamitl,* not a soul would understand what was meant, and the questioners would very likely laugh in one's face. It will therefore be easily understood why I could not make up my mind to use this otherwise admirable name.

Not until I had explored the ruins of Seibal and Altar de Sacrificios in 1895, did circumstances take me to Yāxchilan, where I remained two days (July 14th and 15th). At that time the river was very high and only the topmost stones of the little *cuyo* appeared above the water, so that we were doubtful as to whether we had arrived at the site of the ruined city or not. Fastening our cayuco to a tree and walking a short distance, we reached the Templo de la Ribera, in which we took up our quarters. I took no photographs on this occasion, because to do so always necessitates elaborate preparations and incurs great expense, and I had no men and no provisions with me. I limited my activity to an inspection of the principal buildings, and to drawing plans of the Templo de la Ribera and of the Temple with the headless figure of Ketsalkoatl. I dismissed my cayuco-men, or *vogas,* a short distance beyond the ruined city, and went to Tenosique by land, by way of Mr. Torruco's montería, situated at this point, and of El Cayo and Piedras Negras.

When after many eventualities fate once more brought me to the glorious banks of the Usumatsintla, I was able on the 30th of June, 1897, to leave the montería of Anaité and embark in the cayuco I had borrowed, with my five men and the necessary baggage, this time to undertake the serious exploration of Yāxchilan.

There must have been heavy rainfalls in distant Guatemala and Eastern Chiapas, for the Usumatsintla was excessively high, having risen to the very edge of the high banks, which made progress up the river exceedingly difficult, since the poles by which the cayuco is propelled could not reach the hard bottom. Under such circumstances forked branches are made fast to the end of the poles, and with these *horquetas* the men seize the overhanging branches of the trees and shrubs and thus push the cayuco forward, while those not occupied with the poles, grasp the branches, if possible, with their hands, and pull with all their might. This procedure is exceedingly laborious, and progress is slow. In this manner it took us a day and a half to overcome the short distance between Anaité and Yāxchilan (about thirteen kilometres). When the river is in this condition no one ever attempts to go upstream, the labor and the danger are too great. In point of fact, we had a terrible struggle. We had to force our way through branches of trees projecting out of the water, and often we had to use our machetes to remove the obstacles impeding our way. In spite of all our exertions, we were frequently whirled round by the force of the current and carried downstream. Masses of trees which reached far out into the river could not be surmounted, nor powerful rapids overcome, without two or three successive attempts.

The trees which grow on the banks of the river are chiefly of the kind that is here called *huitz,* their Aztec name being *cuauhxinicuil* (kwauhšini-kwil). They have blossoms formed of great white stamens and the seed forms in long green pods. There are besides a great many *amatl,* which are here called *chimon* (tšimon). On the low shore different kinds of grass, reeds and *guadua* make up for the absence of trees.

When we rested at night we fastened our cayuco to the branches of a great chimon and protected ourselves and our baggage as well as we could with oiled cloths against the heavy night rains. It was not possible to go on shore, as everything was flooded. At noon of the second day we finally arrived at the ruined city, the location of which one of my men recognized by certain signs. The *cuyo* on the low shore, which generally serves to mark the spot, had entirely vanished under the water. We now breathed more freely, and, glad of having thus far surmounted all difficulties, we fastened our cayuco to a tree. My men admired each other as heroes, and each one asserted that had it not been for *him*, we never could have come up the river.

In the mean time we sought shelter in the neighboring "shore temple." But as the entire stone structure was soaked with rain and all the ceilings dripped with moisture, my men constructed for themselves a palm-leaf hut, *una champa*, while I, after discovering the "Labyrinth" (Edifice 19), settled myself within its walls with my most important baggage, for the ceilings were dry, and the great stone benches were very convenient for sleeping purposes or for spreading my things out upon them.

It was rather dangerous to spend the nights quite alone in that solitary ruin on account of the tigers. But fortunately we escaped all collision with these felines, which are always to be greatly feared. We were so fortunate as to have a month of glorious weather, which greatly lessened the difficulties of my work among the ruins. It generally rained at night and hardly ever by day. Even the Usumatsintla soon sank again to a less dangerous level. But we had another trouble to contend against. Our stock of provisions had run very low, because the men when living at some one else's expense eat enormously and know no moderation. I therefore hastened all my preparations for photographing the façades and sculptures.

Keeping one man to assist me, I sent the rest as soon as I could spare them, in the cayuco to the nearest ranchitos to buy food, in which they were only partially successful. No one in this country, upon which nature has so lavishly bestowed her gifts, is willing to sell food to another. In spite of this luxuriance of nature a regular famine prevailed, which naturally affected us also. My men shot birds and monkeys, or frequently succeeded in catching a fine large fish of the scaleless kind called *pezcado bobo*. In this manner we got along as best we could.

Working incessantly and exploring the forest in which the extensive ruined city lies, in every direction, I convinced myself that I had found everything worthy of note, with the exception perhaps of objects that were lying too deeply buried under the ruins. Plans were drawn of all the important buildings. I succeeded in discovering three magnificent temples, never yet visited by Europeans, at the southern end of the mountain range of the great Acropolis. I photographed with magnesium light at night under great difficulties the lintel sculptures still in position over the entrances to the temples. Others, already fallen to the ground, and some wholly buried and excavated by me, I placed in such positions that they could be photographed in sunlight. I also prepared a dozen mortuary or deity stelae for photographing. Of these stelae I found only one still in an upright position; all the others had fallen to the ground; many were broken in pieces and sunk in the earth. Notwithstanding the lack of provisions which greatly hampered us, the result of my explorations (July and August, 1897) may be said to have been on the whole very satisfactory. Leaving the excavation of additional pieces of sculpture for a future occasion, I returned for the time being to Yucatan by way of Tenosique and El Cármen.

After I had completed my second exploration of Piedras Negras in December, 1899, I continued my voyage up the river. In El Cayo I procured a cayuco, had the necessary paddles made, and, leaving my animals behind, embarked with my men and my baggage.

The voyage to Yáxchilan was again fraught with very great difficulties. The dangerous *Raudales de Anaité* had recently claimed several human lives. Besides this, several cargoes had been sunk, the oarsmen, however, having been able to save their lives. Instead of blasting away the most dangerous rocks, the authorities at Tenosique preferred to forbid the shooting of the rapids on pain of a heavy fine. As the forest trails are in an unheard of condition, the pack animals cannot survive on them. It is almost an impossibility to convey a *carga* by land. In spite of all dangers, therefore, most of the wood-cutting firms prefer the water-way.

I had succeeded in bringing my rather old and fragile cayuco as far as the *Raudal grande*, where we all disembarked, leaving the baggage in the boat, which my men, who had climbed up on the rocks, now slowly and carefully towed along by means of long ropes. It was a very difficult piece of work, because the cayuco, gliding along at the foot of the sheer rock, remained invisible to those handling the ropes, which had every now and again to be slung over projecting angles of the rock or bushes, which threatened to impede progress. We finally reached the last headland, down which we clambered and made the cayuco fast. I then had it unloaded and everything placed on the lowest rocks, for at this point the water dashed over half-concealed boulders with such force that we could not think of towing the boat through with its load. The sight of the stupendous walls of rock, which we had just passed, the din of the water, forced between rocks and rushing along at the most frightful speed, caused my men utterly to lose their heads, though they had always considered themselves excellent *vogas*. They were terribly frightened, and only the utmost exertion on my part had brought the trembling fellows thus far. Our attempt at towing the cayuco over the rapids was unsuccessful. It filled with water, the ropes broke, and, dashing to pieces against the rocks, it vanished in the whirling flood. It was no great loss. All my baggage, the paddles even, and my men, who had so greatly feared for their precious lives, were saved. Notwithstanding the accident, we could still consider ourselves very fortunate, for we had now passed the most dangerous rocky narrows and rapids. The rest of the voyage henceforth offered no great dangers.

In the meantime, however, I established my camp on the rocks and sent two of my men through the forest to Anaité, about two leagues distant, to procure another cayuco in which to continue my voyage. They succeeded in obtaining a large one, which I afterward bought for sixty pesos, from a ranchero, José María Jiménez, who had settled somewhat farther up the river. The men were accompanied on their return by my old friend Lamberto de La Cruz of Amaité, and another cayuco arrived at the same time with people on their way to El Cayo. Thus we were at last able to continue our voyage, though not without loss of time.

I was only half annoyed at my enforced stay of several days on the rocks, for the chasm cut by the river at this point affords such a magnificent sight that I was actually sorry to part from this scene of wild beauty. I had made good use of my time in collecting some rare specimens of butterflies and beetles, and I had been successful in capturing a male and a female of the great beetle called *el cornezuelo* in Tabasco. This beetle is probably the largest in America. It is not found in other parts of Mexico.

Guided by Lamberto de La Cruz, we now passed the rapids called *El Raudal chico*, which are smaller than those previously passed, but by no means without danger. Here also a high rock had to be surmounted on foot, while the cayuco was towed along by a long rope. From this point all danger ceased.

After allowing my men a day of rest at Anaité, we continued on our way to the ruins of Yáxchilan. Above Anaité the river, bordered on both sides by low mountain ranges, offers a succession of magnificent views, which further up are not again equalled in beauty. Arrived at the ruins, we all took up our quarters in the "Labyrinth."

First of all, I turned my attention to the terraces of the three South Temples, convinced that more stelae and circular altars could be brought to light there. In point of fact I succeeded in excavating nine stelae, so that the total number of stelae found by me in Yáxchilan amounted to exactly twenty.

After being convinced that it was not possible to find more stelae,—unless a group of more distant buildings should some day be discovered,—I began a second very thorough search of the half and wholly ruined structures for lintel-carvings. Having familiarized myself with the method of construction employed in building the principal edifices, when drawing their several plans, it was a comparatively easy matter for me to find out, even with regard to the most shapeless mass of débris, whether I was dealing with a structure of one, two, or three entrances, where the latter must have been, and about how far their lintel-slabs must have fallen forward in the general downfall. Thus every excavation produced the sought-for lintel-slab with almost mathematical precision, without further loss of time. There only remained the question as to whether it was ornamental or plain.

In this way I succeeded in excavating no less than fourteen lintels, ornamented with the most interesting picture or inscription carvings imaginable, also a fragment of a fifteenth, the most important part of which had doubtless been carried off.

As sculptured lintels are never plentiful, and one is often glad enough to have found two or three, or even a single one, the result of my exploration may be looked upon as very extraordinary. The number of sculptured lintels found at Yāxchilan, after my second expedition, had accordingly increased to forty-six, inclusive of those that had been sawed off by previous visitors.

The work of these excavations had consumed three whole months, January, February, and March, 1900. Then everything had been photographed, several paper moulds had been made, and my general plan of Yāxchilan was completed.

While we actually suffered from famine during the first expedition, we fared very well this time, for we had a superfluity of provisions. I had brought along a little machine for grinding maize, *el azteca*, so that my men could daily make fresh maize bread, *tortillas*. José María Jiménez, who had settled a little way above the ruins, opposite the embouchure of the Yāxchilan, from time to time brought us maize, beans, bananas, and even a little pig. Besides, we frequently succeeded in shooting birds and little mammals, which afforded us savory roasts. Passing cayucos occasionally sold us spirits, which largely contributed toward keeping the men contented.

When my work in Yāxchilan was finished, my men were completely discouraged with regard to undertaking further explorations and ardently longed to return to Tenosique. Such is the character of these people that even for the highest wages and with the best treatment, they cannot be induced to continue at one pursuit for any length of time. My success in having secured their services for seven months may be regarded as the utmost that can be accomplished. Nevertheless it was my wish to push forward at least as far as the lower course of the Rio Lacantun, not so much to undertake any serious work—especially as my photographic material was exhausted—as to institute inquiries at the neighboring monterías as to whether further ruins had been discovered within their precincts. I therefore persuaded my impatient men to follow me as far as the Lacantun River. They finally consented to do this, since it involved only what might be regarded as an excursion without any hard work.

Our superfluous luggage and the paper moulds were concealed in an abandoned temple to be called for on our return. In this way the difficulty of the reconnoissance was materially simplified.

About two Mexican leagues above the ruined city, opposite the mouth of the seemingly insignificant Arroyo de Yáxchilan, lie the ranchitos of José María Jiménez . . . and of his sons and kindred, where we passed one night.

Notwithstanding the fact that in their search for caoutchouc, *hule,* Jiménez and his people are accustomed to traverse the entire Guatemala shore as far as El Cayo, they had never seen anything but *vestigios* and nothing that could be called standing ruins. Otherwise they would readily have guided us. It is extremely difficult, generally speaking, to discover a ruin containing anything of interest, and this is in part due to the fact that chains of cities, so to speak, attained architectural developments along certain lines and not along others.

To gratify those who desire to have as full a description as possible, I may add that the actual and larger Yáxchilan River flows in a direction opposite to that of the smaller stream of the same name, and as a matter of fact into the Rio San Pedro(-Limon). As it is easy to lose one's way in this wilderness of which no topographical charts have ever been made, travellers, on reaching the smaller stream mentioned above, believed it to be the true Yáxchilan and therefore gave it that name. Subsequently, this was found to be an error, but in popular usage both rivers are called by one and the same name. Hence I designate the river flowing to meet the San Pedro-Limon, "el Yáxchilan grande," and that emptying (directly) into the Usumatsintla, "el pequeño Yáxchilan," which will obviate all confusion.

We took advantage of our stay with Jiménez to buy provisions for the trip up the river, and thus fully equipped we started on our journey to the montería "Orizaba" situated four leagues farther up. This montería belongs to a German-American by the name of Schindler, and is situated on the left (Mexican) shore.

A short distance above the entrance of the Yáxchilan, the Usumatsintla again winds along through a low mountain range. For some distance the ascent is rendered difficult by numerous beds of rock, between which it was necessary for us to force our way. Enormous caymans, basking on these rocks, plunged noisily into the water at our approach. After a rather toilsome journey we reached the montería Orizaba, where we temporarily stored our luggage.

I had previously ascertained that there were some heaps of ruins in the forest behind the present location of the huts of the woodcutters. I therefore availed myself of this opportunity to inspect the most important of these ruins and to search for sculptures. The principal structure must once have been by no means insignificant. Remains of a stone stairway can still be distinguished, leading up to a terrace the superstructure of which is in utter ruins.

At this montería we succeeded in persuading an intelligent man, Manuel Reyes by name, to accompany us to the Guatemala side on a visit to the only Indian living there, Andres Bolon by name, who was well acquainted with the region and whose final opinion as an expert I wished to obtain as to whether there was actually nothing of interest in the region on the right bank.

When we were ready we embarked, accompanied by Reyes, in order to travel three kilometres down the river again to the place where a small stream "El Arroyo de Bolon" empties into it on the right. We entered the stream for the purpose of fastening our cayuco at a spot hidden from passers-by. Places where one embarks or lands are called in this country "el paso," hence the point where we landed is called "El Paso de Bolon," because that Indian's place is reached from here, and at this spot Bolon himself embarks when he wishes to go to some other montería.

On the right bank of the arroyo we pushed forward into the magnificent forest of tall trees frequently interspersed with guano and corozo palms. While traversing the very first league we came to a small ruin, where, as several heaps of débris bore witness, stone buildings had once stood.

After travelling almost four leagues (about thirteen kilometres) we emerged on a savanna covered with succulent grass, through which we had to walk in order to reach Bolon's huts. On nearing these, I sent Reyes ahead, who was on friendly terms with the family, in order not to alarm them, and to apprise them of our coming.

In these huts we met two of Bolon's wives with their children and his eldest son, a lad of about fifteen years of age, Bolon himself was absent. Our reception was a friendly one and an empty hut was assigned to us. The women soon brought to each of us *una sarta de pezcados,* which is the name given to a *bejucco* (piece of vine) having strung upon it a dozen half-cooked fish dried in the sun (*mojarras*), and some large bananas and tortillas. Here was a repetition of what I had so often experienced; namely, wherever the Indians are not affected by the Spanish element, food is remarkably abundant. Wherever the people have come under Spanish influence, we have sometimes been unable to obtain a single miserable fish even at a high price. Now each of us received a dozen large delicious fish, which we could hardly consume in three days.

We were rather weary and also quite hungry and therefore enjoyed a repast of the fish and bananas slightly roasted at the fire; we also made coffee and then sought our night's quarters, fully protected, under our *mosquiteros,* from the gnats which swarmed hither in dense multitudes from the laguna near by.

Regarding the circumstances of this man,—who preferred the free life in the wilderness to the constraints of a civilization which had conferred but little good upon him,—the following can be said: Bolon is an Indian or half-breed from Tenosique and was the *mozo adeudado* (that is, one who serves another for debt) of a business man of that town. The name Bolon is an abbreviation, the full name being Bolonchac (*bolon-tšak* = nine-red), which is the Indian name for a favorite species of quail the plaintive call of which in the silence of the night or in the early morning is heard at a great distance. Overwhelmed by his debt and seeing no better future before him, he went many years ago among the Lacantun Indians, who at that time were settled on the right bank of the Usumatsintla. Bolon therefore belongs in the category of those who in this republican land are called *mozos huidos;* but it may be incidentally mentioned that subsequently he cancelled his indebtedness with caoutchouc, *hule,* and at the present time he has nothing more to fear. As a Maya-speaking Indian from Tenosique he had no difficulty in making himself understood by the Lacantuns, whose dress and customs he adopted, and who gave him a wife. In the course of time many of these Indians moved to distant inaccessible wildernesses, others died, and in this way more women and children fell to Bolon. The last chieftain of the race, when dying at an advanced age, even conferred upon Bolon his priestly office, and earnestly impressed upon him his obligation to watch over the graves of the departed, and enjoined upon him that, when he in his

Dugout canoe

Photograph by Teobert Maler. From *Researches in the Central Portion of the Usumatsintla Valley,* 1901. Copyright 1901 by Peabody Museum of American Archaeology and Ethnology, Harvard University. Courtesy of Peabody Museum of Harvard University.

turn should see death approaching, he should place in the temples at Yáxchilan the incense vessels which are in the temple hut by the graves.

This Indian settlement, where the incense vessels still remain, and where Bolon and the remaining women and children yearly burn copal and offer sacrifices, must be about two or three leagues (two or three hour's journey) below Bolon's present establishment.

Although it is not to be supposed that any valuable historical or religious traditions could have been preserved by these people, considering the extremely low intellectual condition into which they have all degenerated, it is nevertheless interesting to note how the last remnants of this race have adhered, amid every hardship, to a kind of ancestor worship, and how the memory of the former greatness and sacredness of Yáxchilan has endured among them. At any rate, we may take it for granted that Bolon has acquired a full knowledge of the habits and customs and also of the religious conceptions of the Indians with whom he has lived for so many years. Whoever should succeed in gaining his confidence might acquire much interesting information, though presented in a vague and confused style.

Thanks to our *mosquiteros,* we passed a comfortable night. We invited young Manuel Bolon to take breakfast with us, and chatting with him about indifferent matters, I introduced questions relative to that which interested me, and thus tried to find out from him whether there were any ruins or sculptures on this side of the Usumatsintla. The young man stated that he had never seen a ruin, but he knew of a *cueva* (cave) on the top of the mountain on the eastern shore of the laguna. If we wished, he would guide us thither. We accepted his offer so that the day might not pass quite unprofitably.

We had to go only about three hundred paces from the huts to reach a small lake, the greatest extent of which in the dry season may measure about one and a half kilometres. As this lake has no name, I gave it for the time being the full name of the Indian owner of the montería, "La Laguna de Bolonchac." There is said to be a series of small lakes in this region which have never been explored by Europeans.

Fortunately Bolon had a cayuco—a boat made of a hollowed-out treetrunk—in which we embarked. Without stopping in the more shallow parts of the laguna, we rowed toward the mountain range, where the water attains a considerable depth and where fish are exceedingly plentiful. Water-fowl of various species enlivened the mirror-like surface. We were especially interested in some large black and white ducks, which, however, were frightened and flew away before we could get ready to shoot them. High in the air circled some beautiful *coscacuauhtli,* "king vultures" (*Cathartes papa* Linn.), whose black and white plumage glistened in the sun. This noble bird—which the Spaniards call "El Rey de los Zopilotes"—can very rarely be observed in its wild state.

We soon reached the wooded slopes of the little mountain range and fastened our cayuco to the roots of an overhanging tree. The ascent was very steep and rocky. After reaching the summit of the mountain, we examined the slope on the other side and soon found the rather spacious open cave, which in ancient times probably afforded an acceptable shelter to Indians hunting in the adjacent forests or fishing in the lake. I at once examined the walls to see if there were not pictures of some kind cut in the rock.

In the centre of the cave where the ground had been somewhat levelled, there was an almost vertical boulder about two and a half metres high. On the wall back of this rock an oval stalactite had formed in the course of years. Into this two round holes for eyes, two quite small ones for nose, and a short line for the mouth had been cut, perhaps by people of a long-vanished race. It is easy to imagine that this rock in front of the human face served in the most primitive fashion to hold incense vessels or small sacrificial gifts.

On searching the corners of the cave for potsherds, I found a few, which seemed to belong to the general Maya-Lacantun period.

I named the cave "La Cueva de la Cabeza," and made a little sketch of the cave with the stone altar and the face on the stalactite.

A heap of stones near the cave seemed to me to be the remains of a building once standing in the vicinity. As we paused on the mountain top and gazed in the direction of Peten-Itza over the boundless wilderness intersected by mountain ranges of not inconsiderable dimensions, we beheld nothing but a vast uninhabited and unexplored tract of country.

Then we descended to our cayuco to explore further the laguna and to fish in the most favorable places.

My men threw in their hooks and with such success that at each throw a fish rose almost instantly to the bait. These fish were *mojarras,*—or *tencuayacas,* as the natives call them,—and were from 25 cm, to 35 cm. long, having eight black spots on each side. In a short time we caught fully a hundred of these delicious fish, so that the entire bottom of the cayuco was covered with them. We also saw great numbers of small fish, *sardinas,* which probably served as food for the *tencuayacas.* In the distance huge alligators swam lazily about.

A gorgeous vegetation is developed on these shores. Many trees, like the *macuilishuatl* and *chutté,* showed a profusion of beautiful pink and white blossoms. We also saw a great deal of *palo de tinte,* which no one here thinks of turning to profit.

Late in the afternoon we returned to the huts in a contented frame of mind, without, it is true, having made any important discoveries.

While we were engaged in cooking, Andres Bolon appeared upon the scene. When Reyes had explained the purpose of our visit, Bolon came into our hut to pay us his respects and to offer his services. At first, of course, I refrained from asking him troublesome questions. Not until late in the evening, after Bolon with his wives and I with my men had eaten an abundant repast, and Bolon had come again to our camp-fire, did I attempt to settle the most important question as to whether he had ever seen ruins in the wide tracts through which he roamed.

I regret to report that the result of our conference—at which Reyes faithfully assisted—was negative. Bolon positively asserted that he had never seen a standing structure like those in Yáxchilan; that only here and there foundations, remains of walls, heaps of stone (*cuyos*), etc., were to be found, nothing worth photographing: . . . *hay cimientos . . . pedazos de pared . . . cuyos . . . en fin vestigios donde se conoce que há habido población . . . pero ruinas en pié, como las de Yáxchilan, no las hay en ninguna parte!* . . . Furthermore, Bolon offered to guide me to the *vestigios* of which he knew.

While convinced that a journey through this wilderness to all the picturesque lakes and little mountain ranges would be of very great interest to the naturalist or to the artist, I decided to leave such an expedition for some future occasion and at present to return to "El Paso de Bolon" in order from there to continue the voyage up the river. On the next morning, therefore, we prepared for the return journey and took leave of Bolon and his wives in the friendliest manner.

Casting a final glance upon this paradisiacal little spot of earth, I could not refrain from thinking that it might be regarded as a remarkable fact that I, Teobert Maler, in the last year of the nineteenth century, had encountered in that vast wilderness on the right bank of the Usumatsintla—opposite the ancient Yáxchilan—a single inhabitant—a *mozo huido*—with the wives of deceased Indians and a very few children, the last remnant of their race.

Conqueror and conquered have both vanished from this region, leaving no trace behind. The forest primeval has again asserted its rights.

• • •

EIGHT

Edward H. Thompson 1904

That Great Water Pit

[Edward H. Thompson—who dredged the famous Sacred Well at Chichén Itzá, Yucatán, and brought up from its murky depths treasures in gold and jade, thus confirming an ancient legend that it was the Cenote of Sacrifice into which the Indians cast offerings to the Rain God—went to Yucatán, as he himself expressed it, "by way of Lost Atlantis." When he was still a student at the Worcester Polytechnic Institute in Massachusetts, he wrote a romantic article entitled "Atlantis Not a Myth" which was published in 1879 in *Popular Science Monthly*. The article came to the attention of Stephen Salisbury, Jr., then vice-president of the American Antiquarian Society, who, six years later, was instrumental in having Thompson appointed an American consul to Mexico, to be stationed in Yucatán and Campeche with instructions to devote all possible time to exploration and investigations of the Maya ruins in that area.]

I am an enthusiast by nature and so completely did I give myself to my work in Yucatan that some of my contemporaries spoke of me as impractical. I carried out many explorations for such institutions as the Peabody Museum of Harvard, the Field Columbian Museum of Chicago, and others, but when there was an expedition to be made and no great foundation at hand to sponsor it, I was wont to undertake it all the same, on my own account. I purchased and restored the great plantation of Chichen, which included within its bounds the ruined group of Chichen Itzá, ancient capital and sacred city of the Mayas, so that I might the better study this, the greatest

The quotations by Thompson are, in the order quoted below, from Edward Herbert Thompson, *People of the Serpent: Life and Adventure among the Mayas* (Boston and New York: Houghton Mifflin, 1932), pp. 4–5, 102–8, 123–26, 268–74. Copyright 1932 by Houghton Mifflin Company. Reprinted by permission of the publisher.

monument of a vanished race. I have squandered my substance in riotous explorations and I am altogether satisfied. The reward of a labor of love lies in the performing of it, and I can look back upon a career as full of incident and adventure as any man has the right to expect.

Edward H. Thompson

As veteran of a long campaign in the forests and jungles of Middle America, I bear certain honorable scars. I am slightly deaf because of eardrums injured while I was diving in the Sacred Well of Chichen Itzá to prove that this venerable water pit was once used for human sacrifice. A poisoned trap set by Indians in the remote hinterland of Yucatan left me with a lameness in one leg. Several bouts with jungle fever robbed me of my once luxuriant locks earlier perhaps than they would have passed in the normal course of nature. On a number of occasions I have been in imminent danger of death in various unpleasant forms. But there were many high moments in my life in Yucatan any one of which outweighs the sum total of these debits.

Such a moment it was when I first gazed upon the glistening temple and palaces of Xkichmook, the Hidden City. Others are linked with discoveries which will probably be recorded as my most important contributions to this branch of archaeology. These were, first, the finding at Old Chichen of the tablet of the Initial Series, or date stone, which has thrown considerable light on Maya history; second, the proving that ancient traditions concerning the Well of Sacrifice at Chichen Itzá were true; and third, the discovery of the Tomb of the High Priest in a hollow pyramid at Chichen, the only one of its kind yet brought to light. The thrill I experienced in any one of these finds made years of work and hardship seem well worth while.

[The story of Thompson's dredging of the Cenote of Sacrifice at Chichén Itzá has been retold many times—it was one of the most dramatic discoveries in the history of Maya archaeology. Some of Thompson's other experiences are less well known and I shall quote from them here. The first occurred during his investigations at the ruined city of Labná.]

One of the singular facts about Labna was that it seemed to have depended entirely upon the rainfall for its water supply. Every large edifice within this ancient city had at least one reservoir or cistern called by the Mayas *chultunes,* built into the structure of the terrace on which the edifice rested. They were, therefore, really subterranean chambers.

In the scientific investigation of Labna, one of my interesting duties was to descend into these *chultunes,* take their measurements, calculate their capacity, and investigate the materials that had accumulated on their bottom. Often I found things there of real archaeological value, jade beads, pendants of polished stone, and shell objects, either thrown in as votive offerings in some forgotten ritual act, or else, like the terra-cotta water-vessels, dropped in by accident while the water was being drawn. On the smoothly finished stucco walls of the *chultunes* I sometimes found, moulded in relief, figures representing waterfowl, turtles, frogs, and snakes, all very naturally done.

In the material of the terrace that supported the Palace, was an unusually large and well-made *chultun*,* in shape and structure like the smaller chambers of the Palace. A large circular pavement raised above the terrace served as a watershed that conducted the rainfall on the surface through a man-hole about three feet in diameter, down into the cistern.

In preparing to enter subterranean places of this character, I wore a high-crowned hat with a narrow brim, the crown of which was filled with rags or leaves, and I held between my teeth a heavy and very sharp hunting-knife. Then with one foot in the noose of a stout rope and one hand free, my men let me over the edge and down into space. The rag-packed crown served to receive and to ward off harmlessly what might otherwise be a knockout blow if a falling rock should hit me, while the sharp and heavy hunting-knife came in very handy at times when I had to snip off the heads of a small but very poisonous species of rattlesnake that lived in the rock crevices, before the reptile could fasten its fangs in my face. I carried the knife between my teeth while on my way up and down for the reason that my right hand was thus left free and ready for quick action when needed.

Thus equipped, I was let down one day through the man-hole and into the water chamber. It had been, when in use, a very fine *chultun*. Of course the settling of the soil and the wrenching of the tree-roots during centuries of neglect had cracked its walls and opened seams in the well-made floor. But it still kept its pristine shape as a water chamber, although it no longer held water.

As I went down, I noticed, in the dim sepulchral light that entered through the opening at the top, the loosened stones in the roofing, the cracks in the walls caused by the settling, and the large mound of débris that had fallen through the man-hole. I landed lightly on the mound and, stepping to one side, began to take measurements. As I scraped the dust away from a corner, I heard a sound that I well knew, the rattle of a rattlesnake, and it came from the stone mound on which I had just stepped. I looked at the spot intently and saw a big triangular head come from the mound, raise itself a foot or so, and then the wavering head with its lidless eyes gazed at me fixedly. I looked at the snake while the snake looked at me; meanwhile his body was gliding smoothly out from that pile of débris, until I began to believe that what I thought to be a mound of rock and dirt was mostly rattlesnake.

It was a very large rattlesnake. He had probably fallen through the man-hole when young and inexperienced in the handling of his body, and perforce stayed there. The rain and dew that from time to time entered was sufficient for his needs, while the incautious and inquisitive rats, moles, lizards, and toads that fell in were sufficient to keep him alive and thrifty. So he waxed big and strong and very venomous. Everything considered, he must have had rather an easy, uneventful life until I came and made him a very mad rattler by squeezing his body as I stepped on the rock pile.

* Edward H. Thompson. *The Chultunes of Labna.* Bulletin [Memoir] of the Peabody Museum, vol. 1, no. 3, 1897.

The situation grew rapidly acute, for his eyes were turning bottle green, his jaws dripped saliva, and a strong odor like musk filled the unventilated space of his chamber, and gave me a feeling of nausea. It was clearly time for me to make a move.

At first thought it would seem that at least I could pick up a rock and smash the snake's head. But all the rocks were close to where the snake lay coiled. Where I had been stopping to take the measurements by the wall, there were only tiny twigs and the dust of ages. There was nothing in that idea. I might have shouted and so brought help from my men, but I had proved long before that, unless I could take my stand directly under the opening above, no matter how loudly I called or how distinctly I spoke, my voice would reach the surface only as an inarticulate howl. The men might have detected an urgent note in the howl, it is true, and sent one of their number down to investigate. The nearly naked native would have come swarming down the rope onto the rattlesnake and straight-way I should have had a dying Indian on my hands.

I might have shot his head off with a bullet from my heavy revolver, but the heavy discharge in the confined space might have brought the roof stones in a pile on me. A still better reason for not using my revolver was that I did not have it with me. I am very rarely parted from my revolver while marching through the jungle or making excursions of this nature, but with the cartridge-filled belt and holster it was heavy around my waist, and so I had just hung the belt and revolver on the limb of a near-by tree, where it could now do me no good.

The rattlesnake was working himself into a cold-blooded rage while I leaned against the wall of the chamber and watched him tightening his coils and changing the upper one into the striking S. If anyone says that a rattlesnake strikes directly from a coil, you may tell him from me that, in the jungles of Yucatan at least, he does not. He throws the last coil back into a kind of a double curve and then launches his attack the length of that double curve; no farther and often much less. But, even so, that would be far enough for him to reach his mark. I had raised my booted leg, hoping to receive the threatened stroke on its leather surface, when the miracle happened.

The walls of the *chultun* were made, like those of the Palace itself, of stone and mortar rubble, faced with cut stone and surfaced with a hard finish of mortar. The last surface of mortar was much thicker in the *chultun* than in the Palace chambers above, that the stored water might not seep through it.

During the centuries that had passed since the structure was deserted, the terrace had settled and with it the *chultun*. This settling had caused the thick mortar surface of the *chultun* to buckle in places from the faces of the wall stones, and it was my good fortune to lean directly against one of these buckled places. I felt the surface give and at once understood what it meant. Pushing back with all my strength, I felt the mortar crack. To reach behind me, grab a thick fragment, and throw it at the rattler was the work of a moment. I missed the head and neck, already tense for the spring, but struck the coiled mass of the body. I must have hit it hard, and fractured a vertebra, perhaps, for the head and neck fell to the floor of the chamber and writhed there uncertainly for a few seconds. Then this creature seemed to recover, for he once more raised his head, but too late.

Those precious seconds that he lay prone were sufficient for my purpose. They gave me time to seize and throw two other fragments of mortar that stunned the reptile. Placing the limp head through the dangling noose, I held it there by putting one foot on the neck in the noose and shouted to be drawn up. The men must have understood the urgency of my call, for they hauled me up so quickly that both skin and flesh was torn from the knuckles of my left hand by the rim of the man-hole. Even to this day there are times when I cannot move my fingers freely.

There was a curious aftermath to this adventure. I took two or three baths a day with fragrant herbs and aromatic buds added to the hot water to get rid of the smell of the snake, and yet, for days after, every time that I perspired freely, I could smell that musky odor of that rattlesnake.

My favorite riding-horse was an animal so attached to me that he would follow me around like a dog if I let him. When I wished to use him, I would only have to give the low and soft but penetrating whistle of the quail, and he would come up with a whinny and nuzzle me for a piece of cane sugar. After this affair with the rattler, he would come readily at the call until he caught the snake odor. Then he would stop abruptly, his nostrils would widen until I could see the red, and he would snort and rear until it took two men to hold him while I mounted into the saddle.

One afternoon, we found ourselves by the edge of a small lake, called by the natives Akal. Yucatan has almost no brooks or running water, and for four long years my ears had not heard the sound of singing brook, nor had my eyes been gladdened by the sight of rivers flowing on the surface. So this little bright lake in the midst of the dark forest was to us like an oasis in the midst of a desert to the sight of the thirsty traveller. We encamped then and there and bathed long and luxuriously. One of the men, a famous cook among his people, took advantage of the stop to cook in the earth, with all the requirements of the occasion, forest herbs, little wild peppers, and all, a large wild fat turkey that we had killed. That meal was a banquet that anyone would have enjoyed, although the menu might perhaps have puzzled him.

The meal over, we lay back comfortably, looking up into the dense foliage far above us, where a family of *tigrillos*—little tiger cats—were frolicking. Either they thought themselves too far above us to be in danger; or, more probably, had never before seen man and so had not learned to fear him.

My men were about to teach them something, but I forbade them to fire. The *tigrillos,* about double the size of a common house cat, although much more slender, are harmless to all except the smaller game and the hen-roost.

Before we slept, we told the nightly stories around the campfire. On this occasion most of them were about the bloody doings of the *Sublevados,* and, as we rolled ourselves in our blankets and gave ourselves up to slumber, all save one silent watcher crouching by the fire, doubtless our last waking thoughts were of them, for we were well within their country.

We slept soundly and well, as tired men, well fed, should; I in my hammock, swung between two trees, and the natives on the ground around the fire. How long we slept thus I never knew, but I was suddenly awakened by a series of hideous yells, and my surprised eyes dimly saw, half-naked, brown-skinned bodies dancing wildly around the fire. My fingers gripped my ever-ready pistol. As my naked feet touched the ground, a thousand red-hot needles pricked me, and then another figure, a white-skinned one, joined the dancing group. The explanation was simple enough. An army of black foraging ants having designs on something more distant, found the half-clad bodies of the slumbering men intercepting their path, and after the manner of their kind, proceeded to sample them. A thousand keen little forceps simultaneously set to work on each of the four brown bodies. The frenzied yells and the agitated dancing followed as sunrise follows the dawn. For over an hour we were forced to keep at a distance from the fire, and let the ants go about their business without interference. By and by, the solid black mass grew thinner, and finally faded away entirely; then we went back to our belongings and took account of stock.

Everything had been sampled, even to the leather binding of my boots, but nothing was seriously damaged. A little black line showed where too inquisitive ants had tried to reach the lard, in its tin pail, and had tumbled in. They had even investigated the campfire, and a ring of half-burned bodies, shrivelling up in the heat, lay entirely surrounding the coals. For a while we sat nursing our bites, and then, "turned in again," to sleep soundly until the scolding of the great blue birds, the *cheles,* woke us up once more.

Early the next day, just after the broad disk of the sun, the great golden disk that the primitive people delighted to worship, swung up above the forest ridge on which we stood, we saw in the distance the massive walls and majestic form of an imposing stone structure, "the walls of which shone like silver," in the sunlight. "Xkichmook," I said softly, more to myself than otherwise. "Xkichmook, *no hoch hach tzutz*"—"how big and beautiful"—echoed my Indians in tones as soft and as awed as my own.

We approached the ancient group through the remains of an artificial watershed; then we had to climb the walls of a stone terrace and cross the level platform, up to the towering base of a massive stone building, blank and severe as a fortress wall. Skirting this with difficulty, because of the fallen masses of stone, we passed through a narrow archway into a hollow square.

On the south rose the high temple, on the east and on the west were one-story structures, wings of the temple, while that on the north was ruined and shapeless.

We climbed slowly upward, over the fallen blocks and columns that covered the broad stairway leading to the altar platform, on the top of the temple.

From time to time we stopped to let the breeze refresh, and to admire the landscape as it unfolded itself before us. Just before we reached the top, a stone rolling down made us look in the direction from which it came. A handsome female jaguar had just glided out from beneath the altar structure and was gazing at us with unblinking yellow eyes, uncertain whether to fight or run. A heavy American ball and a large native-made lead slug reached her vitals at almost the same instant. Her blood sprinkled the altar base as she gave her last convulsive spring. She was offered up as a blood sacrifice for our discovery of Xkichmook.

I have referred before to an article, "Atlantis Not a Myth," written during my college days, and of the important bearing it had on determining my future course. It was while hunting up material for this article that I first came upon an old volume written by Diego de Landa, one of the earliest Spanish missionaries to Yucatan and later bishop of that diocese. Among other things recounted in quaint old Spanish in this book was a description of Chichen Itzá, the capital and sacred city of the Mayas. The wise priest laid special emphasis upon the traditions concerning the Sacred Well that lay within the confines of the city.

According to these traditions, as told to De Landa by his native converts, in times of drought, pestilence, or disaster, solemn processions of priests, devotees with rich offerings, and victims for the sacrifice wound down the steep stairway of the Temple of Kukil Can, the Sacred Serpent, and along the Sacred Way to the Well of Sacrifice. There, amid the droning boom of the *tunkul*, the shrill pipings of the whistle and the plaintive notes of the flute, beautiful maidens and captive warriors of renown, as well as rich treasures, were thrown into the dark waters of the Sacred Well to propitiate the angry god who, it was believed, lived in the deeps of the pool.

From the moment I read the musty old volume, the thought of that grim old water pit and the wonderful objects that lay concealed within its depths became an obsession with me. Then, long years after, by what seemed to me almost an interposition of Providence, I became the sole owner of the great Chichen plantation, within whose confines the City of the Sacred Well and the Sacred Well itself lay.

For days and weeks after I purchased the plantation, I was a frequent worshiper at the little shrine on the brink of the Sacred Well. I pondered, mused, and calculated. I made measurements and numberless soundings, until, not satisfied but patiently expectant, I put my notebook aside and

awaited the accepted time. It came when I was called to the United States
for a scientific conference. After the session was over, at an informal gathering I told of the tradition concerning this Sacred Well of Chichen Itzá, of
my belief in its authenticity, and the methods by which I proposed to prove
it.

My statements brought forth a storm of protests from my friends.

"No person," they said, "can go down into the unknown depths of that
great water pit and expect to come out alive. If you want to commit suicide,
why not seek a less shocking way of doing it?"

But I had already weighed the chances and made up my mind. My next
step was to go to Boston and take lessons in deep-sea diving. My tutor was
Captain Ephraim Nickerson of Long Wharf, who passed to his reward a
score of years ago. Under his expert and patient teaching, I became in time
a fairly good diver, but by no means a perfect one, as I was to learn some
time later. My next move was to adapt to my purpose an "orange-peel
bucket" dredge with the winch, tackles, steel cables, and ropes of a stiff-
legged derrick and a thirty-foot swinging boom. All this material was crated
and ready for immediate shipment when ordered by either letter or wire.

Then, and not until then, did I appear before the Honorable Stephen Salisbury of Worcester, Massachusetts, and Charles P. Bowditch of Boston, both
officers of the American Antiquarian Society and of Harvard University of
which the Peabody Museum is a part. To them I explained the project and
asked the moral and financial aid of the two organizations they represented.
Although I had headed several important and successful expeditions under
the auspices of these institutions, I found both of these gentlemen very reluc-

The Cenote of Sacrifice, Chichén Itzá, dredged by Edward H. Thompson

tant to put the seal of their approval upon what they clearly believed to be a most audacious undertaking. They were willing to finance the scheme, but hesitated to take upon themselves the responsibility for my life.

I finally argued them out of their fears, and all other obstacles having been overcome, the dredge and its equipment were duly installed on the platform to the right of the shrine, and close to the edge of the great water pit, the Sacred Well.

During my preliminary investigations I had established what I called the "fertile zone" by throwing in wooden logs shaped like human beings and having the weight of the average native. By measuring the rope after these manikins were hauled ashore, I learned the extreme distance to which sacrificial victims could have been thrown. In this way I fixed the spot where the human remains would probably be found. Regulating my operations by these calculations, I found them to respond with gratifying accuracy.

I doubt if anybody can realize the thrill I felt when, with four men at the winch handles and one at the brake, the dredge, with its steel jaw agape, swung from the platform, hung poised for a brief moment in mid-air over the dark pit and then, with a long swift glide downward, entered the still, dark waters and sank smoothly on its quest. A few moments of waiting to allow the sharp-pointed teeth to bite into the deposit, and then the forms of the workmen bent over the winch handles and muscles under the dark brown skin began to play like quicksilver as the steel cables tautened under the strain of the upcoming burden.

The water, until then still as an obsidian mirror, began to surge and boil around the cable and continued to do so long after the bucket, its tightly closed jaws dripping clear water, had risen, slowly but steadily, up to the rim of the pit. Swinging around by the boom, the dredge deposited on the planked receiving platform, a cartload of dark brown material, wood punk, dead leaves, broken branches, and other débris; then it swung back and hung, poised, ready to seek another load.

For days the dredge went up and down, up and down, interminably, bringing up muck and rocks, muck, and more muck. Once it brought up, gripped lightly in its jaws, the trunk of a tree apparently as sound as if it toppled into the pit by a storm of yesterday. This was on a Saturday. By Monday the tree had vanished and on the pile of rocks where the dredge had deposited it only a few lines of wood fibre remained, surrounded by a dark stain of a pyroligneous character. Another time the dredge brought up the bones of a jaguar and those of a deer, mute evidence of a forest tragedy. And so the work went on for days.

I began to get nervous by day and sleepless at night.

"Is it possible," I asked myself, "that I have let my friends into all this expense and exposed myself to a world of ridicule only to prove, what many have contended, that these traditions are simply old tales, tales without any foundation in fact?"

At times, as if to tantalize me, the dredge recovered portions of earthen vessels undeniably ancient. I resolutely threw aside the thought that these might be the proofs I sought. Potsherds, I argued, were likely to be found anywhere on the site of this old city, washed from the surface deposits by rains. Boys are boys, whether in Yucatan or Massachusetts, and have been for some thousands of years. The instinct of a boy is to "skitter" any smooth hard object, stone or potsherd, across smooth waters like those of the deep water pit and then it rests amid the mud and rocks at the bottom until brought up by the dredge. I could not accept these chance potsherds as the proofs that I required.

One day—I remembered it as if it were but yesterday—I rose in the morning from a sleepless night. The day was gray as my thoughts and the thick mist dropped from the leaves of the trees as quiet tears drop from half-closed eyes. I plodded through the dampness down to where the staccato clicks of the dredge brake called me and, crouching under the palm leaf lean-to, watched the monotonous motions of the brown-skinned natives as they worked at the winches. The bucket slowly emerged from the heaving water that boiled around it and, as I looked listlessly down into it, I saw two yellow-white, globular masses lying on the surface of the chocolate-colored muck that filled the basin. As the mass swung over the brink and up to the platform, I took from it the two objects and closely examined them.

They were hard, formed evidently by human hands from some substance unknown to me. They resembled somewhat the balls of "bog butter" from the lacustrine deposits of Switzerland and Austria. There, ancient dwellings were built on piles in the midst of the lake to protect them against raiding enemies. The crocks of butter were suspended by cords let down between the piles and immersed in the ice-cold water for preservation. Despite all their precaution, raids did occur and the dwellings were destroyed by casual fires as well as by raids; so the crocks of butter fell unobserved from the charred piles down through the icy waters to rest unheeded in the increasing deposit until ages of time changed them into the almost fossilized material known to archaeologists as "bog butter."

But these two nodules could not be bog butter, for unless the known data are strangely wrong, the ancient Mayas kept no domestic animals of any kind, much less cows or goats. They seemed to be made of some resinous substance. I tasted one. It was resin. I put a piece into a mass of lighted embers and immediately a wonderful fragrance permeated the atmosphere. Like a ray of bright sunlight breaking through a dense fog came to me the words of the old *H'Men*, the Wise Man of Ebtun: "In ancient times our fathers burned the sacred resin—*pom*—and by the fragrant smoke their prayers were wafted to their God whose home was in the Sun."

These yellow balls of resin were masses of the sacred incense *pom*, and had been thrown in as part of the rich offerings mentioned in the traditions. That night for the first time in weeks I slept soundly and long.

NINE

• • • •

Sylvanus G. Morley 1916

Murder on the Trail

[Sylvanus Griswold Morley (1883–1948) was the best known Maya archaeologist of his generation. For half a century he explored the jungles of the Maya area, always seeking unreported ruins and, more especially, stone monuments with carved hieroglyphic inscriptions, on which he had become the world's authority. Sometimes called the "Little Friend of All the Americas," he was well known and affectionately regarded from New York to the remotest villages in the Guatemala rain forest. He charmed everyone with his friendliness, his great knowledge, and his store of anecdotes of travel in the bush.

[Alfred V. Kidder called Morley "that small, nearsighted, dynamic bundle of energy; of warm, outgiving friendship; of love for beautiful things; and above all else throughout his professional life, of preoccupation with, and determination to forward the study of, the ancient Maya. . . . Heat, cracking sunburn, thirst, saddle-soreness, rock bruises, cactus stabs, nothing discouraged him. I can see him now, a quick, small figure in high boots and khakis and an enormous straw hat that was always falling off, stumbling about among the fallen walls and along the rimrocks, perilously close to nasty drops. Why he never broke his neck in the McElmo canyons or afterwards among the Maya ruins is a mystery—he never looked where he was going. He'd trip and go down, and pick himself up and keep on, cheerfully whistling."

The quotation by Kidder, above, is from Alfred Vincent Kidder, "Sylvanus Griswold Morley, 1883–1948," *El Palacio* (Santa Fe, N.M.), Vol. 55, no. 9 (September, 1948), pp. 267–70. The letter from Morley, quoted below, is from Arthur Carpenter, "The Death of Lafleur: Two Letters from Morley." In *Morleyana: A Collection of Writings in Memoriam, Sylvanus Griswold Morley—1883–1948* (Santa Fe, N.M.: The School of American Research and the Museum of New Mexico, 1950), pp. 23–45. Copyright 1950 by the Museum of New Mexico and the School of American Research. Reprinted with permission of the publishers.

[An entire book of anecdotes about Morley has been published. I have chosen to reproduce here his own account of the murder of an expedition companion, Dr. Moise Lafleur.]

El Cayo, British Honduras,
May 22, 1916.
My dear Dr. Woodward,—

On May 19th, as soon as I could gather and verify the essential facts, I advised you by wireless of the death of Dr. Moise Lafleur, the expedition's physician, which occurred two days earlier (May 17) at three o'clock in the afternoon. The more detailed account which follows has been prepared after repeated consultations with Mr. Carpenter, and the two colored boys, Andrew and Marius Silas, the only other eye-witnesses of the tragedy besides myself.

In order that you may understand clearly just what happened, it is first necessary for me to outline the movements of the expedition during the past four weeks, and to describe briefly, not only the geography of the country in which it had been operating, but also the attendant political circumstances.

The expedition left Belise on the 17th of April five strong, Mr. Carpenter, Dr. Lafleur, myself, and our two colored servants, Andrew and Marius Silas. We reached here (El Cayo), the head of navigation on the Belise River, three days later; and at once began to arrange for a three weeks trip into northern Peten, the adjoining department of the Republic of Guatemala.

Having gathered the necessary outfit, guides, mules, supplies, etc., we left El Cayo on April 25th taking a generally northwesterly direction into the Peten bush, our objective being a newly reported archaeological site some nine days journey in.

The northern half of Peten is a gently rolling plain traversed by ranges of low hills, and is completely overgrown with a vast tropical jungle. The only roads are occasional narrow winding trails cut by chicleros (*i.e.*, the chicle bleeders), and the only human habitations in the region, their constantly shifting camps. You should note that these trails spread fan-like from El Cayo as a base. Here all the mule-trains discharge their cargoes, and from here it is shipped to Belise by water. To the west and north lies a vast trackless jungle whose only point of egress is at this frontier village of El Cayo.

Along one of the blades of this fan of trails we were now making our way. The first night out (Ojo de Agua) one of our guides, to whom I had advanced money after the custom of the country, decamped, presumably returning to El Cayo. The next morning (April 26) I went back to look for him, leaving Mr. Carpenter in charge with the understanding that he would conduct the expedition to Laguna that same day and await me there.

On reaching El Cayo I heard some startling news. That very morning at day-break, a party of about forty revolutionists, composed mostly of Mexican chicleros actually recruited on British soil, *i.e.*, from El Cayo and Benque Viejo, had captured the nearby frontier village of Plancha Piedra without bloodshed, and had seized the chicle and mule-trains there. They were issuing manifestos to the effect that nobody would be harmed, and that their movement was directed solely against the Government of Guatemala, and the . . . abuses which have crept into the chicle business there.

I felt that I must return at once to Laguna, and acquaint the other members of the party with this totally unexpected development, and by a long ride I succeeded in reaching there before dawn that same night.

We considered the situation carefully, debating whether to continue on our way, or whether to return to El Cayo at once. Because it was impossible to foresee all the contingencies which might arise if we went on,—though personally I had no misgivings as to the wisdom of such a course,—I did not care to assume the entire responsibility for the decision, and the question was left to an open vote of the field staff: Mr. Carpenter, Dr. Lafleur, and myself.

Sylvanus Griswold Morley
Courtesy of *American Antiquity*.

Sylvanus G. Morley (left) and Thomas Gann standing by stela, Copán
From Thomas Gann, *Ancient Cities and Modern Tribes*, 1926. Copyright 1926 by Thomas
Gann. By permission of Charles Scribner's Sons.

We found ourselves unanimous as to the advisability of continuing our journey, which opinion, indeed, was held by all the others, the native guides, muleteers, and camp servants. . . .

The next morning, therefore (April 27th), we continued our journey into the bush, turning our backs upon civilization, and largely forgetting the matter for the next fortnight.

This is not the proper time for presenting the scientific results of this trip, probably the most successful I have ever undertaken, since it includes among other things, the discovery of the oldest Maya monument yet reported, so I will pass over the intervening fortnight between April 29th and May 13th without further comment other than to say that we made the journey successfully; spent six days at the ruins near a chicle camp called San Leandro; and returned back along our trail reaching the chicle camp of Triumfo on May 15th, where we heard the first accurate news in two weeks on the conditions obtaining ahead of us.

We learned that the revolutionists had abandoned Plancha Piedra almost immediately after they had taken it, and marching to Laguna had taken that village without opposition on the 28th of April, the day after we left there. The Government troops in the meantime had reoccupied Plancha Piedra, and had fortified themselves there. In these two places the respective forces were encamped, apparently watching each other.

The only weak point about this news was its age, being then (May 13th) over two weeks old. We did not know, nor had we any means of finding out, what had happened since. The entire trouble might have blown over in that time, or might equally well have reached serious proportions. In this dilemma we decided to wait over a day at Triumfo, particularly since another mule-train, whose advance runners we had met on the previous day, were due to arrive the next day, and its leader, so my own head muleteer told me, knew more about the situation ahead of us than we did since he had left El Cayo after us.

The next day this mule-train arrived (May 14th), and with it began the first of those adverse circumstances which in a vicious train so linked themselves together as to eventuate in Dr. Lafleur's death.

There arrived that same day at Triumfo another mule-train also en route for El Cayo. With it came a Mexican, Ladislao Romero, a chicle contractor, and for the last seven years a resident of El Cayo. He had been sent into the bush from El Cayo by a Mr. Waight, another chicle contractor, a British subject, for the purpose of hiding Waight's chicle in the bush until the trouble should have passed over. He carried a passport from the Commissioner of the Cayo District, the local colonial administrative official; and to provide against possible encounters with the revolutionists, he had gone first to Laguna and had secured from the chief, one Trinidad Flores, a passport permitting him and his associates to pass freely through the revolutionary lines.

Romero approached me at Triumfo that afternoon (May 14th) and told me that a mutual friend, no less than the revolutionary chief himself, whom I had known slightly at El Cayo, sent me his best wishes and the message that if I cared to return to El Cayo through Laguna I would not be molested in any way. He then showed me his passport signed by this Trinidad Flores, which in fact gave him and his associates free passage through the revolutionary lines. At the same time he showed me another passport from the District Commissioner of the Cayo District giving him permission to leave and return to the Colony for the business in hand.

Romero said the only thing he lacked was a passport from the Guatemalan authorities. Of the latter I had taken elaborate precautions to provide ourselves, with what I thought was an adequate supply for any emergency that might arise. Both Mr. Carpenter and I had letters from the Minister of Foreign Relations in Guatemala City bespeaking for us the usual courtesies extended to scientific expeditions, and in addition I had a letter from Don Clodeveo Berges, the Governor of Peten, recommending me to the care of all the civil and military authorities of the Department. Finally, beside these, we had our own American passports and your official letter, sufficient credentials, if examined, to guarantee the peaceful and altruistic character of our mission. By traveling with Romero we would be safe if we encountered any of the revolutionists, and so far as any government troops were concerned, we naturally anticipated no danger from that source. Moreover, by joining forces with this other mule-train we increased our number from 9 to 18, a greater number than any picket of the revolutionists which we would be likely to encounter.

We left Triumfo the next morning (May 15th) and proceeding by more circuitous and less used trails than the ones by which we had entered, we reached Dos Aguadas that evening and the Rio Holmul the next (May 16th). By this route we had made a big detour to the south and west in order to avoid the revolutionary headquarters at Laguna. We had at last reached the region where trouble—if there were to be any—would most likely occur. You will note that from the Rio Holmul to El Cayo is only a matter of thirty miles, and from this point the trails converge more or less rapidly. This last stretch lay directly between the two hostile camps, and we imagined must be fairly well patrolled by both sides. Unfortunately there were no other trails available since as I have already explained, all trails emerge at El Cayo; and we had no guides who would lead us through the untracked bush, even had our failing food supply permitted such a course. No one, not even the natives, expected any serious trouble, since we had passports from both sides, and indeed the worst we ourselves anticipated was that we might be stopped and some of our outfit taken from us.

I now come to the last day (May 17th), that on which Dr. Lafleur was killed. We left Rio Holmul at 7:50 A.M., our party going out in two sections, one taking the pack-animals over the Bullet-tree Falls trail, and the other, in which Mr. Carpenter, Dr. Lafleur, and myself all rode, going by way of Chunvis.

We approached this latter place with an extreme of caution. The bell had been removed from the bell-mare; no one spoke aloud; all shouting at the mules, the usually inevitable accompaniment of mule-driving in this country, was eliminated for once; and our really large mule-train made little or no noise. When within two miles of Chunvis three runners were sent ahead to find out whether or not the coast was clear. By missing the trail at this point we also missed the boy they sent back to inform us that all was safe and come ahead in, but this was of little consequence since we ourselves reached Chunvis a little later finding everything there perfectly quiet and normal.

The two chicleros in charge of the camp told us that the government troops were still at Plancha Piedra from which they had not moved since they occupied it three weeks before, and that the revolutionists were still at Laguna from which they had not moved since they captured it. Furthermore that there had been no encounter between the two forces, and that all was, and had been, quiet. Indeed, a mule-train had been engaged for the past week in making daily round-trips from Buena Vista in the Colony of Chunvis and return for chicle, and finally this train had left for Buena Vista only three hours before we got in.

This then was the information we received at Chunvis and it dispelled all our misgivings. Everything was, and had been, quiet since the original outbreak more than three weeks before. The regular business of hauling out chicle was going on uninterruptedly as always, and indeed over the very trail we were about to take to El Cayo.

The day was early, just noon, and the horses while not fresh, were by no means exhausted: and the remaining distance not more than eighteen miles. We were unanimous in the decision to push through to El Cayo, get our mail, and the first news of the outside world in over three weeks. Back of this decision also, was the feeling that a short ten miles separated us from the frontier, and once across this line and on the British soil, we could dismiss all further anxiety over the revolutionists.

But here a quandary arose. The head muleteer of the pack-train said his pack animals were too tired to go on, and he was not coming in until the next day. This left us without a guide. I asked some of the chicleros if they would show us the trail to Buena Vista, but they said they could not leave their chicle. Finally Romero said he would go with us as far as Buena Vista, from which point on in to El Cayo I myself knew the trail. I closed the arrangements with him, and at 12:30 P.M. we started six strong: Romero, Mr. Carpenter, Dr. Lafleur, Andrew and Marius Silas, and myself, all mounted. Andrew Silas led, in addition, a horse which had been hurt on the way.

The guide Romero rode first; I came second after my usual custom. The other four constantly shifted their positions in the line behind us. The coun-

try between Chunvis and the border is a succession of low hills covered with
the same dense bush as elsewhere. The trail bears a little south of east as it
approaches the frontier, it ascends a little low hill cutting across the slope—
in the direction we were going—from right to left.

Just a few minutes before the [shooting], perhaps fifteen at the outside,
occurred an incident which had an important bearing on the matter, since it
probably determined (without our knowing it) that Dr. Lafleur was to lose
his life instead of myself.

At 2:30 a sudden brief shower came up. The water collecting on the lenses
of my glasses, so interfered with my vision that I took them off to place in
my pocket until the rain should be over. In doing so they fell to the ground,
and I was obliged to dismount to pick them up. At this point Dr. Lafleur,
who had been riding well toward the rear, pushed up ahead of me saying
as he passed, "I am going up next to the guide, Morley, to talk to him." Andrew Silas leading the lame horse also passed me before I remounted and
fell into line.

This trivial incident, you will note, caused an entire shift in our relative
positions in the line. Romero the guide was still first, but Dr. Lafleur had
taken my place as second, and Andrew Silas and the lame animal had come
forward to the third place. I then fell back to fourth place, Mr. Carpenter
came fifth, and Marius Silas last. This could not have been more than five
minutes before the shooting.

We proceeded noisily enough through the bush, with no thought of con-
cealing our presence there, talking back and forth to one another, all fears at
rest. The frontier was within a quarter of a mile. I had told Romero to advise
me in advance when we approached the line so that we could take the readings of our watches since Mr. Carpenter was carrying out observations for
longitude. He had just called back to me that we were getting very near the
line. We had entered a space about 125 feet long where the underbrush had
been cleared back from the trail some distance on the left hand side and a
few yards to the right hand side leaving us in a little clearing. Ahead the
thick undergrowth closed in again.

Suddenly, without warning of any kind, not the stirring of a leaf, there
burst from the bush just ahead of us and to the right and left as well, a volley
of ten or fifteen rifle shots, and this was immediately succeeded by sustained
irregular firing.

Simultaneously with this first volley the guide Romero gave a violent cry,
at the same time falling to the ground where he lay crying and writhing
about, apparently mortally wounded.

Doctor Lafleur after the first volley jumped from his horse, and paused
to pump a shell from the magazine into the chamber of his rifle, a Winches-
ter 38 calibre carbine, which he was in the habit of keeping at hand while
traveling, for hunting purposes. An instant later he sought cover to the right
of the trail. It is doubtful in the minds of Mr. Carpenter and myself whether

he ever succeeded in firing a shot; particularly since the autopsy seems to show that his right arm was almost immediately disabled.

The boy Andrew, who occupied third place in line, dismounted with maximum celerity, abandoning his own mount and the lame horse he had been leading, and retired to the rear post-haste, back down the trail toward Chunvis.

During these few seconds I retired a few feet—still mounted—until I was abreast of Mr. Carpenter, who had just dismounted. By this time the firing was very fast and heavy and none of the party remained between us and the firing line, which was not more than 25 yards distant at the maximum, and probably about half that. We stood here engaged in conversation between 35 and 60 seconds, the open target of uninterrupted fire from the ambuscade. I said: "What are they doing?" Mr. Carpenter replied: "They are shooting at us." I returned the question: "What had we better do?" He answered: "I am going to shoot." At this point the boy Marius, who had not moved from the beginning, broke in by saying: "Mr. Morley, I only have four cartridges; we'd better go back." Mr. Carpenter had in this interval drawn his pistol, released his horse, which dashed forward through the ambuscade, and had fired twice. Up to this moment none of us had seen any member of the ambuscade, though we assumed from the first that it was the revolutionists.

Mr. Carpenter believes that as his horse passed through the ambuscade he saw one man rise to reach for it, at whom he fired the two shots mentioned, but that he did see a man at this time is not entirely certain, however, since the head of the clearing was already filled with dense powder haze.

At this point I began to realize the extreme peril of our open position, and called first to Mr. Carpenter: "Arthur, we must get back," and then gave the general command: "Back! Back! Back! For God's sake, everybody back!" I spurred my horse, wheeled and dashed down the trail around the first bend followed closely by Marius and at a greater distance by Mr. Carpenter, both on foot. Here we paused an instant and then set off at a run overtaking the boy Andrew about 150 yards from the first bend. At 200 yards we came to the bottom of the slope and stopped.

A hurried consultation was held. Mr. Carpenter decided against my wishes—since I believed that Dr. Lafleur was dead—to return and approach as near as possible through the bush with the object of ascertaining whether Dr. Lafleur had survived the opening fire, and if so to carry him cartridges which he lacked. I instructed him to return to Chunvis within the hour, to which he refused to agree. He started back toward the shooting, which had largely subsided, carrying his pistol and some cartridges but leaving everything else. I started for Chunvis with the two servants. We had scarcely gone a hundred paces when two rifle shots were heard in the direction Mr. Carpenter had taken. I said: "They've got Carpenter, or that is the end of the poor doctor," whereupon we quickened our pace, fearing pursuit. Subsequently the servants said they heard faint shots, but I did not. Two hours later we were in Chunvis.

Owing to the fact that unless I close this report here, the whole must be delayed another week, I feel it better to forward this section which sets forth the principal incidents of the tragedy and the events leading thereto, reserving for the second installment an account of the escape of Mr. Carpenter and myself and the subsequent steps taken to recover the body of Dr. Lafleur, remove it to El Cayo where it was interred, salvage the expedition equipment which remained at Chunvis, and finally to ascertain definitely that our assailants had been Guatemalan Government troops.

I enclose also the original copy of the report of the medical examiner whom I engaged to perform an autopsy. Mr. Carpenter and I expect to return to the States on the next steamer leaving here June 2nd, barring instructions from you to the contrary. I shall look up Dr. E. Lafleur, who lives in Opelousas, Louisiana, and deliver to him the personal effects of his brother. We should be in Washington about June 10th.

I have suppressed in the foregoing account as much as possible reference to the personal feelings of both Mr. Carpenter and myself, but naturally the shock we have sustained has been very great and as yet I am unable to measure its full extent. The horror of those few crowded minutes has not left my mind free for a single instant, either waking or sleeping, ever since. I remain,

Very respectfully yours,
Sylvanus G. Morley.

====

TEN

Gregory Mason and Herbert J. Spinden 1924

Through the Mouth of a Cauldron

[In the early 1920's, the *New York Times* financed an expedition of archaeological exploration to the east coast of Yucatán, a largely unknown part of the peninsula that is famed for its ruined cities of the ancient Maya. The expedition was led by Gregory Mason and Herbert J. Spinden, the latter at that time an assistant curator of Mexican archaeology and ethnology at the Peabody Museum, Harvard University. Mason's book, *Silver Cities of Yucatan,* reported on the expedition. I shall quote first from the preface by Spinden, and then from Mason's account of their discoveries.]

Eastern Yucatan is a coast of adventure where the trade winds of the tropics pile surf on coral reefs and where white temples of the ancient Mayas serve as landmarks for ships that wisely stand off. There is memorable beauty in the outer islands with slender palms leaning out from dunes of wave-broken coral. The shore line of the mainland appears low and monotonous but on closer inspection vast shallow bays are revealed with mangrove mazes which once offered hidden harbors to the buccaneers. The level unbroken forests of the Mexican territory of Quintana Roo are guarded by vigilant Mayas who still cherish in these wilds crumbling buildings of their ances-

The selections from Mason and Spinden are, in the order quoted, from the following works. Gregory Mason, *Silver Cities of Yucatan* (New York: G. P. Putnam's Sons, 1927), pp. vii–xii, 147–51, 152–53, 155–64, 296–301. Copyright 1927 by Gregory Mason. Gregory Mason, *South of Yesterday* (New York: Henry Holt and Company, 1940), pp. 103–22. Copyright 1940 by Gregory Mason. Reprinted by permission of Holt, Rinehart and Winston, Inc.

tors. For generations these Indians have fought to stave off modern commercial civilization that on the raw edges of its expanding front shows anything but a pleasing parade of virtues.

There is glamour and mystery enough in a quest of ancient cities in Central America, yet the finest part of the adventure is intellectual rather than physical. The thrill of breaking through the frontiers of history into an unknown age is much deeper and more satisfying than that of merely entering closed territory at a slight risk of life and limb. After all, the chances of violent death are probably greater in modern cities than in the most backward lands. Eastern Yucatan will remain in my memory, not as a region where thorns scratch, insects bite, and boats capsize, but as a region where crumbling temples bear the unmistakable stamp of one of the New World's greatest personalities.

Quetzalcoatl, emperor of the Toltecs, and conqueror of the Mayas—priest, scientist and architect in one commanding individual—was a contemporary of Henry II and Richard the Lion Hearted. He died in far off days before a reluctant King John signed the Magna Charta of English liberties. His holdings in Mexico and Central America were several times more extensive than the holdings of those puissant monarchs of the Angevin line in France and the British Isles, his philosophy of life was richer and his contributions to the general history of civilization were greater than theirs. Old stone walls in eastern Yucatan are mute evidence of the commerce, religion and art that Quetzalcoatl built up as the expression of his practical and ideal State. He encouraged trade that reached from Colombia to New Mexico, he preached a faith of abnegation and high ethics which later led speculative churchmen to identify him with St. Thomas, and in sculpture and architecture he formed a new and vital compound of the previous achievements of two distinct peoples, the Toltecs of the arid Mexican highlands and the Mayas of the humid lowlands. We can restate three of Quetzalcoatl's personal triumphs in astronomical science corresponding to the years 1168, 1195 and 1208. We know that he conquered the great city of Chichen Itza in 1191 and erected therein a lofty temple which still bears his name and a round tower which is still an instrument for exact observation of the sun and moon. We know that Quetzalcoatl set up a benign system of local self government among conquered tribes of Guatemala which made those peoples relate his praises in song and story. We know that after his death he was made a god because during his life he had been "a great republican."

The archaeology of eastern Yucatan belongs for the most part to the three centuries which intervened between the reign of Quetzalcoatl and the coming of the Spaniards. The buildings of Chichen Itza are copied in Paalmul and Muyil, settlements which pretty clearly grew up along one of the important trade routes from Chichen Itza to the far south. To be sure there are some vestiges in the region of the much older First Empire of the Mayas, several monuments having been discovered in recent years which bear dates in the fourth and fifth centuries after Christ. But the cultural facts of the splendid First Empire are already known from a score of magnificent ruins on the plains of Peten, and in the valleys of the Usumacinta and Motagua rivers. Science was really in greater need of evidence on the last phases of Mayan civilization and this evidence we found in the territory we visited.

There is a more tragic story not without interest to the student of the rise and fall of civilizations, namely, the narrative of a clash between two races, the American Indian and the white man of Europe. In eastern Yucatan the unequal contest of brown breasts against bullets has waged since 1519. Some persons may see in the broken men who survive in little independent communities of rebellious Mayas only degradation and inferiority. Yet over and over again the Spanish colonists, for all their coercive engines, were driven out of this territory which was the first part of Mexico on which they set foot.

The terrible War of the Castes devastated Yucatan some eighty years ago, one of the causes, according to a scholarly work recently published in Merida, being the exportation of Maya Indians to Cuba as slaves. The eastern portion of the peninsula has not been reconquered since that time. One encounters in the darkening forest Christian churches which are no less ruinous than the more ancient temples of the Indians. It seems that Father Time is impartial when the figures of European saints and the grotesque faces of pagan gods fall beneath the weight of his hand.

Although the *Indios sublevados* of Quintana Roo have managed to maintain their independent status their numbers have pitifully diminished. Under President Díaz a vigorous campaign was waged against them for twenty years but the recalcitrant natives allowed the Mexican generals to hold precariously only the town of Santa Cruz and a few lines of communication. Then, as political strife developed in the Mexican capital itself, the garrisons were withdrawn. In 1918, the aboriginal population found a still more deadly enemy in the world epidemic of influenza. Recently American silver has been more successful over this renegade people than Mexican lead. The insistent demand for chewing gum among the children and salesladies of the United States has brought about a benevolent penetration into Quintana Roo of hand mirrors, glass pearls and alcohol flavored with anis seeds.

When offered the opportunity of joining with Mr. Gregory Mason and several others in an exploring expedition to Cozumel Island and the adjacent mainland, I gladly accepted, first because the region was difficult of access and offered great promise of finding unknown ruins of the ancient civilization, secondly, because the narrative of adventures and discoveries would direct public attention to the grandiose archaeology of the Mayas. I shall let Mr. Mason tell what we found.

In preparing the book that is before us—which is directed to the general public whose support archaeology needs—Mr. Mason has had the coöperation and good wishes of his fellow adventurers.

HERBERT J. SPINDEN

The schooner has already proved to be a good sea boat. And on McClurg's trip up the bay she proved to be all that he hoped when, with a bottle of beer at Belize, he christened her "a good mud boat." A dozen times the mud clutched her, says McClurg, but she extricated herself each time without any such elaborate measures as we had to take on Hicks' Key.

On Pinto's advice we anchored at the mouth of a narrow bay between the mainland and Allen Point. Ambrosio confirms the word of the Belize fisherman that this inlet connects with the ocean at Boca de Paila, and that Allen Point is not a peninsula at all as our chart indicates, but is merely the southern extremity of a long thin island, a mere sand bar supporting some fifteen miles of guano palms and coconut trees.

Pinto said the ruin was near three conspicuous palms about three kilometers from the position of the *Albert*. But these three coconut trees were not reached until the *Imp* had anchored off a pretty little beach a good ten kilometers from the schooner. Then there was a delay about finding the ruin. Pinto had chanced upon it when gathering firewood for a fishing boat two years ago, and he had never returned till now.

He indicated the general direction to follow, and we spread out at intervals of twenty feet, Spinden, McClurg, Whiting, Pinto and I. So thick was the brush that even at such close quarters we often lost sight of each other. But in pauses between his own attacks on the bush each man could hear the swish of other *machetes*, and hear the cries of, "Do you see it yet?" . . . "Is this another 'sell' of Venus's like yesterday's shrine?"

As luck had it I caught the first glimpse of the first Maya ruin found by the expedition. Through the falling green ahead of me as I raised *machete* for another blow I saw a low grayish structure.

"Here it is," I shouted, "a poor thing, but our own!"

It is a tiny building, only sixteen feet long by eight feet ten inches wide—outside measurements; only ten feet and a half by four and a half inside. The door is only three feet five inches high and the walls four feet. The roof, which has fallen in, was probably of stone slabs, for we found several of these within the walls. In short, it is a characteristic example of those curious little shrines much built during the last period of Maya architecture, those shrines whose diminutive size led earlier explorers of active imagination like Dr. Le Plongeon to the erroneous hypothesis that the builders had been dwarfs.

Because of its location between the booming ocean and the placid salt lagoon we had just left Spinden thinks that perhaps fishermen once came to this little temple to burn incense to some watery divinity. Appropriate to this suggestion there are fossil shells imbedded in the coral rock which is the material of which the building was made. As it is of late-period Maya architecture it probably is not more than seven hundred years old.

We have called it "Chenchomac," using the name which Ambrosio says the Indians apply to this locality. In Maya Chenchomac means "Well of the Fox."

"In Maya?" it may be asked. That is in the language of the modern Indians of this country, whom scientists agree to call Mayas. It must always be remembered, however, that these Indians use Spanish characters when they write their language, or rather, Spanish characters are used by the learned men who construct Maya grammars and make other linguistic studies in the hope of finding some connection between the modern language and the baffling hieroglyphs. For these Indians of today cannot read a single hieroglyph.

We cast through the bush for an hour, hoping vainly to find more buildings. Tired of fighting thorns and mosquitoes we sat down on the ocean beach and watched the waves burst into clouds of white. This beach of fine creamy sand extended both north and south as far as we could see. I suppose some day the realtors will find it, and there will be another Florida boom. But thank God, I shall be as dead as the Mayas who built that shrine to their Turtle Deity.

Here is yet a place where one may escape the tawdriness, the filth, the aching confusion of ugliness and noise with which man has seen fit to ruin the placid green face of the earth.

We took off our boots and wiggled our toes in the sand, in the little uphill rivers of clean foam and clean green water,—the last fillip of those ponderous swells which rolled in from Africa. Here I could never know, thank God, those chaotic fears, those indefinable feelings of inferiority which an hour in New York or London or Chicago always awake in me. There was noise enough here, but a simple noise which did not daze the brain but rather whetted it, the oldest noise in the world, the shout of the leaping wind and the thunder of the tumbling sea.

That wind grew and whipped froth around our boat's stern as she scudded for the schooner through a gray, angry dusk. But we were well content with the world and with each other.

It is a small thing, that shrine of Chenchomac. But it is a beginning. We have discovered something of that which we are seeking, and our appetite is sharpened for more.

Chumyaxché has been a name, a cross pencilled on a bare map. Yes, and a living hope. But now it is a conviction, a vivid conviction of buildings shrouded by brush, buildings gray with weather except where some falling tree has scraped off the patina of dead centuries and shown the true white of the limestone.

The *Albert* got underway at dawn and picked a hole in the reef about a mile and a half east of Allen Point. The wind dropped rapidly, but it had been enough east of north to leave tall oily seas, which threw the schooner about with creaking of idle booms and skidding of loose objects like a boathook, my rubber boots and Spinden's cot. Spinden was prostrate again, wedged against the *Imp* on the forward deck. Our temporary mutilations by insects are nothing to what he endures for the expedition.

Boca de Paila is about eighteen miles north of Allen Point.

"Boca de Paila," says Spinden, "is hard to get into, hard to stay in, and hard to get out of."

This statement is admirable, for it is at the same time succinct, pertinent and complete. The Mexican name is well chosen. *Boca de Paila* means "Mouth of a Cauldron." The "mouth" in the reef here is narrow, and the water inside is nearly always turbulent, for the insufficient reef merely knocks the white caps off the sea rollers, does not stop them or even change their rhythm. Of all the alleged harbors along this God-forsaken coast Boca de Paila most strains the allegation. After dodging coral heads all the way in from the reef mouth and bumping bottom twice here we were anchored in the midst of them on none too good holding ground, pitching and lurching in a nasty swell with the foaming beach only four hundred yards under our lee.

Spinden, who had lain in a coma all morning, was now in a fever to start for Chunyaxché. This day was half gone and prudence suggested awaiting the beginning of another before undertaking to reach ruins a vague but considerable distance away over uncharted inland waters which our pilot seemed to know none too well. But our archaeologist's ardent yearning for *terra firma* was a moving sight. With a haste which was regretted later, duffle bags were packed by the shore party, consisting of Spinden, Whiting, Ambrosio Pinto and myself. Griscom was to come into the interior later if we found any land birds for him to skin. Meanwhile he would hunt the beaches and marsh. McClurg had hydrographic work to do, and, as usual, he preferred any schooner to any land. His intense aversion for land and Spinden's equal antipathy for sea continue to be a spectacle for a philosopher to muse upon.

About half a mile directly behind the mouth in the reef is a break in the shore, an opening into a great expanse of lagoons, lakes and swamps. (Ambrosio says that not even the Indians know the exact limits of this "lake country," as they call it.) This inner *boca* like the outer one is guarded by a bar. A small sloop which had crossed this was anchored on the inner side, but our schooner was too deep to follow her. Indeed the surf on the bar looked as if the feat of crossing would be difficult even for our small boats. We got into the larger one.

To make the *Imp* lighter crossing the bar most of the baggage was put into the other tender. In *Delirium Tremens* the Captain now led the way to the bar. (This does not sound like safe pilotage but it served us well.) We were soon in smooth water, the hum of the two outboard motors extinguishing the disappointed roar of the surf we had evaded. Here at its entrance the lagoon offered loveliness to lure us into the mud and mangrove horror beyond. Through deliciously clear tropic water white sand gleamed under our keel, exaggerating the vivid gold and blue and black of swift fish. The lagoon was so narrow that on each side we could almost count the shells on a creamy beach.

The *Imp* used the little sloop as a dock while she took her baggage from the *Delirium Tremens*. This sloop, the *Nautilus*, at fairly regular intervals brings here supplies from Cozumel for the Indians and carries their chicle back. To make this exchange the Indians come thirty-seven miles from their holy city of Chunpom, twenty-five miles afoot or a-mule and twelve miles in fragile dug-out canoes nine feet long and eighteen inches wide.

With our handsome and youthful guide in our bow we left the friendly *Nautilus* and *Delirium Tremens* and turned toward the unknown. The lagoon forked, Ambrosio Pinto waved his hand majestically to the right and we rounded a point of black mangroves which blotted the other boats from our view. Almost immediately we ran aground.

"You say you know this channel, Ambrosio?"

"*Si Señor.*" He added that it was shallow for only twenty feet. We all got out and dragged the boat through six inches of water. When we had gone fifty feet Ambrosio said we were almost out of the shallows. We got out of them after four hundred feet more of this back-breaking pulling. At this point the water was deep enough to float the *Imp* if only one of us walked. Ambrosio was nominated. After another hundred yards he found deep enough water to float his weight with ours. Our little propeller threw up a wake of swirling mud. The lagoon was now a wide shallow lake of brackish water with low shores of the monotonous mangrove.

When we had reached the middle of this lake a jet of water as from a lawn fountain sprang upward from the *Imp's* bottom. We regarded this phenomenon with mild curiosity. It is surprising how short a time one must be exposed to the constant risk of running aground, capsizing and sinking in order to become callous to such matters. Mexican indifference and fatalism was in our blood already. The water was only four feet deep but that was enough to sink the boat and raise havoc with our baggage. And I am sure that if the water had been four fathoms deep our reaction would have been the same. A delicious humor filled our veins. The leak was a matter for discussion, for debate but not for emphatic action.

Spinden suggested it be stopped with my handkerchief. I happened to be carrying two of linen and one of cotton. I wanted the latter to clean my shotgun with but reluctantly began searching for it through stuffed pockets while suggesting that the tail of Spinden's pink shirt would make excellent caulking. No, he had worn the shirt to impress the natives and he would keep it for that purpose, tail and all.

I kept pulling out linen handkerchiefs but couldn't find the cotton one. Much of the lake was now in the boat and the rest was very close to her gunwales. My regard for linen and Spinden's for silk began to be criticized by Whiting, who was running the engine and in its noise was not appreciating the repartee. At this moment Ambrosio finished whittling a plug from a pole we carried. The plug reduced the leak to modest proportions. We were saved a two-mile wade back to the *Nautilus*. And we had discovered a use for the "Venus de Mexico." Ambrosio could whittle.

Now another debate arose. The question might be stated this way: "Resolved, that my baggage shall not be put in the wet bottom of this boat."

Everyone took the affirmative. And everyone suited the action to the word and lifted his belongings to such spots on the commodious seats of the *Imp* as were not occupied by three wrangling Americans and a silent Indian. The boat became top-heavy. This situation was dangerous, but each man's reasons for keeping his stuff out of the wet belly of the boat were good.

Spinden: "Confound it, my bags are full of film, the water would ruin them!"

Mason: "My duffle bag is loaded with beans and coffee and crackers. Do you want them soaked in brackish water?"

Whiting: "My bag is full of ammunition, which is future food. Films are a luxury, soaked crackers can be eaten, but you can't kill a turkey with a water-logged cartridge!"

Someone thought of a happy compromise. Ambrosio's poor little duffle bag was put at the bottom and the oars laid between that bag and the anchor to make a rack for the other luggage. I began to bail with the shell of a gourd.

At last we reached the other side of this expanse of open shallows and entered a channel some hundred yards wide which wound among clumps of mangrove. Herons, bitterns, white egrets and their reddish cousins and roseate spoonbills rose at the buzz of the first gasoline engine they had ever heard. In half an hour or so the channel narrowed rapidly. We tasted the water, it was sweet. The wide, sluggish river had become a freshwater stream with a very perceptible current.

Instead of deepening, however, it was shoaling. And it was narrowing at an alarming rate. Consequently the current was increasing until our motor could barely make headway against it. To add to our difficulties the course of the stream now wound like the path of an erratic snake. Our pilot sat in the bow, his beautiful face set in that vacant expression characteristic of the least cerebral type of moving picture actor. He sat in the bow—and looked backward.

Whiting stood up in the stern, cursing Ambrosio softly and steadily as he threw the metal steering handle from side to side and tried to determine which bank of the twisting rivulet harbored the fewer snags. At each turn our stern would graze the bank and our following wash over-ran the land.

It was like Mississippi navigation on a very Lilliputian scale. Where the current bore around a bend and into the opposite bank there was the deepest water and there we had to go despite the current. The depths ranged from one to three feet, and we drew nearly one. In the midst of some tiny rapids we bumped bottom, hung there a breathless instant, then with the help of an extra oar moved ahead. As we grazed a bank Spinden sighted rare orchids and jumped ashore. He could easily walk faster than we were now going. It was navigation under the most peculiar circumstances I have ever seen, and I dwell upon it because it reflects an interesting light upon the builders of the ruins who poled their canoes laboriously against this swift stream—as indeed do their descendants who sell chicle to the white men today. If you chew gum reflect that its fundamental ingredient may have been brought down this difficult stream in a dug-out canoe.

For another reason this river is interesting; it is the most northerly surface river we have ever heard of in the Yucatan Peninsula, which is a limestone plain famous for its underground rivers, pools and lakes but notorious for the absence of surface streams.

The swamp gradually gave way to savannah.

We swept around a bend, Ambrosio waved a majestic arm, and there was the first temple, dazzling white in the sun!

It is a one-storied, oblong building, rather small—in short, an outpost of the city. It faces a lake about two hundred feet west of it, a lake of which the river we had been following is an outlet. With happy inspiration Spinden promptly named the building, "*Vigia del Lago*" ("The Watch on the Lake," or "The Lookout on the Lake").

There were no trees near the building except a dead one on its roof. But there was a lot of brush and high grass, which had to be cut down before we could get photographs of the front of the temple with its three doors, and an interesting carving over them.

The size of the lake surprised us. Ambrosio says it is fifteen miles long and three miles wide, but it is not shown on any of the maps we brought. It was the narrow northern tip of the lake which we crossed.

The stolid Ambrosio seemed to be leading us directly into a bank of high grass when it suddenly opened and showed us a channel as narrow as the upper end of the river we had left. The more we studied the construction of this the more convinced were we that it was a canal, a canal made by the Mayas centuries ago. It ran nearly straight, and although its banks were covered with grass they were higher than the land behind, and on each side of the water and paralleling it could be seen the long mound made of the earth thrown out when the canal was dug. A barely perceptible current moved against us.

After a quarter of a mile of this we entered a second lake, perhaps a mile and a half broad and two miles long. On the farther side were visible three or four roofs of thatch, and soon we could distinguish two men observing us from a little dock made of logs. A dazzling white beach belted the lake. Behind the yellowish roofs we were approaching rose high trees—

the beginning of the big bush. Altogether it seemed a delightful spot to us weary of mangrove swamps and mud. We could not yet see the insects.

The *Imp* grounded a few feet from the little dock and we waded ashore. One of the two men awaiting us was *Señor* Amado Castillo, head *chiclero* of this region, right-hand man of General Juan Vega, of Chunpom, who is second in command to General May, military commander of all the Indians of Quintana Roo.

"Yes, there are ruins here," said Don Amado, "I'll take you to them." Spinden went off with him while Whiting and I carried baggage, cots and my hammock under a thatched roof supported on a pole framework, a shelter offered us by the hospitable *Señor* Castillo. It was nearly dark, and we began supper. Now we regretted the haste in which we had started. I had forgotten bacon, lard and flour. But we made a makeshift meal of pea soup, rice, dried raisins and tea under the thatched roof which Don Amado lent us for the night.

Spinden returned in high satisfaction. He had seen two buildings, he said, a structure with pillars and a temple on a pyramidal mound, a typical Maya "*Castillo,*" to use the misnomer which has stuck to this type of temple since the uncouth Spanish adventurers first applied it. Dark had fallen before Spinden's guide of the fit name (Castillo) could show him more than these two structures. But Don Amado said there were seven or eight other buildings in the bush, and any quantity of mounds marking where others had already succumbed to decay.

As we listened to Spinden over our crackling little fire Whiting and I forgot our fatigue, forgot the stinging ants which swarmed over us from the ground on which we had stretched our aching bodies. Here was success, complete, dazzling—and now that we had it—ridiculously easy. Forgotten were not only the bites, the bruises, the sea-sickness of today and yesterday, but the foot weariness and the heartaches of the trying days of organization in New York. A city with eight or ten temples still standing!

Spinden and Whiting put up their cots on opposite sides of this shack, and and in the middle I hung my hammock under the great billowing piece of canvas and dangling mosquito net which the archaeologist calls my "hangar." It was a cold night—and the knack of keeping blankets about one in a narrow hammock has never been mine. Then there were tick bites to keep me awake, and above all, wonder about these ruins.

Quietly I reached down for my boots, putting them on in the hammock to avoid the ants which were swarming on the dirt floor.

Fully dressed I slipped out of the hut between my snoring companions and followed the path I had seen Spinden return by a few hours before. A branch led off to the right, and instinct told me to take that.

I had gone perhaps two hundred yards through the mystery of moonlit woods when there rose through the trees at the left of the path the high dark bulk of something which gleamed where moon rays reached it.

I worked around to the west of it, where there was a slight opening. The low moon was now behind me. And there rising before me was a typical-Maya pyramid, four sided with ascending terraces and a wide stairway. And on its top a temple, shining like silver under the moon. A true Maya temple not seen by archaeologist until today. And carved on its corners—one to each corner—the faces of old gods.

For four days we were cooped up at Santa Cruz de Bravo while the heavens deluged the earth. But as we set out on the fifth morning there was not a puddle on the trail. It had all been taken care of by the wonderful natural drainage of this limestone formation. There were holes as big round as buckets, dropping straight downward through the rock as far as the eye could see.

The first night out of Santa Cruz we reached Tabi, but before we arrived it was obvious that Camera is not the guide that he represented himself to be. He was constantly asking the way of his assistant *arriero,* a short, plump little fellow named Pancho. As we made supper at Tabi, within sight of Spanish walls, Spinden asked if the ruins Camera was "selling" us were like these.

"Oh, no," he said, "the ruins are Maya. But we won't reach them till tomorrow noon."

This ought to have made us suspicious.

The following noon we saw ahead the tall *piche* trees which invariably mark the site of an old Spanish or Mexican town. Camera had been losing patience under our frequent queries as to the proximity of the ruins. As we rode into a clearing bounded on two sides by remnants of a Spanish fortification Camera said:

"Here are the ruins, *Señor.*"

"What," roared Spinden, "These are your temples of Tabi?"

"*Si, Señor.*" The *arriero's* eyes were on the ground.

It was simply too disgusting, too cruel. Camera is not a fool. And we have spent hours explaining to him the difference between Spanish and Maya ruins, and have shown him dozens of photographs of the latter. It is just a cheap hoax, perpetrated apparently for the sole purpose of gaining a few days employment driving mules. A cheap contemptible fraud which costs us valuable time and not a few *pesos.*

I exploded into expletives, but what was the use. I sank on the ground and reveled in the denunciation of the despicable *arriero* which flowed from Spinden's lips. His just anger lent him an astonishing facility in Spanish invective, in the biting, scathing dialect the *arriero* knows as none other.

The rest of that day—it was yesterday—was a dull gloom.

But anger has its uses. We rose this morning still in a rage at Camera. The mule driver's delay in starting did not diminish Spinden's choler. For this reason he marched straight through the remains of another Spanish town where the *arrieros* wanted to stop for a bite and a drink, for it was noon.

Spinden was walking in the lead, and when he had plodded an hour or so longer under the broiling sun even he began to realize the necessity of refreshment. As he reached a point where the trail passes a lake filled with bulrushes he called back to Camera:

"You can stop here a few minutes."

Except for Spinden's anger at Camera we had not stopped here—but before this.

And when I walked down to the shallow water and looked across the green level of reeds I noticed a hill on the farther side. A little hill it is, yet unusually conspicuous for this flat country.

On the top of it I perceived a high excrescence, covered with growth but distinctly square and sharp in outline.

"That looks like a ruin," I suggested.

"No, it's just a natural hill, *Señor*," said Camera, "I have seen it many times."

Herbert J. Spinden at summit of unexcavated pyramid, Okop, Quintana Roo
From Gregory Mason, *Silver Cities of Yucatan.*

"It does look like a ruin," said Spinden with a black glance at the *arriero,* "we'll have a look at it after lunch."

We bolt a few sandwiches of dried *tortillas* and canned beef and start up the trail, aiming to cut in at right angles to it as soon as we judge we have passed the end of the lake.

Camera leads through the brush, slashing right and left with his *machete* and still muttering that the high mound we saw is just a "natural hill." When we have gone perhaps three hundred yards I climb a tree. Ahead is a woody knoll. That may be it and I direct Spinden to continue as he is going.

But in pulling my leg over a limb I have been straddling I look around, and there, towering over me, not one hundred yards away, is a thundering big Maya *castillo!* Its size takes my breath, I hang in the tree, like a stunned bird, drinking in the majestic bulk and symmetry of the pyramid. For me this is the biggest moment of the whole trip.

At last I collect my wits, realize that Spinden and Camera are disappearing, and shout for them to turn at right angles. Spinden is skeptical of my directions, but heeds them, half convinced by the ring in my voice.

I slide down the tree, falling the last ten feet in my haste. Running over a small ruin I catch up to the other two, and slashing at the brush abreast we reach the foot of a great stairway. The trees hide the top of the temple, but there is no doubt in anyone any longer. This is no "natural hill" but a whale of a *castillo!*

We toil up the stairway, cutting away wild henequen, its sword-shaped leaves tipped with wicked black spikes. We clamber very gingerly, for many of the stones are ready to give way underfoot and crash down on the man behind.

A doorway yawns above and to the left. Like some of the lofty temples of Tikal this one is built into the top of the great mound instead of being raised upon its summit.

A clump of cactus bars the way to this chamber and we keep on to the top of the pyramid. Out of breath we crawl up to the flat top of the mound, a bush-covered plateau perhaps twenty-five feet square. If we had any breath this view would take it away. On every side is a flat expanse of forest like a great green ocean, melting off at the edges into the blue of the sky.

"God," says Spinden at last, "this by itself is worth the whole journey."

[As he expressed it, Gregory Mason, whose *Silver Cities of Yucatan* I have just quoted, got into archaeological exploration by the back door, via journalism and war correspondence. *The Outlook* sent him to Yucatán in 1916 to investigate a revolution and the state government's monopoly of sisal fiber. On this assignment he took a week off to visit the ruins of Uxmal, and then "knew at once that I wanted to change the direction of my career."

[Mason wrote several books on his experiences, as well as two novels of

Yucatán and Mexico. The following extracts are from *South of Yesterday,* published in 1940. They tell of some of his investigations in British Honduras.]

When we had finished with the San Felipe mounds, we turned our attention to caves. One of our two mule drivers guided us to a cave he had found a year before while cruising the bush for sapodilla trees. It was an impressive big cave of the wide-mouthed variety. The entrance must be about a hundred feet wide and seventy-five feet high.

We had not been three minutes in the natural inner chambers of the cavern before we had found a number of potsherds and a complete pot five and three-quarters inches both in height and in diameter. It was made of rather thick, painted ware and was pleasing in form, with the remains of a black design faintly visible on its tan sides. Like many of the art objects found recently in British Honduras, this pot is something of a puzzle to one accustomed to the conventional and—frankly—better ware which is characteristic of Maya culture at its height.

No more intact pieces were found, but there were enough sherds to indicate that the cave was inhabited for a considerable period, and probably until quite recently. It would make an excellent home for three or four hundred Indians. The wide mouth let in enough of the slanting rays of the afternoon sun to prevent the unhealthy dampness which usually permeates caves in this country. Before we left I found two sherds decorated with bands of the same design. It looked very much like a glyph, although untranslatable now. Probably it was a decoration put on with a stamp, in the way modern potters might stamp some trite motto on their ware: "God Bless Our Home," or "God Bless Our Cave."

The marks left by men who had formerly used the land outside the cave were of more interest to me than the cave itself. There were any number of stone walls which had served as the front supports for agricultural terraces, and there were the remains of two roads, limestone founded. The early Americans terraced hillsides for agriculture very much as modern farmers do in France and in Japan. The vicinity of the cave is hilly. The hills are small, and terraced everywhere. Many of the walls were in excellent condition. It seems probable to me that this is one of the regions where the Mayas, or some of their close cousins, held out until some time after the Conquest. Excavation in such an area should be extremely profitable.

Explorers have a tradition that they must apply a Maya name to any new group of ruins. When a cluster of ruins is known already to the natives by a Spanish or an English name, the bestowal of a Maya name seems to me to be an unnecessary complication—a complication which will make finding the place difficult for the next man with historic or scientific interests who comes along. This cave and the region around it had no name. I called the site Chikin Ac Tun, which means "Western Under Ground" or "Western Cave."

The cave is near the western border of British Honduras and some distance west of the Rio Frio caves toward which we set out after leaving Chikin Ac Tun.

I had purchased information in order to locate the Rio Frio caves. An outline of the transaction would serve as the plot for a story of adventure. Through the kindness of Mr. John Ross, of El Cayo, I heard of an old chiclero who was said to know the location of a cave filled with marvelous pottery. The chiclero proved to be a very taciturn man of Negro and English blood, named Alfred August. When he had been hunting deer in the pine ridge country south of Cayo about thirty years before, he had come upon an aged Indian who had just been bitten by a poisonous snake of a kind known locally as "tommy-goff (fer-de-lance)." August is what bushmen call a "snake doctor." He applied his bush remedies and the old Indian recovered. In gratitude, the patient offered to show August a wonderful cave in the mahogany forest which adjoins this piece of pine ridge on the west. August returned for a rendezvous when the Indian had regained his strength. They went together to a cave "which opens through a slit in the side of a hill and has many, many rooms, filled with pots—pots everywhere," August told me.

His tale sounded convincing. He declared that he had told no one else of the cave until he recently mentioned it to Mr. Ross. He was such a taciturn old man that I believed him. He never had revisited the cave but thought that he could find it, for a consideration. We bargained for a while over Scotch-and-ginger in a back room of Cayo's flea-infested hotel. August agreed to go out and look for the cave. If he was successful in finding it, he would take me to it for forty dollars. The next morning he rode away on his mule. Three days later he returned, with the curt statement: "Found her."

The cave turned out to be all that he had promised. While we were encamped there we found two other caves in the near-by bush. We called them Cave A, Cave B, and Cave C, in the order in which we visited them. The three caves are close together in a dense mahogany forest near an abandoned mahogany cutters' camp called "Schultz's Camp," on the banks of a creek known as the Rio Frio.

Two of the Rio Frio caves—Cave A and Cave C—afforded voluminous treasure. Cave B is the smallest and least interesting. There are two good reasons why it was less used for human occupancy than the other two. First, it lacks a water supply of its own. Second, it is of the wide-mouthed type with few pockets or tunnels inside and would, therefore, be more difficult to defend than the other two. We found a few common potsherds in Cave B, but no other artifacts. It did, however, yield a wide variety of bats, including a species which Oliver L. Austin, Jr., told me was new, as he skinned it for Harvard's Museum of Comparative Zoology.

Cave A and Cave C are utterly unlike each other, but both merit rank among the physical wonders of the earth. The first one sees of Cave A is a wide slit near the top of the western slope of a sizable hill. The gash in the hillside is about ten feet high and forty feet wide, with a bare limestone lip showing above. An extensive division is at the right with several subdivisions or chambers, but the entrance to the main cave is at the left and steeply downward. Most of this entrance had been walled with big stones by the ancient inhabitants. The wall served both as defense against enemies and as protection from loose boulders which might roll into the cave.

The first impression one gets of the cavern is that it is hung with heavy white draperies, deeply folded. The "hangings" are limestone. The cavern is deep and has so many natural passages and chambers at each side that one is bewildered by the possibilities for exploration and alarmed by the possibilities for getting lost. The first time I went in we fastened one end of a ball of string at the entrance and unrolled the ball as we went along. When we came to the end of the string, we stationed candle beacons at intervals of thirty or forty feet.

About two hundred feet northeast of the entrance and sixty feet below it, one comes to what I have called the "cathedral." It is a great round chamber under a high dome of limestone. At different levels—like second and third stories—other apartments of the cave open on one side of the cathedral. A massive limestone pillar, about twenty feet high and five feet by four in cross section, reaches up from the floor of the third story to the roof. It seems at first to be the work of man, and I examined it several times before coming to the conclusion that it is not. Its artificial appearance is increased by the fact that, low down on the side which looks out over the great main chamber of the cathedral, there is an opening like a mouth with what appears to be lower and upper teeth, four or five inches long. At first I thought it was the open jaws of a stone simulacrum of the sacred serpent, such as may be seen at Chichen Itza and other Maya cities. I am convinced now that the teeth are merely small stalactites and stalagmites. However, there were traces of copal incense ashes at the bottom of the "mouth" to show that if man did not make it for ceremonial purposes, he used it for that purpose—and not very long ago, either.

The old Indian who showed the cave to Alfred August escorted him there about 1908. He told August that Indians of the tribe that had inhabited the cave were living, at that time, only about thirty miles away in the Peten District of Guatemala.

From the main chamber of the cathedral we reach the upper stories through a burrow barely large enough to enable a man to crawl thirty feet on his hands and knees up a steep grade. Emerging into a large chamber, we climb its perpendicular eight-foot wall with the help of projecting knobs of limestone. The base of the plateau of limestone must be circled to reach the top, from where that extraordinary pillar reaches to the roof. Another hundred feet on, over some very bad footing, is the edge of a precipice above a hidden creek. There are slimy boulders to climb over and, worse yet, a forty-foot expanse of slippery rock sloping steeply to where it ends with a drop of thirty feet to sharp stalagmites. The precipice includes an almost sheer drop of thirty feet at the south. At the north it is only an exceedingly steep and slippery hill, ending in an easier slope to the creek perhaps eighty feet below and one hundred and fifty feet west. We could not see the water, but, when we threw down stones, a series of clicks as they bounced off rocks always ended with a faint splash.

One end of our light rope was made fast around a big boulder at the top of the incline. A small but fearless Nicaraguan laborer named Chinda took the other end in his left hand and went down. We tried to augment the illumination from his flashlight by throwing the rays from our own *focos* ahead of him. When he hooted, to signal that he had reached the water, my foreman followed. While an old Negro called "Mistah Brooks" remained to watch the fastened end of the rope, I began to descend. I advanced in a sort of crouch, except when forced to stand up where the rope led over a high boulder.

The creek is only three or four feet wide at the foot of this incline, which is at the middle of the stream's visible course through the cavern. The stream wells up out of the rock at the south and flows about two hundred feet before disappearing under the rock at the north. Its water is the most limpid imaginable—sweet and cool.

We found a shallow saucer of rough sandy ware grown into the limestone in the bed of the creek. It was the only artifact we discovered along the creek, although we found a few intact pots and a number of broken ones of several varieties throughout the rest of the cave. I believe that it was here that Alfred August saw "dozens of pots, each with a little hole in the bottom," thirty years ago. I believe that this particular cache of pots has been stolen, very likely by Indians, since August saw it; and that August, like many another guide under similar circumstances, is seeking refuge in a lie when he says that he cannot find the same approach to the creek which he used before.

Having explored the little river, I sent Chinda and Smith, my smallest laborers, into two tunnels too narrow for me to enter. These tunnels seem to be natural fissures through the limestone, but some of them are so regular in shape that it is easy to believe that man had a hand in making them.

The first of the tunnels ended in a chamber in which only broken pieces of common pottery were found, but the other brought us better luck. It started with a perpendicular drop of five feet, then turned horizontally into a wide, shallow chamber containing many fragments of large water jars and corn jars. Beyond this chamber the tunnel became too small for me to enter, so I waited at the mouth of the perpendicular shaft while Smith and Chinda went on.

They had been gone half an hour when I heard their voices directly over me and saw their lights through a hole in the stone ceiling. As the hole was too small for them to squeeze through, even if we had had a ladder, they were forced to spend another half hour returning the way they had gone. They reported having found a maze of tunnels and chambers, and having sighted several water jars intact, besides the pieces of better stuff which they brought with them. Four of the pieces were found to fit together, making a very nice wide, shallow plate, with a geometric design painted on in orange and black and with red flowers in the center. They also brought out a large piece of a vase with a design in red, orange, and black, including what may be glyphs. Experts consider it not unlikely that there were other written languages in Central America besides the Maya, or that there were variations of the Maya glyphs so different from the conventional style as to be unrecognizable at first.

The first time August guided me into the cave, he found an orange vase encircled by a band of red glyphs. Mistah Brooks, exploring a chamber which the rest of us had overlooked, found two other vases of this character, but with more decoration than the one August found. Each of them contained ashes, but before I could save the ashes for later analysis, one of the men spilled them into the river.

These three vases are of a very valuable variety. The first is cylindrical, seven and a half inches high, and six inches in diameter. It is made of a thin red ware, with a yellow band one and three-fourths inches wide around the outside of the top. In this band is a row of red hieroglyphs or designs—it is hard to say which, though it is not any known glyph—which encircle the vessel. They are repetitions of the same sign, which looks something like the symbol for fire ceremony.

One of the other vases is five and seven-eighths inches high and five and a half inches in diameter. The color is orange. Below a black line, a black glyph, or design, repeated seventeen times, encircles the top of the vase. Below that, in four black circles of three inch diameter, are four red glyphs, or designs, which seem to have the serpent motif.

Jade earplugs from Río Frío Caves, British Honduras
From Gregory Mason, *South of Yesterday*, 1940. Copyright 1940 by Gregory Mason. By permission of Holt, Rinehart and Winston, Inc.

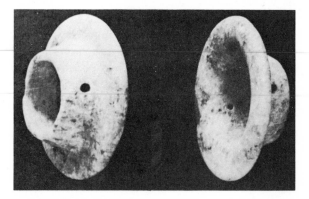

The third vase was my first choice when I divided the collection with Captain Gruning of the British Museum, in accordance with Colonial law which allowed me to keep only half of my collection for the Museum of the American Indian, Heye Foundation. It is six inches high, and five and one-fourth inches in diameter, of orange-yellow ware three-sixteenths of an inch thick. At the top, between black borders, sixteen red glyphs encircle the vase, no glyph being repeated. The background on which they lie is a clear yellow, a lighter tint than that of the body of the vase. Encircling the middle of the vessel are six ovals of red, and below them three one-eighth-inch black bands and a one-fourteenth-inch red band, all somewhat unsteadily drawn.

Nearly everywhere in Cave A, we encountered necks and other pieces of *ollas* which probably had been used to hold water and grain. They varied from eight to eighteen inches in height, their diameter usually nearly equaling their height, and in a few cases exceeding it. They were of a thick, coarse dark-grayish ware, unpainted, but often bearing encircling punctate designs below the neck. In many cases the designs were wavy. Some bore eyelets under the neck, to facilitate carrying with a cord. There seemed to be no standardized type of lip or neck. One olla had a neck with an outside diameter across the lips of only five and seven-sixteenths inches, while another had a diameter of seventeen and three-sixteenths inches. None of the ollas had legs, but some of them had circular bases.

I do not believe this cave was used as a tomb. There was not enough earth to make burials sanitary for the living who occupied the cave, and the quantities of pots and potsherds indicate that it housed a large population for hundreds of years. The only feature which suggested a grave, within the cave, was a small terrace of earth and rock near the opening. We took this terrace apart and found only a few pieces of rough pottery. I believe the terrace was made originally to reduce erosion.

Cave A was an ideal home for primitive man, as well as for his more cultivated descendants who made the pottery. The age, both of the cave and the pottery, is difficult to fix, but I believe the cave was used by some pre-Maya people. The hills are Tertiary limestone, much older than the Quaternary limestone of Yucatan.

Cave C is just as remarkable as Cave A but is entirely dissimilar in form. Cave C opens wide and high at each end and is illuminated to some extent by daylight throughout the nearly four-hundred-yard length of the main cavern. It looks more like a high, covered canyon than like the usual Central American cave. Its lofty sides contain some pockets and branch caverns, but they do not compare in number or extent of floor space with the labyrinthine subdivisions of Cave A. That cavern impresses you by its mystery; Cave C, by its scenic beauty and by an air of well-proportioned spaciousness suggesting a huge Gothic cathedral.

We discovered Cave C coming up the bank of the little Rio Frio from the south-southwest. A long sandbar stretched ahead of us to the foot of a little waterfall which was at the bottom of a great stone mouth in the base of a steep hill. The mouth was a hundred and fifty feet wide and equally high, its upper lip barely brushed by a tall tree growing in a steep bank just outside the cave. The whole edge of this horseshoe-shaped mouth was bare, grayish limestone.

From the southwest entrance, the cave runs about twenty degrees east of north. In the middle, the great natural tunnel swings about sixty degrees more easterly. We went in on the southeast side of the river, on the right bank going upstream. The ground rises sharply from the river and the cave widens to about two hundred and fifty feet just inside this entrance, leaving considerable space, which humans might occupy, on each side above high water mark. This space is wider on the southeast side than on the opposite bank, and it was on the southeast bank that we discovered most of the artifacts and other evidences of man's occupation.

Almost at the very entrance to the cave is a big boulder. There is just room for a man to pass between it and the wall of the cave in order to reach a hole which is waist-high. I was not able to enter until I broke off some sharp four-inch stalactites, which threatened to rake the back of anyone who might crawl the nine and a half feet that the passage runs. It opens into a cavity about thirty feet long and from five to ten feet wide, but only about four and a half feet high. The opening was too small for any of us except the diminutive Chinda, named the Human Ferret by the other men. He promptly wormed through it, scratched about with his machete on the dirt floor of the interior for a minute, and then passed out a beautiful jade earplug. It was carved from one piece of stone but looks as if it were made of two hollow disks of jade, connected by a collar half an inch long. The entire piece is a hollow disk half an inch high, two and a half inches in diameter at the top and one and one-fourth inches in diameter at the bottom. Later, Chinda found another and smaller jade earplug in this same place, at a depth of from four inches to a foot in the loose earth. He also found a pendant of jadeite, probably worn on the chest, and six dishes, mostly alike in shape, varying in height from one and a half to two and a half inches, with a top diameter of from four inches to seven and one-fourth inches, and a bottom diameter of from three inches to four and a half inches. In three of them, the bottoms were roughly rounded.

Chinda found fragments of human bones, and I have no doubt the place had been used as a tomb. The Mayas were a small people. Many of their modern descendants are as small as Chinda, who is five feet two inches tall and weighs a hundred and ten pounds.

A few feet further in the cave was a structure which seemed to be an altar. It was thirty feet long, nine feet wide, and four feet high, built out from the perpendicular wall of the cave, and constructed of loose stones without mortar. The stones ranged from four inches to two feet in diameter. The small stones were at the top of the altar, and the large ones at the bottom. The altar ended against a great boulder which hung out of the side of the cave, leaving a space about seven feet wide and ten feet long, with two or three feet of head clearance beneath it. Three feet from the southern end of the altar there was a round hole in the floor of the cave. When I dropped into this manhole, I found a little tunnel winding through the altar to the space under the boulder. On top of the altar we found one shallow saucer of rough ware. Before the altar there were many fragments of pottery, including pieces of two incense burners studded all over with nipple-like projections one and one-fourth to one and seven-eighths inches long, and a ball of limestone two and one-fourth inches in diameter—the latter probably a slingstone.

Later, we took the altar apart. Under its junction with the big rock we found four jade beads, many small, broken pieces of jade, and a jadeite button. At least, the last object was much like a button on one side, with a depression in the middle; but the opposite side is pierced from the flat surface to the rim by two small holes, suggesting a Japanese *netsuki*. There were many ashes under the boulder at the edge of the altar, very likely the remains of ancient ceremonial fires. And under the boulder, in the loose sand, I found another small dish, like the ones Chinda had found in the tomb.

Before the job of taking down the altar was begun, we made an exploration of the whole cave, with special attention to the cavities high up its perpendicular sides. Smith and Chinda reached one of them, thirty feet above the floor, and ten or fifteen yards north of the boulder. In a small chamber, which would have been an excellent hiding place in time of war, they found half a dozen small saucers of plain sandy ware, two inches high and three and three-fourths inches in diameter.

On the southeast side of Cave C, the ledge on which the altar was built continues, with some breadth, half the length of the covered canyon, ending in a wide platform of flat rock. The natural supposition that this cave would have been much used by the ancient inhabitants was confirmed by the presence of many potsherds in the thin layer of dirt over the stone. Ordinary walking was impossible any further along the wall, but Chinda went up the perpendicular side like a fly, creeping from crevice to crevice and probing every crevice with his flashlight. In several of them he found pottery remains, betokening an early human existence here that suggests the cliff dwellers of our own Southwest.

On the opposite side of the river, the largest space suitable for human occupation is toward the northeast entrance of the cave. We crossed the river, over slippery stones, and ascended terraces of hard-packed sand suggesting the bad lands of Arizona. Above were terraces of creamy limestone, covered with fine earth, which the prevailing easterly wind was sifting into the cave at this very moment. A human aversion to this mild, but more or less continuous, sandstorm may have been one reason why the southwest end of Cave C had been used more than the northeast. Several feet of drifted dust would have to be removed before one could expect to find sherds on the main terraces at this side of the river. Smith went up the steep side of the cave, opposite where Chinda was playing the human fly, and found sherds in another pocket, this one almost under the lofty roof.

There were several pockets which even the agile Chinda was unable to reach. One should not conclude from this, though, that they were never used by early man. They could have been reached with crude ladders, and they offer such an obvious retreat in the event of the capture of the main cave by an enemy that it is quite possible they will be found to contain traces of human occupation.

In order to get as much work as possible out of my men, I instituted a system of bonuses for everything valuable which they found. The chance at extra money made the men almost too zealous. I had not secured permission from the government to do any digging, and had brought along a pick and shovel merely to open up narrow passages in Cave A, which had baffled us on our first brief visit there. The last day in camp Mistah Brooks sneaked out early without any breakfast. When I reached Cave C at eleven o'clock, after exploring a mile of the river with Austin, I found he had made a dozen small excavations. In one of them, which he had made under the big boulder at the southwest entrance to the cave near the entrance to the tomb, he found, at a depth of fourteen inches, a well-preserved human skull. It crumbled when he tried to get it out of the closely packed earth, but I managed to bring away both jaws, which contained a number of teeth in a good state of preservation.

The other bones of the skeleton were pretty far gone, yet I doubt if this was either a very ancient or a very important burial. I believe the skeleton was that of an aborigine of fairly late and low culture, and probably an individual of little importance; for there was nothing resembling a stone grave about the bones, and either a slab grave or a cist seemed to have been used in this region for important interments, judging by the excavations of several archaeologists, including myself.

As for the tomb, the burial or burials in it were made, I believe, a good many hundreds of years ago. The type of dish found in this tomb was not found in the other caves I explored, and more nearly resembles certain Egyptian things than anything from Central America which I have ever seen. It would be absurd, however, to seize upon this slight coincidence as an excuse for reviving the ancient and well-riddled theory of the Egyptian origin of the Mayas.

George Vaillant, an expert on the classical pottery of the Mayas, who has seen what I found in these caves, says that it rather baffles him, as it does me. This is a credit to his honesty and no reflection on his ability as an archaeologist, which already has been brilliantly proved. It is, however, a reflection of the truth known to every thoughtful student of early Central American culture: that archaeologists have, as yet, barely scratched the surface in their search for remnants of the culture of ancient Middle America.

No dishes of the type found in the tomb of Cave C were found in Cave A or Cave B, although both caves are only about a mile away. Big water jars and corn jars of the type found plentifully in Cave A have not been found in either Cave B or Cave C. Neither of these types of pottery were found in the cave at the other new site I discovered in the Cayo district, Chikin Ac Tun.

From the Rio Frio Caves, I went back to my living quarters in El Cayo—a garret over the grocery store of Mr. Lisby, the Negro gentleman who had given me permission to excavate the burial mounds on his land at Monkey Falls, San Felipe.

A young American archaeologist whom I knew came to see me there to give me some earnest advice. It seemed that I had violated a law of the Colony by taking archaeology out of the Rio Frio Caves. The law required that, before doing any work, an archaeologist must get the status of a "concessionaire" from the Colonial Government. I had come here to make a collection of ethnology of the products of the living Indians for the Museum of the American Indian, Heye Foundation, of New York. I had stumbled on the caves, more or less by accident and had, naturally enough, taken out what I had found.

Word of this had got around, and a British archaeologist, who had once been told of the caves but neglected to visit them—probably because all conservative archaeologists regard caves with suspicion as "Rider Haggard stuff" —had informed Dr. Gann that I had violated the law of His Majesty's Colony. Thomas Gann was a picturesque old Britisher who was skinny and rather crabbed but likable. Formerly he had been Port Doctor of Belize, with card playing and archaeology as his hobbies. The point of the young American archaeologist's visit to my garret was to tell me that Gann had informed the Colonial Government to take my collection away from me when I reached Belize. It would be a disarming tactic, thought my friend, for me to wire the Acting Governor that I had found archaeological treasure of some value and should like to discuss the disposition of it with him when I reached the coastal capital.

I sent the wire, and a few days later called on the Acting Governor. He was all friendliness and smiles. He thanked me for my telegram and said he did not need to look at my collection. Certainly, I might box it and ship it to the Museum of the American Indian in New York.

Twenty-four hours later, my collection was boxed and on the dock, waiting for tomorrow's steamer. I went back to the Belize Hotel to have a drink in celebration of my good luck. I had the drink and was leaving the barroom when someone tapped me on the shoulder. It was a man named Brunton, the Surveyor General.

"Do you realize you have violated the law of the Colony in taking out that stuff from the caves without permission?" he asked.

"But I have the permission of the Acting Governor."

"Did he put it in writing?"

"No . . . I asked him what to do about my stuff and he said that I might have it. That's all."

"Then he has violated the law himself. Only the Colonial Council can give you such permission—and then it would be permission to take out only half of it. By law, one-half of all archaeological collections made here remain the property of the Colony."

So I had to hire a dray to take all my boxes to the Council chamber, where they were opened, and my vases and jade earplugs and potsherds spread on the two long council tables under the portraits of the British King and Queen. They remained there, closely guarded, for more than a month. And I had to postpone my departure for Guatemala.

First, there was a delay of two weeks before the Council could be assembled. When they did meet, however, they very generously voted me—ex post facto—the status of a concessionaire. That meant that I should get half of the collection anyway. Naturally, that pleased me, but it pleased me doubly because it showed me that I had the affection or, at least, the respect of most of the leading citizens of Belize. The seizure of my collection by the Surveyor General had become the chief subject of conversation at the Polo Club and the Golf Club. Many a solid Belizian told me confidentially that the action of Mr. Brunton, in overriding the generosity of the Acting Governor, was rather resented.

There was now another delay while the Council arranged for the division of the collection. The law stated that a coin should be flipped between the actual collector and a man appointed to represent the Colony. Whoever won the toss was to have first choice, the other man second choice, and so on, alternately, through the whole collection.

The delay now was due to the fact that Dr. Gann had just sailed for Europe, and there was no Britisher in town of sufficient archaeological training for the Council to trust him as their representative. Several sly questions were put to me as to what I considered was the best thing in the collection. I had been so well treated thus far that I gave my honest opinion that the polychrome vase, with sixteen curious designs on it which might possibly be glyphs, was the piece I valued most. Two somewhat similar vases and the large jade earplug were certainly "museum pieces" also.

After several days more, I was notified that a British archaeologist named Clive-Smith would soon arrive from the British Museum diggings at Luba-antun, in the south of the Colony, and that he would be asked to flip the coin with me.

Mr. Clive-Smith asked me out to the Polo Club for a Scotch-and-soda. Over the third one, he said:

"I suppose you'd rather have the best polychrome vase than any other piece if you win the toss."

"That's right."

"Well, I'll tell you something, Mason. As an archaeologist, I think the Colony is taking too much when it takes half of a collection it perhaps never would have seen except for your industry, and the money your museum backed you with. I think, at the very least, they ought to give the first choice to the man who gets the stuff. If I win the first choice, I am going to take that big jade earplug. Seems to me that's only sporting.'"

Two days later, I was told it had been decided that such a young fellow as Mr. Clive-Smith lacked the necessary experience to choose for the Colony. So I should have to wait a few more days until Captain Gruning, of the British Museum, came down from Benque Viejo. Gruning would be asked to choose for the Colony.

By now, everyone in Belize was agog over my collection. You would have thought there was a clue to the lost gold of the Mayas involved.

A week later, after Gruning's boat had come down the river, he took me out to the Polo Club, and over his first Scotch-and-soda, he made a speech in which he expressed the very views of Clive-Smith.

"It's only sporting," said Captain Gruning, "that the man who finds the stuff should have first choice. If I win the toss, I shall choose that big jade earplug. You may depend upon it."

Well, he won the toss, and chose the earplug. Taking them by and large, the British are very good sports.

•
══

ELEVEN

Thomas Gann 1924-1931

A Visit to the Year 1000

[Dr. Thomas Gann was a doctor of medicine by profession and an archaeological explorer by avocation. As port doctor of Belize, British Honduras, he had constant opportunities to hear about ancient Maya ruins and to travel in the crown colony and the archaeologically rich department of El Petén of adjacent jungle Guatemala. Gregory Mason, excerpts from whose writings I have already quoted, described him as "a picturesque old Britisher who was skinny and rather crabbed but likable." These qualities are reflected throughout his books and their photographic illustrations. Gann's attitude toward the natives of this area was one which many colonial officials develop toward their subjects, and which doctors often show toward their more uneducated and underprivileged patients: an amused but not always forbearing scorn for their ignorance, their superstitions, their preference for the less subtle physical pleasures of life, and their other "shortcomings." Probably because of his colonial and medical experiences, he dealt with them in what might be considered today a rather cavalier, authoritarian manner, but one which the field archaeologist is frequently forced to adopt, no matter how thorough his anthropological training or how sincere his professional tolerance of other ways of life.

[Gann was an inveterate traveler. Like Morley, he obviously hated the vicissitudes of the bush, yet rarely passed up an opportunity to explore it further. He is credited with the scientific discovery of several major Maya

The selections from Gann are, in the order quoted below, from the following works. Thomas Gann, *Mystery Cities* (London: Duckworth, 1925), pp. 23–39, 58–60, 66–68, 78–80, 81–83, 97–101. Copyright 1925 by Duckworth. Reprinted with permission of the publisher. Thomas Gann, *Glories of the Maya* (London: Duckworth, 1938), pp. 21–24, 25–27, 28, 37–38, 42–45, 47–48, 49–52. Copyright 1938 by Duckworth. Reprinted with permission of the publisher.

ruins, such as Cobá, Tzibanché, Ichpaatum, and Xumaché. Besides several monographs and articles that appeared in professional periodicals, Gann wrote six volumes of popular accounts of his experiences. We shall quote from two of these; first *Mystery Cities* (1925) and then *Glories of the Maya* (1938).]

From Belize we set out on June 28th for Cayo, the frontier station between the colony and the Republic of Guatemala, this being my first trip into the interior. The first part of our journey, up the Mopan River to Banana Bank, had to be done by pitpan, and from thence on horseback to Cayo. These pitpans are curious craft, in which a great deal of the river-travel throughout Central and South America is done. Ours was dug out from a single immense cedar-tree, measuring 35 ft. in length and 5 ft. 6 in. beam. Bow and stern were square, and clear of the water for the last two or three feet of their length. In the centre a small tarpaulin-covered space gave very

Thomas Gann at Lubaantún, British Honduras

scant accommodation for the passengers; the bow was occupied by the four paddlers, and the stern by the steersman, armed with a paddle six feet long, which served both as propeller and rudder. Shortly after 6 A.M. all the crew had turned up at the wharf, with the exception of an old negro known as "Sicky," a notorious character in Belize, who had unfortunately been run-in the previous night for being drunk and disorderly, and it was not till he had been brought before the magistrate, and I had paid his fine, that we could make a start. On leaving the court-house, he formed the centre of a triumphal procession down to the wharf, clad in a lady's pink silk blouse, holding two green parasols over his head, loudly chanting his opinion of the law in general and its representative with whom he had recently had an interview in particular, and accompanied by half the little nigger-boys in the town, yelling and shouting for all they were worth.

Passing through the lower reaches of the river, the banks were covered with dense mangrove swamp, whose branches and aerial roots arched above us, forming a stifling, airless tunnel which hemmed us in on every side, and shut out the sun and breeze, while the combined smell of mud, decaying vegetation, and alligators filled our nostrils. I was bitten on the hands and face by the doctor-flies which swarm here. These miserable insects, about the size of an ordinary house-fly, are of a vivid green and yellow colour. The bite is not particularly painful at first, but in ten or fifteen minutes swells rapidly, and for hours afterwards itches intolerably. By the time we had passed through the mangrove belt my fingers were so swollen I could hardly bend them, my eyes were almost closed, and my nose a shapeless, itching lump twice its natural size. That evening we put in at The Boom, a small settlement on the bank, so called because it is said that in the old days a great chain stretched across the river at this point to intercept the mahogany logs floated down the river from camps in the interior. The place was literally swarming with mosquitoes, which after sundown attacked us in battalions. I could not sleep, and from the sounds of subdued swearing, punctuated by vigorous slaps on bare hide, it was obvious that no one else could either. I therefore determined to make an early start, so, after a cup of coffee and a biscuit, we pushed off about 2 A.M., into a raw, damp fog, which hung like a pall over the river. The way the men paddled throughout the whole day was simply amazing—hour after hour under the blazing sun, without halt or rest, every now and then dipping their heads, hands, or paddle-handles into the stream, and going on without the least sign of fatigue. During most of the day they kept up a sort of low, droning, improvised song, or chant, describing incidents of their work, their amusements in Belize, very highly-seasoned amorous adventures, and—most popular of all—graphic accounts of the peculiarities and peccadilloes of the principal white citizen of the colony. When one performer had finished, another would take up the song, till each had had his turn, all joining in a sort of chorus at frequent intervals. Whenever we came to a stretch of river where the current was particularly swift the chorus increased in volume, and quickened in time to keep pace with the more rapid strokes of the paddles. About 5 p.m. we reached a little clearing called Indian Camp, and, as it was raining heavily, determined to stop for the night. The only house in the place was a small one-roomed affair built of bamboo, with considerable intervals between the sticks for ventilation, which also freely admitted the rain. The owner, an old Indian of seventy-five, with his six children, the youngest only five, all lived in this single room. Each in turn before tumbling into their hammocks (three children to one hammock), came and knelt at their father's knees, and said their "Aves" or "Paters." The old man was not averse to a little whisky, after two or three glasses of which he became quite lively, sang us several Indian songs, and showed us how they danced the "*mestisada*" when he was young. There was no room to swing my hammock, but my host provided me with a huge mahogany washing-bowl 5 ft. long by 3 ft. across, which at least had the merit of being clean, and, curling myself up in this, with my sheet wrapped round me from head to foot to keep off mosquitoes, and my hammock as a mattress, I soon fell asleep.

Next morning we made another early start, bidding adieu to our host, who was not in the best of tempers, and evidently rather upset by his dissipation of the previous night. About eight o'clock we pulled into the bank to allow the men to cook their food. Each man is allowed four pounds of salt pork and seven quarts of flour weekly as a ration. The cooking is simple in the extreme. A large fire of dry sticks is made, over which is hung the common cooking-pot, and into this is dropped each man's piece of pork (with a string attached, hanging over the side, by which it may be identified, and pulled out when done), and his flour made into a round ball of dough. In about ten minutes the half-raw hunks of pork and sodden dough-balls are pulled out, and each man swallows his portion as rapidly as possible. The broth, being common property, is lapped up in calabashes by each in turn. Some of the men carry a private supply of plantains, which are cooked in the common pot, and, as all carry guns, a little game is sometimes procured to help out this meagre ration. Early in the afternoon I shot an iguana, a species of lizard, nearly four feet long. The men had spotted the reptile stretched out asleep in the shade along a bamboo branch projecting over the river. I shot him in the head, and he promptly dropped into the water and sank like a stone, but Marcelino, the Carib bowman, dived over the side like a flash, clothes and all, and soon fished the carcase up from the bottom. This was a very welcome occurrence, and the men insisted on stopping at once to cook and eat the prize, so at the next landing-place they halted, in a twinkling had a fire lighted, and without in any way preparing the reptile—skinning, cleaning, or even decapitating—they hung the hideous carcase on a tripod of sticks over the fire, and, allowing it to cook half through, tore it limb from limb and ate it, the blood still streaming from the flesh. They wanted me to try some, but though the flesh, which is not unlike chicken, looked quite good, the method of cooking had been too revolting, so I declined.

That night we arrived at Beaver Dam, a large mahogany camp on the river bank, to which logs cut in the interior are hauled down on great, solid sleds by teams of oxen, along passes cut through the bush, and dumped in the river to find their own way to Belize and the sea. This, however, they not infrequently fail to do, as the river in a heavy flood will sometimes rise eight or ten feet in twenty-four hours, and it is no uncommon thing to see a giant log of mahogany perched snugly on the bank, or in the branches of some great tree ten feet above one's head. Next morning we found the river had risen fully eight feet during the night, and was roaring down like a mill race, rendering it quite impossible for us to make a start. During the day it continued to rise, and brought down great tree-trunks, dead animals, roofs of thatched houses, and one dead Indian. Later, bales of goods, barrels of pork and flour, rolls of cotton, and innumerable other goods, came hurtling down—sure signs that one or more pitpans had been upset higher up the river. Some of this treasure-trove was secured by the mahogany-cutters on the bank, who put out for the purpose in small cedar dug-outs into the raging flood, at serious risk to their lives, for, had any of them been upset, if they escaped drowning, they stood an excellent chance of being picked up by one of the alligators which swarm here and are always more on the alert and more voracious during a flood. These constant upsets of pitpans made goods of all kinds extremely expensive in the interior. At the little town of Flores, in Guatemala, which is three days on mule-back from Cayo, a bottle of lager beer costs twelve to fifteen shillings. The natives have christened it vino Americano—American wine—and drink it out of wine-glasses on state occasions much as we take champagne.

Next morning I woke at 5 A.M. to find the rain falling in torrents, and the floor of my hut covered with over a foot of muddy water, in which most of the baggage, saturated and filthy, was floating about, while heavier objects, such as guns, machetes, toilet utensils, cartridges, canned food, etc., had to be fished up by groping for them over the muddy floor. I moved, with all the baggage, to one of the labourers' huts higher up the bank, and beyond the reach of even a top-gallant flood, but the change to this poky little place, with mud floor, leaky palm-leaf roof, and bed made of round sticks arranged in rows on a wooden framework, was decidedly one for the worse. We were kept in all five days at Beaver Dam, and amused ourselves by fishing and shooting. The only fish we caught were vaca, a species of cat-fish, which were quite plentiful and not bad eating, though the flesh of some of them was full of small white worms. We shot two deer, two peccari, or wild hog, and four gibnut, a large rodent closely resembling a guinea-pig, but rather larger than an English hare. We also brought down a dozen parrots and quite a few pigeons as they flew over, but a good many of these fell in the high bush and in the river, whence it was impossible to retrieve them. The deer and peccari were driven across the bush track by a pack of half-starved mongrel curs, which had been trained to range ahead, accompanied by their owners, and drive the game across the track as near to the sportsmen as possible. The burrows of the gibnut were discovered by these same curs, and the animals smoked out with a smudge of damp leaves and some pepper-bushes, and shot as they bolted from their holes, very much as one shoots rabbits when ferreting. With the exception of the parrots and pigeons, both fishing and shooting provided but poor sport. Fresh fish and meat, however, were a welcome change from a straight diet of salt horse, from which we had been suffering for over a week, though the old parrots proved so tough that even the labourers could make nothing of them.

On the fifth morning, the river having gone down considerably, we made a fresh start at 7 A.M.; the current, however, was still running very strong, and the men frequently took to the poles, as they could make no headway against the stream over shallow runs, but, even with poles, one watching the bank would wonder for seconds at a time whether the old dug-out was making any way against the current, or only just holding her own. Once, going over a specially swift run, the water caught her bow, switched it round, and turned her, completely out of control, broadside on to the current. She canted sideways, shipping enough water to fill her nearly to the thwarts; then, just as I was preparing for a swim to the bank, the men succeeded in grounding their poles and got control of her again, with no worse misfortune than the saturation of everything on board. Going round a bend in the river where the water was comparatively smooth, we almost ran into a tapir swimming the river, and about one-third of the way over. He was a young animal not much bigger than a large mastiff, and evidently very much flurried by our sudden arrival on the scene, as he first tried to turn back, but the pitpan headed him off from the near bank, the men making an awful din by beating the water with their paddles and shouting at the top of their voices. He then started for the far bank, followed closely by the pitpan, which soon overtook him. I was very anxious to get a live tapir for the Zoo, so shouted to the bow paddleman to try and lasso him instead of killing him with a machete, as he was about to do. With some considerable difficulty he succeeded in slipping a loop of rope over the animal's head, and, paddling upstream, we began to tow him astern; but the poor little beggar was making very heavy weather of it, for, as he could not swim as quickly as we paddled, he was being towed under and half strangled, half drowned. On approaching the bank I stopped the boat, slacking the tow-rope with a view to getting him on board and carrying him there trussed up. Finding himself in shallow water, he soon found his feet, stood up, and giving his head a sideways twist, slipped out of the noose in the most marvellous manner, and, before I could even put a cartridge in my gun, was up the steep clay bank and off into the bush. I rather sympathised with him as, though a mere baby, he had put up such a gallant fight, but the men were very sore that so much good tapir meat on the hoof should thus easily have escaped them.

That evening we arrived at Banana Bank, where I spent a couple of pleasant days, and on the third morning set out on horseback with a guide—a taciturn Spanish Indian—for Cayo.

On fording the river, we crossed a stretch of beautiful open grass country with magnificent wild cotton and Santa Maria trees dotted everywhere, which might well have passed for an English park had it not been for the tall, stately cuhoon and royal palms which were plentifully scattered over it. Crossing this, we entered an old mahogany truck pass, where, owing to the sticks, which had been laid down transversely to form a corduroy road for the heavy trucks to pass over, having rotted from years of exposure, the going was very bad and full of holes; bush also had grown from the sides and filled the pass, so that in places it was very difficult to find the way. Coming to a place where a great frond from a cuhoon palm had fallen across the track, just too low to ride under, I stretched out my arm to lift it up, when, with a sharp *"Cuidado, señor,"* the guide brushed alongside me, and sliced the frond in two with one blow of his machete, severing at the same time a small, yellow-jawed tamagass—one of the most poisonous snakes in the colony—which had been lying stretched out along the leaf, the two wriggling halves falling on each side of the trail. He had seen some movement on top of the frond, and knowing the danger of handling such things, which are favourite places for snakes to take a siesta upon, had intervened just in time.

About 4 P.M. we arrived at the good-sized, but forlorn and dismal Indian village of San Francisco. The huts were wretched, tumble-down affairs, consisting of a few upright sticks roofed over with rotting palm-leaf, wind and rain finding their way freely through both walls and roofs. Even the women were dirty and bedraggled, a most unusual thing with Maya women, who are generally spotless. The wretched, pot-bellied children were making languid efforts to play in the dust, but scuttled off like rabbits into the bush at our approach. The few men who were lounging about did the same, and the women made a bee-line for their huts. We rode up to the largest and least miserable-looking hut, and there found the *Alcalde,* or chief man of the village, suffering from a severe attack of malarial fever. He told us there was no food of any kind to be had in the place, and the utmost he could offer us in the way of hospitality was a hammock each for the night. I saw the guide examining the hammocks carefully.

"What are you looking for, *hombre?*" I said.

"Come over and look for yourself, señor," he answered.

I did so, and found that the loops, to which the suspending ropes were attached on both hammocks, were literally seething, crawling masses of brown bugs and their ova. These loathsome insects retire to this part of the hammock during the day, but at night come down in battalions to attack the luckless would-be sleeper. The sky was overcast, and we were evidently going to have rain, but I determined to push on, as even a night in the bush would be preferable to one at San Francisco. The guide told me that this was the worst village in the district; half the men were wanted by the police of the colony and the neighbouring republics; not one of the couples living together in it was married, and whenever the people could club together sufficient money, it was expended in purchasing demijohns of native rum for a debauch in which both sexes joined, and which usually ended in a free fight. Several murders had been committed there, but the perpetrators had never been brought to justice. From their pot bellies, earthy colour, and lack of energy, I could tell that most of the children were earth-eaters. I caught one wretched little naked girl of about eight in the act of scraping up some reddish earth from the side of the house, where the parasite-infested pigs wallowed during the night. She was either too weak or too indifferent to all mundane affairs to run away. I asked her how much she ate in a day, and she answered, with a ghost of a grin, by putting her two little claw-like hands together and scooping up a small double fistful, to show me that that was about her daily allowance. I tried a fragment of this earth myself, and found it of a sweetish and not unpleasant taste; the danger to the children, however, lies in the fact that it is full of the ova of numerous parasites, from the pigs' and other animals' droppings, including hookworm, from which fully eighty per cent. of the Indians suffer.

Shortly after leaving San Francisco we passed a cluster of mahogany-cutters' huts known as Mount Hope, which we knew to be just twenty miles from Cayo. A couple of miles beyond this, the rain, which had been long threatening, came down in torrents, and the night rapidly closed in. So dark did it soon become that I unloosed my picket-rope, and the guide and I each took hold of it so that we should not lose each other, which, in the pitch-dark bush, with the pouring rain, it would have been quite easy to do. Riding was most uncomfortable, not to say dangerous, as the overhanging branches, which are difficult to avoid in the daytime, kept scratching our faces, and a "wait a bit" thorn caught me just over the eyelid, tearing a gash in my forehead from which I could feel the blood trickling down into my eye. Fortunately it was not half an inch lower, as in that case I should probably have lost the eye. After what seemed hours of riding, we came to the conclusion that we must have lost our way, as we had encountered nothing like the creek at which we knew we should have arrived about two hours after leaving Mount Hope. I determined to call a halt till dawn, for we stood a good chance of either losing our way entirely in the bush, falling over the steep bank into the creek, or getting blinded or stunned by some overhanging branch. As a last forlorn hope we gave the horses their heads to see if they would make for home, but, instead of doing so, they turned round in their tracks and headed in the opposite direction. We dismounted—as miserable a couple as it would be possible to find, for we had no grub, and had had nothing to eat since breakfast—tethered the horses, off-saddled, and, wrapping ourselves up in the blankets which are always used as *numnahs,* with our saddles as pillows, lay down in the pouring rain to try and get a little sleep before dawn. One would have thought that the downpour of rain would have kept off the mosquitoes, but, far from doing so, it only appeared to make them more bloodthirsty. At last they became unbearable, so, pulling my saddlebags to me, I managed, after a lot of fumbling in the dark, to unearth three dirty handkerchiefs, one of which I tied round each hand and one round my face, and, lying down again, having beaten the mosquitoes, I went off into an uneasy doze. I seemed to have been asleep only a few minutes when I was suddenly awakened by something coming down "flop" into my lap from the tree above; partly freeing my right hand from its handkerchief, I stretched it out to discover what had disturbed me, when to my horror I encountered the clammy coils of a small snake. Fully awake in an instant, I jumped up and ran till I was brought up by the bush; no doubt it was only a harmless tree-snake, which, having, if a snake can be said to do so, missed his footing up aloft, and been half stunned by the fall, was probably more scared than I; I have, however, always had a particular loathing for snakes of all sorts and sizes, and this one, falling as it were from the heavens, I must admit, scared me considerably. I did not lie down again, but, fagged as I was, paced up and down the track till the first faint streaks of dawn began to make their appearance through the bush. As soon as it was light we discovered that we were on the trail from Mount Hope to Cayo, but had turned around (no doubt at one of the so-called "cut offs," which Indians make round large trees fallen across the track, sooner than take the trouble to cut through the tree-trunk) and were actually retracing our steps towards Mount Hope. The horses had been right after all in wanting to turn when given their heads, and their instinct had been more reliable than our reason.

Soon after dawn the rain held up, and, the sun warming our miserable chilled bodies, we set out in better spirits and reached Cayo shortly after noon. On each side of the river a smooth, park-like savanna, dotted over with giant shade trees, sloped up from the banks to a height of from 50 to 100 feet. The houses, forming a belt, surrounded this park-like amphitheatre, through the centre of which wound the river, clear and limpid, with clean, shingly bottom. Women, naked to the waist, clad in gaily coloured print petticoats, were washing clothes, or rather pounding them with wooden clubs on the rocks by the side of the river, chattering and laughing amongst themselves like a flock of parrots. On seeing two *caballeros* at the ford, those whose garments were deficient below as well as above the waist hastened to hide their nakedness under water, with an assumption of modesty to which their impudent, laughing glances gave the lie.

Though we had had no food since the previous morning, and our clothes were torn to ribbons, our faces and legs covered with scratches and wounds, we neither of us were really any the worse for the experience, which, when it was over, I was glad to have gone through, as it gave me some faint idea of what the life of a mahogany-cutter living in the bush is like.

Cayo is a good-sized village, with an extraordinarily mixed population, consisting of Guatemalans, Mexicans, Honduraneans, negroes, and Maya Indians, with a few French, Americans, and English. It is the last outpost of civilisation, and portal to the impenetrable and unexplored jungle beyond, which stretches north to Mexico, south to Guatemala, and east and west from the Atlantic to the Pacific. All the way up the river I had found patients awaiting the coming of an English medico; though bush-doctors, snake-doctors, obeah-men, shamans, and all kinds of quacks are plentiful as blackberries in autumn, the arrival of a genuine doctor is a rare occurrence. Fees varied a good deal with the commercial rating of the patient, ranging from a few sweet potatoes or corn cakes (the East-End surgery fee), through a dozen eggs or a brace of parrots or pigeons (perhaps about the average general practitioner's remuneration), up to a sucking pig, a gibnut, or a couple of hens (the Harley Street consultant's fee). One of the first patients I was asked to see in Cayo was a well-known character, old David Arland, an ancient African, who as a child had been captured with his parents by slavers on the West African coast, and liberated by a British ship of war. He had come to British Honduras as a plantation hand, and drifted to Cayo, where, in the combined professions of pitpan steersman, cattle doctor, and obeah-man he had acquired a good bush house, and a considerable amount of money and live stock. For a long time he had been suffering agonies from an internal tumour which had got quite beyond the possibility of operation, and, though he could eat nothing, still clung on to life. When I got to the house he called me into the bedroom, and, having first turned his family out, showed me his left hand, between the middle and ring fingers of which a small, hard lump was to be felt. This, he explained, was a piece of charmed metal, which when he was a boy in Africa, had been grafted into the flesh by a celebrated obeah-man. It was guaranteed to bring constant good luck and prolong life indefinitely. The good luck he admitted had been his, but now, affected as he was by a painful and incurable disease, he was (much as he wished it) unable to die and end his sufferings, owing to the presence of the charm. Would I remove it, and so let him pass in peace? This I accordingly did, and found it to consist of an oblong piece of some rather soft metal, greyish outside, silvery within, ½ inch long, ¼ inch broad, and ⅛ inch thick. He seemed greatly relieved after the little operation, and, curiously enough, that same evening passed peacefully away. On visiting the house next day, I found his bed neatly made, and, laid out on a small table by the side of it, a substantial meal of pork, plantains, beans, sweet potato, and corn cake, all smoking hot. On seeking an explanation, his wife told me he had left all his property to her, on the sole condition that for one month after his death she should twice a day prepare a good hot meal, and lay it beside his bed, as he meant to return in the spirit and regale himself on the smell of the food; which condition she faithfully carried out, and his spirit must have enjoyed a series of repasts far superior to anything he had ever enjoyed in the flesh for such a long period.

[Nine miles from El Cayo is a large Indian village, Benque Viejo. From here Gann planned to visit the ruins of Xunantunich, accompanied by his Negro, Jim, and "Muddy Esquivel," a guide and general utility man who had worked at one time or another for most of the American and British archaeologists in this region. Muddy was half Irish, a quarter Spanish, and a quarter Maya Indian. A Guatemalan *arriero* or muleteer transferred their equipment across the river and to Xunantunich.]

We suffered a good deal from the scarcity of water, as the nearest creek is a mile away in the bush, over a very hilly path ankle-deep in mud, and it had to be fetched by two Indian boys carrying large hour-glass-shaped calabashes on a long pole. The water was none too good when one got it, as it formed a milky mixture with tea, and had to be drunk in strict moderation by me, as it acted like a mild dose of Epsom salts. We were a good deal puzzled as to where the ancient dwellers in this city obtained their water supply, as it is hardly conceivable that they should have sent so far for it as the creek; on the other hand, we found no trace of those great underground tanks or cisterns known as chultuns, hollowed out in the limestone, in which the ancient Maya at many of their cities stored water; yet it is quite possible that these may exist, and that the narrow circular openings have in the course of the centuries become choked up by fallen tree-trunks, limbs, and other vegetal débris.

One never realises what a boon a bath is till one has gone without it for a week or two in a tropical climate, and the warm sponge-over taken from a small tin dishpan containing about two quarts of this rock-hard water was one of the greatest luxuries I ever enjoyed. It was preceded by a good rub-over with a mixture of kerosene oil and tobacco-juice to loosen the ticks and red bug accumulated during the last few days. Insects are undoubtedly the main curse of the bush. Ticks of all sorts abounded here (though it was the rainy season), varying in size from a large split pea to microscopic little chaps into whose nests along the bush trails one is constantly brushing, when a veritable shower of these bloodthirsty little beasts is scattered over one's trousers or coat, spreading rapidly in all directions, and "digging in" on the inner side of the thighs, all round the waist, and in other spots where the skin is thin, and incidentally tender, and the anchorage is good. Unless removed with kerosene or tobacco-juice, they hang on like grim death, and suck blood till they turn into tiny distended bladders. Red bug, called by the Spaniards *coloradillo* (minute scarlet insects which can only be seen by the aid of a small magnifying glass), are even worse than ticks, as they burrow deeper into the skin, causing intolerable itching, and are much more difficult to get rid of. Mosquitoes of all sorts and sizes abounded, but one gets used to them; and here, buried in the depths of the bush, there is no micro-organism of malaria, yellow fever, or filariasis for them to carry, so their attacks can be borne philosophically. Worse than the mosquito, however, is the batlas-fly, a minute peripatetic suction pump whose bite itches intolerably, and leaves a little red circle of blood, about the size of a small pin's head, extravasated beneath the skin, which in a day or two turns black, and does not wear off for weeks. I have seen a white man's hands turn almost black on the backs after a few weeks' residence in the bush where these flies abound.

I was introduced that afternoon, while searching the bush for burial mounds with one of my Indian boys, to the water ti-ti, a dark-coloured, rough-barked liana, about as thick around as my wrist. Though very thirsty, I did not like to drink the creek water without boiling, and told Pedro so, on which he went a few yards into the bush, and, seizing a great rope of the liana hanging from a branch 50 ft. up, sliced off a section about 2½ ft. long with two blows of his machete, and, holding it over his head, allowed the water—of which it contained about an ounce, clear, pure, and cool—to drip into his mouth. I proceeded to follow his example, though it took a dozen sections to relieve my thirst. Many an Indian has been saved from death by thirst by this ti-ti, when lost in the Yucatan bush, where streams are not, and water holes are few and far between. Fruits, nuts, and edible roots abound, and game is incredibly tame, so that food-supply presents no difficulty, but, with the exception of this liana and a large, broad-leaved cactus which holds water in the spaces between its rows of leaves, practically no water-supply exists. The water in the cactus, being open to the air, affords a combined drinking-trough and bathroom to myriads of insects, who not infrequently use it also as a convenient place in which to commit suicide, so that it usually smells aloud, is of a soup-like consistency, and it is not to be compared for a moment with that supplied by the liana.

This particular morning there turned up at the ruins a celebrated local character amongst the Indians, Urbano Patt, the most renowned shaman, bush-medico, and snake-doctor in all the district. He was a curiously thin, wizened, dried-up, little Indian of indeterminate age, but possessing a look of far greater intelligence than the majority of the Maya, who, notwithstanding their ancient and lofty lineage, are, it must be admitted, somewhat bovine in aspect and intellect. His appearance was not impressive, dressed as he was in cotton shirt and pants—none too clean—an old pair of moccasins, a dreadful old straw hat, a tiger-skin bag hanging over one shoulder— the one modest badge of his office visible—and a great machete strapped to his side. Yet there was not lacking a certain dignity and assurance in his manner, which was courteous and urbane, as one celebrated physician meeting another of a different school, a smile on his face, hat raised, and hand outstretched in greeting. He bade me welcome to Xunantunich, which I learnt for the first time was the Indian name for the ruins. The word means in Maya, literally, "stone maiden," and its origin, as told by Urbano, is somewhat peculiar. Some years ago, when the Maya first settled in Benque Viejo and discovered the ruins, one of their number started out hunting one morning with his three dogs, and climbed the temple mound in search of the freshly made hole of a gibnut, as it was a favourite place for this animal to burrow. Crossing the mound just below the base of the temple, he was suddenly brought up "all standing" by the sight of a beautiful statuesque Maya maiden, of heroic size, clad in *huipil* and *pik*, standing motionless by the side of the mouth of the passage, which runs beneath the temple. She appeared of a dazzling and supernatural whiteness, as she stood full in the rays of the rising sun, and looked with fixed and stony stare, as it appeared to him, across the intervening bush to the valley, where later the Indians built the village of Succots. On recovering a little from his first shock, he promptly turned tail, and, throwing aside his gun, bolted incontinently down the hillside and made for the river. He reported the matter at once to the *Chaac*, or native priest, and both of them started back for the ruins. Arriving at the mound, the *Chaac* took the lead, and soon came to the mouth of the tunnel, only to find that the stone maiden had disappeared. They found the gun thrown aside in the bush, but of the three dogs and of the Xunantunich nothing was ever seen again. It is probable that the dogs, entering one of the limestone caves of the neighbourhood, encountered a jaguar instead of a gibnut, while the lady can only be regarded as the creation of a singularly lively and vivid imagination, though the tale is firmly believed by the Indians to this day.

As none of the men would dig because it was Sunday, I determined to cut a path from Xunantunich to some entirely new ruins which had been recently found by the Indians, distant about two miles to the north. Though they strongly objected to digging, they had no objection whatever to cutting passes through the bush, and the only explanation I could get of this apparent inconsistency was that digging was considered work, and a breach of the fourth commandment, whereas felling bush was not. There was a track leading to them from Succots, but as this was a long way round and full of red bug, I decided to cut a trail of my own through the forest. Muddy, with two men, started early for the new ruins, while two were left with me. Muddy and his men, on arriving at their destination, started cutting a picado, or trail, through the bush in a general southerly direction, while my men, having given the others time to reach the ruins, cut in a general northerly direction towards them. Both parties blew at frequent intervals on curious conical horns, made by twisting thick tough palm leaves into a cone, and blowing through the smaller end. The note may be varied by altering the diameter of the cone, and the extraordinary bleating noise which the horns make can be heard for miles through the bush on a calm day. They take the place, in fact, of the conch shell trumpets used by the Coast Indians and Caribs. In less than two hours both parties met, almost in the middle, having cut a nearly straight pass through two miles of bush, no mean feat when one considers the density of the undergrowth.

We had now twenty men reporting for work every day, and with them that morning came the Succots Indian who had hired me, for twenty-five cents daily, the dug-out in which the men crossed the river every morning. He now demanded one dollar per day, grounding his claim on the fact that whereas at first only a few men crossed, now twenty crossed daily, and it was useless to explain that the twenty-five cents was a flat rate for the use of the boat for about ten minutes every day, so it made no difference to him if a hundred men crossed in her. She was a crazy old craft, dug out of a wild cotton trunk, the softest and cheapest wood used for the purpose. When new she had been worth perhaps ten dollars, but now when one crossed the river in her she leaked through a dozen cracks, imperfectly caulked with pieces of tough bark, reinforced by fragments of old garments, and it was only by constant baling that the opposite side, perhaps fifty yards away, was reached. Five dollars would have been an extravagant price for her, and yet her owner demanded one dollar per day hire! Even a war profiteering shipowner would have nothing to learn from these poor primitive Indians, who have bought their experience dearly from chicle contractors and Armenian store-keepers. Fortunately for me another dug-out owner offered to lend me his boat for nothing, on which the profiteer volunteered, as a great concession, to keep to the original 25 cents, which offer I was delighted to be able to turn down. When we passed by a week later the old tub was sunk at her moorings, where she will probably remain till she rots.

One of the men who had worked with me for a few days when I first arrived passed through camp that morning on his way to the chicle bush. He had four or five months' killing labour to look forward to, sleeping under a palm-leaf shelter, hardly ever dry, with nothing but corn cake and beans to eat, yet he was as cheerful as a lark, and full of chaff for my other men who had not the enterprise to leave home, brave the hardships of the bush, and take the chance of making big money or nothing at all. The *mulada,* or mule train, to which he belonged, had left three days previously on its eight days' journey into the heart of Central American bush, but he had been unable to tear himself away from the señoritas, the *vino del pais*—wine of the country, or white rum—and the fascinating games of *chingalingo* and *parapinto* provided in the village of Benque Viejo. He had started three times to follow the mule train, but the attractions of Benque had each time drawn him back at night; now, however, if he were to catch the *mulada* at all, he was really obliged to go, as he would have to cover in five days the distance they had travelled in eight. His luggage consisted of a small shot bag, slung over his shoulder, and a guitar in a waterproof cover, carried in his arms with more care and solicitude than if it had been a baby. But this guitar was to him what his harp was to the wandering minstrel—the price of many a meal, many a cigarette, and many a drink of rum round the chicle camp fire, under the flimsy palm-leaf shelter, with the ping of the mosquito, the quack of the tree frog, and the howl of the jaguar, the only other sounds to break the silence of the bush by night.

Chicleros are extraordinarily improvident, and swayed solely by the whim of the moment. One frequently passes chicle camps, in which their owners, after the season is over had left behind such articles as guitars, pots and pans, crockery, spurs, lamps, food, and even blankets and hammocks, not wishing to be encumbered with these in their mad rush back to the dissipations of semi-civilisation, perhaps four or five long days' tramp through the bush. They are great gamblers, and having no other stakes available in the bush, play for blocks of chicle, using the fragments left over in trimming each block as small change. Recently Indian and Mestiso girls have taken to accompanying the men into camp, and it is no uncommon thing to find a mother bemoaning the loss of her daughter who has eloped with some gallant chiclero to the bush. Once the girls have got into the habit of this free untrammelled life, they find it almost impossible to break, getting ready as each season comes round to accompany their chiclero—though rarely the same one for two consecutive seasons—back to the wild.

The men clearing the new ruins returned that evening, and reported that on the summit of the main temple they had found a small fallen-in chamber from which they had disturbed a large yellow-jawed tomagoff, one of the most poisonous snakes in the bush, and that on seeing them he had made off and taken refuge in a hole in the wall of the temple about half-way up. I told them to be sure and kill him next day if he returned.

[Gann decided to visit some of the more remote Indian settlements in the bush, where a white man was seldom, or never, seen. Accompanied by an interpreter he set out on horseback for the village of Chorro, thirty miles distant from Cayo, a small exclusively Maya village containing about forty or fifty huts.]

We found considerable excitement in the settlement as a baby had been missed that same morning, and a search-party formed by the men when they returned from work in their corn plantations in the afternoon. The remains of the child—a little girl perhaps two years of age—were discovered about a quarter of a mile from the village, and a truly ghastly spectacle they presented, hardly anything but the gnawed, bloody bones and scraps of cartilage being left. The poor little thing had evidently wandered out, while her mother was busy washing clothes, to the edge of the bush, where she was seized, carried off, and devoured by a jaguar, which was probably on the look-out for a stray pig from the village. The Indians, feeling sure the jaguar would return, tied up a small porker as a lure for him just within the edge of the bush, while the child's father and myself sat with our guns loaded with buck-shot on a platform of sticks erected in the lower branches of a great ceiba-tree, within easy shot of the pig. The first night we sat, or rather squatted, in an extremely constrained and uncomfortable position, unable either to talk or smoke, till nearly 2 A.M., when I gave it up as a bad job, and retired to bed, though the child's father stopped on till sunrise. On the next night, however, we had hardly taken up our positions on the platform for an hour when the pig began to squeal and pull hard on his picket rope, evidently in mortal terror. Beneath the cieba-tree the bush was comparatively clear, and we could distinctly make out, in the bright moonlight, a dark shadow slowly creeping round the edge of the clearing towards the pig. We fired simultaneously, and the noise of the reports was followed immediately by the sound of the animal crashing his way through the bush. We both felt sure we had hit the brute, but neither of us had the least inclination to follow him up by moonlight. Next morning we found blood on the ground in the clearing, and, following this into the bush, where it was plentifully smeared on the leaves of the undergrowth, and lay in gouts upon the ground, we came upon the jaguar stone dead, not a hundred yards from where he had been shot. He was a magnificent animal, and I had his skin tanned by a local moccasin-maker and made into a rug, though its beauty was somewhat marred by having been riddled with buckshot holes over the head and one shoulder.

I found it very difficult to obtain quarters for myself and the interpreter in the village, as all the huts were already overcrowded; he at length discovered a nice, clean little hut, occupied only by a young widow named Petronilla Can (Petronilla Snake in Maya), generally called by the Maya diminutive Xpet, who agreed to take us in and feed us for the few days we remained in the village. She gave me a remarkably comfortable cuhoon palm-leaf bed, and made a shake-down out of the same leaves for the interpreter on the floor, retiring herself to sleep in a little cubby-hole, screened off from the *sala* by a wall of upright sticks. I had been up after the jaguar the greater part of the first night, and made up for lost time by sleeping most of the following day, but on the second day I noticed that she seemed very miserable, and her nose and eyes were red, evidently from crying, so I enquired what was wrong. It appeared that her husband had died of small-pox the day before we arrived, and, moreover, had died on the very bed, and covered with the same blanket, that I had used. I tried to rub in the criminal carelessness of her conduct in letting me sleep in an infected bed, under an infected blanket, but she was so thoroughly a fatalist that I had to give it up as hopeless, and, having seen the bed and bedding burnt, we took up our quarters in a little bush chapel, which was really the most comfortable building in the place. This poor widow had come with her husband quite recently about twenty miles across the Guatemala border, from a village which had been decimated by small-pox, hoping to escape the infection—her fatalism evidently extending only to those in whom she had no special interest—but a few days after their arrival the husband was stricken with the disease, and in less than a week was dead. The Chorro people, I feel sure, did not realise the danger of the infection, or they would never have allowed the couple to settle in their village, and it would have been well for them had they not done so, for shortly after the death of the man the disease spread through the village and carried off a number of the population, hardly a house but was left mourning the loss of some member of the family.

These Indians are intensely superstitious, and believe firmly in Xtabai, or evil spirits, in the form of beautiful women, who lure hunters on to follow them in the bush, and then murder them; in the *pishan,* or souls of the dead, who at certain times of the year are permitted to return to the scene of their former existence, in the Galatea-like coming to life of those dwarfish clay figures of the ancient gods found decorating the outer surfaces of incense-burners, which they sometimes dig up, and which I have been assured by more than one Indian he had seen dancing in the moonlight; and, lastly, in the existence, and occasional appearance of, a personal devil of the orthodox kind. I determined to test this belief in the last, and, with the aid of Velasquez, obtained a large round calabash, which I hollowed out, and cut eye-holes, a mouth, and a nose in the shell. Fixing this on a stick, and placing a candle inside, I drew a little cotton blanket round the stick and myself, so that it looked like a ghastly white figure seven feet high, with fiery eyes, nose, and mouth. I may say I borrowed the idea from my schooldays, using a calabash, as no turnip was available. The Indians are in the habit of squatting about in the streets after their work is done, gossiping about the maize crop, the scarcity of game, the iniquities of the *Alcalde*—in fact, very much the same subjects as interest more civilised people. I knew, therefore, that my best time would be about eight o'clock, for the moon had not yet risen then, and it was not late enough for them to have retired indoors for the night. When everything was ready, I sallied forth from the back of the little chapel and stalked slowly and majestically down the street. Nobody saw whence I came, and, for all they knew, I might have descended from above, or more probably ascended from below. They did not stop to enquire, but bolted into their houses as if the devil were after them. Down the front street and up the back street I went; people everywhere flying from me in terror, children howling, women screaming, and men blocking up the door behind them to keep out the devil. I managed to get back to the chapel unobserved, and was greatly interested the following day in getting detailed accounts of the personal appearance of the devil from various eye-witnesses, no two of which were alike. Next morning Velasquez appeared after breakfast looking somewhat abashed and sheepish, quite a new role for him. He intimated he had something important to say, so I bade him go ahead.

"Well, señor," he said, "you have found Xpet a good cook, is it not so?"

"Quite true," I replied.

"And clean?"

"And clean also," I admitted.

"And she is still young, and for an Indian not so bad-looking?"

"That also," I admitted, beginning to see which way the cat was about to jump.

"Señor," he continued, "there are in this village more women than men and, saddened though she is at the loss of her husband, the girl feels she should have a man to take care of her. Will you take her back to Cayo to cook for you?"

"José," I said, "you have the morals of a monkey; but worse, you are a fool, for what should I do with an Indian girl, however beautiful and clean, and skilled in making corn cake, when I leave the district?"

"True, Señor Doctor, I never thought of that; but would there be any objection to Xpet accompanying *me* back to Cayo?"

"José," I replied, "if I hear one more word about the *viudita* (little widow) you return to-day to Cayo, and on foot."

[Several years later, Gann was again in Belize when the colony was rebuilding after the disastrous hurricane and tidal wave of 1931.]

From Belize we went to Gale's Point, Manatee, in my motor launch, spending a very uncomfortable night on board, as a cloudburst flooded us out and left us like drowned rats in the morning. Here we hired a thirty foot dug-out to take us and our outfit for the trip up the Manatee River. The crew consisted of my man, Muddy Esquivel, a black guide, and Ikal, a Kekchi Indian, a tall, powerful, copper-coloured lad with an immense mouth, from which a broad smile was seldom absent. He prided himself on his knowledge of English, and although he spoke Spanish fairly well he would seldom converse in that language and became conveniently deaf when addressed in it. His English, though fluent, was quite unintelligible, which made matters rather awkward at times. We ascended the river in the launch for a couple of hours, then embarked in the dug-out, as beyond this point the river was a series of falls and runs up which the launch could not go. At five in the afternoon we arrived at a great perpendicular cliff of limestone rock, about one hundred and fifty feet high, at the base of which appeared a small, dark, arched tunnel from which the river emerged, and into which, after lighting the gasoline vapour lamps, we plunged in the dug-out.

Navigation along this subterranean tunnel was not easy, as the current against which we had to make our way was very swift, sharp bends were frequent, and the idea of being plunged, in Cimmerian darkness, into the cold, black river, was by no means reassuring. The water was too deep for poling and the current too swift for paddling, so we made our way by clawing along the rocky side.

During the flood time the tunnel is evidently filled to the roof with water, as the lamp showed us trees and logs, caught up at all levels on the shelves and projections along its walls. We were very thankful to emerge into daylight on the upriver side of the tunnel.

The vast wall of limestone through which the river passes is not more than three hundred feet in breadth, but the passage through it is very winding and much longer. It divides the upper from the lower valley of the Manatee River, making the former a sort of archaeological "Land which Time Forgot," for no archaeologist has entered it since the last of the ancient Maya inhabitants perished there miserably.

The wall is a very remarkable formation, and, covered with ferns, creepers,

Dugout pitpan
From Thomas Gann, *Mystery Cities*, 1925. Copyright 1925 by Thomas Gann. By permission of Gerald Duckworth & Co. Ltd.

liana, and flowering shrubs which have taken root on its perpendicular sides, and topped by a fringe of virgin bush, it presents a beautiful and unique spectacle, whose regular stratification would almost lead one to suppose that it was the work of human hands.

We pitched our camp on the river bank, and next morning, poling up the river for a short distance, came to the mouth of a little creek. Ascending this as far as the dug-out would go, we arrived again at the barrier wall, here about one hundred feet high, presenting the appearance of a vast building at the base of which was a high arched entrance through which the creek flowed.

Entering this, we found ourselves in a large cave, the roof of which was covered with stalactites of all sizes. On following the cave for about two

Gann's expedition negotiating rapids

From Thomas Gann, *Mystery Cities*, 1925. Copyright 1925 by Thomas Gann. By permission of Gerald Duckworth & Co. Ltd.

hundred yards, we arrived back at the point from which we had started, as it was formed round a great circular core of limestone.

In a cupboard-like recess in the wall we discovered two large round-bottomed water jars of coarse pottery, one of which was supported in a circular rim broken from another jar. Near them was a big amphora-shaped vase, broken in three pieces and firmly cemented all round by limestone concretion deposited by the dripping stalactites. Behind the amphora stood a stalagmite two and a half feet high, to the side of which clung many hollow calcareous tubes, evidently the stems of creepers which had been covered with concretion and were now rotting away, leaving only the hollow pipes behind. The dripping has now stopped from the roof, and it is impossible to say how long it required for the concretion round either the pot or the liana to collect, owing to the great variation in the formation, not only in different places but even in the same place at different times.

At Lubaantun we found, in a small stream, living snails so covered in lime concretion that the exit from their shells was almost blocked up, and thousands of snail shells in which the occupants had been killed by complete occlusion of their front doors, showing that here at any rate the process must have been a very rapid one.

In the floor of the cave was a large hole, on descending which we found ourselves in another cave, also circular, and running parallel with the first but beneath it. On the floor of the lower cave were fragments of charcoal and ashes, some potsherds, a broken conch shell, and part of a cracked human thigh bone. The roof of this chamber was covered with stalactites of various sizes, some of which, when struck with a long thin piece of broken stalactite, gave out beautiful, clear musical notes of varying tone.

Muddy, who is musically inclined, succeeded in playing a simple tune on one of them, the notes sounding rather like those of a xylophone.

Next day we explored a great limestone wall, from twenty-five to seventy-five feet high, running first east and west, then turning at right angles and running north and south. It was terraced, and looked at first sight like a gigantic stairway, honeycombed by many caves at various levels.

On the floor of one we found, lying together, half the lower jaw of a peccary, a cooking pot of rough pottery, fragments of conch shell, and part of a human leg bone, evidently the remains of a somewhat mixed feast. The human tibia showed teeth marks, and had evidently been knawed by a rodent while some animal matter still remained on it. On the floor of a second cave were fragments of the bones of some large mammal, probably a tapir, fragments of a human skull, potsherds, and ashes.

Whether or not the ancient Maya were addicted to cannibalism has always been a controversial point with archaeologists. Accepting the evidence of writers contemporaneous with the Conquest, it would appear that they were, but that the custom was of a purely ceremonial nature and was confined to human victims which were offered as sacrifices to the gods, and of whose bodies small portions were eaten with a view, probably, to acquiring some of the characteristics of the god to whom the sacrifice was made.

This part of the country, from soon after the Conquest, seems to have formed a refuge for runaway slaves and apostate Indians from the Spanish dominions in Yucatan on the north, and Vera Paz on the south, chiefly, no doubt, owing to its inaccessibility and the facilities for concealment which its innumerable caves and underground passages afforded. But these advantages must have been more than counterbalanced by the difficulty in obtaining food; for the land was not suitable for the cultivation of maize, the staple food of the Indian throughout Central America, and no long seaboard well supplied with fish was available as at Ambergris Cay. Moreover, even if they had had anything with which to trade with their neighbours for food, contact with these was almost completely cut off by the Spanish colonies on all sides of them.

These poor Indians, then, persecuted and harried on all sides, had little opportunity, even if the land had been suitable, of cultivating their corn plantations, and were consequently driven by sheer starvation to the horrid practice of cannibalism, as has happened to more civilised communities throughout the world in all ages. The place may well be termed the "Valley of Death," for those who were not devoured there probably died of starvation. One curious characteristic is common to the cannibals of Ambergris Cay and those of the Manatee valley: both seem to have deserted the gods of their ancestors and to have set up new gods for themselves, which, judged by their images portrayed on the clay censers found in both places, were grim-visaged, horrible, and malevolent, entirely in keeping with the miserably debased condition of their worshippers, from which it would almost seem as if the practice of eating human flesh wrought some sinister change in the spiritual outlook of those who became addicted to it.

We discovered, eleven years ago, in the south-eastern corner of Yucatan, buried in the virgin bush, and never before visited by a European, a group of large stone temples, standing upon steep, lofty, stone-faced pyramids. In one of them was a wooden lintel, still *in situ*, upon which was inscribed a Maya date.

On returning to Belize from the Manatee River we were told by some chicleros, who had been bleeding the sapodilla trees which abound in the district, that they had discovered an even larger temple a few miles to the north of the first group, which we had named "Tzibanché," or "writing on wood."

In 1929 these ruins were flown over by the Carnegie Institution's expedition under Colonel Lindberg [*sic*], and again, in 1931, by the University of Pennsylvania's expedition.

In consequence of the reports brought in by the chicleros my wife and I left Belize for Corozal, the most northerly town in the colony, and the best place in which to prepare for the journey to the ruins, as here a mule train, with muleteers and labourers, can be hired for the trip into the interior.

We put up at a cocal, or coconut plantation, on the south side of the mouth of the Hondo River, where I kept my little motor launch and our very considerable impedimenta consisting of tents, bedding, tinned food, with rice, pork, and flour for the men, moving picture and ordinary photographic outfit, and scientific instruments. . . .

At last the welcome news came that the mulad[a] and all the men would be awaiting us at Sac Xan on the following day at noon.

Accordingly, at sun-up next morning we got under way in my motor-boat, the *Alfonsina,* for Payo Obispo, the capital of the Department of Quintana Roo and our port of clearance for the Mexican side of the Rio Hondo.

It is not easy to clear a small boat, either on entering or leaving a Mexican port, when one wishes to explore places in the hinterland of the Republic. The Customs officers and quarantine authorities have first to be interviewed, then the immigration, forestry, and preservation of ancient monuments departments have to be satisfied; and finally a special permit must be obtained from His Excellency the Governor of the territory himself, before one is allowed to penetrate into the interior of the country. But we were treated with the greatest courtesy and consideration by all the authorities whom we had to interview, and indeed in my experience there is no country in the world where travellers, especially "turistas"—for Mexico, like most other countries, is out for the tourist trade—are so courteously treated by Government officials on entering the country as they are in Mexico.

We were soon on our way up the Rio Hondo, passing first the opening of the Sahumal Lagoon, where the great Captain Cook was wrecked in his early days, when on a mission from Belize to Merida, in Yucatan. On the opposite side of the river we passed San Antonio, the site of a number of large ancient burial mounds, where it seems that only the prominent inhabitants of some large city, now buried in the primeval bush in the neighbourhood, had been interred, for such of these mounds as have been excavated contained beautiful examples of Maya ceramic art, many of them painted and engraved, with exquisite jade ornaments and some pearls. There is here a fruitful field for the archaeologist who can come to some arrangement with the Mexican Government satisfactory to both parties as to the sharing of the objects found.

Higher up, we passed the mouth of Chac Creek, which leads into the Bacalar Lagoon and down which, more than a century ago, came to attack the colony of British Honduras a little armada which, at the battle of St. George's Cay, met with an even warmer reception from the colonists than that accorded its predecessor in the reign of Elizabeth. At the mouth of this creek are still to be seen a number of large, heavy, muzzle-loading iron cannon, perhaps left behind by the ill-fated expedition.

About midday we arrived at Sac Xan, a miserable little Indian village, built on the side of a hill near the river bank, owing its existence to the fact that there is good maize land in the vicinity and that it is a convenient port from which to ship the precious chewing gum, brought out on mule-back from the forests of the hinterland.

Later in the day we passed out of the acaiché into high bush and, arriving at a spot about two miles from the place where the chicleros reported that they had discovered the temple, pitched our camp by the side of a small water hole, the only known supply of drinking water for many miles.

Near the camp was a little temple which stood on top of a great, steep, stone-faced pyramid. Early next morning, on climbing to the top of this, we were able to see about two miles to the north a bush-covered mound standing out like a lighthouse in the unbroken flat plane of the bush, which the guide informed us was the temple discovered by the chicleros.

We took the bearings of this and at once detailed a small gang of men to cut a path through the bush towards it with their machetes. This work was not finished till well on in the second day, and while waiting for its completion we amused ourselves by exploring various other ruined structures in the vicinity, chiefly stone temples perched on the summits of truncated pyramids, up one side of which flights of stone steps ascended to the temple entrances. All these structures were built of well-dressed stone, held together by tough mortar, and covered, inside and out, with layers of hard stucco. Perhaps the most remarkable thing about them was the narrowness of the rooms, which in some cases did not exceed two feet in breadth, and it was obvious that originally they must have been used for purely ceremonial purposes, and not as palaces for the rulers nor as dwellings for the priests.

The group forms part of the ruined site which we discovered and which we called Tzibanché, or "writing on wood," from the fact that on two of the wooden lintels of a temple were inscribed some Maya dates which have not yet been elucidated.

As soon as the men had finished cutting a path through the bush we set off along it on mule-back and, after an hour's ride, arrived at the lofty structure we had seen from the top of the little temple.

Here an amazing spectacle met our eyes. We stood at the base of a vast stone-faced pyramid, divided into three terraces, up one of the steep sides of which led a broad stone stairway. The pyramid was quadrangular in shape and was completely covered with great forest trees, through the foliage of which we could just discern the outline of a large building, perched, as it seemed to us, in the clouds.

On climbing the pyramid, we found the ruins of a magnificent Old Empire Maya temple, which probably no white man, certainly no white woman, had ever before set eyes on, and which may have lain buried in the depths of the virgin bush, hidden even from the eyes of the native Indians, ever since its builders deserted it, for some unknown reason, more than ten centuries ago.

The temple was not a single building but consisted rather of a group of buildings, placed at various levels on the great flat top of the stone substructure. It contained four storeys, or rather four sets of buildings placed at different levels, for no storey was actually built over the one beneath, but immediately behind it, an architectural necessity to Maya builders both in the New and Old Empire, since, not having yet discovered the principle of the true arch, they were compelled to make use of the cantilever arch, which necessitated such thick walls that the lower storey was unable to support the tremendous superincumbent weight of a second storey built immediately above it. In possessing four storeys the temple is a veritable aboriginal American skyscraper and appears to be unique amongst the Maya buildings discovered up to the present in the Central American forests, for the largest of these does not exceed three storeys in height.

Lubaantún

Up the centre of each of the terraces upon which the building stood ran a flight of stone steps leading to the terrace above, till at last the great building on the summit was reached, from the top of which a magnificent view of all the surrounding country was obtained, stretching as far as the eye could reach in every direction and covered to the horizon by a sea of unbroken bush. Five other bush-covered mounds were visible from this elevation, indicating the presence of at least five other temples standing on their pyramidal substructure.

The main temple faced almost due south, the north wall being entirely without opening of any sort and springing straight up from the substructure, which is here almost perpendicular. The south wall, in which was the en-

Mound at Lubaantún

From Thomas Gann, *Mystery Cities*, 1925. Copyright 1925 by Thomas Gann. By permission of Gerald Duckworth & Co. Ltd.

trance, is in a very ruinous condition, owing, no doubt, to the collapse of the wooden door lintel, following on centuries of exposure to the tropical rains and the attacks of white ants. When this lintel collapsed it brought with it the great mass of super-incumbent masonry which it supported, together with a great part of the side walls and the roof of the chamber of which it formed part of the doorway. This chamber was twenty-five feet long, but only five feet broad, its length, like all the other structures examined at Tzibanché, being out of all proportion to its breadth. It was covered throughout with a layer of smooth white stucco almost as hard as stone, and the outer walls of the main temple and of all the secondary buildings constituting the group had been covered with similar stucco. This was originally painted a bright red, but, except in certain little niches where it was protected from the torrential rains of this region, the colour had entirely disappeared.

The north, east, and west walls were in a fair state of preservation, and were surrounded by two rectangular cornices, between which the stucco had not entirely perished.

This part of the temple was ornamented by a series of niches and decorations, consisting of representations of the Maya day Ahau, which also means "lord" or "ruler," sunk in deep lines in the stucco.

These day signs, when accompanied by a numerical coefficient, usually possess a calendric significance, and when accompanied by other calendric hieroglyphics they often enable one to read the date of the temple or of the stela on which they are inscribed. In this case, however, no definite numbers written in the usual Maya bar and dot method could be made out; furthermore, the Ahaus themselves were extremely ornate, with long rays projecting from their outer edges to meet both the upper and lower cornice; consequently we came to the conclusion that they were purely decorative in function.

The temple must originally have presented a truly magnificent spectacle. The great building with its lofty roof comb rising, terrace on terrace, all covered with bright blood-red stucco, perched on a vast substructure, sheathed in shining white, gleaming in the rays of the tropical sun, must have been a sight to inspire awe of his gods, and of the priests their servants, in the heart of every Maya who gazed upon it, from the humble agriculturalist tilling his cornfields on the neighbouring plain, to the noble in his stone palace in the city at the edge of the acaiché. These temples, and other minor ones which we visited during this and our previous visit, together with the innumerable ruins, burial mounds, and remains of stone walls, with which the whole countryside abounds, indicate that there must once have flourished here a large and thriving city.

While searching round the base of the great temple pyramid, we came across a small, circular impression in the earth, in the centre of which was a round hole, some two feet in diameter. On looking down it, we were unable to see the bottom till we turned the electric torch into it, when this became clearly visible about ten feet below. As the sides of the opening shelved away from the entrance we realised we were looking into a cavity of considerable size.

The men were all rather reluctant to descend, as they were afraid of encountering snakes or other objectionable vermin, which had fallen in through the opening and been unable to get out again owing to the shelving sides of the chamber. I realised, however, that whatever had fallen in must very soon have died of starvation, for even a snake cannot live indefinitely without food, and if it had to exist on the occasional small animals which inevitably become trapped in these underground chambers and perish there of starvation, it would find it a long time between meals.

I had the men construct a crude ladder from two long sticks cut in the bush, with cross pieces bound on with liana, which is almost as good as rope and serves the Indians exclusively for that purpose.

Armed with a torch, I descended by this and found myself in an oval chamber cut in the limestone, about ten feet high, and tapering off at each end so that in shape it somewhat resembled an egg-shell cut in two lengthways. Scattered over the floor of this, and especially beneath the opening, were the skeletons of innumerable small animals, chiefly rodents; rats, mice, squirrels, and native rabbits. A few of these were quite fresh and had evidently fallen in recently, while others were represented only by little heaps of white bones, and had perished in this natural trap many years before. Upon the floor were numerous fragments of the roof, part of which had fallen in from time to time. As before mentioned, these chultuns, or underground chambers, cut in the limestone formation, whatever their original purpose may have been, were frequently used finally as sepulchral chambers. I hoped, on descending, to find that this chamber also had been used for that purpose, but it seemed to be absolutely empty with the exception of the portions of ceiling which had fallen in. I noticed, however, that on the floor, almost directly under the opening, there was a small mound of mixed earth and droppings from the roof, most of which I ascribed to débris from the surrounding forest, blown or washed in through the open hole in the roof, though there seemed to be too much material to have been accounted for in this way. I began digging in this little mound with my machete, with but a very remote hope that it might contain something of interest.

My hope, however, was far from vain, for I soon came down to the floor of the chamber and uncovered a piece of the upper end of a human thigh bone in a very advanced state of disintegration. Near this were a number of green jade and nephrite objects, lying quite close together, and covering an area of perhaps four square feet. There were fifty pieces in the cache, probably ornaments belonging to the owner of the thigh bone. Beads predominated, but amongst them were three small representations of human faces, perforated for suspension, the features of which were very crudely carved. The eyes were mere circles, made with the hollow drill, across the centre of each of which a straight line was incised, to indicate the pupils, the mouth was represented by a horizontal line, and the nose by a small triangular projection. None of these objects was made of exceptionally fine jade, and none showed any great skill on the part of the maker. With them, however, was an object which, on closer examination, proved to be of exceptional interest, well rewarding us for all our trouble even if we had found nothing else at the site. This consisted of a beautifully polished block of nephrite, of a light green colour, through which ran veins of a dark laurel green. It measured two and a half inches in length, one and three-quarter inches in breadth, and one inch in thickness, and had probably been used as a gorget or similar ornament, for it was perforated by two oblique holes at each of the upper corners, evidently for suspension.

The most interesting point about it was that upon its front surface was incised a Maya inscription, consisting of three hieroglyphs, two of which were accompanied by numerical coefficients. The inscription measured one and one sixteenth of an inch in length, by five-eighths of an inch in height. The first hieroglyph was undoubtedly the Maya day sign Ahau, above which was the number twelve, expressed in the usual way by two bars and two dots. The next hieroglyph was equally unmistakably the Maya sign for the Katun or period of twenty years, and the last sign was also a Katun symbol, above which was the number 4, expressed by four dots, surmounted by an ending sign, signifying that this date was the end of the period indicated. Now, ordinarily, there would have been no difficulty in reading the first and last hieroglyphs of this date as 12 Ahau, the end of a Katun 4, and as the only place in which this date fits in the Long Count is at Katun 4 of Bactun 10, we should have been justified in reading the date recorded as having occurred 10 Bactuns of 400 years each, 4 Katuns of 20 years each, 0 years, 0 months, and 0 days, after the opening date of the Maya Calendar, which, according to Spinden's correlation between Maya and Christian chronology, would have been in the year 650 A.D., or adopting the Thompson Teeple correlation, now more generally accepted by archaeologists, 260 years later.

TWELVE

Frans Blom 1924

Dwellers in the Jungle

[Frans Blom was born in Copenhagen, Denmark, in 1893. He first visited southern Mexico in 1919 as a member of an oil survey team, became fascinated with Middle American antiquities, and worked at Palenque, Chiapas, in the early 1920's. In 1924 he joined the staff of the Department of Middle American Research (now the Middle American Research Institute) at Tulane University in New Orleans, and a year later became its director. He led three expeditions to the Maya country: the first resulted in the book *Tribes and Temples,* from which I quote here; the second recorded in detail the Nunnery Quadrangle at Uxmal in Yucatán, part of which was reconstructed as a museum at the Century of Progress World's Fair in Chicago in the early 1930's. In 1943 Blom moved to Mexico to live. He spent the remaining twenty years of his life exploring, with his wife, the vast Lacandón Forest of lowland Chiapas, helping the Indians of that region who were suffering from disastrous crop failures, and maintaining a library and research center for scientists working in southern Mexico. He died in 1963 and was buried in a small Indian cemetery at San Cristóbal Las Casas. He was described by Pie Dufour of the *New Orleans Times-Picayune* as "a colorful, adventurous, brilliant, if erratic figure. . . ."

[*Tribes and Temples* was written in collaboration with the Pulitzer Prize-winning novelist and short story writer, Oliver La Farge, who at the time was a research associate at Tulane. The narrative I quote first tells of their discovery of some fine stucco sculptures in tombs at Comalcalco, Tabasco.]

The selections by Blom are, in the order quoted below, from Frans Blom and Oliver La Farge, *Tribe and Temples* (New Orleans: Tulane University, "Middle American Research Institute Publications" No. 1: 1926), Vol. I, pp. 115–30, 203–9, 218–19, 235–36. Copyright 1926 by The Tulane University of Louisiana. Reprinted with permission of the publisher.

All our work had been finished. We had drawn ground plans and sections of the temples, made a general map of the ruins, taken notes on art and construction. It was late in the afternoon and we were ready to leave Comalcalco the next day. Only a small ruined room remained to be placed on the general map. This room lay hidden by thick undergrowth, on the western slope of the Palace mound quite near Temple 2. It was a small room, probably an old burial place. Most of it had fallen in, and what was exposed did not appear to be of great interest. "Brick clad with stucco. Ceiling of room and some of east wall exposed. 1.75 meters long and 1 meter broad. Nothing much to note." That is how the notebook runs. The sun was standing low, and its rays fell on the east wall of the room. "What was that on the walls—some stucco ornaments?" Eagerly we scraped away a great mass of fallen leaves and dirt. The feather ornaments of a helmet appeared, then a face, all modeled in stucco low relief. More feathers, and part of another face. After all we had not finished our work at the ruins. Here before us was a burial chamber with delicately modeled figures on its walls. We must clean this out before leaving. Thrilled with what lay in store for us we rode back to the town through the short tropical dusk.

Early the next morning we were ready to clean out the burial chamber. Only five Indians were employed, as there was not much room in the narrow chamber. Our excitement seemed to communicate itself to our Indian workmen. With the greatest care they removed dirt and stones, and by noon we had exposed the upper part of nine figures, three on the south, three on the east, and three on the north wall. The entrance to the chamber had been from the west, and on this side we found the blocked door. These nine figures delicately modeled in low relief are some of the finest pieces of art as yet found in the Maya area.

By noon the next day the small chamber had been cleared. We had reached its highly polished red cement floor.

On this floor stood four low pillars built of brick, and from the dirt around these we extracted a large amount of clam shells, all squared and filed, and with two holes in each for suspension. They had once formed part of a necklace worn by the noble or high-priest who had been laid to rest in the chamber. All these shells had been painted with a red earth. Some fragments of human bones were also found, and these too were covered with the same red substance. Whether this is a case of secondary burial with painted bones, or whether the red colour came from the great amount of shell ornaments found all over the floor of the grave, we were not able to judge.

It looked as if a wooden slab had been placed on the pillars on the floor of the chamber and on the table the body had been laid. Due to moisture percolating through walls and ceiling of the chamber, all had decayed except the shell ornaments and a few bits of bone.

Standing at the western end of the chamber, we look at its back wall—the east wall. Here we see three figures. The central one is undoubtedly intended for the most prominent person of the nine pictured on the walls.

The head of this figure (No. 5) is shown in right profile, the shoulders and body in front view. He is turning to a person on the right (No. 4). On his hand is a simple helmet, in his ears are earplugs, around his neck a string with a large pendant, and around his waist a loin cloth. The body is nude, and the face and shoulders are badly weathered.

Figure No. 4 is shown in left profile, turning towards No. 5, and with his right arm lifted in gesticulation, as if to emphasize what he is saying. He wears a helmet and earplugs. On his arms are cuffs, and on his breast hangs a pendant in form of a bar. His loin cloth is very elaborate. He turns his shoulders in front view, but there is a twist in the drawing indicating that he is on the verge of turning towards No. 5.

Back of No. 5 stands a man, No. 6, shown in right profile, head as well as body. He stands stiffly erect with his arms crossed over his chest, a servant standing at attention by his master.

Frans Blom at Uxmal
Courtesy of Middle American Research Institute, Tulane University.

Three groups of hieroglyphs may explain this scene. Some parts of the glyphs have disappeared, and the ones preserved belong to those which we as yet cannot read. None of the glyphs in this tomb are calendrical, so we have to estimate its age by artistic criteria.

On the south wall, we see three more figures, Nos. 1, 2, and 3. *No. 1* standing stiffly erect with his arms crossed over his chest is shown in left profile. Before his face is a column of glyphs. The central figure, *No. 2*, in right profile with body in front view, is bending slightly towards No. 1. Part of his head-dress and his left arm have disappeared. In his right hand he holds a bag, and around his neck is a string of beads.

No. 3 is the best preserved of them all. A standing man is shown in right profile with downcast eyes. The whole figure shows repose, one might say sadness. His head-dress is smaller than the others. On his chest hangs a large pendant, probably meant to represent a face carved in jade.

Of the three groups of glyphs on this wall, the greater part has fallen away, only showing impressions in the stucco where they once were placed.

On the northern wall there are three more figures, all with nude bodies,

Tomb sculptures, Comalcalco, Chiapas
Courtesy of Middle American Research Institute, Tulane University.

dressed only in loin cloths and hats. Figures No. 7 and 8 are shown in left profile, Figure No. 9 in right. We were fortunate in being able to make a paper squeeze of the head of Figure No. 7. This head is exquisitely modeled, and ranks among the finest pieces of Maya art.

Of Figure No. 8 only the shoulders and the lower part of the face is preserved. Bricks from the ceiling had fallen and crushed it long ago. Enough, though, remains to show us that this figure wore a bead necklace and a large earplug. The face turns the left profile towards the spectator, and the shoulders are seen in full view.

And last we come to Figure No. 9, a fat-bellied elderly gentleman shown in right profile with stumpy nose and heavy chin, and apparently a hunchback.

This completes the array of figures. Every one is different from the other, every face showing character. No doubt they are all portraits. They may be a picture of the dead ruler and his foremost court attendants and servants. It is distressing to have to refer to them by numbers. One is tempted to give them names and to try to imagine their lives. Bishop Landa tells us that the

rulers of Yucatan, at the time of the Conquest, kept troupes of actors and jesters. Was our hunchback the court jester, grown sorrowful, now that his chief had died? The feet have been done in a conventional way, the loin cloths with more care, and the faces with a rare mastery of relief. No doubt the Maya artist knew the full value of shadows thrown by the relief, and utilized this to give expression.

In this small chamber we stand before the best stucco work yet found in the Maya area. Even the fine stucco figures in Palenque do not reveal such mastery and freedom of line.

Both the figures and the walls of the tomb were painted in the same deep red color as the floor.

When the tomb had been cleared we spent a day in cleaning the figures carefully with soft brushes and filling all cracks with cement so that these magnificent figures would be protected against destruction by the elements. The Municipal President of Comalcalco, Don David Bosada, was fully aware of the artistic and historical value of our discovery, and he at once ordered a roof to be built over the chamber to protect it against the tropical rains.

Again it was late afternoon. The rays of the setting sun fell on the central figure of the back wall, perhaps the picture of the dead chief. Let us give imagination a free rein for a moment, and see the tomb ready to receive the lifeless ruler. His career had ended, and as the sun, worshipped by him and his people, was setting and its rays fell on his picture on the back wall of the tomb, they laid him to rest on the wooden table on the floor of the chamber. Around him stood his friends and servants mourning, as we now see them pictured on the walls.

And as the last rays of the sun fell on the picture of the chief who had died about 1,400 years ago, and whose portrait we had again brought to light, we left the ruins to continue our journey through the country where his race flourished long ago.

For some hours we followed the valley towards the east, then swung due south and started to climb towards a mountain pass. Luckily this climb was not nearly so steep as the Cojolite pass. Here and there we had to stop to cut our way around a fallen forest giant, but the going was comparatively easy.

Reaching the top of the pass we frightened a drove of wild pigs, or pecary, the kind which have a musk gland on their backs, from which they emit a white, foul-smelling liquid when frightened. They rushed away grunting and squeaking, and my attempt to get one with our .22 rifle was unsuccessful.

As we descended the southern side of the range the faint trail before us turned more to the southwest, and this was the main bearing of our travel for the next two days.

Chicle trees became frequent, and with them signs of the activities of the chicle bleeders.

Chicle is the name of the raw material for chewing gum, and is tapped from a tree called Chico-Zapote, found only in the Central American forests. It is a tall tree having very hard wood, so hard in fact that when dry a nail cannot be driven into it. The ancient Maya used the wood of this tree for beams and lintels in their temples. Its gum was also used by them in offerings to their gods.

This sap is tapped from the tree by the so-called Chicleros, or chicle bleeders. They climb the tree with the help of such spurs as are used by linemen climbing telegraph poles. With machetes they cut zig-zag grooves in the bark of the tree, and snow-white gum oozes out in these scars down into a small bag tied to the foot of the tree. That sounds easy and simple, but when one has watched these men and the life they lead the story is quite different.

The tree produces gum only during the rainy season, which means that the chiclero has to spend the worst time of the year in the heart of the forests, sheltered by small palm roofs, living far from supplies, and having to buy these at exorbitant prices. Day and night it rains, and the chiclero is not far from being an aquatic animal. Generally he is a beast. All kinds of riff-raff run together in a chicle camp, mostly men who are "wanted" somewhere by the law. Fights in the camps are frequent, drunkenness is usual, and stealing and smuggling are daily occurrences.

When he has gathered his bags with the white gum, the chiclero boils it down in small pans, and finally melts it together in a block of a dirty brown colour, weighing 100 pounds. Anything goes into the boiling pot to make the block a little heavier, and it is fortunate that the raw gum is thoroughly cleaned and sterilized before it is placed on the market.

Two blocks make one mule-load. From the collector's camp these blocks are hauled out to the rivers, often requiring days and weeks over trails where the poor mules sink to their bellies in mud. Sometimes enterprising bandits hold up trains of 20 to 30 mules and mules and gum disappear, leaving only a few dead chicleros as mute records of what has happened. Fantastic are the tales that can be heard in the evening around the chicleros' camp fire, and most of them are true.

Chewing gum and Maya archaeology are closely related, strange as it may sound. When the chiclero wanders around the forest on the look-out for zapote trees, he often runs across ruined buildings, stone monuments with inscriptions, or large pyramids. When the season is over he goes out to the small towns along the edge of the forest, and there he runs into the archae-ologists who start into the forest as soon as the weather is dry enough to allow them to work with their cameras and other equipment. Often the chiclero guides the archaeologist over the trails he has broken in his efforts to satisfy the gum-hungry world. The waterhole which served the chiclero now serves the archaeologist, and the millions of ticks which were brought to the waterhole by the chiclero's mule team hungrily attack the white skin of the explorer.

We rode towards the sun all day, making a great semi-circle around the end of the Cojolite range. La Farge and I each shot a faisan, the large bird called curassaw* in English, and "ish" in Tzeltal.

Our Indians were a cheerful crowd. All day long they would walk ahead of us cutting the trail; now and then stopping to cut the heart out of a small palm and eating it as a great delicacy, especially when fresh. At other places they would break open the huge nests of the white ants and with their machetes dig for bags of honey deposited by some small bees who favor these ant nests for their hives.

About four o'clock in the afternoon, we stopped to make our camp on the banks of the small Mistolja stream. The horses were unloaded, and while some of the boys made a clearing where we rigged up our fly-sheet, others cleaned the two birds we had shot and planted the meat on sticks by the fire. Others went into the forests to cut leaves of the breadnut tree (Ramon) and a certain kind of small palm to feed our animals. In the big forest there is no grass; the animals have to be fed on leaves. This is sufficient for mules, as the sturdy animals can stand such a diet for many days, but horses very soon lose weight.

At nightfall we sat around the campfire, eating our birds, and listening to the Indians chatting. It was our first camp in the real, big jungle. Soon we climbed into our hammocks, and for a time lay listening to the thousand sounds of the tropical night, the monotonous singing of insects, small noises of nocturnal animals, and the murmur of the stream close by our camp.

Evening in the jungle is beautiful; dawn is magnificent. We sat wrapped in our blankets drinking coffee when light began to appear high up in the tops of the trees, at first very sparsely and a pale gray. Little by little the light sifted down, and as it reached the bottom of the forest the sun threw a glimmer of gold on the tree-tops. The night insects became quiet, and the birds began to fly around and sing. He who has watched the daily awakening of life in the jungle will never forget it.

The day was a strenuous one, for literally every step we advanced we had to cut down undergrowth. It looked as if every tree which had fallen for the last few years had chosen to fall across the faint trail we were following. Sometimes we could hardly distinguish the trail, and once we followed a path leading towards the north hoping that it soon would turn in the direction we should go. It did not, so we did.

In one place we came across large mud holes, whirled up by the hoofs of innumerable wild pigs, one of their great bathing places. No birds were seen all day, so when we discovered some large black-faced monkeys (*batz*) high up in a tree, our Indians asked us to shoot one for supper. I fired shot after shot at one with the rifle and hit him, but the brute hung on with all

---

* Editor's note: The curassow (family Cracidae).

four hands and his tail. Finally he came down with a thud, and La Farge scornfully suggested that it was the weight of the lead I had pumped into him which had brought him down. One of the Indians loaded Mr. Batz on his back, and we trotted along until we reached the Bascan river.

The Mistolja and the Bascan run into the Tulija river, above Salto de Agua. The crossing of the river was negotiated with some fear. The flow was swift, and there were deep places, but we were fortunate in getting everything across without it being wet. The Indians undressed and bundled their clothes on their heads.

A short stop was made for the Indians to drink their posole, a habit we were also acquiring. This drink is the midday meal. One meal in the early morning, another when in camp in the afternoon, and posole for lunch. If we stop at noon to have a regular meal, the result will invariably be that the Indians will "call it a day," and it is next to impossible to get them started again.

We followed the left bank of the Bascan, now headed towards the west, hoping to reach the direct trail from Palenque to Finca Encanto. The forest was nearly impenetrable and it took us a couple of hours to cover a little more than a mile. As soon as we saw that we would not be able to reach the main trail before dark, we made camp on a small stream running out into the Bascan, and hardly had we got our tent-fly up before a strong rain started. There was no time to build a palm-leaf shelter for the Indians, so we all huddled together under the tent.

When a lull came, two of the Indians rushed away to skin the monkey. It is, by the way, an ugly sight to see a flayed monkey. Lazaro looked after his dear "niños" as he was calling the horses, and we helped the other Indians with the firewood and cutting leaves for shelter. When a second burst of rain came everything was in order, and steaks of monkey meat were roasting on sticks under a roof of leaves built over the fireplace.

The Bascan Valley appeared to be quite broad in some places and somebody will undoubtedly find ruins in it one day, but we did not have such luck. The river is full of small falls built up of travertine, with long stretches of water navigable for canoes. With some portage it could well have been used for transportation in olden times.

It was a great relief to reach the main trail about eleven o'clock. The manager of Finca Encanto, Mr. Linke Timler, expecting our coming, had sent Indians out to do some clearing along the trail. None the less we found that the hardest was yet to come. The climb up to the Mirador pass was steep, the soil slippery from the rain, and the new cutting difficult to negotiate in many places. Up and up we climbed. Our animals, accustomed to the level trails of Tabasco, had much trouble with the rocky climb. Again and again they slipped and tumbled. Then we had to unload them, which was difficult, as they always found the worst places to fall. When freed of the pack, we had to set them up on all fours, and again put the load on. Innumerable times we had to stop to swing our heavy pack boxes on the beasts, generally standing in anything but a level place. We sweated and swore, packed one animal and advanced about a hundred meters, only to find that another animal had fallen. It certainly tested both our patience and strength.

Not until after three o'clock did we reach the top, and then we had to change the cargo from two of the pack animals to two of the saddle horses which were not so tired, as we had climbed on foot most of the time.

From the highest point we slid and rolled down for about an hour until we reached a small arroyo, Zachalucum, where we made camp for the night. We were not the only travellers at this place. The "hotel" was already occupied by four Indians sitting under a palm-leaf shelter cooking their food as we arrived. They hardly stirred at our approach, though we must have been a formidable sight with our animals and guides.

Soon the camp was in order, and our boys planted the legs and arms of the monkey we shot the day before on sticks around the fire for roasting.

We were up at dawn, and saw our neighbors preparing for departure. A bite of cold meat and a gourd full of posole was their breakfast. Then they gathered their belongings into nets, loaded them on their backs, and trotted off for a day's march.

After a short ride from our camp we reached a descent, famous because of its steepness and because of the grim story of how the rebel general, Pineda, lay in ambush below when the federal troops tried to catch him. The soldiers coming from above could only advance in Indian file, and as they were shot one by one, rolled down the mountainside giving place for the next one. Quite a practical place for an ambush. Now a few bones lie as silent records of the battle.

Frans Blom watching flight of Indian arrow
Courtesy of Middle American Research Institute, Tulane University.

Down we went and again a horse tumbled. Then up a hill and another horse slipped. At last we were down in the Tulija valley, and halted on the river bank where the boys drank their posole.

We crossed without difficulty. A short distance further on we reached a road, a real road laid with corduroy, and alongside which grew thick juicy grass. Our poor animals immediately went after it and we had difficulty in keeping them going, but as we were now near our destination, the Encanto ranch, where the horses could rest and get plenty of fodder, we drove them on.

Crossing another stream we rode along a broad, well made road lined with rubber trees and royal palms. As we neared the finca, the dogs began to bark, and when we rode up in front of the main house, we were most cordially greeted by an old friend, the manager Mr. Linke Timler.

We then embarked in our big dugout canoe and proceeded upstream on our return trip to Finca Encanto. Progress against the current was slow and the sun was blazing hot. The Indians were pushing us forward with long poles; starting at the bow of the canoe placing one end of the pole at the bottom of the river, the other to their shoulder, they plod towards the stern; reaching it they swing the poles over their head and walk forward balancing them to allow those that are still poling towards the stern to pass by. They made a kind of endless human chain and the monotonous clatter of their bare feet on the bottom of the canoe made us drowsy.

It was late in the afternoon when we reached the mouth of the Encanto river, and we decided to proceed to Agua Clara and return from there to Encanto on foot instead of sleeping on a bank of the river. Where the two rivers meet is a group of mounds in advanced state of ruin, which we named the Agua Clara mounds.

Agua Clara is a ranch now partly abandoned. A Mexican caretaker and a few Indians live there. From it a good trail runs along the side of the valley to Encanto. The sun was getting low as we started, but by fast walking we succeeded in reaching the Finca Encanto just after dark.

Sunday is always a day of celebration on the fincas. Both the Mexicans and the natives spend the day getting drunk. We were sitting on the porch of the main house enjoying the beautiful surroundings and fixing up our notebooks when Don Arturo Tovilla, in charge of the coffee plantation Cacate-el belonging to Encanto, came running towards the house and told us that one of the carpenters of the finca had drowned. The two carpenters belonging to the place had spent the morning in getting themselves thoroughly drunk whereafter they went for a trip on the river in a dugout canoe. When they tired of this, one decided to take a bath and carefully placed his hat on the river bank and went in with clothes and shoes on. The swift current and the rum got him. When we arrived his corpse was being dragged ashore. He was blue in the face with froth out of mouth and nose. We worked with him giving him artificial respiration for two hours without result.

Then he was laid on a board and carried up to the carpenter's shop to be laid out in state, as is customary here, and candles appropriately set in empty bottles were placed around him. While all this was going on his partner was sitting on a rock by the river, moaning and crying hysterically.

Our chief guide, old Lázaro, had also taken a part in the morning celebration, but, being of a more balanced temperament, he selected the middle of the main road to the finca as the best place he could find to sleep. After a while he got up and went to his room, and when he returned to life towards evening and heard about the afternoon's accident, he at once reported for duty in the crowd of mourners who stayed up all night with the body, singing songs and lamenting the death of one carpenter while the other carpenter beat time on the nails of the new coffin he was making. The drowning of the carpenter stopped us from going into the forest the next day as a statement had to be written and we were expected to report to some kind of local official who was coming from a distant village. We, therefore, spent the day in collecting data on the life of the Indians, making studies of their houses, and collecting words of their language.

La Farge was attending to the linguistic work, and the writer was going to join him when three of the Indians who had worked for us on the river trip to Chuctiepá came towards the store carrying the fourth. The latter had been bitten by a poisonous snake, and though Sebastian Gomez, the foreman, was considered to be the leading medicine man of the settlement he had done nothing but lay a ligature of vines above the bite, which was in the boy's leg. The poor Indian was blue in the face and spitting lumps of blood. His right leg was dark blue and swollen to double its natural thickness. Sebastian would not cure him as he had nothing with which to pay for the services and could not buy the rum, without which no medicine man dares to deal with holy things. Therefore, they had brought him up to the finca and he did not come under our treatment until three hours after he had been bitten.

We at once got out our medicine kit and cut the bite just over the two small red holes made by the fangs of the snake. Then permanganate crystals were smeared into the cut and more cuts were made lengthwise down his leg that he might bleed freely.

After a while his sister arrived and had him carried off to her hut where she would try to persuade a local medicine man to pray over him. We later heard that the Indian snake doctors had refused to help him because we had touched him. Fortunately for us he pulled through and a week later when we left Finca Encanto, he was walking briskly around.

We spent several days at Encanto as there was much work to do. La Farge was busy with his studies of the Indian customs and the writer occupied himself with making sketches of the pottery found at Yoxihá. It was work and rest at the same time.

La Farge had collected much data on the Indians, but one thing that he had not seen was an Indian burial ceremony. We could not very well kill an Indian for that purpose, but as it happened the Indians themselves furnished us with the missing data.

While I was making water colour sketches of the Yoxihá pottery, an Indian came running with the news that there was a dead man lying in front of one of the Indian houses. Following him, I saw an Indian lying on the ground, face down. For all I could see, he might be drunk and taking a rest. Turning him over I saw that he had a large hole in the abdomen. He had been shot from a short distance with a shotgun, and was quite dead. Two or three Indian women sat around wailing and screaming. One of them was quite a pretty girl.

The murderer had escaped, and in bits and fragments I got the following story. Sebastian Moreno, Indian, had a pretty sister with whom he led a married life. None the less, Pasqual Guzman, already married, wanted this girl and was courting her much to the disgust of Sebastian.

For a long time trouble had been brewing. They had both got drunk. Sebastian had drawn his machete, and given Pasqual some bad slashes in the shoulder, whereupon the latter jumped into his hut, grabbed a shotgun, and fired at Sebastian a few feet away. Bleeding badly from his cuts, Pasqual ran for the forest.

A small detachment of the Mexican employees of the finca at once set out in pursuit of the murderer, but soon returned without having found anything but bloodstains on the bushes.

Meanwhile those who stayed behind had locked up Pasqual's wife. Everybody insisted that he would return to get his wife, and that she would follow him to some secure place far back in the forest, where they would build their house and make their fields, living outside the reach of the authorities. I thought this rather doubtful, but towards the afternoon some of the Mexicans came walking in with the murderer securely tied. They had found him stealing towards his house and caught him as he tried to enter.

It was a strange sight. One-half of his body was white, his cotton trousers and shirt; the other half was red from blood streaming out of a deep gash in his shoulder.

Murderer or not, I at once attended him, washing his cuts, and treating them with antiseptics. He had one cut under his chin, and was minus the tip of one finger from gripping the blade of the machete which Sebastian was wielding. Worse was the cut in the shoulder, clear to the bone.

All the time I was treating the wounds, he did not show the slightest sign of pain. He just looked at me. He was afraid he would be hanged, and it was pitiful to watch him being led away, securely bound, to be held till the authorities from San Pedro Savana could come for him.

That night the family of the dead Sebastian held a wake, and the next day at noon he was buried. La Farge attended both of these ceremonies.

THIRTEEN

Ann A. Morris 1926

The Treasure of the Plumed Serpent

[Visitors viewing the magnificent Temple of the Warriors at the Mayan ruins of Chichén Itzá, Yucatán, find it hard to believe that this great structure with its "Court of the Thousand Columns" was, until the middle 1920's, almost completely buried in a huge mound of earth, covered with forest, with only a few building stones outcropping here and there to suggest that a structure lay underneath. The enormous task of excavating and restoring this temple fell to Earl H. Morris of the Carnegie Institution of Washington. The official report of this project appears in a massive two-volume technical account, but the informal story is told by Morris' wife Ann in her popular book *Digging in Yucatan*. Just when everyone thought the work was nearly done, Morris made a startling discovery.]

The season of 1926 was drawing to a close. It was the second year of work on the Warriors' Temple, and we all calculated that by the time the rains began the thing would be done—and an impressive, clean-cut architectural unit would stand resurrected from the past.

On a Saturday afternoon, after the men had been paid off, a few of us were visiting the temple and admiring our handiwork. The tension of hurry was slackening, and our week-end was our own to enjoy as we pleased, but like the bus man who takes his holiday by going bus riding, we were drawn back to the spot as by a magnet. We wandered around to the north side, idly

The selection quoted below is from Ann Axtell Morris, *Digging in Yucatan* (New York: Junior Literary Guild, 1931), pp. xv–xvii, 236–41. Copyright 1931 by the Junior Literary Guild. Reprinted with permission of Elizabeth Ann Morris Gell and Sarah L. Morris.

looking the place over, and I remember Earl remarked to Dr. Morley: "Well, now the Warriors' is so nearly done, what will we tackle next?"

Truly the Maya gods must have laughed aloud to hear him. The Plumed Serpent himself hovering over his ancient home must have relaxed his rigid snarl to smile a moment in derision before he loosened a tiny pebble from the slope and rattled it down at Earl's feet. We looked up to see whence it came and noticed a great stump protruding from the pyramid; some careful native had that morning been undermining its base preparatory to uprooting it. It was a gnarled old stump clutching with frantic roots at its precarious hold, and was very picturesque. Someone unslung a camera, saying, "That ought to make a good picture. Help me get a set up, somebody," and clambered up

Ann Axtell Morris at Chichén Itzá

From *Digging in Yucatan*, 1931. Copyright 1931 by Ann Axtell Morris. Courtesy of Elizabeth Ann Morris Gell and Sarah L. Morris.

the steep slope. Earl followed, using the stump itself to hoist himself the last yard or two. As he sought a foothold in the cavity beneath it, he noticed a bit of carved stone clasped between the roots. It stood vertically, as if in position, but even then he thought it might be only a detached bit of carving dragged in by the mason's helpers as they might any ordinary bowlder. The pyramid was salted with such examples of sculpture, some worthless, but a few had proved to be intrinsically beautiful and valuable in themselves. With his pocket knife he gouged out a bit more dirt, laying bare a strip of stone a few inches high, and then, burrowing deeper, he perceived that the carved block he had first seen rested upon another and that the two were firmly cemented together. He says now that when the portent of these two stones began to dawn on him, the hair at the back of his neck rose in a cold chill of apprehension and excitement, and that many times since he wished he had covered his find quietly and hastened to bury it forevermore behind the sheathing of the pyramid.

The first we knew of anything untoward was his hoarse command, "Bring me a pick." And then, with the activity of a squirrel excavating for some choice long-buried nut, he flew into the dirt beneath that stump, clinging with one hand as well as he could, while with shortened grip on the pick handle he tore away dirt and rubble. The top of a square column emerged, then stone below stone, until at a depth of seven feet a red polished floor appeared.

Temple of the Warriors, Chichén Itzá, after excavation and restoration by Earl H. Morris, Carnegie Institution of Washington.

It was plain now that in our two long years we had been working only on the frosting to our cake, while all the time there was buried in the pyramid's heart an older building. I imagine that the Plumed Serpent must have given a triumphant lash of his tail before he settled down to another two years of contented apathy, waiting for a conscientious archeologist to follow out the new clue which was to result in even further glorification to his temple.

For a while we had no way of knowing whether much of the older build-ing was buried in the pyramid or whether only the single tell-tale column emerging near the corner remained to trick us into our high hopes. Obvious-ly the thing to do was to trace the line of the floor along the pyramid faces until its boundaries were reached. It was dangerous work, for the platform upon which the Warriors' Temple was built was high above the new col-umn's face, and on the north side this platform was so narrow that much undercutting would carry one beneath the none-too-secure massive temple walls.

Earl clung to a rope which he fixed to a series of stumps and worked along the line of the floor toward the east, laying bare its broken edge. Finally the floor line stopped sharply and a few inches farther a series of plaster-covered blocks sloped sharply downward. This boded well for it appeared that one limit of the buried structure had been reached, and that it had been com-prised of some kind of a colonnaded hall built upon a pyramided base even as was the great Temple of the Warriors.

Thence, returning to the original corner, he burrowed into the west face of the pyramid where presumably the crest of a second column stood. It was there. Then a third was found, and finally the stub of an upright wall. Thus the size of our building was established. It apparently measured about fifty feet square, and with rueful heart Earl realized that the major portion of it lay directly under the Temple of the Warriors.

For a time he seriously debated whether or not it would be worth while to go to the terrific effort and expense necessary to clean this second temple without harming the beautiful building above. The new structure seemed to be nothing but a rather exact replica of the later one, although built on a much smaller scale, and it was questionable whether one would be justified in working it in spite of the interest of its position.

Then an unexpected discovery set all his doubts at rest, for one morning Manuel raised an excited shout from the little platform he had dug for him-self before one of the column faces. Earl hurried up the slope to find the man staring fascinated at a block of stone emerging from the rubble at his feet. It was one of the most magnificently colored things either of them had ever laid eyes on—all hues of the rainbow intensified a hundredfold.

"Oh, Engineer, what is it?" breathed Manuel.

As Earl recovered from a paralysis of astonishment at finding such an ob-ject where only dirt and stone were to be expected, he snatched Manuel's shovel and in a few moments laid bare a serpent's head—a yard square, much like those found the previous year, but infinitely more richly colored. Close by it was another, and then came a series of blocks made from the fallen jamb of door, glorious in color as the day they were new.

"By the Great Plumed Serpent himself!" ejaculated Earl. "This place is a treasure house. Manuel, go brush clear a little space on the wall where we found that projecting stub, and tell me what you find."

Manuel worked carefully a few moments with the trowel, then shouted, "Color, Engineer—like those others—only more color."

That settled it. The Buried Temple would have to be excavated. From the rain-washed stones above, we thought we had found adequate pictures of an original Maya temple, but this place, which had been purposely covered while still fresh, revealed their true state to have been magnificent beyond anyone's previous conjectures.

There were a hundred incidents that filled those days in Yucatan, but probably none which moved me more than our very last night in Yucatan—a night of full moon, brilliant white as only a tropic moon can be, when Earl, my husband, and I stood and looked at the great Temple of the Warriors, complete and finished after our years of work, planted monstrous and squat on its pyramid like a crouching animal, quiet with the ominous stillness of a reptile, and beautiful, but hideously so.

Four years before it had existed as nothing but a forest-covered and ragged hill without shape or meaning, but a mound that had about it some innate provocation which seized upon Earl's thought, turning him aside from other plans, almost, it seemed, bending him to its will. Nor would it release him, until after stupendous labor it had step by step returned to being—time itself turned backward—a ghostly materialization from the Land of Things Destroyed.

I had thought sometimes I would have given a great deal to be able to view life in that old temple as it was being lived before the Spaniards came. But that night I shivered in the realization of what it would mean really to see it come to life—for gorgeously decked priests to pass in solemn procession, for golden bells to tinkle and drums to throb, for the wailing of old chants to be renewed by huddled crowds below temple steps. If I would reawaken all this, at the same time terrible gods would rise up from their sleep of death—gods with the heads of poisonous snakes and the claws of fierce birds, gods who hated men and drank their blood, gods who fed on the warm beating hearts of thousands of young men, gods who smothered the New World with fear, and finally failed only because of the astounding courage with which they were fought by Spanish and Christian gentlemen.

Such gods are well lost, no forest can ever bury them deeply enough. But there is another and better way to read the great story of ancient times, and it is taught to us by archeology.

FOURTEEN

Phillips Russell 1929

Chichén Itzá, Izamal, and the Jungle Doctor

[For my taste, this century's best travel writers on the Maya country are Louis J. Halle, Jr. (whom I quote elsewhere) and Phillips Russell, a professor of journalism at the University of North Carolina. I had the pleasure of knowing both of them briefly—Halle when we were students of archaeology at Harvard, Russell when I taught at North Carolina. Both were charming people, and it does not surprise me at all that their writings delight me. Their narratives are forthright; they are emotional but not maudlin; their stories are believable and, where they overlap with my personal experience—and this is often—completely reliable. Russell's history of Chichén Itzá and Izamal, written over thirty-five years ago, has, it is true, become somewhat outdated.

[Rather than give an archaeologist's description of Chichén Itzá, let us see it—and then Izamal—through a journalist's eyes.]

Tropical exploring was once—indeed, until a very few years ago—accompanied by heartbreak, backache, and ticks. In the Yucatan jungles, white-dotted with shining but irretrievably lost cities, the traveller suffered most, aside from heat and fevers, from the virulent tick known as the garrapata. But now the explorer in Yucatan goes tickless.

He rises in the soft but strangely chilly pre-dawn of Merida; has his *café con leche y pan dulce,* coffee with milk and sugared bread; and rides softly in a high-pooped Meridan cab to the railway station where he boards a miniature train filled with women, all in clean and flowing white, having the grave faces of the gentler Roman senators, and with little brown men having at one extremity an enormous, decorated straw sombrero and at the other sandals tied with twine to small, shapely feet. Their deportment is perfect. They mind their own business with unusual ability.

The little train spins cheerfully through dry miles of grey and green Yucatan jungle-bush. Passengers sleep; the women draw their *rebozos*, shawls, no two colored alike, farther over their eyes; the men drop their heads back and snore candidly through plump open lips occasionally edged with a bit of black mustache. There is no staring; no rudeness; the Yucatecans, extraordinary people that they are, do not quiz, catechize, or otherwise harass each other without cause. The conductor is always affable. He does not forget to call you when your station arrives, and waves an *adiós* with a flash of fine teeth.

For five hours you ride through henequen fields, heat shimmers, and cactus, and then you dismount at Dzitas, once a village with palm-thatched huts sleeping under hibiscus blooms and cocoanut leaves. It still has these, but has become more metropolitan now, being the receiving and shipping point for the Carnegie Institution, which has undertaken to excavate and restore the chief buildings at Chichen-Itza, twenty miles distant. Here, a thousand years ago, was the Mecca of all devout Mayans and at one time their queen city.

At Dzitas you no longer hire from the nearest hacienda horses or mules to carry you over the liana-crossed trail to Chichen-Itza; you hire a *fotingo*, as Mr. Henry Ford's hardworking Model T is affectionately called by all Latin-America. The metal of this veteran car is wrapped with wire. Wire or string drops from its top to all parts in need of support. It resembles Brooklyn Bridge seen from a distance. Its tires are in ribbons. It is driven by a neat little Indian, in short white trousers over which hangs the long, close-fitting Yucatan undershirt. You bargain about the fare. He accepts a third less than

El Castillo, Chichén Itzá

he originally asked. While he fills his steaming radiator, you hunt for a thirst-quencher, for you know the ride will be hot and dusty. On the station platform stands your man. For a few centavos he will serve you pineapple or papaya crushed in ice or the iced juice of a green cocoanut, all unspeakably delicious.

At last you are off. Off is the word, for you seldom touch the ground except when an unusually large boulder projects from the road. Your Indian driver simply opens the throttle and steers reasonably clear of chickens, pigs, turkeys and loose donkeys. But at the outskirts of the village he halts. It is a cantina. Will you have beer or something? No, then, with your permission, he will. He returns, wiping his wisp of a mustache, but not alone. This is a friend who lives on the road to Chichen. He would like to ride with us; otherwise he would have to walk, carrying his bundles of chickens, turkeys and dry goods.

Very well; he is welcome; let him pay in proportion to the length of his ride.

But unfortunately, señor, he has no money.

You suspect something is behind all this and shake your head with a carefully cultivated, hard-boiled finality.

The friend is pushed away. The chauffeur turns to his crank, but his countenance is sunken. The friend stands back mournfully.

Oh well, if he is a good friend of yours, tell him to come along.

Two faces lighten instantaneously. In hops the friend, sticking chickens and turkeys in odd corners. The *fotingo* starts with a rush over the straight, relatively improved road and does not slacken for an hour. We are halted by a flat tire. While the two *Indios* sweat over it, you step out into the road. The heat quivers from flattened boulders of limestone. The bush is a solidly woven texture mostly grey in color, for the rains are still two months off. Two parakeets rise chattering in the air. The long-tailed Mexican jay screams from a tree. Iguanas crash into the bush. The air is speckled with drifting butterflies in blue, green, and black. Beside the road is a round spot two feet across. It is composed of dead butterflies. They lie not heaped upon each other, but side by side. Each is intact, but all are dead. What could have killed them? The earth is slightly moist. Did they drink up some poisonous dew? You cannot guess; it is one of those mysteries of which all jungles are full.

You start again with an even more furious speed. Rocks and ruts—your Indian takes them all with a little extra gasoline. Butterflies are dashed into your face and fall into your lap, quivering as they die. Their under-wings are marked with a crimson streak startlingly like blood.

At last comes a sudden bend in the road and a steep pyramid looms between the trees. It is crowned with a low, square, flat-topped building which appears glistening white in the Yucatan sun. You recognize it at once. It is the *Castillo* of Chichen-Itza, the loftiest structure in the Mayan Mecca, so placed that approaching pilgrims could see it from miles away.

We are alone among the gods of ancient days. Though it is not yet noon, the workers on the restoration project have gone dripping to their shower baths. The sun is too withering to permit white men to toil under it between the hours of 11 a.m. and 4 p.m. But at the moment a breeze has arisen that cools the air enough to make possible a tour of the ruins whose contents are as yet imperfectly known.

On our left are row after row of shining white pillars, marking the site of the Court of a Thousand Columns. Behind them rises the terraced majesty of the Temple of the Warriors, the most splendid structure yet uncovered in the city that was once lost but has been found again. The entrance is guarded by two gigantic Feathered Serpents in stone, their gaping jaws resting upon the floor, their curled tails once reaching the roof. The unending sculptures which cover walls and pillars, the vast amount of masonry, must have required the labor of hundreds of artists and thousands of slaves.

On our right is the Temple of the Jaguars, around which runs a frieze of sculptured jaguars, once richly painted and so instinct with the graceful, stealthy movement of life that one's eyes return to them again and again, even though irresistibly diverted by the weird sights of an exotic land—muscular iguanas flattened against heat-quivering walls, their heads thrust into a crack for shade; a solemn procession of leaf-cutting ants crossing the path, their burdens carried by the edge like so many sails; the hoots and whistles of tropical birds; the long-necked zopilote, the Latin-American buzzard, cutting the air in graceful spirals.

Temple of the Jaguars, Chichén Itzá

Attached to this delicately sculptured temple are high walls enclosing a long and imposing rectangular stadium. Here was played the sacred game of *tlaxtli*, which on festal days attracted thousands of eager fanatics. It is improbable, however, that they yelled, or indulged in the other antics of American football fans; rather did they preserve a sacred silence resembling that of English spectators at a cricket match.

The ball is plainly sculptured on the temple walls. It was made of crude rubber and was apparently dimpled somewhat like a huge golf ball. On opposite sides of the long walls hung, twenty feet from the ground, great stone rings four feet in diameter. One of them has fallen, but the other is still in place. Both are engraved on their flattened sides with a design of intertwined serpents. The game seems to have resembled a combination of hand ball and basket ball. Its object was to drive the ball through the rings. Skilled players were allowed to strike the ball with their hips only, wearing leather protectors for this purpose. A clean goal must have been a rarity and the successful *jugador* received special honors. A court of the same kind existed in Mexico City, where games were played before Montezuma.

From the Castillo stretches a stone-laid causeway, Gothic-arched now, as it must have been then, with grey-trunked trees. This was the Via Sacra, or sacred path to the Cenote de los Sacrificios, an awesome well over one hundred feet across and sunk a hundred and fifty feet deep through stratum after stratum of grey, blackened, root-hung limestone. When the milpas, cornfields, were parched and the heavens were as brass, certain persons were

Ball Court and El Castillo, Chichén Itzá, before restoration

selected by the priest to be sacrificed to the Rain-God. If the drought were severe, the ecclesiastic choice fell on virgins. At daybreak a preliminary ceremony was held on the steps of the Castillo, where all might see.

Followed a solemn march, slow, funereal, down through the overhanging trees to the great rocks on the brink of the grey and black Cenote. Here, one by one, the young women, many of them, if we may judge by the remnant of their tribe left today, delicately formed and Oriental of feature, were hurled into the deep water seventy feet below. After them were flung jewels of gold, jade and turquoise. Ornaments of this description have been dredged up within recent years. At the sound of each falling body, prayers were chanted and magic litanies uttered.

Hidden behind the ever-climbing bush are three more impressive buildings. One of them is the only round structure found at Chichen, the Caracol, or astronomical tower, from which observations were taken and calculations made that have caused modern mathematicians to take off their hats to the Mayan calendrists. Another is the House of the Dark Writing, a long low squat building with parallel rows of windowless cells. A third is the most ornate structure in Chichen: the House of the Monjas or Nuns. Here the Mayan sculptors gave themselves free rein and covered the exterior with exuberant, if carefully executed, decorations. It was this building, with its

El Caracol, Chichén Itzá, after restoration by Karl Ruppert, Carnegie Institution of Washington.

numerous curved noses or tongues projected from row upon row of serpents' faces, that caused an early explorer to proclaim to the world his belief that the Mayans were Asiatic in origin, since in his opinion these curled projections represented elephants' trunks. Scarcely less pronounced is an imitation of lattice work, or X design, cut into the stone.

The Mayan sculptor, culturally speaking, was a barbarian. He belonged to the Stone Age. All his tools were of stone, flint, or obsidian; and yet with these crude instruments he was able to cut lines scarcely surpassed for delicacy and grace. To feathers in an ornate headdress, for instance, he could impart the utmost airiness. His chief weakness was a tendency to overcrowd his space. He could not abide a vacuum, nor did he know how to make it a part of his design. Wherever he found an empty corner he filled it with hieroglyphs or symbolic decorations. Wherever he erred or slipped, the painter came to his rescue. It must be remembered that Mayan architectural sculpture which is largely in bas-relief, was intended only to provide a design to which masses of color were to be applied.

All the buildings in this religious capital were richly painted on their exteriors as well as sculptured. Surrounded as they seem to have been with terraced banks of tropical flowers, the effect on the pilgrim, coming from his palm-thatched home in the parched bush, must have been dazzling beyond description.

It is plain that Chichen, which was dominated by the priestly craft, was laid out so as to awe and impress. The city as a whole covered a space of two square miles, and including Chichen-Itza and the earlier group of structures known as Old Chichen. Each building was constructed, with every appearance of solidity and permanence, upon a mound or terraced pyramid filled with rubble and faced with cut stone. The pilgrim, approaching over Yucatan's low, flat miles of sand, bush, and limestone outcroppings, could not doubt that here was the Eternal City. In the distance its grey buildings shone white and dazzling. As he came nearer, he could distinguish their bands of color—blue, red, green and yellow. A walk through surrounding glades of trees, interspersed with sacred cornfields, brought him into a city whose temples towered far above his head, sharply outlined against a sky of intense blue, and with every detail distinct in a transparent atmosphere.

Here he found everything which could provide him with a complete emotional *Katharsis*—bloody human sacrifices to arouse his terror, processions to gratify his love of spectacle, cavernous temples to provoke his awe, naturalistic representations of gods to create his submission, and ball games to divert and excite him. Around the outskirts of the holy ground was a considerable city composed of homes much like those in which Mayas live today—palm-thatched huts made of poles daubed with mud, floors of beaten earth, and with hammocks for beds.

Chichen Itza was settled, about eight hundred years before Columbus discovered America, by the Itza tribe of Mayans, who called it "Chi-Chen," from "Chi," mouth, and "Chen," well, or Mouth of Wells. Almost exactly a thousand years ago they mysteriously abandoned it. The precise reason never has been determined, owing to the destruction of the Mayan records by the Spanish bishop Diego de Landa, who regarded them as the unholy chronicles of a devilish paganism. Various hypotheses have ascribed the desertion of the city to a persistent plague; to the orders of priests who believed they had discovered omens threatening to the future of the city; and to increasing starvation due to exhaustion of the surrounding soil. The plough and the use of fertilizers are even at this date virtually unknown on the Yucatan peninsula. The rural Indian clears a patch of ground by burning it off and plants his corn by making holes for it with a thrust of a stick. The humus in most parts is only a few scant inches deep. Below that is the hard rock of ages.

In the middle of the thirteenth century the Itzas returned to Chichen as mysteriously as they had left it, and upon its re-occupation the city flourished more grandly than ever, becoming the religious capital of the new Mayan empire, while Uxmal, to the southwest, became the political capital.

About thirty years before the coming of Columbus, prolonged civil war broke out and the Itzas were worsted. They then abandoned Chichen forever and moved to the forests of Guatemala. They left the painted city to be inhabited only by the iguana, the tick, the army ant, and the buzzard, and in time to be overwhelmed by the bush through which ran the jaguar and

Las Monjas (Nunnery), Chichén Itzá

the spotted ocelot. Tropical vegetation, so long kept underfoot by the heavy stones of the Mayan builders, came back with a rush. Roots and lianas, at first yellow-green and tender, pushed their way gradually through mortarless crevices, until they became strong and brown. Then with the pressure exerted by sap and expanding cells, they rose up and felled to the ground all but the most solid and best balanced masonry. Lintels, hewn out of the tremendously resistant zapote wood, in time rotted away, allowing the walls above them to pour down in cascades.

At the foot of every mound lay sculptured serpents' heads and the broken limbs of gods, priests, and warriors in painted stone. Today many of these heaps of graven stones lie just as they fell. The Thousand Columns were buried deep under dust and the matted bush. Streets and even paths disappeared, and Chichen became a "lost" city, known only to silent Indians until a wandering explorer found it again about seventy-five years ago. Since that time the work of explorers and archaeologists is gradually unravelling what once appeared to be one of the irretrievably knotted mysteries of ancient American life.

That Chichen and other Mayan centers are so remarkably preserved today, despite the attacks of time and the jungle, is due to three factors: the absence of frost, which can rend even the hugest boulders; the erection of buildings on tall mounds which impeded the encroachment of vegetation; and the feature of Mayan building for which their architects have been most

La Iglesia, adjoining Las Monjas, Chichén Itzá

criticized—the "false" or triangular arch, sometimes called the American arch, to distinguish it from the round or Roman arch.

The Mayan never knew the principle of the keystone, hence it never occurred to him that an arch might have a rounded top. He simply carried up his walls to a certain height and then began to draw them together by "stepping" one stone upon another. As soon as these inner walls almost touched, he capped them with a slab of stone, thus forming a large **A** or truncated triangle. The result was a building curiously narrow but unlimited in length. This method was immensely wasteful of stone and labor, but it is unlikely the Mayan cared about either sufficiently to economize in it. His stone was quarried, worked, and erected by slaves, of whom he captured thousands in battle. However defective these arches appear to be from the modern architect's viewpoint, their sheer weight of stone gives them an enormous solidity, and to them is largely due the preservation of Mayan cities in the relatively sound state in which they exist today.

The Mayan sculptors, painters and calligraphers were very apt in portraying the racial physiognomy. What are evidently faithful portraits in bas-relief indicate that the Mayans were a well-formed but stocky people with smooth, yellowish skins and a plumpness which concealed their high muscular development. Their most conspicuous facial characteristic was a curving and sometimes hooked Roman nose through which the men wore a long plug frequently tufted at the ends. Their foreheads slanted sharply backward, due to the practice of binding boards on the heads of infants. They were also virtually devoid of chin, so that the face came to a point at the lips, which were thick and projecting, the lower lip sometimes slightly pendulous.

They were fond of wearing elaborate costumes and felt most imposing when masquerading as birds, animals or reptiles. They cured the skins whole and warriors thrust their heads through the open mouths of alligators or jaguars to appear in dances or processions. Most attention was paid to the headdress which was of towering height, containing feathers or flowers which fell over in graceful loops behind their backs. Another conspicuous feature of their dress was a broad girdle whose ends made aprons in front and behind. A similar apron, the *maxtli,* is worn by their descendants today. It is usually made of blue cotton cloth and protects the white trousers of laborers when at work.

A short mantle was sometimes worn over the shoulders of Mayan warriors. It was a network of leather and had angular ends which somewhat resembled modern epaulets. Leggings, wrist-guards and anklets were also common, and their short, plump feet were always protected by sandals with unusually high backs. Tattooing on the face and body was freely indulged in, and the incisor teeth were frequently filed to a sharp point. In fact, there was scarcely any part of his body which the Mayan did not adorn and decorate for festal occasions. He liked a good show and contributed himself to it with enthusiasm.

Fighting men wore armor of quilted cotton, made of two layers with sand or salt packed between. It afforded good protection against light missiles, but was of course worse than useless when the Spaniards came with their bullets. Mayan warriors carried spears and short clubs of wood into which flints were fitted like saw-teeth. These weapons could inflict terrible wounds and were capable of cutting off a man's head at a blow. Their spears, headed with chipped flint, were of two lengths—one as long as a man, and the other short and pointed somewhat like an arrow. The bow and arrow were late arrivals in Mayan life and were probably borrowed, as were many other institutions, from the Mexicans of the North.

The early Mayans were not a pugnacious people and preferred to attend to their crops, promote their religious affairs, and develop the arts of peace. But a change came after contact with the Toltecs and Aztecs of the North. Wars then became more frequent, but the Mayan never developed into a slayer on a large scale. It was his object to capture his enemies rather than to kill them; captives were not only sacred to the Mayan gods, but carried out the heavy labor of temple construction, and furnished the subjects for the elaborate human sacrifices which the Mayans celebrated with imposing ceremonies. On sacrificial days the priests painted themselves blue, which was a sacred color. Their victims were also painted blue on the nose and around the eyes, the rest of the body being sometimes decorated with vertical red stripes.

Mayan women, though devout, took little active part in religious affairs, and did not mingle with or eat with men in public. They dressed with far less splendor than the proud and exuberant male. They wore no clothing above the waist except an occasional short shoulder mantle. Their skirts came below the knee. As a screen from the sun they tossed a rebozo over their heads, and used the same garment to make a back-sling in which to carry the baby. Domestic scenes pictured on various walls reveal Maya women living in the same palm-thatched houses, making the same tortillas, and wearing the same rebozos that characterize their descendants today. In a thousand years the Indian women of Yucatan have not changed their essential habits.

Their sculptures, paintings, and picture-writings make it plain that the Mayas possessed a civilization far in advance of any other existing at the time on the North American continent. Their architectural planning and building indicate that they were a strong, progressive and imaginative people singularly gifted not only in the practice of the arts but the sciences. No one can stand among Mayan ruins and gaze upon their fallen Babylons without feeling that it was a misfortune to human history that their rise was broken short, like a mutilated stump, and that they were not permitted to complete their rounded cycle in the expansion of civilization.

The Great Stone Face of Izamal. We had heard of it as one of the wonders
of Yucatan; it was fixed in the side of a mountain and was almost as big;
it had the inscrutable expression of the Egyptian Sphinx and was better
preserved. True, Stephens, who visited Izamal about 1842 and saw the Face,
was more temperate as regards its size, but his description was sufficiently
interesting:

"It is seven feet eight inches in height and seven feet in width. The
ground-work is of projecting stones, which are covered with stucco. A stone
one foot six inches long protrudes from the chin, intended, perhaps, for
burning copal on, as a sort of altar. It was the first time we had seen an
ornament of this kind upon the exterior of any of these structures. In sternness and harshness of expression it reminded us of the idols at Copan, and
its colossal proportions, with the corresponding dimensions of the mound,
gave an unusual impression of grandeur."

The mound mentioned here is one of eight which on the wide flat plain
that supports Izamal do indeed appear to be mountain high. They undoubtedly supported the temples and other buildings which composed the old
Indian town, whose chief was a mighty man named Ulil. Legend says the
town's original name was Itzamal, so called after the Itza tribe which dominated this region.

As soon as we reached Izamal, we inquired for the location of the Great
Stone Face. Two Indian lads could only shake their heads and say, "It is
not here."

"It is not here? Then where is it?"

They did not know. Further inquiry brought out the saddening information that the Great Stone Face of Izamal is no more. Several years ago the
family whose backyard contained the Face, which was built into the stone-
work supporting the base of a mound, became annoyed by the increasing
stream of curious visitors and destroyed it!

A similar fate has overtaken other Mayan monuments. The modern Yu-
cateco has little regard for his country's antiquities, and the Indian is prone
to regard them either as a source of building stone or a nuisance. Worked
stones with Maya inscriptions have been found in the cornices of modern
buildings, and one rare stone was found, miles from its place of origin, doing
duty as a support for a horse-trough. Knowledge of such incidents causes
visiting archaeologists to moan in their sleep.

Though mourning the destruction of the Face, there was compensation
for us in the discovery in this time-worn old town, so Spanish in some
respects, so Indian in others, of the only specimen of his kind extant—an
American doctor who was born in Yucatan and brought up as a Yucatecan.
Noting the American name on his shingle, we stopped at his office, filled
with shiny-eyed Indians, to extend greetings.

Dr. G. turned out to be a tall, spare, blond man of forty-six years, simple
and hearty in his manner, the son of an Indiana physician who, having a

taste for natural history, came to Yucatan years ago to study its plant and animal life. Before completing his stay, he was commissioned by the British Museum to gather and send to it a collection of Yucatecan fauna and flora, including the smallest humming bird in the world, a creature with a body no larger than one's little fingernail. It took ten years to form the collection, but at last it was complete, and was shipped to England and on a sailing vessel. In mid-ocean the ship caught fire and burned to the waves' edge. Everything on board was lost, including the collection. The doctor at once started another, in time completing it and shipping it safely. Meantime, he had settled down to practice in Yucatan, where his children were brought up. He has since published a four-volume study of the plants, birds, insects and animals of the peninsula, issued in Spanish by the Mexican government.

On the father's retirement, the son, who had obtained his medical education in the States, took up his practice, much of it being among the natives, whose language he speaks fluently. He told us that modern Mayas suffer chiefly from grippe and amoebic dysentery. There is also some pellagra. But their vitality is, in general, astonishing.

One of his recent patients had been an old Indian woman eighty-two years old. In her backyard she had kept a yearling bull, tied out to graze. One day she went out to move the animal which, though previously mild-tempered, suddenly turned on her and gored her through and through. She fell to the ground, where the bull attacked her again, lacerating her so furiously that her intestines fell out. It was in this condition that her relatives found her. They placed her in a hammock, but dared not touch her otherwise, and called the doctor. Though deeming the case hopeless, he washed and replaced the viscera, which happened not to be torn, sewed up the wounds, and asking her people to notify him when she had expired, made out the death certificate. The relatives came to report, as requested; but instead of announcing her death, they voiced her complaint that she was receiving an insufficiency to eat! Two months later she was not only alive but on the road to recovery.

Both the doctor's hands were badly scarred. One wound came from an alligator's bite, the other from a giant ray's barb, both animals being at the time supposedly dead. The alligator had been harpooned and hauled into the doctor's boat while he was fishing with natives off the coast. With expiring energy the brute bit through his left hand, severing a vein.

Bad as this was, the other wound was much more serious. The doctor and his native companions had found basking in the warm Gulf water a giant stingray, one of those marine beasts with a broad, flat body and a poisonous barb sheathed in its tail, which grow to monstrous dimensions in tropical waters. They killed it and towed it to land where the doctor, then young and inquisitive, intended to dissect it. As the ray was apparently lifeless, he took hold of it by the tail to drag it up on the beach. The beast with a galvanic effort, drove his barb through the young physician's right hand, where it broke off. The stingray's dart is covered with a poisonous slime and is so constructed that it can be drawn through flesh in only one direction. There was no remedy at hand except brandy, and of this the doctor drank copiously, to maintain his circulation, while the Indians opened the back of his hand and drew out the barb. He then lay down to give battle to the poison. For seven hours he was violently ill, his body seeming for part of the time to be on fire and again as cold as if packed in ice. It was two days before he recovered sufficiently to be taken home, and he was ailing for three months afterward.

On recovering completely, he experienced a marked aversion from all forms of sea food, of which previously he had been very fond. Eventually he tried a dish of oysters, but the very taste of them caused severe nausea, and his repulsion for sea food persisted for seventeen years longer.

Interior of temple room, Chichén Itzá

We felt it to be good fortune when the doctor laid aside his work for half a day and joined us for a trip through the bush to a henequen plantation; for with his enthusiastic interest in all forms of Yucatecan life, he was teaching us more in a minute than we would otherwise learn in a week. He pointed out the boneta tree, with pods flanged like an arrow head; a silk-cotton tree three feet in diameter at the base, whose bolls bear a soft, curly fiber; a lemonillo, bearing the green limes of commerce; a ciruela, whose cherries are green when ripe, and finally a bitter-orange and sweet-orange tree grafted together by the native method. A young tree of the bitter variety is planted near a larger sweet one. When their limbs begin to mingle, they are broken off and their ends tied together, the joint being plastered over with clay. The sweet orange being the stronger, its sap compels the bitter tree to yield sweet fruit.

We came upon a clearing where the little golden bees of Yucatan were drinking themselves to death on the odorous blossoms of the flor de Mayo, Mayflower tree. Their native owner took us behind his house to show us their hives—short lengths of hollow logs, stopped at the ends with clay and piled up like cordwood. In Yucatan you do not eat honey but drink it. The native showed us how. Picking up a hive-log, he made a hole in it, bidding us lift and drink. We did so, and the honey ran out like water.

Owing perhaps to the hot climate, Yucatecan bees do not build solid hexagonal cells like their burly cousins of the North. The liquid honey would

Maya hollow-log beehives, Yucatán

not stay in such structures. Instead, they make large, multiple cysts, somewhat like the nests of bumblebees.

The doctor being an enthusiastic apiarist, he once imported a colony of bees from the States. The queen was seventeen days making the journey, and though her majesty was sadly jolted and arrived in a temper, she was soon mollified and at once set about the creation of a large family. Nearby was a colony of native bees, who were surprised and made indignant one day when the Americans—doubtless wearing horn-rimmed glasses and talking through their noses—swarmed over and robbed them. The native bees complained to the government, but when nothing, as usual, was done, they girded their loins and went over and robbed the Americans. While the unpleasantness lasted, neither colony did any collecting but spent their whole time robbing and re-robbing each other. Their owner had to break up the cross-raiding by moving the warring colonies far apart.

As we passed one of the outlying Izamal mounds, we witnessed a sudden battle between a spider and an army ant. The ant had appeared from around a corner and poked his head into a small crevice. He must have made a noise or dislodged a grain of sand, or perhaps he truculently shouted a challenge into the darkness; at any rate the spider, of the same color as the rock and the same size as the intruder, bounded out from a side exit and began a search. His bristling demeanor plainly said: "Who is prowling around here? Doesn't he know this is private property?"

As soon as he spied the reconnoitering ant, he rushed upon him. The two little insects rolled over and over, separated, and rushed together again. They fought over a field of about four square inches, the ant wildly clashing his hooked mandibles and the spider no less wildly trying to use his dagger. Neither seemed able to get a permanent grip on the other or reach a vital spot. At last in the midst of a locked wrestle the spider saw an opening and sank his sting in the ant's stomach. Instantly the ant rolled over dead and slowly slid down a slope, finally tumbling over a precipice, at the bottom of which he lay motionless. The spider looked gloatingly over the edge and, still wildly excited, searched his estate for other possible trespassers before turning back to his castle with an air that said: "If there are any more of those bandits around here annoying peaceful citizens, they will get the same medicine."

This was not our first sight of Yucatan's formidable insects, and we had many times tried to see if we could break up the long lines of leaf-cutting ants, seen everywhere in tropical Mexico, each of which carries his burden on edge, so that they present the appearance of a fleet embarking under tiny green sails. Each ant can be lifted by his sail, the edge of which he carries between his strong mandibles while he balances the leaf, which may be several times his weight, across his back; but he holds on with terrier-like persistence, and if lifted to a tree limb, he in time makes his way back to the ground and rejoins his toiling brethren, still grasping his bit of green.

In planted areas their appearance is greeted with horror, for they will cut a garden or orchard to pieces unless headed off by water or fire. In Yucatan it is common to see wells with broad stone tops trenched through the middle and carrying a moat of water. This is to keep out the ants who are capable of marching solemnly down the interior of the well and dropping into the water by millions, simply because no order is given to halt.

One day I was standing within a Mayan ruin, wondering at the number of wasps' nests on the walls, when a few army ants, a half inch long, climbed up, cautiously inspected the nests laden with grubs, and withdrew. These must have been scouts. Doubtless they submitted a glowing report to the commanders keeping their divisions marking time outside, for in a few minutes the army appeared at three different doors of the building. On reaching the perpendicular walls it deployed and sent up half a dozen narrow lines. These lines were escorted and kept in order by large ants carrying much heavier mandibles, acting as officers, flank guards, and military police.

The shock troops which led the advance rushed upon the nests and began tearing at the cell covers. The parent wasps at once realized the danger, set up a shrill buzzing, and furiously attacked the ants with jaws, feet, and stingers. For a moment they successfully fought off the advance guard, but the first narrow lines were now widening from two to four, six, and a dozen ants abreast, and the supporting regiments were pouring over the thresholds below in rivers.

I followed these lines back and found them blackening the steep stone steps and terraces all the way down to the ground, where their starting place was obscured under low bushes and piles of stone fallen from the ruin. I put obstacles such as sticks and stones across their paths, but they surmounted these without even losing step. A shallow trench likewise gave them no trouble, but a deeper one, with vertical walls two inches high, threw them into confusion. They fell into it by hundreds and seemed unable to climb out except after much delay. Latecomers gathered on the edge of the trench in a thick black line, waving their mandibles and feelers. Officers and guards came hurrying up, ran around in circles, conferred, and went away. They evidently reported the serious depth of the trench back to the high command, which doubtless gave out the necessary orders, for the marching line began to thin and then disappear. A new road had been located three feet away, and over this the army was now rushing, to the entire disregard of my trench.

By the time I returned to the ruin, half the wasps' nests had been mopped up. Resisting owners were seized by wing or leg, buried under knots of swarming ants, and torn limb from limb. The nests were overwhelmed, cut to bits, and looted. The pieces fell at the foot of the walls like rain. Even the stumps of the nests were sheared off and demolished. Soon there was an emptiness and silence where a few minutes before there had been a humming and active wasp city.

Yucatan's welfare depends on henequen, the American agave related to the cactus which produces the sisal rope of commerce. It is odd that in a soil so thin and stony the other plants maintain themselves upon it with difficulty, henequen grows green and stout, loving the sun and miraculously extracting from the dry, calcareous sand sufficient moisture to make its great sword-like blades fat and pulpy. Its fibers were known to the Mayan builders, who twisted them into ropes with which to haul the vast stones of their temples.

It is grown on great plantations, "fincas," having something over one thousand plants to the acre which radiate in spiky rows from the Big House or hacienda, where dwells the owner or manager in what was, up to a few years ago, a patriarchal, semi-feudal style. If the *haciendado* was a good man, his Indian workers planted and gathered the henequen crop patiently year after year, looking to him for all their needs. If he was brutal and grasping, the work went on just the same, except that there were occasional outbursts of burnings and killings. The Revolution laid the foundation for a change which is not yet complete, but under which the government pro- tects the worker, and his own Leagues of Resistance, or labor unions, regu- late his hours and wages.

At any hacienda the stranger is welcome, for time sometimes drags heavily through the long Yucatecan day, and the owner is eager for news. We were several times entertained at these haciendas, which usually sit, cool and somnolent, in a cluster of trees and windmills. At one a few miles from Izamal, the managers and foremen put aside everything to show us the expensive machinery which grinds up the leaves, extracts the pulp, separates the fiber, and twists it, when dried and bleached, into rope and cordage.

Afterwards they brought us to the great arched veranda, cool under its thick stones, and sent a boy up a palm for cocoanuts from which to drink. They introduced us to the oldest worker on the place, a grizzled Indian whose brown skin was burnt almost black by over three-fourths of a cen- tury of sun, but his withered arms and legs were still fit for active work. He took off his torn sombrero and bowed to us with a pathetic dignity, walling the whites of his eyes at us like an old hound that fears he may not be spoken to gently.

During the World War the price of henequen soared and planters be- came rich. Then came the slump and the reaction. Governor Felipe Carillo, the former train-brakeman, was captured and shot, his body being thrown beside those of his three brothers. Men were assassinated at night in their homes and town plazas were fouled with swinging corpses.

In any state of Mexico the fragrance which rides the breeze bears at its end the charnel odor of history, and the gayest music is threaded with a chord of mourning. Even in Yucatan, whose people love pleasure and have no taste for blood, life wears over its shoulder the arm of death. In the tropics there is no annual pageant of spring with its shouting promise, no winter with its kindly rest. There are only two seasons, the wet and the dry, and decay hangs from the same limb that blossoms. Death works beside life in order that life may not be drowned in its own plenitude. Under the spur of moist heat, Nature, with a trowel in one hand and a knife in the other, has no time and no mercy, hurrying that each job may be rushed to completion and then cut down to serve as a base for a new structure. By such a close alternation of life and death men are bound to be influenced in their thoughts. Throughout Mexico we heard two words used more often than any others. They were "bonito," pretty, and "triste," sad. A thing is one or the other, and sometimes it is both.

The next morning I rose early and walked up the coral beach to a clump of bushes where I undressed and enjoyed a vivifying plunge into the frothy, apple-green surf. While I was dressing, a trio of Maya maidens came up a nearby path, walked into the water, and began to bathe. They did not doff their clothing but kept on a white cotton shift, probably worn as a protection against the already blistering sun rather than as a concession to the careful.

In Yucatan, as in other parts of Mexico, it is common to come upon parties of native ladies bathing without a shift or anything else on but sunlight. In the presence of males they neither scream nor leap for cover, but merely turn their backs, if that. The brown bodies of the younger women, often of several different tones, are usually full, strong, and *esbelto,* this last being a toothsome Spanish word meaning neat and shaped. Brown skins impart no suggestion of nudity, but in hot climates strike a harmonious sexless chord with sun, air, and soil. Mexican Indians have to use their bodies too much to concern themselves with concealment, and in a land where all the members of a family must frequently live, eat, sleep, and die in a single hut, there is no room for any self-consciousness regarding lack of clothing, nor any ignorance regarding the oddities of the human anatomy.

FIFTEEN

J. Eric S. Thompson 1926-1936

To Cobá on the Great
Stone Road

[J. Eric S. Thompson is generally conceded to be the foremost living Mayanist scholar. Born and educated in England, he became interested in Maya hieroglyphics and archaeology while a student at Cambridge. In 1926 he took part in the Carnegie Institution of Washington investigations at Chichén Itzá in Yucatán, then joined the staff of the Chicago Natural History Museum (then the Field Museum of Natural History) and, later, the research staff of the Carnegie Institution of Washington.

[Thompson is best known for his contributions to the study of Maya hieroglyphic writing and decipherment of Maya calendrical inscriptions. This work, however, should not overshadow his pioneer studies of Middle American ceramics, his fine ethnological research among the living Indians, and his studies of Middle American art, architecture, and other remains. His summaries of what we know about the Maya and their neighbors—modestly entitled "trial surveys"—were for years our only authoritative general syntheses of Maya prehistory, and were superseded only by Thompson's own book, *The Rise and Fall of Maya Civilization*, from which I quote on the following pages.

[Thompson has made numerous trips to Mexico and Central America, and has conducted excavations or other investigations at many of its most

The selections from Thompson are, in the order quoted below, from the following works. J. Eric S. Thompson, *The Rise and Fall of Maya Civilization* (Norman: University of Oklahoma Press, 1954), pp. 4–12. Copyright 1954 by the University of Oklahoma Press. Reprinted with permission of the publisher. J. Eric S. Thompson, *Maya Archaeologist* (Norman: University of Oklahoma Press, 1963), pp. 44–64, 72–74. Copyright 1963 by the University of Oklahoma Press. Reprinted with permission of the publisher.

famous ruins, among them Chichén Itzá, San José, Cobá, and Bonampak. Now retired and living again in England, he continues to produce an astonishing amount of research—his latest technical publication being a large catalogue of Maya hieroglyphics—plus, we are glad to say, a book of personal reminiscences and incidents of his long and interesting archaeological career, *Maya Archaeologist,* from which I also quote below.]

On that visit to Tikal, over twenty years ago, we arrived on muleback after losing our way and spending an uncomfortable night in an abandoned, flea-infested camp of chewing-gum gatherers. There was something Chaucerian about the journey of seven days from that modern Tabard Inn, the ramshackle International Hotel in Belize, up the Belize River two days in a launch, and then five days by mule from El Cayo via another Maya city, Uaxactún. We were in a sense pilgrims journeying leisurely to a great shrine, and, as the mules jogged stolidly through the forest at three miles an hour, we had ample time, denied to the air traveler, for speculation on what awaited us.

On earlier journeys in the rain forest of Central America, the exotic surroundings had excited my interest, but with repetition the novelty had worn off, and the impression of the forest on my mind had become one of overwhelming monotony. On this journey, as on a dozen others, we followed endless, narrow, winding tunnels cut in the forest by chewing-gum gatherers. The trees met far overhead, letting through occasional dapples of sunshine or allowing a fleeting glimpse of blue sky or cloud. Below, the serried tree trunks merged in a dull gray mass, and fallen trees wore the brown of decay. The dense foliage excluded the bright colors one associates with the tropics. Except for a careful eye for an overhanging branch eager to deal one Absalom's fate and a perpetual and largely unconscious struggle between mule and rider, one was free to dwell upon the past, when Maya civilization cut its first teeth on this self-same jungle and partly subdued it on reaching maturity.

The descent of the trail into the great *bajo* of Tikal fetched me back into the present. That low swampland, perhaps a lake when Tikal flourished, is a sea of mud in the rainy season, but it was dry when we crossed it. The few feet of descent brought a complete change, very much for the worse, in the vegetation. Spanish cedars, mahogany, the ubiquitous sapodilla, from the wrinkled trunk of which, when it is slashed with a machete, raw chewing gum drips, and graceful cabbage palms gave place to a low, thorny shrub, from the branches of which numberless stinging ants might descend, like paratroopers, upon the rider who incautiously knocked against trunk or limb. The sun beat down on mules and riders as though in punishment for our hours of playing hide-and-seek with him in the tall forest; the strangely distorted branches of the thorn trees writhed like souls in Dante's hell.

The trail, which had been meandering southward, swung to the west before ascending sharply into rain forest once more. Suddenly we glimpsed an awe-inspiring sight. Four of the great pyramids of Tikal, clad in foliage and surmounted by ancient temples of limestone, grayish white against the sky, rose high above the surrounding treetops, like green volcanoes with summits wreathed in white cloud. The pilgrims were at the gates of their New World Canterbury. Just as Chaucer's riders must have lost sight of the cathedral as they hurried through the narrow streets of the city, so we lost our view of the Maya temples as we plunged into the forest in that abrupt climb from the edge of the swamp to the heart of the city.

The trail ascended for about 150 yards to where it crossed an ancient Maya causeway leading southeastward to an outlying group. There we were, so to speak, in the outer downtown district. Two hundred yards farther west, our eyes were caught by the great mass, to the right, of one of Tikal's huge pyramids, the blurred outline of its immense bulk rising through the sea-green foliage like the base of a submarine mountain. To the left were the dispiriting remains of two parallel mounds, which, in better days, prob-ably had been the sides of one of those courts in which the Maya played their ball game with a solid ball of rubber a millennium before our western civilization had any knowledge of rubber or rubber balls. Imprecations of the muleteer, whose mules heeded only the task of skillfully picking their way across heaps of root-entwined rubble, echoed in another key the shouts of players and watchers and the thud of ball on pad or wall—a brighter wall not then in disrepair.

Beyond that narrow passage between pyramid and supposed ball court the trail enters the great court or plaza of Tikal, great not because of its size, but because, like the Forum of Rome, it is enclosed by great structures raised by the toil of thousands to a glory now passed and knit with a faith which was in vain. We unsaddled and hitched our mules to trees, units in what I would have called the virgin forest which compassed us about, had I not known that the forest had been felled in 1881 by the British archaeolo-gist, Alfred Maudslay, and again in 1904 and 1910 by expeditions of the Peabody Museum of Harvard University. Each time the tide of vegetation had engulfed the ruins anew; with the years, saplings had grown to giants, anchored to the thin soil and the Maya-built floors beneath by buttressed roots. Lianas—some almost as thick as fire hose—hung from branches or were looped from tree to tree. A troop of spider monkeys chattered high in the trees that swept up the pyramid guarding the west end of the great court, a New World version of Omar Khayyam's "They say the lion and the lizard keep the courts where Jamshyd gloried and drank deep."

We scrambled up the eastern pyramid, clambering over the slides in the great stairway with the aid of some root working to displace yet another stone of the step or some sapling which now must be a giant. The terraced sides of the pyramid, broken by the actions of roots and rain, were masked by ferns and vines. As we got higher, the cactus-like pitahaya vine with thorny stems triangular in section warned us to climb carefully. The trees thinned out, and we were on the flat crown of the pyramid facing the temple on its summit. We turned to look down the broken stairway we had climbed. The height of the crest of the temple above the level of the court (allowing a few feet for collapse) is almost 160 feet, and each side of the base of the pyramid is a little over a third of a city block in length. So far as we know, there is no natural elevation enclosed in this mass, every cubic foot of which was built without anything that could be termed machinery. The builders were men, and, probably, women and children, who inhabited what is now this forested region twelve hundred years ago; and they erected this vast structure not long after Augustine built the Saxon predecessor of the early Norman church, in turn replaced by the Canterbury Cathedral Chaucer's pilgrims journeyed to see. Gangs brought rock and rubble for the core of the pyramids; they faced the building stone with primitive tools; they cut the wood to heat the lime kilns; they shaped the sapodilla beams for the temple; and, finally, some of them may have given their lives to the building as sacrificial victims at its dedication. It is likely that their bones or their decapitated heads, each neatly enclosed between pairs of pottery bowls placed lip to lip, are beneath the walls or floors of the temple behind where we stood, or below the bottom steps of the stairway facing us.

From the doorway of the temple, we looked out over the treetops whose range of hues was not unlike the contrasting green tones of shoal water. Here and there trees with myriads of scarlet blossoms heightened the effect of a seascape, for they seemed like giant jelly-fish floating on the water's surface. Directly in front, to the west, the gray-white walls of three pyramid-supported temples rose like coral islands above the sea of foliage. A fourth, due south, could be seen by turning to the left. Nearer at hand, a swell in the foliage told of a large building below, not tall enough to break surface. At sunset or dawn deep shadows mapped the contours in better detail.

In ancient times one would have had an uninterrupted view across the city with its clusters of smaller pyramids topped by their temples, its multi-chambered buildings (miscalled "palaces" for convenience), facing courts at different levels, and its endless surfaces of cream-white stucco relieved only by shadow and an occasional building or floor finished with red plaster.

In the great ceremonial court and in various smaller courts stood the stelae, like sentinels, before the approaches to platforms and pyramids. Those limestone shafts, carved or painted with the static portraits of gods and with their hieroglyphic texts always recording that overwhelming preoccupation of the Maya with the mystery of time, are milestones in the history of the city. Every five or ten or twenty years a new one rose to carry forward the story of conquests, not of neighbors, but of the secrets of time and the movements of the celestial bodies. Such impersonal topics would have been unthinkable to the rulers of Egypt or Assyria, eager to commission the texts which commemorated the triumphs of their reigns.

Tikal

Photograph by Teobert Maler, 1895. From *Explorations in the Department of Peten, Guatemala,* 1911. Copyright 1911 by Peabody Museum of Archaeology and Ethnology, Harvard University. Courtesy of Peabody Museum of Harvard University.

Tikal

Photograph by Teobert Maler, 1895. From *Explorations in the Department of Peten, Guatemala,* 1911. Copyright 1911 by Peabody Museum of Archaeology and Ethnology, Harvard University. Courtesy of Peabody Museum of Harvard University.

Just as we forced our way through the tangled vegetation that crowded the courts and surged up mound and across terrace, so, in ancient times, a late arrival at some ceremony must have shouldered his way through the congregation which, packed in the court, intently witnessed a ceremony held on the top of a pyramid before the temple door. I could visualize the priest-astronomer, anxious to check his theories on the length of the solar year or the lunar month, threading his way from stela to stela to see what calculations his predecessors had recorded in the then distant past, or I could conjure up the acrid, sooty smoke of copal incense rising from clay braziers to a sky then fully visible from the great court.

We wandered through the forest, entering temples, climbing pyramids, and once disturbing a herd of peccary feeding on the cherry-like fruit of the breadnut. As darkness fell after that interlude of dusk so brief in those latitudes, we ate, in the ceremonial court, Maya black beans and canned Chicago pork. The mingling of the two foods—one the product of ancient agricultural techniques, the other processed in a modern factory—seemed to symbolize archaeology's task of bringing past and present together.

The rest of the party bedded down in the great court; Agustín Hob, my Maya boy, and I, storm lantern in hand, climbed to one of the Maya palaces on the south side of the court. Passing through a room, the plaster walls of which still showed crude sketches of daily life incised in the plaster a thousand years ago, we slung my hammock, in a second room, from cross-bars of sapodilla wood placed in the vault even before the graffiti were made. Agustín, lantern in hand, returned to the court, and I was left alone with my thoughts.

I thought of those sketches in the adjacent room. One showed a scene of human sacrifice, the victim tied to a frame; another represented a Maya god; several were of temple-crowned pyramids; others were little better than scribbling. Who had made them? Surely not the Maya priests. My thoughts went back to schooldays and idly and crudely drawn caricatures of schoolmasters, of Dido and Aeneas, and of a football hero making a pass, and then I had the answer. Of course, this must have been the building in which the Maya novices were lodged before initiation at some great ceremony. Tired as I was, I tried to picture those youths of a thousand years ago. Were they full of ideas for setting the world to rights? Did they accept authority, or were they in revolt against their elders? Did they accept the gods without question, or were they skeptical? Surely they complained to each other about the long periods of fasting and vigil. Or did they? What right have we to suppose that they reacted as modern young men would?

Why? How? What? When? Like the soporific rhythm of a Pullman car passing over points and rail joints, the questions repeated themselves as I dozed in my hammock. How did this civilization arise? Why, unlike any other civilization in the world, did it come into being in tropical forest? When did it flourish? What hidden forces made it succeed? Why is it so like, but also so unlike, the ancient civilizations of the Old World? The questions danced across the vaulted room. The sand flies began to bite as a full moon rose behind my head, floodlighting the temple atop yet another huge pyramid to the south. In the immediate foreground its beams strove to penetrate the foliage in the deep gully below, once dammed, probably to serve as a reservoir.

The sybaritic Mr. Keith of *South Wind* remarks in the course of one of his frighteningly long monologues, "I like to understand things because then I can enjoy them. I think knowledge should intensify our pleasures. That is its aim and object, so far as I am concerned." Man is by nature curious, and he is most curious about himself and his surroundings. Knowledge, even when not applied in a utilitarian manner, adds to our pleasure. If on a walk one can identify trees or birds or geological formations, his pleasure is increased.

Knowledge, then, gives pleasure. Any knowledge? Well, hardly. Consider the kind of unrelated scraps of information one gets on a quiz program: the diameter of the moon is 2,160 miles; St. Catherine of Siena was born in 1347; the second largest city in Arizona is Tucson; the tallest Maya stela is thirty-five feet high. All are facts of importance in their own contexts, but without intellectual stimulus if presented as isolated statements worth remembering. If we look at Maya civilization as a jumble of odds and ends, a sort of poking around the back of an antique shop, we shall get little real satisfaction; we must look at the civilization as a whole to find out why it got where it did, and we should stroll around the gallery of civilizations and take a look at the other pictures.

[In 1926 Thomas Gann, some of whose experiences in the Central American bush have been presented earlier in this book, told the Carnegie Institution archaeologists at Chichén Itzá of ruins, stelae, and the remains of an ancient Maya *sacbe* or stone road that he had visited in the Quintana Roo forests. A. V. Kidder, Eric Thompson, and two friends set out to explore this interesting city of Cobá further, taking the railroad to its eastern terminus at Valladolid, where they hired mules for the long hard journey ahead.]

We were up at daybreak, but there are always delays in getting a pack train off. Three hours' riding along a wide rock-strewn road brought us to Kanxoc, a large, attractive Maya village with a huge ruined church, relic of the Franciscans, beside the grass-covered plaza on which cows and horses grazed. Beyond, we followed a track which threaded its way through forest interrupted by occasional milpas, the Maya maize fields.

Early in the year the Maya makes a clearing of about ten acres with axe and machete. Burning off the felled trees as soon as they are dry, he plants the seeds in holes dug with a pointed pole in the ash-covered soil just before the rains in early May. Milpas are allowed to revert to forest usually after two seasons (the Maya say that they get too weed-ridden after that to work again and the yield also drops), and a new section of forest is cleared. This primitive system of agriculture derives from ancient times, but it is suited to local conditions, for the soil is thin—often in small pockets in the living limestone rock, which is either exposed or has only a very shallow covering; plows could not be used. We passed these milpas in March when the land had been cleared but not yet burned. Elsewhere were abandoned weed-choked milpas and other parts where the young trees were beginning to dominate the secondary growth.

After riding eight hours we reached Bolmai, a settlement of two families. Here we recruited as guide an elderly Maya, Tomás Cupul, on his claiming in very broken Spanish to know well all the forest region around Coba, where he used to hunt. With his striking figure and pure Maya features, he looked as though he might have stepped out of a sculptured column at Chichen. He might, in any case, have been a descendant of one of those carved figures, for the Cupuls were the ruling family around Valladolid at the coming of the Spaniards. His clothes reminded me of St. John the Baptist rather than the ancient Maya, for he wore nothing but sandals, short white drawers rolled to his knees, and a sack "girt about his loins"; when he drew out some tortillas, I was almost shocked they weren't locusts and honey. Like many elderly Maya, he had about a dozen long hairs on his chin, for the American Indian is singularly lacking in body hair. In Maya art, gods or personages sometimes have a sort of sparse goatee, which probably represents a form of flattery; old Cupul's dozen hairs were above hirsute average.

About two miles beyond Bolmai—from there to the east coast there isn't a permanent settlement—we struck the great Maya stone road which runs west from Coba to Yaxuna, a small site about twelve miles southwest of Chichen.

This great monument to Maya engineering is thirty feet across, wider than most English roads. There isn't a curve and only four changes of direction (none of more than nine degrees) in the whole of its sixty-three miles, a veritable speed fan's paradise, but the jaguars which moved along it had four legs, not four wheels. It averages about three feet above ground level, but across swamps it may be up to eight feet high.

The bed is of great boulders over which is a layer of rocks and stones set in mortar with a surface, now disintegrated, of the rotted limestone called *sascab* or of stucco such as the Maya used for floors. Its construction must have called for an army of laborers, yet it served no utilitarian purpose.

The Maya had no wheeled vehicles and no beasts of burden, so the road was used only by travelers on foot or in litters, and for them a road six feet wide would have been ample; it must have been for ceremonial pageantry. A procession of priests decked in jade and all their splendor with their panaches of quetzal feathers waving in the breeze would have presented an overwhelmingly impressive spectacle of barbaric pomp. Strange that the Maya could achieve such a feat of engineering yet fail to discover the true arch, balance scales, or the wheel (they knew of them for toys but never grasped their application).

To us, among the first dozen white men ever to ride along it, the road presented a very different appearance. A heavy growth of forest (more rain-fall brings higher forest in the eastern part of Yucatan) covered the surface. Decaying tree trunks across the scarcely perceptible path made by modern Maya hunters introduced an air of melancholic decay which the surrounding dull-hued tree trunks, dingy ferns, and scant undergrowth did nothing to dispel. In many places generations of falling trees had churned the surface with their torn-out roots, so that it was more like the dry bed of a stream.

Sometimes we walked, mule halter in hand, for riding at a mule's pace is tedious. Much conversation is impossible because a rider can't turn his head for long to speak to the rider behind him for fear of a crack on the skull from the low branch of a tree, and a good deal of effort and noise goes in trying to keep mules up to the standard three and one-half miles an hour, for naturally with pack animals one can't proceed at trot or canter!

Having no lanterns, we halted as night fell at the edge of a swamp about two miles short of Coba. We had been twelve hours in the saddle. We teth-ered the mules, made a fire for supper, and swung our hammocks from pairs of correctly spaced trees. It rained in the night, adding to the discomfort inevitable when one makes camp after dark.

We were up at dawn, and another mile brought us to a large thatched hut, standing at the edge of Lake Coba, which had formerly been used as a chicle store. From it there was an enchanting view of sparkling blue water set amid the varying hues of the encircling forest. At the east end, the tree-clad bulk of the highest pyramid rose high above lower swells and humps of vegeta-tion above lesser pyramids and mounds; at the west end, a brighter green and a low horizon marked the swampy area by which we had camped.

We set forth for the ruins, Tomás Cupul leading the way. We passed many scattered mounds and plunged into a stand of primeval trees with immense buttress—roots which flowed out along the surface in search of soil in imita-tion of the sinuous lengths of immense boaconstrictors. Crossing a narrow neck of land, we reached another lake, about half a mile long, called Ma-canxoc, on the north shore of which the pyramids and courts of Coba were massed.

We clambered over collapsed buildings from which grew huge trees, made our way across courts filled with fallen rubble and more trees, peered into rooms with vaults which still stood, and, grabbing trees and bushes, climbed up the fallen remains of a stairway to the little one-room temple at the top of the highest pyramid. The roof had gone, but there was red stucco still on the walls, as well as a plain stela set against the back wall. The thick-ness of the walls suggested that many of the stones scattered far below us had once formed a roof-comb. This type of ornament, often set on the roofs of Maya buildings, is like a high wall decorated with niches and masks and figures in stucco. It served no structural purpose, but it added grandeur and a fine field for display of symbols of the chief deities. With such a roof-comb or roof crest the building would have risen to about 140 feet above the lake.

In masonry and in its compact plan of pyramids and multiple-roomed buildings grouped around courts, set at different levels but joined by broad stairways, Coba was quite different from Chichen and other cities of Yucatan; instead, it closely resembled cities of the Classic period in the Peten district of Guatemala far to the south. Indeed, Coba was a typical ceremonial center of the Central area, as the dated stelae subsequently confirmed.

"Ceremonial center" is a better term than "city," because it is clear these places were never urban centers but places to which the people whose homes were scattered over the surrounding country came for important religious festivals, for markets, and to attend courts of justice and to be kept informed of details of local administration. Except on such occasions, the great centers lay empty, unless, perhaps, for a small staff for upkeep. This picture derived from archaeological sources is confirmed by the "empty towns" of some Maya groups of the present day in Chiapas and the highlands of Guatemala. These towns are almost without permanent inhabitants, but on Sundays and other

Giant tree roots penetrate ancient Maya vault, Cobá, Quintana Roo

From J. E. Thompson, H. E. D. Pollock, and J. Charlot, *A Preliminary Study of the Ruins of Cobá, Quintana Roo, Mexico.*

days of civil and ecclesiastical importance the people converge on them from their outlying rural settlements, families of wealth moving into their town houses for the occasion.

The ceremonial center was the symbol of the small group of priests and nobles (the two were often indistinguishable) who ruled the peasants, directing almost every detail of their lives. This was a small theocracy which had its part to play: the peasants produced the food and supplied the labor and materials to build all those temples, pyramids, and palaces, enlarging and extending them at such frequent intervals; the priests, with their divine knowledge, were the intermediaries between the peasant and his gods of the soil. As long as they did this, the peasants seem to have been content to shoulder the physical burdens—and what burdens they must have been. But there came a time when the theocracy appears to have been seduced by new ideas and paid more attention to new-fangled deities than to the old gods of rain and the crops, beloved by the peasants. The result, apparently, was a revolt by the peasants and the massacre or perhaps expulsion of the small ruling class.

A rough comparison might be made with those old ecclesiastical principalities, such as Salzburg, with the archbishop ruler living in pomp surrounded by his cathedral, administrative buildings, nunneries and friaries, on which were lavished all the art of the age, or, from the religious and ec-

Structure 33, Cobá

From J. E. Thompson, H. E. D. Pollock, and J. Charlot, *A Preliminary Study of the Ruins of Cobá, Quintana Roo, Mexico.*

clesiastical sides alone, one can think in terms of an English cathedral close. Perhaps we shall not be too far from reality in regarding the Classic period, *mutatis mutandis* as a sort of exotic background for Maya cousins of Archdeacon Grantly, Mrs. Proudie, and Mr. Harding, not in top hats but in quetzal plumes, and sipping not the 1820 port—"it's too good for a bishop, unless one of the right sort"—but the native *balche.* Indeed, every important Maya ceremonial center might be viewed as a sort of tropical Barchester, and on a mural at Bonampak there is a splendid portrait of Mrs. Proudie watching the bishop at the seat of judgment. Only as long as the right sort were in control did the Classic period endure.

In the course of our explorations we came across smallish fragments of two stone rings, like those in the ball court at Chichen. They lay in debris between two parallel mounds with sloping sides. We paid little attention to these odd-shaped stones, for at that time it was not known that the Maya also used ball courts with sloping sides, and in any case the ball game was believed to have been introduced by the Mexicans at a much later date than the obvious occupation of Coba. It was not until three years later when Blom identified a series of ball courts in various cities of the Classic period that the Coba court was recognized as such, a nice lesson in how preconceived notions can blind one to obvious facts.

At the edge of Lake Maconxoc we came upon a small stone dock of which Gann had spoken. Here canoes for fishing or for use in sacrificial ceremonies in the lake must have been moored.

In 1930 when my wife and I and Harry Pollock were at Coba, we found that three Maya roads had actually been built across parts of Lake Maconxoc, presumably to avoid necessary changes of direction had they skirted the water. For most of their lengths the roads or causeways are now under water, but one can pick them up at each shore and follow their submerged courses by reeds growing on them. One pictures processions along the causeway and canoes converging for some sacrifice in the lake, such as we know the Aztec performed. Dredging the lake would quite likely bring up treasure, as at Chichen. Moreover, such finds would probably be largely of the Classic period, a great haul, for at present we have practically no perishables of that early date.

From the top of the highest pyramid two tree-clad masses were visible a mile to the northeast. They were obviously artificial, and one was enormous. We asked Cupul to take us there, but he was full of excuses, saying that the intervening growth was impenetrable; we wondered whether there were traces there of modern pagan rites he didn't wish us to see (we had come across evidence of offerings to the stelae in Coba itself).

Eventually he agreed to try, and on his return we set out. Most of the way led through an abandoned milpa of *chicleros* (chewing-gum gatherers), a low dense mass of two years' growth, and Tomás had not lied. As the hard work of clearing largely fell on him and he wasn't in the slightest bit interested in ruins, I can't say that I blamed him for his reluctance.

On the far side, Tomás led us to a pyramid almost as high as the tallest at Coba, up which we scrambled. On top was a small temple with roof intact and three niches in the façade. One was destroyed, but we gasped at the figures in the others, for each held a semi-human semi-insect being head downwards as though diving through space. Similar diving gods were known from Tulum and other cities of the east coast (later, an example was noted at Sayil in western Yucatan), but they were believed to be very late. Coba had given us two jolts—a type of masonry and architecture and a style of decoration, neither of which had a right to be there according to current ideas. There was, too, the delayed jolt of the ball court.

There were weathered stelae at the base of the pyramid and, less than two hundred yards away, although we did not then know it, was the termination of the great road along which we had wearily urged our mules and which we had left when we had camped.

Nearby we found the enormous mass we had seen from Coba. It was a colossal platform 120 yards long, 140 yards deep, and about 55 feet high, but on the flat summit there were only a few low walls, foundations for small houses of perishable materials. A great many stone metates for grinding maize were in and around them, confirming our conclusion that these were the houses of peasant families. Presumably the Maya had intended to use this as a foundation for a series of courts and temples even more impressive than the main group at Coba, but the project was never completed. The site was abandoned, and then, one supposes, peasant families moved in.

Elated with our discoveries, we returned to camp for a bathe in Lake Coba before supper. Two months later we found that we were not the discoverers of the Temple of the Diving God; Teobert Maler, an old-time explorer of Maya ruins, had visited Coba and photographed the diving figures thirty-three years before our "discovery." We christened the group "Nohoch Mul," "great mound," the term old Tomás Cupul had applied to that "ill-weaved ambition."

On a subsequent visit we found a mass of mounds and courts, including a second ball court in the area between Nohoch Mul and the start of the great Yaxuna road. Three-quarters of a mile west of that point Road 3 crosses it at right angles. The intersection takes the form of a small octagonal court in the middle of which stands a little pyramid with the remains of a temple on top. The whole was very much like a modern traffic circle. However, instead of easing traffic jams, the Maya arrangement may have had the opposite effect, for litters were probably parked there while their occupants ascended to the little temple to pray and make some offering for a safe journey. There were stairways on all sides of the pyramid, so one may imagine the litter bearers making the half-circle to await their masters on the far side.

We started back for Valladolid, but not in litters; the mules, heading for home, made slightly better time. Soon after nightfall we stopped at Kanxoc for a meal, eating in the road by the flame of a candle which burned without flickering in the windless night. In twos and threes the Maya men gathered round to watch our meal. White cotton vests and drawers caught the candlelight, but the owners were invisible against the curtain of night. With fifty pairs of eyes on us as we ate bread and sardines from the tiny local store, conversation in Maya passed from side to side of the ring. Occasional Spanish words with accentuation shifted to Maya usage indicated that our forks, something the Maya did not use, were one topic of conversation. Three hours' riding through the night brought us to Valladolid. Never did sultan salute his wife so eagerly as we did the Sultana of the East!

Two months later I was again on my way to Coba. Carmen Chai, one of our masons at Chichen, who had once lived near Bolmai, told me of "stone men" he had seen when hunting near Coba. From his account it was clear that the stone men were stelae with carved human figures on them and that they were in a part of Coba we had not visited. As Morley would have cheerfully crossed the peninsula of Yucatan to record a legible hieroglyphic inscription, he readily gave me permission to return to Coba with Carmen. Jean Charlot, my roommate came, too, to make drawings of the "stone men."

The fourth member of the party was Eugenio Mai, a most *simpático* Maya who had worked with me on the Caracol. He was a native of Valladolid, but had moved a few years before to Piste, where he had lodged with a widow and her young, but decidedly plain, daughter. According to Piste gossip he owed his landlady a few pesos for laundry and, unable to pay, offered to marry the daughter if the debt was canceled. The old lady jumped at the bargain, and Eugenio's laundry bill was remitted on his becoming her son-in-law. Eugenio insists the story isn't true, and in any case domestic efficiency means more to a Maya swain than good looks.

Carmen was that rare bird among the Maya, a bachelor of mature years, undoubtedly because he had lived most of his life in Merida. In a Maya village a wife is essential to make tortillas, cook meals, and draw water, whereas in Merida one can buy cooked meals and water isn't only in a cenote. Even Carmen had found bachelordom impossible when he had lived at remote Chulutan, for there he had had a temporary wife. Nevertheless that spell of illegal uxoriousness hadn't changed him, for he was a regular old maid, withal a nice one, the only Maya old gossip I have known.

Following the same route as before, we reached Chulutan late in the afternoon and stayed the night there in an empty hut in deference to Carmen's many pleas. Perhaps that temporary wife of days gone by still lived there, but, if so, Carmen didn't confide in me. Chulutan was a small collection of huts round the ruins of an old hacienda building destroyed some eighty years earlier in the war of the castes when the Maya almost drove the Yucatecans into the sea. We were up soon after 3:00 A.M., but delays in saddling the mules and a final disappearance of Carmen, perhaps for sad farewells, held us up, so that we didn't get off till 5:30. It had rained in the night and rained on and off all day. We were wet through the whole time, every tree letting fall a shower as we brushed against it.

Next morning, with Carmen and old Cupul, whom we had picked up at Bolmai, we skirted the main ruins to reach yet another Maya road, this one sixty feet wide. After leading us along for a mile or so, Carmen warned us we were close to the stone men. Some pyramids came into view and then a scene which thirty-five years later is still vivid in my memory. There amid the trees a large shaft of grayed limestone stood on a small artificial platform. We hurried forward to examine it more carefully. The principal personage, with elaborate headdress profusely decorated with quetzal feathers, had his head in profile, but his body faced to the front. His feet, turned out at a wide angle, were planted on two hapless captives, who crouched beneath his weight, their wrists securely bound. Two other kneeling figures balanced the composition. The back of the stela was carved with a rather similar scene.

I scarcely had eyes for the sculptured figures; they were focused on the hieroglyphic texts, which were unusually long but had suffered much from exposure to the air for over a millennium. It was tantalizing. I ran from back to front of the monument like a dog with two tails, as I recognized on each side badly weathered but undoubted examples of the Initial Series introducing glyph which announces that a date in the involved system of the Maya Initial Series is to follow. Next I made out the Maya glyph for four hundred years and the number nine in front of it. So there were going to be dates of the Classic period, of which only three other examples were then known in the whole of Yucatan. Then I got the glyph for the twenty-year period with the number twelve in front of it. In all the pictures of Initial Series I had read there had never been such a weathered, illegible lump of limestone as this!

Carmen led us to the other stone men. There were eight of them, and several had dates late in the first half of the Classic period. All were a bit weathered, but of the readings there could be no doubt. The style of the carved figures agreed with the dates. Old Carmen had certainly done us proud; a bit of an old maid, perhaps, but, bless him, he had more than delivered the goods. I don't remember whether I gave him an *abrazo*, the embrace with back patting so loved by the Yucatecans; I ought to have. We called the little group Macanxoc as it was close to the lake of that name.

That evening, sitting round the fire in our hut by Lake Coba, we learned from Carmen of another site south of Coba. This was called Kukican by the hunters, he told us, because of a large stucco snake on the façade of the building.

Next morning with Carmen and Tomás we visited them.

Beyond the neck of land separating the two lakes, Carmen brought us to yet another Maya road—he seemed to know them as a taxi driver knows the streets of London. An hour's walk along this with stops to open the trail brought us to an intersection with yet another road, and a ruined building. Its location reminded me of a toll house, but it probably served as a halting point for religious rites; it was too near Coba to be a resting place, such as the *tambos* along Incan roads. Since much of the way was through dense secondary bush (a forest fire had swept the area some years before) where the trail had to be opened with machetes, it took three hours to cover the five miles to Kukican.

Kukican proved to be a small group with two large standing buildings. One had seven rooms, five of which, one behind the other, were enclosed by transverse rooms at each end to form a rectangular block. The front room, with no less than seven doorways, was eighty feet long, and the capstones were sixteen feet above floor level, a most noble building for such a small site. On the exterior were the battered remains of the stucco snake. The second building was of three stories. Usually, the Maya, on adding a fresh story, filled the lower rooms with rubble to carry its weight, but they had not done so here. Indeed, the walls of the third-story rooms rested on the capstones of the second-story vaults, where the support was weakest! Yet this bold experiment had succeeded, for a vault of the second story still stood.

On our return we found a narrow passage with corbeled vault which passed beneath the road, at that point over ten feet high. Probably there was a village nearby, and as the sides of the road were perpendicular, this underpass was a necessity.

Back at Chichen again, I was unable to persuade Morley that I had read the texts correctly; only his own eyes would convince him that such early dates could exist there. Then his enthusiasm flared up, and he proposed that we set out again for Coba that very afternoon. Another two days on muleback through that monotonous forest didn't appeal to me at that moment—I was full of ticks and my backside was tender from contact with what passes for a saddle in the remoter parts of Yucatan. We postponed the trip for a few days.

The mule ride that time was shortened. Morley persuaded the owner of a Model-T Ford in Valladolid to drive us to Kanxoc. The nine miles along that glacier bed of a road took just on two hours; we bounced from side to side and banged our heads against the roof. The driver came out best, for, after we had mounted our mules, he did a bonanza business driving the modern-minded element around Kanxoc plaza at five to ten centavos a ride, for ours was the first car ever to reach the village.

Next morning, on seeing Coba, Vay turned to me and said: "Eric, this can't be a Yucatan site. We must have traveled south for ten days and landed up in the middle of the Peten. I don't doubt your readings of those early dates any longer. They fit right in with this architecture and assemblage and even with the vegetation."

Two days later Vay returned to Chichen; Carmen, Eugenio, and I stayed at Coba a few more days. In later years he used to claim that I had forced his return by the tea I served. I was cook and, as a good Englishman, served tea three times a day. The water could not be drunk untreated, so it was a choice between what I regarded as rather weak tea and chlorinated water. Vay complained that the spoon wouldn't sink in that infernal Limey brew and his stomach lining was being corroded rapidly with tannic acid. Finally, he claimed to have found a pair of my dirty, sweat-impregnated socks in the tea can, charging that I had put them there to add even more strength and flavor to the deadly potion. I never heard the end of that incident.

Vay had a slide made of a sketch map I had prepared of the Macanxoc group. Unfortunately, a couple of fly specks got on it and were reproduced on the slide, which he used in a lecture tour of the season's finds. To my horror, attending his lecture in Chicago, almost the last of a series he had given from one end of the U.S.A. to the other, I noticed that one fly speck had been labeled "Stela 1"; the other, "Stela 4." Vay touched the first with his pointer, and with a dramatic pause, said, "At this spot was found the magnificent stela you have just seen." Moving his pointer to the second, he added, "Here was found the companion monument." The first fly speck was precious close to the location of our temporary latrine.

In 1930 I returned to Coba, on my honeymoon. Coba was a pretty tough spot for a honeymoon, so we delayed our departure until about three weeks after our marriage in Chicago, crossing to Progreso from New Orleans in that old tub, the *Munplace*.

In Merida I had arranged to meet Carmen Chai in the bar of the Gran Hotel—the patched-up romance with the *querida* which I suspected might have resulted from our stop at Chulutan four years before had not eventuated or had not endured, for Carmen was back in bachelor's quarters in Merida. I took my bride to the barroom to await him. I had failed to realize that women never went there, nor did I notice that I had seated her bang in front of the urinal, one of those Latin affairs not overcloaked with modesty. While we were awaiting Carmen, a rather seedy-looking Yucatecan, somewhat the worse for drink, steered a slightly weaving course in its direction. Catching sight of my wife, he stopped, raised his straw hat, bowed to her, and then entered the convenience. On coming out—his head and legs had not been out of sight—he again bowed and raised his hat to my wife. It was for her a strange first instance of the courteous ways of Yucatan which I had previously praised to her.

Morley was also in Merida, and we dined together that night to the music of a couple of troubadours complete with guitars who were entertaining a group at the next table. I rather enjoy their music, but there is a lot to be said for Morley's view: "old blisterers who wail and screech like cats for hours on end about *traición, almas, y amor* [lover's deception, souls, and love]."

After a few days at Chichen, we left for Coba with Harry Pollock, of the

Carnegie staff, Eugenio Mai, and Carmen. We again slept the night at Chulutan, in the hut of Carmen's brother. Carmen and two Maya boys had gone ahead to erect palm-leaf shelters, one for my wife and me, the other for Harry Pollock, the hut by the lake having collapsed.

We reached Coba next evening. It had been a long, hard ride for Florence, and she was ready for her hammock. Alas, the marching army ants, making a sweep of the Maya court, began to stream into our shelter, and we had to evacuate it. It was a fascinating sight to watch them pour through in thick, endless columns, and it was half an hour before they had passed through, sending detachments swarming up the posts in a fruitless search of the new palm thatch. Marching army ants well deserve their name. They will encircle an area, such as a hollow in the ground, and close in on the entrapped insects. First two or three ants will cling to some luckless beetle, stinging as hard as they can. As its pace slows, more swarm on its body till life is extinct. Yet the army is welcome if one is in an old hut, for it will quickly rid the place of scorpions and tarantulas. I have seen scorpions thus dislodged fall from the roof with a few ants on them amidst battalions of ants waiting for just that to happen.

Our camp was in a court in the ruins with trees towering high above us, which kept it reasonably cool but sheltered innumerable mosquitoes. Harry and I went off to work each morning, leaving Florence to cook our meal. She is an excellent cook, but the equipment wasn't all it might have been. We had brought a side of bacon thickly protected with tar, to cut through which she had the choice of a penknife or a two-foot-long machete; for cooking she had tin lard pails so thin that anything not completely liquid inevitably burned. Half a morning's struggle cutting bacon went down our throats in two or three minutes. Still, the marriage hasn't yet gone on the rocks.

The days passed rapidly in mapping the various groups, searches for new stelae, and tracing the course of each *zache*, "artificial road," as the Maya call the old roads. All together we located fifteen of these in addition to the great Yaxuna-Coba road. No such elaborate network exists anywhere else in the whole New World except in Inca territory.

Shortly before we left, Florence and I climbed the great pyramid at Coba to watch the dawn, which for me has always had a greater attraction than sunsets. Down below in the forest it was still dark, but up where we were, it was getting light. The view to the east as we waited for the sun was a strange one. All kinds of depressions and bumps in the surface of treetops, not visible in full day, showed up clearly. They corresponded to the courts and mounds of the outlying groups. It was like noting how all the little bumps on a road show up in the headlights of a car. Mist hung in the depressions, further accentuating the unevenness of the treetop roof. Essentially it was the view the high priest of Coba must have seen when he watched for the rising of the morning star and then the sun, save that then the pyramids and courts in the foreground would have been plainly visible in their sharp geometric shapes, not, as we saw them, as gentle swells in the forest. I have sometimes thought that one reason for the great height of Maya pyramids was to get above the mist which often must have hindered astronomical observations at a lower level.

Gradually the eastern sky took to itself a faint red glow. Then a single ray, like a searchlight beam, shot above the low-banked cloud on the horizon, and Lord Kin, the sun, had once more emerged from the land of the dead for his march across the sky.

It was the start of a propitious day. On the way to work we disturbed two ocellated turkeys, which flew off with a great whirring of wings, and a covey of chachalacas (*ortulis vetula*) filled the forest with their shrill calls. The men discovered two new stelae, one of which had fallen face down. When we managed to turn it, we found the sculptured figure in almost perfect condition. Unfortunately, the top left corner, which would have given the date of the dedication, was missing.

Soon we were jogging along the Yaxuna causeway again—for me the eighth time. We stopped at Chulutan for the night, but the many fleas and a fair number of mosquitoes decided us to get up about 1:30 and continue our journey, as the moon was full. Our muleteer tied a hurricane lamp on the first and last mules of the train, and with our ship's lights for the darker patches of forest which the moon did not penetrate, we rode sleepily on.

Valladolid was sizzling in midday heat. We caught the afternoon train by the skin of our teeth and with a couple of bottles of rum to celebrate our return to civilization. Both Carmen and Eugenio, who had had a few on their own in Valladolid, were pretty happy by the time the train reached Dzitas. That evening we went to a *jarana* dance in Piste, but we weren't sorry to leave early after a day which had started at 1:30 A.M. Next morning Vay told us that after we left the dance he had run into Carmen as drunk as an owl. Vay asked him how much he had had. "*Pues, solamente una copita, Do'tor*," "Only a liqueur-glass full, doctor." It must have replenished itself as miraculously as the widow's cruse of oil.

British Honduras seemed to be a magnet for "Explorers," who, after following well-beaten tracks and keeping an ear open in the bars of United Fruit Company steamers, returned to the States or England with tales of astounding adventures. I particularly enjoyed one story of a fierce encounter with an enraged iguana; it had me on tenterhooks, for an enraged iguana equals in the savagery of his onslaught the angriest rabbit. That same explorer had been at Lubaantun, the same site in southern British Honduras for which I was headed that following year. Later, having exhausted the credulity of England, he appeared on one of the national broadcasting systems in the United States. Each Sunday evening he was on the air, introduced amid the throbbing of African tomtoms as "the greatest living authority on ancient Central America."

In the course of his talks he described his life at Lubaantun, where he sat night after night repelling the attacks of prowling jaguars, which invariably bit the dust, and where the climate was so deadly that no white man could survive for more than three weeks. As I had been there on and off for months, I began to rummage around the family tree for my ancestry. He had penetrated the interior of British Honduras to discover this immense mysterious city, which in fact had been known to archaeologists and European residents since the last century and had been described in print many years before. Worst of all from an archaeological point of view, he had workers build a wall on one of the terraces to make a more impressive photograph. Later he and a collaborator wrote a book, *Land of Wonder and Fear;* to me the wonder was how he could write such nonsense and the fear how much taller the next yarn would be.

Another "Explorer" described in a well-known American magazine a terrible encounter with the "fierce" Maya of the east coast of Yucatan and how he survived the showers of deadly arrows they shot at him. Well he might, for no Maya in Yucatan has used a bow and arrow for well over a century. Another gentleman, English by birth but Californian by adoption, burst into print and on to the lecture platform with stories of having explored the impenetrable jungle of Yucatan alone save for two native guides. It turned out that he had visited Uxmal and the other sites in the vicinity, and by the time he came to explore them the roads were considerably better than when we *drove* along them. Yet another, who had visited my camp with a string of mules long enough to cross the Gobi Desert, bravely flew the flag of the Explorers Club of New York a mile from El Cayo, capital of the district of that name in western British Honduras. I could continue with such tales, but enough is enough. The shorter the visit, the taller the yarn.

SIXTEEN

Addison Burbank 1939

Artist in Paradise

[We have read a conservative New York lawyer's shocked reaction to the partial nudity and what he regarded as general carelessness of dress he encountered more than a century ago in Guatemala. We have noted the quite different reaction of a twentieth-century journalist, Phillips Russell. Now let us hear from a professional artist, Addison Burbank, who gave a charming account of his travels with paintbox and brushes through Guatemala in the 1930's. Burbank found his ideal of the tropics, and of the beauty of its women, fulfilled in San Sebastián on the Pacific slopes of Guatemala.]

Don Conrado offered me a horse to ride during my stay, but I preferred, despite the heat of *tierra caliente,* to follow my usual practice of scouting the country on foot. It is the only way to discover pictorial material.

The rancherias of the *colonos* were scattered through the hills and were exactly like any Guatemalan Indian villages. There was no formal settlement like the tidy concentrated camp on Mocá. Some of these tiny villages, set in tropical vegetation, were exceedingly picturesque, but I found that whenever I visited them a second time with the intention of making a painting, the women would call their children and shut themselves up in their ranchos.

When I asked Don Conrado about it, he said it was only natural that the women should be frightened by the appearance of a strange white man amongst them when all of their men were absent in the fields.

After this I never tarried in the villages, but wandered off into the hills

The Burbank selections are, in the order quoted below, from Addison Burbank, *Guatemala Profile* (New York: Coward-McCann, 1939), pp. 131–35, 145–51. Copyright 1939 by Addison Burbank. Reprinted with permission of Coward-McCann, Inc.

where the jungle grew densely and the trails were sometimes dangerously confused. More than once I thought I had lost my way, and I don't mind admitting that I was scared. There is always, in the tropical forest, a suggestion of suffocation, mystery, and evil, arising from the suspicion of venomous reptiles, inimical insects, and poisonous plants. Before long indeed Don Conrado was treating me for *matasamoras*, a fungus growth that eats away the flesh between the toes, and *chichicaste*, a poisonous nettle, from which my hands had become so swollen and stiff that I was obliged to bind my brushes to my fingers with strips of cloth.

Wherever I went, I had the feeling of being watched, spied upon, and occasionally a wild halloo would echo through the hills. If I met an Indian woman walking alone, she invariably took to her heels.

One morning I chanced upon five Indian women and three children bathing and laundering clothes in a little stream. One of the women, who was stripped to the waist, was young and tall and had such a beautiful face and form that I thought the Tlascalan princess who enchanted Alvarado must surely have been such another. Her eyes, which were slightly elongated, and her hair, which fell in rippling blue-black waves below her sleek thighs, were of exceptional beauty. Her skin, though browned by the sun, glowed with a

Indian woman milling corn, San Sebastián, Retalhuleu, Guatemala

Reprinted by permission of Coward-McCann, Inc. from *Guatemala Profile* by Addison Burbank. Copyright 1939 by Addison Burbank.

SAN SEBASTIÁN - RBU

warm sheen, and she had the usual fine Indian teeth, and beautifully shaped breasts, arms, and hands. She was, at the moment, shampooing the head of a small naked boy.

Wanting to paint her at this task, and remembering the complacency of the bathers of San Cristóbal, I stepped over to the bank and sat down upon a stone. Nothing happened, so after allowing a little time for them to get used to my presence, I opened my paintbox, but the instant I did so the women dropped their wash, grabbed their children and fled, as if in abject terror of their lives.

My efforts to recall them being ineffectual, I cut off through some fields with the intention of showing them that I was going away and leaving them free to return to their tasks. When I last saw them, however, they were still standing in the road with an air of indecision, as if suspecting a ruse.

I found myself in a wild valley, and in the absence of any paths, I followed the banks of a creek that ran through it. Every now and again a hidden Indian would give a bloodcurdling halloo from the bush that would be picked up and repeated the whole length of the ravine. Although I could see no one, I was under constant surveillance, and I was aware that my movements must seem strange, like those of a fugitive. Not caring to give this idea, I cut back up the steep side of the ravine, through brushwood that tore my hands and clothes, in the direction of the road. But upon reaching the road whom should I meet but my five women from the stream. They were jabbering excitedly, but the instant they saw me they stopped dead in their tracks, speechless, as if confronted by a *duende*.

I was standing on the high bank above the road, but they held back as though I were blocking the way. Greatly puzzled, I smiled reassuringly (I hoped) and told them that the road was theirs. After a low-voiced consultation, the oldest, a hag with long flat breasts drooping from her bony chest crossed herself and stalked stiffly by, head held rigid, repeating aloud some strange Indian litany or incantation against evil. One by one, as I watched in amazement, the others did the same, the last to pass being the good-looking young mother with the small boy.

When they were all reassembled a short distance up the road, they turned on me with a shrill torrent of purple epithets, their eyes flashing angrily. The old hag stooped and picked up a stone and made a threatening gesture with it, while the one whom I thought had the beauty and bearing of a Tlascalan princess, very unbecomingly thwacked her shapely buttocks and cried, "Mire, señor! bese mi cula." Everything I said to calm them infuriated them the more.

Their angry cries brought two Indian men armed with murderous-looking machetes to the scene. The women besought them to drive me away, and the bolder of the two climbed the embankment to where I stood. I met him halfway, told him what had occurred, and asked him to talk reasonably with the women. He stood studying me in indecision. It occurred to me that he might be the husband of the beauty, and that perhaps he thought I had meant to attack her. Jealousy is the one emotion an Indian is apt to give way to. Anything, I realized, might happen.

By this time a great many Indians had gathered on the opposite ridge of the narrow ravine, and were shouting and hallooing. The amusing episode by the river had grown into a grave situation. Here I stood unarmed facing a man very adept at using the machete he held ready to swing, while five irate women were urging him to action, and across the ravine, an excited group was raising a kind of hue and cry. A good deal depended upon my next move.

I looked about and saw near by the ruins of the former *casa grande,* where I had come with Don Conrado on the evening of my first day in *tierra caliente,* and had gazed in awe at the smoldering Santa Maria and her bloody volcanic whelp. Now, in the virginal morning light, I could see the burning boulders spewed over the rim of Santiagito, rolling down the charred slopes, and trailing clouds of dust, like steaming tears coursing down the cheeks of the eternally damned.

I turned to the Indian with the machete and pointed to my paintbox. He took a step backward and gripped the handle of his swordlike tool.

"Oiga," I said. "I am an artist-painter. I wanted to paint the women in the stream, but they did not understand and ran away. Tell them to go back to their work and not to be afraid, for I am going to stay here and paint the volcano."

With this, I sauntered over to a small tree and sat down in its shade facing the blasted, fuming mountain. I left behind me a loud silence. Even the hallooing Indians over on the ridge became quiet. Opening my box, I began to paint. I thought the rumpus was over and became absorbed in my work. Then—whish! Something sped past my head and struck the trunk of the tree with a dull thud. The object rolled back toward me. It was a stone the size of a baseball.

Looking around, I saw the Indian women standing on the hillside above me. The good-looking one was out in front; undoubtedly it was she who had thrown the stone. I picked it up to put it in my paintbox; and the women, misinterpreting my action, took to their heels. But they went only as far as the road, from which blind position they continued to pelt me ineffectually while I painted.

At length the patter of missiles gave way to the clatter of horses' hooves, and Carl rode up on his white horse and drew rein. Leaning forward upon the pommel of his saddle and looking down at me with a quizzical smile, he said:

"I heard you were frightening the women."

"Does this look like it?" I asked, showing him the stone that had come nearest its mark. I told him briefly what had happened, and he became grave and summoned the women.

"Why did you stone my friend?" he asked them severely.

The old hag spoke up.

"*Por Dios, patrón,* he has the evil eye. He goes about looking and looking, and God only knows what is in that box he always carries. *Vaya!* we were afraid."

Carl chided them for their foolish fears, and showed them my painting. They stared at it and said that it was *muy chula, muy guapita.*

"See! There is nothing in the box but paints. Next time, *no tengan ustedes cuidado*—don't be afraid."

They looked in my box and not finding it filled with dead lizards and old chicken bones like a sorcerer's kit, burst into mirthless Indian laughter. Ha, ha, ha! Then they went off, gabbling like a flock of excited geese. Months later I was to meet again under strange circumstances the tall beauty who had so nearly brained me with a well-aimed stone, and on my account she was to receive a severe beating from her husband. But this is anticipating.

Carl dismounted and sat beside me, his little white horse standing behind him impatiently nuzzling him in the neck. When I finished my painting, he accompanied me home.

The Mezgers were disturbed over what had happened. Don Conrado said that he had heard that word was being passed among the Indians to watch

Indian woman and child, San Sebastián, Retalhuleu, Guatemala, 1934

Reprinted by permission of Coward-McCann, Inc. from *Guatemala Profile* by Addison Burbank. Copyright 1939 by Addison Burbank.

out for a tall white man who looked like a German and acted like a thief. He wanted me to take a boy with me when I went out again, but I declined this kind offer with thanks, thinking that I now understood the Indian mind somewhat better and should be able to take care of myself.

The true San Sebastián costume is simple but time-hallowed: a *corte* for the women, a loin cloth for the men—a costume perfectly adapted to the climate. But the law, in the name of respectability and with an eye to collecting fifty-centavo fines, requires the women to wear blouses and the men to put on pants.

As I passed from the plaza around the far corner of the schoolhouse, I stumbled upon some rock-sculptured monsters, and pausing to examine them, I saw that they were ancient Mayan idols. I asked a boy where they had come from, and he told me that they had been found in the debris of the old church after the earthquake had destroyed it. These old pagan gods, cast down by the priests but safely hidden in the church altar by the wily

Bathers, San Sebastián, Retalhuleu, Guatemala

Indians, seemed to smile mockingly at the newly rising columns of Christianity.

Wandering through the village, I came to a *plazuela* dominated by a pretty little church painted a bright blue. While I stood admiring, women and children passed, lightly carrying their water jars, baskets, and babies. Some had slipped one arm out of the hateful blouse, others wore it as a sort of bib covering only the breasts, while a few had discarded it altogether. They were the tallest Indian women I had seen, and superbly graceful. They walked with a slow, stately, free-limbed movement, and against the blue background of the church, they were like figures in a decorative frieze.

The farther I strayed from the center of town, the more the Spanish influence waned and the more Indian originality asserted itself. The Indian tropics—the tropics of my dreams—became a reality.

Cobbles gave way to hard-packed volcanic sand, and houses no longer fronted on the street, but hid behind hedgerows, observing no order in their placement beneath the giraffe-necked coco palms and scraggly limbed *achiotes*. Dusky figures moved in the spaces of shadow and color. Now and again I discerned a woman leaning against her loom, while others stood in doorways combing their lustrous hair, which never grows gray. Squatting on the ground, a woman was sewing a *suyucal*, a palm-leaf rain cape such as every traveling Indian carries during the wet season.

A woman's voice through the whitewashed slats of a rancho: "*Mire, señor!* what have you to sell?" My paintbox was a perpetual puzzle to the Indians.

Before long I came to an umbrageous rivulet. Citronella grass, elephant ears, spider lilies, wild plantains, *guarumos*—all the lush vegetation of the tropics—profusely covered either bank, while overhead the sky was hidden by leaning coco palms and the dense foliage of breadfruit trees. The humid air was heady with the cloying perfume of ever-decaying, ever-blooming tropical growth. From a plantain blossom, a jewel-like humming-bird hung by its beak, its little wings fluttering so furiously that they seemed to emit iridescent light. Gorgeous butterflies dipped and flashed above the water.

The brook tinkled over its bed of stones like a toy marimba as it dashed past my feet and rounded a leafy bend, whence came the tantalizing sound of splashing waters and merry feminine chatter and laughter. Stepping from stone to stone to the opposite bank, I saw, through a curtain of living greenery, that the waters widened into a pool in which many women and children were playing as well as attending to the more serious details of life. Remaining unseen, I stared in febrile delight.

As an artist, I love the flesh, but for years my mind has revolted from the brain-racked studio nude. The studio nude is a hot-bed hybrid which has nothing in common with the unconscious clean pagan nakedness of primitive countries. The nude belongs to the pagan world.

As I looked upon these bathers, clean-limbed as marble statues, but warm, glowing, alive, and all unaware of the external eye, I saw naked beauty as the ancient Greeks knew it, but as it has never been known to the Christian world.

A girl whose body had the early maturity of the tropics sat listlessly on a rock, long legs dangling, toes playing in the water, rhythmically running a small wooden comb through her luxuriant dark hair, coppered by the sun. In the lines of the legs, the curve of the back, the beauty-giving touch of the crooked fingers holding the comb, the light palpitating upon the fresh round bosoms, was momentarily caught the fugitive, unposed beauty that maddens the artist's mind. . . . A brown baby splashed in the shallows. . . . A woman whose shapely thighs were wrapped in her *corte* as tightly as the corn in its shard, stood in the water scrubbing clothes on a flat-topped stone, her soft bare shoulders rising and falling with rippling energy, her dangling breasts swaying gently. . . . A little girl stood with hanging arms, taut fingers, and screwed-up face while her mother shampooed her head. . . . One woman scrubbed the back of another, the scrubbed one leaning forward with an expression of sybaritic enjoyment. . . . Nearest to me, but turned away so that I saw her back and the rounded profile of her breast beneath her raised right arm, was a young woman sitting on her heels in the river and languidly pouring water over her shoulder with a gourd *guacal*. Her head was turned at an exquisite angle, and her freshly washed hair, streaked with shiny blue lights, was twisted carelessly about her head and tied in a knot over her low forehead. A rich terra cotta to her slim straight waist, below the line of her corte her bare thighs gleamed whitely. From the near-by bank a large handlike leaf reached out as if to touch the nape of her slender neck.

While I stood watching, I saw a woman come down the path to the river with the slipping grace of a panther. She carried a water jar on her shoulder, as the women often do when it is empty, not putting it on the head until full. Molded by knowing hands, it was a beautiful jar, such as civilization has forgotten how to form. . . . Further downstream, a woman appeared with a pig, which she had led into the water and proceeded to scrub as thoroughly as if it had been her own child.

I knew it would be impossible to paint this scene; if I declared my presence, these nymphs and dryads would either fly from or at me; if they remained, they would be silent, sullen, and unnatural. Every detail of the rapturous picture was indelibly engraved on my mind, but it would remain among the unpainted paintings in the portfolio of memory.

I wanted to slip away unobserved, but I had taken only a few steps when crack! went a twig, and like wild animals at a watering hole at the crack of the game-hunter's rifle, all the women and children darted for the bank and their *cortes* and blouses.

I hurried away.

Walking further in the direction of the outskirts, I came to a long street

like a swath cut by a giant's machete through the thick of the jungle. Here
and there a smoke-blackened grass roof peeped out of the greenery, but there
was no evidence that a wheel ever turned in this secluded byway. It was
Guatemala before Alvarado.

Not quite!

When I sat on a stone and began to sketch, I saw a woman coming down
the street leading a pig. That pig came from Spain. The chickens that
scratched dirt over my shoes were also of Spanish origin. The dog that sat
on his haunches in the shade scratching its fleas was another foreign note;
the fleas, no. The man who came to the door of his rancho had an American
machete gleaming in the crook of his arm. But these were the only outside
touches; the rest of the picture was pure pre-conquest. It was as far from the
center of San Sebastián as San Sebastián, Spain, is from Bali; for the un-
Puritanical costume makes the comparison with Bali inevitable.

The endless pictorial interest of this place could never grow monotonous
to Nordic eyes. It would be shocking to see a comely young woman,
unclothed but for a bright-striped cloth wrapped about her thighs, walking
down Fifth Avenue with a naked baby held to her milk-distended breast,
but here this natural and beautiful sight evokes no stares. A *virginita* follows
her mother, leaning far to one side to balance the weight of a baby almost
as big as herself, which she is carrying on her hip like a grown-up. The
baby's riding days will soon be over, and he may never know any other form
of locomotion than his own feet for the rest of his life.

There is no hurry and no idleness. Life has a slow, rhythmic, unwearied
tempo. But the tropics as a land of lotus-eaters is purely a white man's vision.

Women came up from the stream carrying baskets of sweet-smelling,
stone-scrubbed wash on their heads. They hung it in bright patches on the
bushes in the sun. From the nearest ranchos came the pat-pat-patting of
hands making *tortillas*. Into the street came a young girl with hips of an
hermaphroditic slimness, as graceful as a snake standing on its tail. Across
the street, a woman laid a *petate* on the hard sand and spread upon it some
red chili. As she stooped to her task, her fleshy polished back revealed a
thousand charming curves, and her breast, pressed between thigh and thorax,
swelled like a ripe peach about to burst its skin. Near-by sat a little boy
with a belly as big as a budget, eating dirt, as children will the world over.

As the sun assumed the vertical, the shadow curled up at the foot of the
trees and bushes, and every detail took on robust form and color. Of the
women who passed to and fro, few were ugly and even the ugly ones had
that unmatchable grace of carriage which comes from balancing objects
upon the head from childhood. For the most part, these women, with their
ebony hair, marvelous orange-tinted skin, roundness of arm, smallness of
foot, and daintiness of hand, had the splendor of exquisite health, which
made them seem beautiful. They are daughters of the sun, in whose bodies

are united voluptuousness and strength, rich lines, satiny gloss and transparent tone with firm, compact thighs, smooth limbs, and supple, muscular loins.

I worship beauty of form above all things. But beauty is born, not made; a flower that cannot be sown, a pure gift of heaven. The eternal Evelike beauty that does not outmode is never found in civilized cities, but in the far corners of the world where civilization has not yet spread.

Life in Guatemala is always pictorial and invariably a picture that tells a story. It is a subject for the healthy brush of a Rubens and not that of artists who wade in "the sickly surf of symbolism."

I painted all day, pausing only long enough to eat a banana and drink the cool, sweet liquid of a water coconut. Then, when the evening shadows grew long, I went back to the plaza to await Don Conrado.

The sun was setting as it sets only in the tropics. The volcanoes and the jagged mountains flanking them took on unimaginable hues; the cliffs and crests caught the fabulous rosy light, and the clouds of smoke and mist that rested wearily upon the green pillow of the hills were shot through with rainbow gleams. In the enormous crater of Santa Maria and in all the seams and sinews of the mountains were deep blue shadows. The mountains seemed clothed in changeable silk; but, *poco a poco*, the resplendent colors died away, melting into purple half-tones, shadows invaded the lower slopes, the light withdrew to the higher summits and the valley sank in gloom. At last only the golden crown of Santa Maria sparkled in the serene sky with the parting kiss of the sun.

SEVENTEEN

■■■

Louis J. Halle, Jr. 1938

Tikal and Palenque:
The Beginning and the End

[Louis J. Halle, Jr., was born in New York City. After attending Harvard College, he became a professional editor and writer. His avocation was ornithology, and his interest in birds is reflected not only in his book *Birds Against Man* but also in his observations and illustrations of birds in his later books on travel, among them *Transcaribbean*, which told of his first journeys in Latin America. In Guatemala he became interested in archaeology and decided to visit the more remote Maya ruins and write about them, but unlike most other "popular" authors he prepared himself by studying archaeology at the Harvard Graduate School before beginning his trip. I was privileged to know him briefly at this stage of his career, which, much later, led him to a professorship at the Graduate Institute for International Studies in Geneva, to membership on the policy planning staff of the United States Department of State, and to five books on international affairs.

[Halle and a friend, Tom Gladwin, another student of anthropology, embarked on a long and arduous journey across the heart of Central America's deepest rain forests, from British Honduras, into the Petén, and down the Usumacinta to the Gulf of Mexico, regions with which we have become familiar on previous pages of this book.

[*River of Ruins* tells of their trek. It is an authentic narrative, often lighthearted in spirit, sometimes thoughtful, and always well written. Halle does

The Halle selections are, in the order quoted below, from Louis J. Halle, Jr., *River of Ruins* (New York: Henry Holt and Company, 1941), pp. 12–20, 278–84. Copyright 1941 by Louis J. Halle, Jr. Reprinted with permission of Holt, Rinehart and Winston, Inc.

not always emerge the valiant hero of his anecdotes; as in this first extract
which I quote, he can look back with humor on his early inexperience with
the jungle, and with respect for the giant forest that he and Gladwin were
later to traverse. Edwin M. Shook, archaeologist with the Carnegie Institution of Washington, accompanied him on his first trip into the bush, bound
for Tikal.]

Most of the ruins to be found in the jungle are hidden from the sky by
dense foliage, so that one can discover them only from below. Tikal, greatest
of all these sites, is properly visible from the air alone.

The morning after our flight, Shook and I left Flores at three o'clock in a
little boat and, just as the sun pricked the horizon, landed on the eastern
shore of the lake, ready to descend into the forest at its brink, into that unknown world of darkness where the great shapes of rooted, tangled vegetation towered in brooding silence. The details don't matter. We had mules,
and there was a trail that plunged from the radiant lakeshore into the twilight of the jungle as into a rock cavern. We followed it, in single file, one
after another descending into darkness. The last gap closed quickly behind
us.

It is like the ocean-floor, and I imagine that the deep-sea diver who
plunges from the surface to the depths has much the same feeling as we had.
In the first place, there is a sort of fear of breathing, as though it would be
dangerous to expand one's lungs too freely. Mentally, at least, one holds one's
breath. Then there is the sensation that sooner or later one must emerge
again, that this is not a world in which men were meant to survive. Not a
man's world at all! Vegetation, monstrous, disordered, and utterly silent, but
still made up of living beings, breathing and growing, fulfills the forms of an
alien world. Time and space are not as we know them above. These gigantic,
silent forms make no response whatsoever. Oh, if a wild beast should attack,
that would be one thing! There is no thought of that here. This world merely is what it is passively; merely by its inhuman scale, by its immutability, by
its lack of any response to man's presence, it warns him away from it. But it
does not attack. A creeper with fine thorns dangling across the trail may be
pushed out of the way or slashed with one's machete. It makes no resistance.
An owl perched in the ragged opening of a hollow tree far up overhead
merely opens its eyes and shuts them again, opens and shuts them. There is
no overt hostility in this world but a vast indifference. Where a creeper has
been slashed another will grow up again, and there will have been no change.
Some owl will always be perched somewhere overhead, opening and shutting its eyes. This world is alien, alien . . . but much too large to be coped
with. The trail, which would be overgrown within a few weeks if it were not
kept open by the constant passage of men with machetes, is your only security. It is human and evanescent. But twenty paces off it to either side men
become lost and go mad. They actually do. There have been cases of it, and

there will be more. It is no use shouting for help, even at a short distance, because the vegetation passively screens the sound of the human voice. It is no use running, because all directions are the same, the same monstrous shapes. It is no use calling on heaven above, for even the sky is cut off from sight and sound. Your only security, if you are a man, is a trail that will not remain open for any length of time, that threatens always to vanish before you. The

Tropical rain forest
Courtesy of Middle American Research Institute, Tulane University.

trail is your life-line, like the rope that connects the diver with the surface of the ocean. If it is broken. . . .

The sensation of not daring to breathe freely is only one of the forms of fear. But, fear, too, can be pleasant. Of all the emotions it is the most exhilarating—for a time, at least, and in measure. Men encounter it voluntarily where there is no motive of greed or vainglory to spur them on. In that spirit they tell each other ghost stories to feel the tingle of the unknown along their spines. Well, this is like a ghost story, this jungle, these cavernous depths in which the disordered forms of trunk and branch, the masses and layers of heavy foliage, remain strangely still, sheltering an unseen life that is not human. The difference is that this is real—there is no suspicion of artful fabrication. It is more real than all the world of human civilization, of motor-roads and public squares, because it came before and will remain after. It tells the adventurous man what the city-dweller never learns, that mankind inhabits a world that is alien to it, alien and colossally indifferent. It mocks man's mortality along with his enterprise, his art with his science, by its shocking and invincible indifference. These forms of aspiration belong to the world that men seek to establish on this sphere where they abide temporarily —but this is the world that is, this is man's final immortality.

The "silence" of the jungle must not be taken literally. It is an impression that overlooks details. Actually there are sounds, continuous, repetitious, unceasing. But if these sounds were in proportion to the visible grandeur of the tropical forest they would be deafening to human ears, like a clap of thunder prolonged indefinitely. It is all a matter of proportion. . . .

Two days after leaving the lake Shook and I came into the ancient city of Tikal. The trail to Tikal, tunneling through this dark and oppressive forest, at last comes alongside a steep hill, almost a wall, buried under vegetation. Nothing shows that this is the site of an ancient city. Though you stand in the midst of the colossal remains, you do not know it. You have to pull yourself up by twigs and vines to climb the stone slope, and long before you reach the level of the tree-tops you are puffing and dripping. Suddenly, then, you emerge from the twilight below into the open sun-drenched sky to find yourself standing on a stone platform before the gaping door of one of these temples, where Mayan priests, dead for over a thousand years, performed the ritual of their religion before worshiping multitudes in the plaza (now hidden by jungle) at the foot of the pyramid. Confronting you across the sea of leaves that almost laps your feet are the three other pyramid-temples that dominate the site, their massive roof-combs towering above them. When you enter the dark interior, which smells of ancient moldy dampness, streams of bats brush out past you into the daylight with a loud fluttering of wings. Yet, for all the time that has passed since these temples were last occupied, the plaster of the inner walls is so smooth and white still that it might have been laid the week before. These temples of Tikal, because of their massive construction, are the best preserved as well as the most imposing monuments of the Mayan civilization. Some of the walls are over thirty feet thick.

The other temples loom very close to you across the roof of the jungle, but they are hard to find from below when you have clambered down into darkness again, just as a foundered ship, though its mast showed above water, might not be easily discovered by a diver in the darkness of the ocean-floor. Machete in hand, you cut your way through the vegetation, stumbling over sculptured stones that lie half-hidden at your feet, and if you do succeed in reaching the temple you are looking for you will not find it until you are almost up against the wall of the pyramid that supports it. But whatever direction you take, you come across other ruins, temples and palaces, that do not rise above the top of the forest and so are not visible from above. Monkeys swarm along branches that span broken walls, parrots fly screaming through open courtyards, toucans balance uncertainly in hanging vines over crumbled roofs. The limits of the city have never been explored, but it is beyond reasonable doubt the most extensive aboriginal site in the New World.

Our first evening out from the lake, Shook and I made camp at one of the rare *aguadas* or water-holes that are found in northern Petén. In a setting that resounded with the evening calls of unseen birds and the dismal barking and moaning of monkeys somewhere in the distance, I hung my hammock between two trees and set about preparing myself to spend the night. I was badly equipped for the purpose, and I mention that fact here because it reveals, what Tom did not know, my inexperience. I had, of course, bought the most obvious necessities for assaulting a tropical wilderness before leaving the city: a compass, a boy-scout knife, a machete, blankets, a hammock, a *pabellón*. . . .

Most important of all was the *pabellón*. Literally translated, a *pabellón* is a pavilion, but in its local usage it means a mosquito-bar. An ordinary *pabellón* for suspending over a bed or cot consists only of four walls and a roof, all made of some muslin that allows as much circulation of air as is compatible with wholly preventing the circulation of mosquitoes. The *pabellón* to be worn with a hammock differs in that it has a long sleeve built in at either end through which the cords of the hammock pass, with drawstrings to close it. My *pabellón*, the ready-made one that, influenced by the smooth tones of a clerk who knew it was just what I needed, I had bought in the city, was an ordinary sleeveless one!

Veterans always expect greenhorns to act their part, and the amusement which the first sight of my brand-new mosquito-bar afforded Shook was, I am sure, a full return for the additional risk he had incurred in having me along. That *pabellón* provides him with dinner-table conversation to this day. What I did—the only thing I could do—was to cut a hole in either end with my boy-scout knife, pass the hammock cords through, and trust to luck and bits of string to keep the mosquitoes out.

But I had not been in my hammock more than a few minutes when, in addition to all the other noises of the jungle, I began to detect a faint whining sound. It was a high-pitched and faraway drone, musical and not very loud, but disturbing. It seemed to recede and approach, approach and recede, and in a few more minutes I was completely surrounded by it. It was everywhere. Several times it came in close, rose to a shrill climax, and stopped. Then, feeling a slight pricking on my ear, on the back of my neck, or on my face, I would swoop and strike with my open palm. My hands were never still for long. No sooner did I settle down to sleep than I was suddenly obliged to strike out again by the whine close to my ear, the abrupt silence, the little stab that followed. I turned on my flashlight and surveyed my muslin room in its beam. Already there were quite a few mosquitoes inside, delicate buzzing creatures with hanging legs, too many for me to deal with. I turned the light off again, reflected that I had better get a good night's sleep even if I did wake in the morning covered with welts, and made up my mind to pay no more attention to such a picayune disturbance. Shook, the two muleteers, and the native cook we were taking along were already breathing heavily and contentedly in sleep. In a few moments, shutting my mind to the increasing drone, I should be doing the same. If I wanted to listen to anything I could concentrate on the whistles, the screams, and the moans from the surrounding forest. When a mosquito bit me I pretended not to notice. I played 'possum and did not move.

The next time I turned on my flashlight I could hardly see to the end of the *pabellón*. The mosquitoes were no longer to be reckoned by individuals. They formed a cloud, a thick droning fog in the beam of light. The muslin walls and ceiling were heavily peppered with them. There was something fantastic and extremely frightening in the sight. All thought of sleep finally left me. A few minutes later I was seized by a fit of temporary insanity and began thrashing about wildly, striking out at the air, beating myself all over, grunting and shouting, and at each blow I killed handfuls of mosquitoes. . . .

In the morning before daylight, when we rose to break camp, Shook complained that he had been awakened several times during the night by boisterous sounds from inside my *pabellón,* a sterling testimonial to his prowess as a sleeper.

The following evening, when we made camp, I found a way to make my *pabellón* secure against mosquitoes by carefully darning the holes at either end with string. The sense of relief with which I sank into my hammock that night was one of those matchless experiences that are recorded only in poetry. I found a hammock extraordinarily comfortable and luxurious, and it was only my second night in one. I would not have exchanged it for any bed. The way it adapted itself to the natural position of the relaxed body was such sheer delight that I deliberately kept myself awake for a few minutes to enjoy it. I listened again to the great nocturnal chorus of the tropical forest, but this time in peace. If I heard the drone of mosquitoes I was at least secure in the knowledge that they were outside my muslin walls.

I was already dozing when the rain came. It came spattering at first, a few big drops colliding with the surrounding foliage. I hardly felt it, though an occasional drop, striking the ceiling of my *pabellón,* sprayed my face. But the sound of spattering was quickly replaced by a roar, which could be heard advancing across the top of the forest like a moving waterfall. And then it struck.

Shook had hung his hammock and *pabellón* under a simple palm-leaf lean-to which some former camper had left here. By the time I was fully awake, our cook, Moisés, had already scampered over to the lean-to and taken shelter on the ground inside Shook's *pabellón.* In a moment I had abandoned my luxurious hammock and done the same. Moisés and I spent that night on the bug-infested floor of the jungle, under Shook's suspended body, which cleared the ground by hardly a foot, and in a space so crowded that none of us could change position except by prearrangement with the other two. And it rained all that night, and it rained all the next day, and for two days and two nights thereafter.

When I came out of the jungle, by the same trail to the shore of the lake, it was alone with one muleteer. But I had with me, now, a proper *pabellón,* borrowed from Shook, and Shook's personal tooth-brush, which I had likewise had to borrow. Twice, during those three days, riding alone, I knew the chilling fear of finding that I had got off the trail. And I did not even have a compass with me! The one I had bought before leaving Guatemala City had disappeared mysteriously from my baggage and did not reappear, again in my baggage and again mysteriously, till after my return.

This one experience of a land-expedition in the tropics was to be our mainstay on the much greater expedition Tom and I were soon definitely planning. It gave me the status of a veteran in his eyes. He agreed to stake his life on it, apparently without the least thought that it might not be a first-rate risk.

[My second quotation from *River of Ruins* illustrates the thoughtful quality of this remarkable book of travel. Although the author was not writing a history of the Maya, or a technical description of their remains, he was constantly aware of the meaning of the ruined cities rather than regarding them merely as curiosities with which to astound his readers. I know of no better description of Palenque, to which we now return, one hundred and thirty-three years and eighteen archaeological explorers after Guillelmo Dupaix.]

It would be hard to imagine a more inspiring setting. In this respect the crumbling city of Palenque has no peer among living cities, unless such magnificently set jewels as Rio de Janeiro and Naples may be judged worthy of comparison. But ancient Palenque not only looks up from below at a screen

of surrounding hills, as do these cities, it also looks down like an eagle from
its aerie over the wide expanse of a world below. The range of forest-clad
mountains into which it is set does not decrease gently in rolling foothills to
the plains; its base falls abruptly, like a coastal escarpment standing out
against the level sea. Surmounting it is a narrow flat shelf that rims the irregular summits of the range. This shelf penetrates back between the hills
in a series of narrow pockets, and in one such pocket are the main ruins of
Palenque. Little streams from the mountains above cross the terrace at short
intervals to fall from its brink in a confusion of tumbling cascades to the
land below. Several of the rivers of Tabasco, which is a country of rivers,
have sources here.

To add emphasis to this dramatic opposition of mountain and plain, the
lowlands seem to reach their lowest just at the foot of the escarpment. A
narrow wooded valley, extending indefinitely in either direction, forms a
moat outside it. Your first view of the ancient city is across this valley from a
ridge on the opposite side. Through a gap in the trees, you see a small
square clearing on the dark scarp of the mountains confronting you, and in
it a compact group of stone buildings that glints like a jewel in the sunlight.
Unlike all the other ruined sites of Middle America, most of which stand at
hazard in the midst of broad plains or valleys, this one seems to hang on the
mountainside, as if not men but eagles had selected it for their abode.

Instead of the usual shambling mule, a sturdy white steed was mine for
the two days I spent in Palenque commuting between Don Ernesto's ranch
and the ruins. This horse was fully equal to taking almost the entire twelve
miles in one gallop, so that it was only an hour each way. But the last quarter mile of the way to the ruins was no galloping matter. Here the trail left
the ridge and ran down into the woods. Two splashing woodland streams
were forded, the trail began to climb again, and then, abruptly, it leaped
straight up the rocky face of the escarpment, so steeply and directly that a
man on foot would have had to use all fours for the ascent. There was nothing more than a series of shallow foot-holds mounting the slope. If a horse
should hesitate halfway up, falter and lose his balance, he might easily go
over backwards to kill both himself and his rider on the ground below.

"Pegasus," I said, hesitating, "what do you think? Shall we be sensible and
go it separately?" But Pegasus had wings to his spirit, if no others, and he
showed no hesitation. He would hurl himself, and me too, to the top of the
scarp, or we should perish together. "*Adelante*, then!" I cried to him, bending
low over his neck as he charged.

It was all over in half a minute. By a succession of tremendous heaves
from his haunches, each one carrying us to the next foot-hold up, we stormed
the heights and gained the citadel. At the summit we found ourselves in the
midst of the incomparable ruins of Palenque.

I had been here so often before, through the reports and photographs and
drawings of others, that there was nothing in the city not quite familiar to

me already. The topography, the plan, and the architecture, that is, were just as I had imagined them. What was strange was the greater magnitude, the more imposing scale, the larger beauty of the vision as I saw it now for the first time directly through my own eyes. Everything that Stephens and Maudslay and Holmes and Blom had described was here, in its proper place —yet the sky was larger, the air was more brilliant with sunshine and heavier with heat, the jungle was bigger and more luxuriant, the elevation loftier, the ruins grander, and the view through that window in the mountainside over the dim plain of the world below had more reach and airiness than text or photographs could ever hope to represent. The emotion aroused by the suddenly revealed scene was like the emotion of a grand passion, that cannot be anticipated by imagination or retained in memory. Of the first arrival in Palenque I can only say that it takes one's breath away.

No one could have portrayed more faithfully than Maudslay, in the "Biologia Centrali-Americana," the forms and dimensions of the ancient city. But he had said nothing of the immensity of human achievement and the solemnity of death with which its ruins fill the imagination. Nor had he mentioned the accompanying music and pageantry of a life that goes on eternally and abundantly without regard for the successes and failures of men. When I arrived, howler monkeys were roaring from the surrounding hills, while two large white hawks circled and screamed over the sun-drenched ruins.

The valley or niche in the hills was some two thousand feet deep and wedge-shaped, so that its upper end was only a cleft wide enough to accommodate the bed of the creek that watered it. Its lower end broadened out into the terrace and came to an end on the brink of sheer space. Surrounding it, on all except its one open side, were abruptly rising banks of the richest kind of tropical forest, walls of lush vegetation through the occasional dark openings of which one caught glimpses of the white framework of trunks and branches, the whole entangled in a living mass of creepers, flowers, and parasitic plants. The floor of the valley had been cleared of bush by the government caretaker, so that from a distance it appeared as neat and open as a golf-course. A group of perfectly symmetrical terraces and mounds covered it, the mounds, raised up on the terraces for the most part, supporting exquisite stone temples in varying degrees of ruin, and an immense palace that, with its tower, its porticoes, and its courtyards, seemed a city in itself.

Over this valley wedged in between the hills, a pair of Ghiesbrecht's hawks circled on extended wings, at intervals uttering long piercing cries. Their plumage was glittering white, with a band of ebony along the hind edge of wings and tail, so that in the brilliant sunlight of a tropical sky or against the verdant foliage of the tropical jungle they seemed utterly anomalous and spectacular, like denizens of arctic snows that had mistaken their place in nature. They appeared to be cruising aimlessly, sometimes roaming close by a fringe of the forest, again drifting out from the brink of the terrace into the radiance beyond.

As Tikal is the first great expression of a culture that has arrived at maturity, so Palenque is its last. Between the beginning of the one and the completion of the other, all the possibilities that were inherent in Mayan culture were realized. What existed before Tikal led up to it; what followed Palenque led downward into the eclectic confusion of the Mayan decadence. The road from Tikal to Palenque, by way of Yaxchilán and Piedras Negras, is the same highroad that leads from the spiritual grandeur of the Gothic cathedrals to the secular splendor of Versailles. At Tikal men had at last mastered the material world and shaped it to the full expression of their common spiritual need. After Palenque, the fulfillment of the spirit had been achieved and craftsmanship became, more and more, an end in itself. In the final Aztec phase, it was subordinated to the service of the omnipotent state.

The palace and its tower, Palenque
Photograph by A. P. Maudslay, 1880. From *Biologia Centrali-Americana: Archaeology,* vol. iv.

Just as the temples of Tikal, different in everything else, remind one of the Gothic cathedrals by their spiritual grandeur and purity, so one appreciates Palenque with the same feeling that one does Versailles. It bespeaks the ultimate refinement of human living, the cultivated good-taste and competence of an aristocracy that stands for genuine spiritual sophistication. Man is no longer a youthful spirit, deeply moved by nature and aspiring to godhead. He is worldly and accomplished, and if he is not already complacent he very soon will be.

Perhaps it is significant that, in contrast to Tikal, the principal edifice of Palenque is secular. The palace, raised up above the ground-level on a stone-faced terrace, is built in vaulted galleries about four inner courts. The galleries are double, each divided from its opposite by a septum and opening outwardly in a series of doorways separated by square piers. These long galleries provide magnificent perspectives. The most spectacular feature of the palace, however, is a square tower, four stories high, with an inner staircase, that stands in one of the courts near the center of the entire structure. The top story, at my visit, was inhabited by a colony of menacing hornets that

Temple of the Inscriptions, Palenque, after partial excavation and restoration by Alberto Ruz L.

Photograph by Otto Done.

had constructed their enormous nest at the stairhead, where one sidled by it at peril of one's life to enjoy the view from above.

The temples of Palenque, like the Petit Trianon at Versailles, are gems of architecture—a term that could not by any stretch of the imagination be applied to the Gothic cathedrals or the temples of Tikal. They are exquisite, rather than imposing; refined, rather than massive. They are quite content with the earth they stand on, and do not, like their predecessors, reach for the sky. Like precious jewels, they are beautiful and complete in themselves.

Palenque is also distinguished among Mayan sites by the fact that most of the sculpture adorning its buildings was modeled in stucco rather than cut in stone. The faces of the square piers in the long galleries of the palace and between the doorways of the temples, the sloping upper façades (or roofs), and the roof-combs, all served as panels for the display of this sculpture, which was originally painted in a variety of harmonious colors, traces of which remain today. In its profusion of forms, in its free-flowing lines, in the cultivated taste of its composition, in the sheer elegance of its conception, it has something in common with the rococo decoration of the 17th and 18th centuries in Europe. The severity and the sullen, primitive stolidity of earlier days has given way to the lightness and refinement of a sophisticated people. The earlier gods (if they are gods) in the sculptures of Tikal, Copán, Quiriguá, seem to represent great natural forces, the forces that cause the maize to grow and the rain to fall; these gods, here at Palenque, are the members of an elegant aristocracy that rules gracefully over the destinies of men. There is a touch of courtliness about them that you do not find in their more barbaric forerunners. Like the buildings that support them, they represent the end and goal of a great cultural development.

Index